Thackray's 2015 Investor's Guide

THACKRAY'S

2015

INVESTOR'S
GUIDE

Brooke Thackray MBA, CIM, CFP

Published in 2014 by: MountAlpha Media:

alphamountain.com

Brooke Thackray is a research analyst for Horizons ETFs Management (Canada) Inc. All of the views expressed herein are the personal views of the author and are not necessarily the views of Horizons ETFs Management (Canada) Inc., although any of the strategies/recommendations found herein may be reflected in positions or transactions in the various client portfolios managed by Horizons ETFs Management (Canada) Inc., securities (if any) discussed in this publication are meant to highlight investment strategies for educational purposes only not investment advice.

Commissions, trailing commissions, management fees and expenses all may be associated with an investment in the Horizons Seasonal Rotation ETF. The Horizons Seasonal Rotation ETF is not guaranteed, its values change frequently, and past performance may not be repeated. Please read the prospectus before investing.

ISBN13: 978-0-9918735-2-4

Printed and Bound by Webcom Inc.

10 9 8 7 6 5 4 3 2 1

To my wife Jane

Acknowledgements

This book is the product of many years of research and could not have been written without the help of many people. I would like to thank my wife, Jane Steer-Thackray, and my children Justin, Megan, Carly and Madeleine, for the help they have given me and their patience during the many hours that I have devoted to writing this book. Thanks must be given to Wade Guenther for helping me source and filter a lot of the data in this book. I would also like to thank the proofreaders and editors, Amanda ODonnell and Jane Stiegler. Special mention goes to Jane for the countless hours she spent helping with writing, formatting and editing. This book could not have been written without her help.

INTRODUCTION

2015 THACKRAY'S INVESTOR'S GUIDE
Technical Commentary

The seasonal strategies that I have included in my previous books have proven to be very successful. The buy and sell dates are based upon iterative comparisons of different time periods measured by gain and frequency of success. Although the buy and sell dates are the optimal dates on which seasonal investors should focus on making their investment decisions, the markets have different dynamics from year to year, shifting the optimal buy and sell dates. Combining technical analysis with seasonal trends helps to adjust the decision process, allowing seasonal investors to enter and exit trades early or late, depending on market conditions.

The universe of technical indicators and techniques is huge. It is impossible to use all of the indicators. Only a small number of indicators and techniques that suit an investment style should be used. In the case of seasonal investing, a lot of long-term indicators provide very little benefit. For example, the standard Moving Average Convergence Divergence (MACD), is far too slow to be of any use in shorter term seasonal strategies. In this book I have chosen to illustrate the use of three technical indicators that have provided a lot of value in fine-tuning the dates for seasonal investing: Full Stochastic Oscillator (FSO), Relative Strength Index (RSI) and Relative Strength. The indicators are used in conjunction with the price pattern and moving averages of the security being considered. Investors must remember that technical analysis is not absolute and there will be exceptions when utilizing indicators and price patterns.

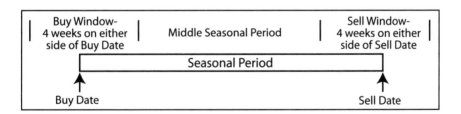

To combine technical indicators with seasonal trends, the indicators should only be used within the windows of the buy and sell dates. The indicators should be ignored outside the seasonal buy/sell windows. The only exception to this occurs when an indicator gives a signal during its middle seasonal period, which is in the seasonal period, but after the buy window and before the sell window. In this case a technical signal can support selling a full position based upon a fundamental breakdown in the price action of a security. By itself, a FSO or RSI indicator showing weakness in a security during its middle seasonal period, does not warrant action, it can only be used to support a decision being made in conjunction with underperformance relative to the broad market, or a major price action break.

Below are short descriptions of the three technical indicators that are used in this book and the metrics of how they are used with seasonal analysis. Full evaluation of the indicators and their uses with seasonal analysis is beyond the scope of this book.

Full Stochastic Oscillator (FSO)

A stochastic oscillator is a range bound momentum indicator that tracks the location of the close price relative to the high-low range, over a set number of periods. It tracks the momentum of price change and helps to indicate the strength and direction of price movement.

I have found that generally the best method to combine the FSO with seasonal trends is to buy an early partial position when the FSO turns up above 20 within four weeks of the seasonal buy date. Additionally, the best time to sell an early partial position occurs when the FSO turns below 80, within four weeks of the seasonal exit date.

For practical purposes in this book, %D, a 3 period smoothed %K, has been omitted. The standard variables are used in the FSO calculation (14 day look back period, and a 3 day simple moving average smoothing constant).

Relative Strength Index (RSI)

The RSI is a momentum oscillator that measures the speed and change of price movements. I have found that the best method to combine the RSI with seasonal trends is to buy an early partial position when the RSI turns up above 30 within four weeks of the seasonal buy date. The best time to sell an early partial position occurs when the RSI turns below 70, within four weeks of the seasonal exit date. Compared with the FSO, the RSI is less useful as it is slower and gives too few signals in the buy/sell windows.

Relative Strength

Relative strength calculates the performance of one security versus another security. When the relative strength is increasing, it indicates the seasonal security is outperforming. When the relative strength is declining, the seasonal security is underperforming. When a downward trend line is broken to the upside by the performance of the seasonal security, relative to the benchmark, this is a positive signal. This action carries a lot of weight and can justify a full early entry into a position if other technical evidence is positive. Likewise, if an upward trend line is broken to the downside, a negative technical signal is given and can justify a full early exit from a position if other technical evidence is negative.

THACKRAY'S 2015 INVESTOR'S GUIDE

You can choose great companies to invest in and still underperform the market. Unless you are in the market at the right time and in the best sectors, your investment expertise can be all for naught.

Successful investors know when they should be in the market. Very successful investors know when they should be in the market, and the best sectors in which to invest. *Thackray's 2015 Investor's Guide* is designed to provide investors with the knowledge of when and what to buy, and when to sell.

The goal of this book is to help investors capture extra profits by taking advantage of the seasonal trends in the markets. This book is straightforward. There are no complicated rules and there are no complex algorithms. The strategies put forward are intuitive and easy to understand.

It does not matter if you are a short-term or long-term investor, this book can be used to help establish entry and exit points. For the short-term investor, specific periods are identified that can provide profitable opportunities. For the long-term investor best buy dates are identified to launch new investments on a sound footing.

The stock market has its seasonal rhythms. Historically, the broad markets, such as the S&P 500, have a seasonal trend of outperforming during certain times of the year. Likewise, different sectors of the market have their own seasonal trends of outperformance. When oil stocks tend to do well in the springtime before "driving season," health care stocks tend to underperform the market. When utilities do well in the summertime, industrials do not. With different markets and different sectors having a tendency to outperform at different times of the year, there is always a place to invest.

Until recently, investors did not have access to the information necessary to analyse and create sector strategies. In recent years there have been a great number of sector Exchange Traded Funds (ETFs) and sector indexes introduced into the market. For the first time, investors are now able to easily implement a sector rotation strategy. This book provides a seasonal road map of what sectors tend to do well at different times of the year. It is a first of its kind, revealing new sector-based strategies that have never before been published.

In terms of market timing there are ample strategies in this book to help determine the times when equities should be over or underweight. During a favorable time for the market, investments can be purchased to overweight equities relative to their target weight in a portfolio (staying within risk tolerances). During an unfavorable time, investments can be sold to underweight equities relative to their target.

A large part of the book is devoted to sector seasonality – the underpinnings for a sector rotation strategy. The most practical rotation strategy is to create a core part of a portfolio that represents the broad market and then set aside an allocation to be rotated between favored sectors from one time period to the next.

It does not makes sense to apply any investment strategy only once with a large investment. Seasonal strategies are no exception. The best way to apply an investment strategy is to use a disciplined methodology that allows for diversification and a large enough number of investments to help remove the anomalies of the market. This reduces risk and increases the probability of a long term gain.

Following the specific buy and sell dates put forth in this book would have netted an investor large, above market returns. To "turbo-charge" gains, an investor can combine seasonality with technical analysis. As the seasonal periods are never exactly the same, technical analysis can help investors capture the extra gains when a sector turns up early, or momentum extends the trend.

IMPORTANT: Strategy Buy and Sell Dates
The beginning date of every strategy period in this book represents a full day in the market; therefore, investors should buy at the end of the preceding market day. For example the *Biotech Summer Solstice* seasonal period of strength is from June 23rd to September 13th. To be in the sector for the full seasonal period, an investor would enter the market before the closing bell on June 22nd. If the buy date landed on a weekend or holiday, then the buy would occur at the end of the preceding trading day.

The last day of a trading strategy is the sell date. For example, the Biotech sector investment would be sold at the end of the day on September 13th. If the sell date is a holiday or weekend, then the investment would be sold at the close on the preceding trading day.

What is Seasonal Investing?

In order to properly understand seasonal investing in the stock market, it is important to look briefly at its evolution. It may surprise investors to know that seasonal investing at the broad market level, i.e. Dow Jones or S&P 500, has been around for a long time. The initial seasonal strategies were written by Fields (1931, 1934) and Watchel (1942), who focused on the *January Effect*. Coincidentally, this strategy is still bantered about in the press every year.

Yale Yirsch Senior has been largely responsible for the next stage in the evolution, producing the *Stock Trader's Almanac* for more than forty years. This publication focuses on broad market trends such as the best six months of the year and tendencies of the market to do well depending on the political party in power and holiday trades.

In 1999, Brooke Thackray and Bruce Lindsay wrote, *Time In Time Out: Outsmart the Market Using Calendar Investment Strategies*. This work focused on a comprehensive analysis of the six month seasonal cycle and other shorter seasonal cycles in the broad markets such as the S&P 500.

Don Vialoux has written many articles on seasonal investing. His writings on this topic have developed a large following, via his free newsletter available at www.timingthemarket.ca.

Seasonal investing has changed over time. The focus has shifted from broad market strategies to taking advantage of sector rotation opportunities – investing in different sectors at different times of the year, depending on their seasonal strength. This has created a whole new set of investment opportunities. Rather than just being "in or out" of the market, investors can now always be invested by shifting between different sectors and asset classes, taking advantage of both up and down markets.

Definition – Seasonal investing is a method of investing in the market at the time of the year when it typically does well, or investing in a sector of the market when it typically outperforms the broad market such as the S&P 500.

The term seasonal investing is somewhat of a misnomer, and it is easy to see why some investors might believe that the discipline relates to investing based upon the seasons of the year – winter, spring, summer and autumn. Other than some agricultural commodities where the price is often correlated to growing seasons, generally seasonal investment strategies use the calendar as a reference for buy and sell dates. It is usually a specific event, i.e. Christmas sales, that occurs on a recurring annual basis that creates the seasonal opportunity.

The discipline of seasonal investing is not restricted to the stock market. It has been used successfully for a number of years in the commodities market. The opportunities in this market tend to be based upon changes in supply and/or demand that occur on a yearly basis. Most commodities, especially the agricultural commodities, tend to have cyclical supply cycles, i.e., crops are harvested only at certain times of the year. The supply bulge that occurs at the same time every year provides seasonal investors with profit opportunities. Recurring increased seasonal demand for commodities also plays a major part in providing opportunities for seasonal investors. This applies to most metals and many other commodities, whether the end-product is industrial or consumer based.

Seasonal investment strategies can be used with a lot of different types of investments. The premise is the same, outperformance during a certain period of the year based upon a repeating event in the markets or economy. In my past writings I have developed seasonal strategies that have been used successfully in the stock, commodity, bond and foreign exchange markets. Seasonal investing is still relatively new for most markets with a lot of new opportunities waiting to be discovered.

How Does Seasonal Investing Work?

Most stock market sector seasonal trends are the result of a recurring annual catalyst: an event that affects the sector positively. These events can range from a seasonal spike in demand, seasonal inventory lows, weather effects, conferences and other events. Mainstream investors very often anticipate a move in a sector and incorrectly try to take a position just before an event takes place that is supposed to drive a sector higher. A good example of this would be investors buying oil just before the cold weather sets in. Unfortunately, their efforts are usually unsuccessful as they are too late to the party and the opportunity has already passed.

By the time the anticipated event occurs, a substantial amount of investors have bought into the sector – fully pricing in the expected benefit. At this time there is little potential left in the short-term. Unless there is a strong positive surprise, the sector's outperformance tends to slowly roll over. If the event produces less than its desired result, the sector can be severely punished.

So how does the seasonal investor take advantage of this opportunity? "Be there" before the mainstream investors, and get out before they do. Seasonal investors usually enter a sector two or three months before an event is anticipated to have a positive effect on a sector and get out before the actual event takes place. In essence, seasonal investors are benefiting from the mainstream investor's tendency to "buy in" too late.

Seasonality in the markets occurs because of three major reasons: money flow, changing market analyst expectations and the *Anticipation-Realization Cycle*. First, money flows vary throughout the year and at different times of the month. Generally, money flows increase at the end of the year and into the start of the next year. This is a result of year end bonuses and tax related investments. In addition, money flows increase at month end from money managers "window dressing" their portfolios. As a result of these money flows, the months around the end of the year and the days around the end of the month, tend to have a stronger performance than the other times of the year.

Second, the analyst expectations cycle tends to push markets up at the end of the year and the beginning of the next year. Stock market analysts tend to be a positive bunch – the large investment houses pay them to be positive. They start the year with aggressive earnings for all of their favorite companies. As the year progresses, they generally back off their earnings forecast, which decreases their support for the market. After a lull in the summer and early autumn months, they start to focus on the next year with another rosy forecast. As a result, the stock market tends to rise once again at the end of the year.

Third, at the sector level, sectors of the market tend to be greatly influenced by the *Anticipation-Realization Cycle*. Although some investors may not be familiar with the term "anticipation-realization," they probably are familiar with the concept of "buy the rumor – sell the fact," or in the famous words of Lord Rothschild "Buy on the sound of the war-cannons; sell on the sound of the victory trumpets."

The *Anticipation-Realization Cycle* as it applies to human behavior has been much studied in psychology journals. In the investment world, the premise of this cycle rests on investors anticipating a positive event in the market to drive prices higher and buying in ahead of the event. When the event takes place, or is realized, upward pressure on prices decreases as there is very little impetus for further outperformance.

A good example of the *Anticipation-Realization Cycle* takes place with the "conference effect." Very often large industries have major conferences that occur at approximately the same time every year. Major companies in the industry often hold back positive announce-

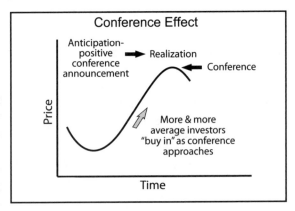

ments and product introductions to be released during the conference.

Two to three months prior to the conference, seasonal investors tend to buy into the sector. Shortly afterwards, the mainstream investors anticipate "good news" from the conference and start to buy in. As a result, prices are pushed up. Just before the conference starts, seasonal investors capture their profits by exiting their positions. As the conference unfolds, company announcements are made (realized), but as the potential good news has already been priced into the sector, there is little to push prices higher and the sector typically starts to rolls over.

The same *Anticipation-Realization Cycle* takes place with increased demand for oil to meet the "summer driving season", increased sales of goods at Christmas time, increased demand for gold jewellery to meet the autumn and winter demand, and many other events that tend to drive the outperformance of different sectors.

Does Seasonal Investing ALWAYS Work?

The simple answer to the above question is "No." There is not any investment system in the world that works all of the time. When following any investment system, it is probability of success that counts. It has often been said that "being correct in the markets 60% of the time will make you rich." Investors tend to forget this and become too emotionally attached to their losses. Just about every investment trading book states that investors typically fail to let their profits run and cut their losses quickly. I concur. In my many years in the investment industry, the biggest mistake that I have found with investors is not being able to cut their losses. Everyone wants to be right, that is how we have been raised. Investors feel that if they sell at a loss they have failed, and as a result, often suffer bigger losses by waiting for their position to trade at profit.

With any investment system, investors should let probability work for them. This means that investors should be able to enter and exit positions capturing both gains and losses without becoming emotionally attached to any positions. Emotional attachment clouds judgement, which leads to errors. When all of the trades are put together, the goal is for profits to be larger than losses in a way that minimizes risks and beats the market.

If we examine the winter oil stock trade, we can see how probability has worked in an investor's favor. This trade is based upon the premise that at the tail end of winter, the refineries drive up demand for oil in order to produce enough gas for the approaching "driving season" that starts in the spring. As a result, oil stocks tend to increase and outperform the market (from February 25th to May 9th). The oil stock sector, represented by the Amex Oil Index (XOI), has been very successful at this time of year, producing an average return of 7.3% and beating the S&P 500 by 4.2%, from 1984 to 2014. In addition it has been positive 26 out of

XOI vs S&P 500 1984 to 2014

Feb 25 to May 9	positive S&P 500	XOI	Diff
1984	1.7 %	5.6 %	3.9 %
1985	1.4	4.9	3.5
1986	6.0	7.7	1.7
1987	3.7	25.5	21.8
1988	-3.0	5.6	8.6
1989	6.3	8.1	1.8
1990	5.8	-0.6	-6.3
1991	4.8	6.8	2.0
1992	0.9	5.8	4.9
1993	0.3	6.3	6.0
1994	-4.7	3.2	7.9
1995	7.3	10.3	3.1
1996	-2.1	2.2	4.3
1997	1.8	4.7	2.9
1998	7.5	9.8	2.3
1999	7.3	35.4	28.1
2000	4.3	22.2	17.9
2001	0.8	10.2	9.4
2002	-1.5	5.3	6.9
2003	12.1	5.7	-6.4
2004	-3.5	4.0	7.5
2005	-1.8	-1.0	0.8
2006	2.8	9.4	6.6
2007	4.2	10.1	5.8
2008	2.6	7.6	5.0
2009	20.2	15.8	-4.4
2010	0.5	-2.3	-2.8
2011	3.1	-0.6	-3.7
2012	-0.8	-13.4	-12.5
2013	7.3	3.8	-3.5
2014	1.7	9.1	7.4
Avg	3.1 %	7.3 %	4.2 %
Fq > 0	77 %	84 %	77 %

31 times. Investors should always evaluate the strength of seasonal trades before applying them to their own portfolios.

If an investor started using the seasonal investment discipline in 1984 and chose to invest in the winter-oil trade, they would have been very happy with the results. Over the last few years, the fact that the trade did not produce a gain in 2010, 2011 and 2012, does not mean that the seasonal trade no longer works. All seasonal trades go through periods, sometimes multiple years where they do not work. An investor can start any methodology of trading at the "wrong time," and be unsuccessful in a particular trade. In fact, if an investor started the oil-winter trade in 1990 and had given up in the same year, they would have missed the following successful twelve years. Investors have to remember that it is the final score that counts, after all of the gains have been weighed against the losses.

In practical terms, investors should not put all of their investment strategies in one basket. If one or two large investments were made based upon seasonal strategies, it is possible that the seasonal methodology might be inappropriately evaluated and its use discontinued. A much more prudent strategy is to use a larger number of strategic seasonal investments with smaller investments. The end result will be to put the seasonal probability to work with a much greater chance of success.

Measuring Seasonal Performance

How do you determine if a seasonal strategy has been successful? Many people feel that ten years of data is a good sample size, others feel that fifteen years is better, and yet others feel that the more data the better. I tend to fall into the camp that, if possible, it is best to use fifteen or twenty years of data for sectors and more data for the broad markets, such as the S&P 500. Although the most recent data in almost any analytical framework is the most relevant, it is important to get enough data to reflect a sector's performance across different economic conditions. Given that historically the economy has performed on an eight year cycle, four years of expansion and then four years of contraction, using a short data set does not provide for enough exposure to different economic conditions.

A data set that is too long can run into the problem of older data having too much of an influence on the numbers when fundamental factors affecting a sector have changed. It is important to look at trends over time and assess if there has been a change that should be considered in determining the dates for a seasonal cycle. Each sector should be judged on its own merit. The analysis tables in this book illustrate the performance level for each year in order to provide the opportunity for readers to determine any relevant changes.

In order to determine if a seasonal strategy is effective there are two possible benchmarks, absolute and relative performance. Absolute performance measures if a profit is made and relative performance measures the performance of a sector in relationship to a major market. Both measurements have their merits and depending on your investment style, one measurement may be more valuable than another. This book provides both sets of measurement in tables and graphs.

It is not just the average percent gain of a sector over a certain time period that determines success. It is possible that one or two spectacular years of performance skew the results substantially (particularly with a small data set). The frequency of success is also very important: the higher the percentage of success the better. Also, the fewer large drawdowns the better. There is no magic number (percent success rate) per se of what constitutes a successful strategy. The success rate should be above fifty percent, otherwise it would be better to just invest in the broad market. Ideally speaking a strategy should have a high percentage success rate on both an absolute and relative basis. Some strategies are stronger than others, but that does not mean that the weaker strategies should not be used. Prudence should be used in determining the ideal portfolio allocation.

Illustrating the strength of a sector's seasonal performance can be accomplished through either an absolute yearly average performance graph, or a relative yearly average performance graph. The absolute graph shows the average yearly cumulative gain for a set number of years. It lets a reader visually identify the strong periods during the year. The relative graph shows the average yearly cumulative gain for the sector relative to the benchmark index.

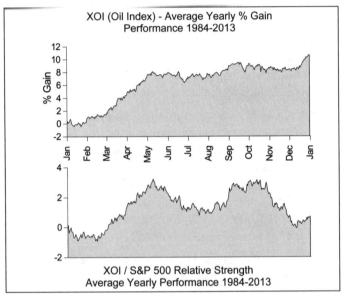

Both graphs are useful in determining the strength of a particular seasonal strategy. In the above diagram, the top graph illustrates the average year for the NYSE Arca Oil & Gas Index (XOI) from 1984 to 2013. Essentially it illustrates the cumulative average gain if an investment were made in the index. The steep rising line starting in January/February shows the overall price rise that typically occurs in this sector at this time of year. In May the line flattens out and then rises very modestly starting in July.

The bottom graph is a ratio graph, illustrating the strength of the XOI Index relative to the S&P 500. It is derived by dividing the average year of the XOI by the average year of the S&P 500. When the line in the graph is rising, the XOI is outperforming the S&P 500, and vise versa when it is declining. This is an important graph and should be used in considering seasonal investments because the S&P 500 is a viable alternative to the energy sector. If both markets are increasing, but the S&P 500 is increasing at a faster rate, the S&P 500 represents a more attractive opportunity. This is particularly true when measuring the risk of a volatile sector relative to the broad market. If both investments were expected to produce the same rate of return, generally the broad market is a better investment because of its diversification.

Who Can Use Seasonal Investing?

Any investor from novice to expert, from short-term trader to long-term investor can benefit from using seasonal analysis. Seasonal investing is unique because it is an easy to understand system that can be used by itself or as a complement to another investment discipline. For the novice it provides an easy to follow strategy that makes intuitive sense. For the expert it can be used as a stand-alone system or as a complement to an existing system.

Seasonal investing is easily understood by all levels of investors, which allows investors to make rational decisions. This may seem obvious, but it is very common for investors to listen to a "guru of the market", be impressed and blindly follow his advice. When the advice works there is no problem. When the advice does not work investors wonder why they made the investment in the first place. When investors do not understand their investments it causes stress, bad decisions and a lack of "stick-to-it ness" with any investment discipline. Even expert investors realize the importance of understanding your investments. Peter Lynch of Fidelity Investments used to say "Never invest in any idea that you can't illustrate with a crayon." Investors do not need to go that far, but they should understand their investments.

Novice investors find seasonal strategies very easy to understand because they are intuitive. They do not have to be investing for years to understand why seasonal strategies work. They understand that an increase in demand for gold every year at the same time causes a ripple effect in the stock market pushing up gold stocks at the same time every year.

Most expert investors use information from a variety of sources in making their decisions. Even experts that primarily use fundamental analysis can benefit from using seasonal trends to get an edge in the market. Fundamental analysis is a very crude tool and provides very little in the way of timing an investment. Using seasonal trends can help with the timing of the buy and sell decisions and produce extra profit.

Seasonal investing can be used by both short-term and long-term investors, but in different ways. For short-term investors it provides a complete trade – buy and sell dates. For long-term investors it can provide a buy date for a sector of interest.

Combining Seasonal Analysis with other Investment Disciplines

Seasonal investing used by itself has historically produced above average market returns. Depending on an investor's particular style, it can be combined with one of the other three investment disciplines: fundamental, quantitative and technical analysis. There are two basic ways to combine seasonal analysis with other investment methodologies – as the primary or secondary method. If it is used as a primary method, seasonally strong time periods are established for a number of sectors and then appropriate sectors are chosen based upon fundamental, quantitative or technical screens. If it is used as a secondary method, sector selections are first made based upon one of three methods and then final sectors are chosen based upon which ones are in their seasonally strong period.

Technical analysis is an ideal mate for seasonal analysis. Unlike fundamental and quantitative analysis, which are very blunt timing tools at best, seasonal and technical analysis can provide specific trigger points to buy and sell. The combination can turbo-charge investment strategies, adding extra profits by fine-tuning entry and exit dates.

Seasonal analysis provides both buy and sell dates. Although a sector in the market can sometimes bottom on the exact seasonal buy date, it more often bottoms a bit early or a bit late. After all, the seasonal buy date is based upon an average of historical performance. Depending on the sector, buying opportunities start to develop approximately one month before and after the seasonal buy date. Using technical analysis gives an investor the advantage of buying into a sector when it turns up early or waiting when it turns up late. Likewise, technical analysis can be used to trigger a sell signal when the market turns down before or after the sell date.

The sell decision can be extended with the help of a trailing stop-loss order. If a sector has strong momentum and the technical tools do not provide a sell signal, it is possible to let the sector "run." When a trailing stop-loss is used, a profitable sell point is established. If the price continues to run, then the selling point is raised. If, on the other hand, the price falls through the stop-loss point, the position is sold.

Sectors of the Market

Standard & Poor's has done an excellent job in categorizing the U.S. stock market into its different parts. Although the demand for this service initially came from institutional investors, many individual investors now seek the same information. Knowing the sector breakdown in the market allows investors to see how different their portfolio is relative to the market. As a result, they are able to make conscious decisions on what parts of the stock market to overweight based upon their beliefs of which sectors will outperform. It also helps control the amount of desired risk.

Standard & Poor's uses four levels of detail in its Global Industry Classification Standard (GICS[©]) to categorize stock markets around the world. From the most specific, it classifies companies into sub-industries, industries, industry groups and finally economic sectors. All companies in the Standard & Poor's global family of indices are classified according to the GICS structure.

This book focuses on the U.S. market, analysing the trends of the venerable S&P 500 index and its economic sectors and industry groups. The following diagram illustrates the index classified according to its economic sectors.

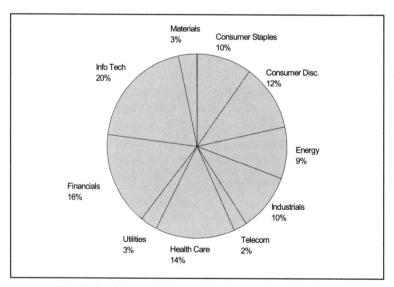

Standard and Poor's, Understanding Sectors, June 30, 2014

For more information on Standard and Poor's Global Industry Classification Standard (GICS[©]), refer to www.standardandpoors.com

Investment Products – Which One Is The Right One?

There are many ways to take advantage of the seasonal trends at the broad stock market and sector levels. Regardless of the investment products that you currently use, whether exchange traded funds, mutual funds, stocks or options, all can be used with the strategies in this book. Different investments offer different risk-reward relationships and return potential.

Exchange Traded Funds (ETFs)

Exchange Traded Funds (ETFs) offer the purest method of seasonal investment. The broad market ETFs are designed to track the major indices and the sector ETFs are designed to track specific sectors without using active management. Relatively new, ETFs are a great way to capture both market and sector trends. They were originally introduced into the Canadian market in 1993 to represent the Toronto stock market index. Shortly afterward they were introduced to the U.S. market and there are now hundreds of ETFs to represent almost every market, sector, style of investing and company capitalization. Originally ETFs were mainly of interest to institutional investors, but individual investors have fast realized the merits of ETF investing and have made some of the broad market ETFs the most heavily traded securities in the world.

An ETF is a single security that represents a market, such as the S&P 500; a sector of the market, such as the financial sector; or a commodity, such as gold. In the case of the S&P 500, an investor buying one security is buying all 500 stocks in the index. By investing into a financial ETF, an investor is buying the companies that make up the financial sector of the market. By investing into a gold commodity ETF, an investor is buying a security that represents the price of gold.

ETFs trade on the open market just like stocks. They have a bid and an ask, can be shorted and many are option eligible. They are a very low cost, tax efficient method of targeting specific parts of the market.

Mutual Funds

Mutual funds are a good way to combine market or sector investing with active management. In recent years, many mutual fund companies have added sector funds to accommodate an increasing appetite in this area.

As the seasonal strategies put forward in this book have a short-term nature, it is important to make sure that there are no fees (or a nominal charge) for getting into and out of a position in the market.

Stocks

Stocks provide an opportunity to make better returns than the market or sector. If the market increases during its seasonal period, some stocks will increase dramatically more than the index. Choosing one of the outperforming stocks will greatly enhance returns; choosing one of the underperforming stocks can create substantial loses. Using stocks requires increased attention to diversification and security selection.

Options

Disclaimer: Options involve risk and are not suitable for every investor. Because they are cash-settled, investors should be aware of the special risks associated with index options and should consult a tax advisor. Prior to buying or selling options, a person must receive a copy of Characteristics and Risks of Standardized Options and should thoroughly understand the risks involved in any use of options. Copies may be obtained from The Options Clearing Corporation, 440 S. LaSalle Street, Chicago, IL 60605.

Options, for more sophisticated investors, are a good tool to take advantage of both market and sector opportunities. An option position can be established with either stocks or ETFs. There are many different ways to use options for seasonal trends: establish a long position on the market during its seasonally strong period, establish a short position during its seasonally weak period, or create a spread trade to capture the superior gains of a sector over the market.

THACKRAY'S 2015 INVESTOR'S GUIDE

CONTENTS

JANUARY

	MONDAY	TUESDAY	WEDNESDAY
WEEK 01	29	30	31
WEEK 02	**5** 26	**6** 25	**7** 24
WEEK 03	**12** 19	**13** 18	**14** 17
WEEK 04	**19** 12 USA Market Closed- Martin Luther King Jr. Day	**20** 11	**21** 10
WEEK 05	**26** 5	**27** 4	**28** 3

THURSDAY	FRIDAY

1 30	**2** 29
CAN Market Closed - New Year's Day	
USA Market Closed - New Year's Day	

8 23	**9** 22

15 16	**16** 15

22 9	**23** 8

29 2	**30** 1

FEBRUARY

M	T	W	T	F	S	S
						1
2	3	4	5	6	7	8
9	10	11	12	13	14	15
16	17	18	19	20	21	22
23	24	25	26	27	28	

MARCH

M	T	W	T	F	S	S
						1
2	3	4	5	6	7	8
9	10	11	12	13	14	15
16	17	18	19	20	21	22
23	24	25	26	27	28	29
30	31					

APRIL

M	T	W	T	F	S	S
		1	2	3	4	5
6	7	8	9	10	11	12
13	14	15	16	17	18	19
20	21	22	23	24	25	26
27	28	29	30			

MAY

M	T	W	T	F	S	S
				1	2	3
4	5	6	7	8	9	10
11	12	13	14	15	16	17
18	19	20	21	22	23	24
25	26	27	28	29	30	31

JANUARY
S U M M A R Y

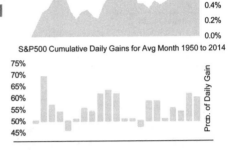

	Dow Jones	S&P 500	Nasdaq	TSX Comp
Month Rank	5	5	1	3
# Up	42	40	28	18
# Down	22	24	14	11
% Pos	66	63	67	62
% Avg. Gain	1.1	1.2	2.8	1.2

Dow & S&P 1950-2013, Nasdaq 1972-2013, TSX 1985-2013

S&P500 Cumulative Daily Gains for Avg Month 1950 to 2014

♦ Recently, from 2005 to 2014, the S&P 500 has only been positive 50% of the time in January and has produced an average loss of 0.9%. ♦ The markets in January tend to act in a schizophrenic manner with most of the cyclical sectors performing well and the defensive sectors performing poorly. ♦ Small cap stocks tend to perform well in January ♦ After the S&P 500 produced a strong 29.6% gain in the year 2013, investors started to question the high valuations of stocks and as a result, the S&P 500 declined 3.6% in January 2014.

BEST / WORST JANUARY BROAD MKTS. 2005-2014

BEST JANUARY MARKETS
- ♦ Russell 2000 (2006) 8.9%
- ♦ Nasdaq (2012) 8.0%
- ♦ Nikkei 225 (2013) 7.2%

WORST JANUARY MARKETS
- ♦ Nikkei (2008) -11.2%
- ♦ Russell 2000 (2009) -11.2%
- ♦ Nasdaq (2008) -9.9%

Index Values End of Month

	2005	2006	2007	2008	2009	2010	2011	2012	2013	2014
Dow	10,490	10,865	12,622	12,650	8,001	10,067	11,892	12,633	13,861	15,699
S&P 500	1,181	1,280	1,438	1,379	826	1,074	1,286	1,312	1,498	1,783
Nasdaq	2,062	2,306	2,464	2,390	1,476	2,147	2,700	2,814	3,142	4,104
TSX Comp.	9,204	11,946	13,034	13,155	8,695	11,094	13,552	12,452	12,685	13,695
Russell 1000	1,219	1,341	1,507	1,444	860	1,133	1,371	1,396	1,599	1,916
Russell 2000	1,551	1,822	1,989	1,773	1,102	1,496	1,942	1,970	2,242	2,811
FTSE 100	4,852	5,760	6,203	5,880	4,150	5,189	5,863	5,682	6,277	6,510
Nikkei 225	11,388	16,650	17,383	13,592	7,994	10,198	10,238	8,803	11,139	14,915

Percent Gain for January

	2005	2006	2007	2008	2009	2010	2011	2012	2013	2014
Dow	-2.7	1.4	1.3	-4.6	-8.8	-3.5	2.7	3.4	5.8	-5.3
S&P 500	-2.5	2.5	1.4	-6.1	-8.6	-3.7	2.3	4.4	5.0	-3.6
Nasdaq	-5.2	4.6	2.0	-9.9	-6.4	-5.4	1.8	8.0	4.1	-1.7
TSX Comp.	-0.5	6.0	1.0	-4.9	-3.3	-5.5	0.8	4.2	2.0	0.5
Russell 1000	-2.6	2.7	1.8	-6.1	-8.3	-3.7	2.3	4.8	5.3	-3.3
Russell 2000	-4.2	8.9	1.6	-6.9	-11.2	-3.7	-0.3	7.0	6.2	-2.8
FTSE 100	0.8	2.5	-0.3	-8.9	-6.4	-4.1	-0.6	2.0	6.4	-3.5
Nikkei 225	-0.9	3.3	0.9	-11.2	-9.8	-3.3	0.1	4.1	7.2	-8.5

January Market Avg. Performance 2005 to 2014[1]

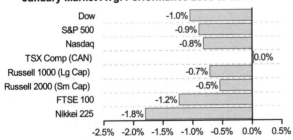

	Dow	-1.0%
S&P 500	-0.9%
Nasdaq	-0.8%
TSX Comp (CAN)	0.0%
Russell 1000 (Lg Cap)	-0.7%
Russell 2000 (Sm Cap)	-0.5%
FTSE 100	-1.2%
Nikkei 225	-1.8%

-2.5% -2.0% -1.5% -1.0% -0.5% 0.0% 0.5%

Interest Corner Jan[2]

	Fed Funds %[3]	3 Mo. T-Bill %[4]	10 Yr %[5]	20 Yr %[6]
2014	0.25	0.02	2.67	3.35
2013	0.25	0.07	2.02	2.79
2012	0.25	0.06	1.83	2.59
2011	0.25	0.15	3.42	4.33
2010	0.25	0.08	3.63	4.38

(1) Russell Data provided by Russell (2) Federal Reserve Bank of St. Louis- end of month values (3) Target rate set by FOMC (4)(5)(6) Constant yield maturities.

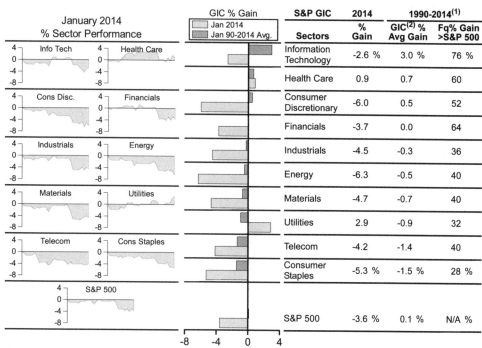

| S&P GIC | 2014 | 1990-2014[1] | |
Sectors	% Gain	GIC[2] % Avg Gain	Fq% Gain >S&P 500
Information Technology	-2.6 %	3.0 %	76 %
Health Care	0.9	0.7	60
Consumer Discretionary	-6.0	0.5	52
Financials	-3.7	0.0	64
Industrials	-4.5	-0.3	36
Energy	-6.3	-0.5	40
Materials	-4.7	-0.7	40
Utilities	2.9	-0.9	32
Telecom	-4.2	-1.4	40
Consumer Staples	-5.3 %	-1.5 %	28 %
S&P 500	-3.6 %	0.1 %	N/A %

Sector Commentary

♦ After a strong year for the stock market in 2013, investors became concerned about an over-heated market declining in early 2014. The energy sector responded by declining 6.3%. ♦ The discretionary sector also performed very poorly, as the extremely bad weather in the U.S. north-east impacted consumer purchases negatively. ♦ The utilities sector increased in value as investors were attracted to its defensive nature and power producers benefited from the very cold weather. ♦ Investors were attracted to the health care sector, not just because of its defensive nature, but also because of the increased number of mergers and acquisitions that were taking place in the sector at the beginning of the year.

Sub-Sector Commentary

♦ In early 2013, bargain hunters started buying gold, which increased by 3.9% in January. ♦ The home-builders sub-sector typically performs well in January, and 2014 was not an exception, as the sub-sector produced a gain of 2.1%. ♦ As investors feared a slowing economy, they drove the steel sub-sector down 12.4% and the metals and mining sub-sector down 9.8%.

SELECTED SUB-SECTORS[3]

SOX (1995-2014)	-1.1 %	4.3 %	60 %
Home-builders	2.1	3.3	60
Silver	-1.0	2.9	68
Software & Services	-0.7	2.4	72
Biotech (1993-2014)	5.0	2.3	55
Railroads	-0.7	1.4	60
Gold (London PM)	3.9	1.3	56
Steel	-12.4	1.0	52
Banks	-0.5	0.3	52
Transportation	-2.4	0.2	56
Pharma	-0.3	0.1	56
Retail	-7.7	-0.1	52
Agriculture (1994-2014)	-9.0	-0.2	38
Chemicals	-3.8	-0.7	40
Metals & Mining	-9.8	-0.8	44

(1) Sector data provided by Standard and Poors (2) GIC is short form for Global Industry Classification (3) Sub Sector data provided by Standard and Poors, except where marked by symbol.

CATERPILLAR
January 23rd to May 5th

The performance of Caterpillar's stock is very much related to the outlook for the worldwide economy. When the outlook for the economy is strong, Caterpillar tends to perform well.

Generally, expectations for economic growth tend to be stronger during the first part of the year compared with the rest of the year. As a result, companies that are more dependent on the economic cycle tend to perform better during the first part of the year. This includes companies in the industrial sector such as Caterpillar.

14.6% gain & positive 84% of the time

From January 23rd to May 5th, during the period of 1990 to 2014, Caterpillar has produced an average rate of return of 14.6% and was positive 84% of the time. During this period, it has also outperformed the S&P 500, 72% of the time.

CAT* vs. S&P 500 1990 to 2014			
			Positive
Jan 23 to May 5	S&P 500	CAT	Diff
1990	2.4%	15.4%	13.0%
1991	16.0	17.2	1.2
1992	-0.3	14.2	14.5
1993	1.9	24.3	22.4
1994	-4.9	14.0	19.0
1995	11.9	5.9	-6.0
1996	4.6	1.6	-3.0
1997	5.6	26.0	20.4
1998	15.8	22.8	7.0
1999	10.0	48.2	38.2
2000	-0.6	-17.6	-17.0
2001	-5.7	23.7	29.4
2002	-4.1	12.1	16.2
2003	5.5	18.5	13.1
2004	-2.0	-6.2	-4.2
2005	0.4	0.7	0.3
2006	5.1	31.6	26.5
2007	5.8	25.7	19.9
2008	7.4	29.7	22.3
2009	9.2	5.9	-3.4
2010	6.8	21.6	14.8
2011	4.0	17.9	13.9
2012	4.1	-6.8	-10.9
2013	8.2	-11.0	-19.2
2014	2.2	16.6	14.4
Avg	4.4%	14.6%	10.3%
Fq > 0	76%	84%	72%

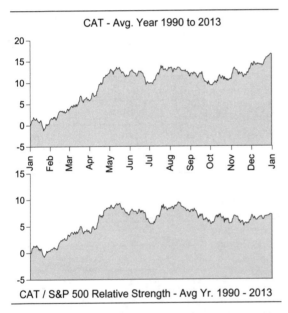

CAT - Avg. Year 1990 to 2013

CAT / S&P 500 Relative Strength - Avg Yr. 1990 - 2013

Although the seasonal Caterpillar strategy has had solid results, there have been years when the strategy has not worked, including 2012 and 2013.

In the year 2000, cyclical stocks including Caterpillar, underperformed during the first part of the year as the technology bubble broke and investors were concerned about the impact on world economic growth. Caterpillar's negative performance in 2004 was largely the result of "consolidating" after producing an 86% gain in the year 2003.

In both 2012 and 2013, Caterpillar started off the year with strong outperformance, but started to underperform the S&P 500 in February as investors shunned cyclical stocks in favor of defensive stocks. Favoring defensive stocks at this time of the year is not typical for investors and often points to a market pull back later in the springtime. In 2014, Caterpillar benefited from strong earnings at the start of its seasonal period, helping it to strongly outperform the S&P 500.

Despite the drawdown exceptions, the overall positive results of the Caterpillar strategy make it a trade worthy of a seasonal portfolio.

CAT - stock symbol for Caterpillar Inc. which trades on the NYSE, adjusted for splits.

2013-14 Strategy Performance

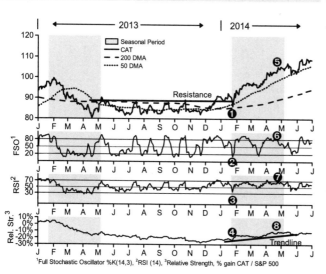

¹Full Stochastic Oscillator %K(14,3), ²RSI (14), ³Relative Strength, % gain CAT / S&P 500

Market Indices & Rates Weekly Values**

Stock Markets	2013	2014
Dow	13,336	16,498
S&P500	1,454	1,838
Nasdaq	3,084	4,151
TSX	12,496	13,586
FTSE	6,016	6,732
DAX	7,771	9,462
Nikkei	10,688	16,291
Hang Seng	23,175	23,177
Commodities	**2013**	**2014**
Oil	92.74	96.78
Gold	1,673.8	1,221.3
Bond Yields	**2013**	**2014**
USA 5 Yr Treasury	0.78	1.73
USA 10 Yr T	1.87	3.01
USA 20 Yr T	2.64	3.69
Moody's Aaa	3.77	4.55
Moody's Baa	4.71	5.35
CAN 5 Yr T	1.43	1.94
CAN 10 Yr T	1.87	2.75
Money Market	**2013**	**2014**
USA Fed Funds	0.25	0.25
USA 3 Mo T-B	0.07	0.07
CAN tgt overnight rate	1.00	1.00
CAN 3 Mo T-B	0.92	0.90
Foreign Exchange	**2013**	**2014**
EUR/USD	1.31	1.37
GBP/USD	1.62	1.65
USD/CAD	0.99	1.06
USD/JPY	87.24	105.08

Caterpillar Performance

Going into its seasonal period, CAT had been consolidating for most of 2013, pushing up against the $90 resistance level unsuccessfully. Overall, CAT was well set up to outperform at the start of its seasonal period, if positive news was able to shift investor sentiment. Just after the start of its seasonal period, CAT announced earnings above expectations, acting as a catalyst for strong performance in its seasonal period.

Technical Conditions– January 23rd to May 5th, 2014

Entry Strategy –Buy Position on Entry Date –

At the beginning of its seasonal period, CAT was below $90 and just above its 50 and 200 day moving averages❶. The FSO was just below 20❷, indicating an oversold level, the RSI was below 50 and trending down❸ and CAT was performing at market❹.

Exit Strategy– Bearish –Sell Position Early –

After performing well since its earnings announcement in January, CAT started to show signs of peaking in late April❺, ahead of its exit date. At the time, the FSO turned below 80, triggering an early sell signal❻. At the same time, the RSI pulled back from 70❼. Within the overall trend of outperforming the S&P 500, CAT had started to perform at market❽.

Overall, the trade was successful, producing a gain and outperforming the S&P 500.

JANUARY

M	T	W	T	F	S	S
			1	2	3	4
5	6	7	8	9	10	11
12	13	14	15	16	17	18
19	20	21	22	23	24	25
26	27	28	29	30	31	

FEBRUARY

M	T	W	T	F	S	S
						1
2	3	4	5	6	7	8
9	10	11	12	13	14	15
16	17	18	19	20	21	22
23	24	25	26	27	28	

MARCH

M	T	W	T	F	S	S
						1
2	3	4	5	6	7	8
9	10	11	12	13	14	15
16	17	18	19	20	21	22
23	24	25	26	27	28	29
30	31					

** Weekly avg closing values- except Fed Funds & CAN overnight tgt rate weekly closing values.

CLX CLOROX— CLEAN PROFITS
①LONG (Jan14-Mar2) ②LONG (Sep22-Nov17)
③SHORT (Nov18-Jan13)

Clorox tends to clean up twice a year with strong gains, once at the beginning of the year from January 14th to March 2nd and the second time from September 22nd to November 17th.

14.5% gain & positive 79% of the time

The strongest seasonal period for Clorox occurs from September 22nd to November 17th when it has produced an average gain of 7.2% and has been positive 79% of the time from 1990 to 2013.

Clorox is part of the consumer staples sector which has on average been one of the top performing major S&P GIC sectors in October since 1990. The sector typically performs well at this time of the year, as investors act cautiously in the transition time between the unfavorable and favorable six month periods that occurs in October.

The one major difference between Clorox and the consumer staples sector is that the consumer staples sector derives most of its revenues from foreign operations, compared to Clorox's 21%. (www.thecloroxcompany.com). This can be a benefit in an environment of a rising U.S. dollar.

① *CLX - stock symbol for Clorox Inc. which trades on the NYSE, adjusted for splits.*

Clorox* vs. S&P 500 1990 to 2013
Negative Short ☐ Positive Long ▨

Year	Jan 14 to Mar 02 S&P 500	Jan 14 to Mar 02 CLX	Sep 22 to Nov 17 S&P 500	Sep 22 to Nov 17 CLX	Nov 18 to Jan 13 S&P 500	Nov 18 to Jan 13 CLX	Compound Growth S&P 500	Compound Growth CLX
1990	-1.3 %	-5.0 %	1.9 %	2.6 %	-0.6	3.9 %	-0.1 %	-6.4 %
1991	17.5	9.3	-1.4	-1.2	8.3	2.5	25.5	5.2
1992	-0.5	18.0	-0.7	0.9	3.3	1.1	2.1	17.7
1993	3.4	6.1	2.6	2.6	1.7	-2.1	7.9	11.1
1994	-1.6	-0.2	0.5	10.1	0.5	0.0	-0.7	9.8
1995	4.1	9.6	2.9	7.0	0.3	-6.7	7.5	25.2
1996	7.1	20.6	7.4	13.3	3.0	-7.2	18.4	46.4
1997	4.1	19.4	-0.5	3.5	0.6	1.8	4.3	21.3
1998	10.0	13.7	11.3	42.7	8.4	-3.5	32.7	68.0
1999	-0.7	12.4	7.9	17.4	2.8	11.5	10.1	16.7
2000	-4.7	-26.1	-5.6	26.0	-3.6	-27.3	-13.3	18.4
2001	-6.4	5.0	17.9	13.2	0.6	-1.4	11.0	20.5
2002	-1.2	14.0	7.6	5.8	1.8	-12.8	8.2	35.9
2003	-9.2	6.7	0.7	3.8	7.4	-1.8	-1.8	12.8
2004	2.5	4.1	4.7	7.5	-0.4	0.9	6.9	10.8
2005	2.8	4.3	2.7	-2.8	3.6	8.2	9.3	-6.9
2006	0.1	4.8	6.3	3.0	2.1	-1.6	8.7	9.7
2007	-3.0	-2.3	-4.4	8.4	-4.0	-7.0	-11.0	13.4
2008	-5.0	-5.5	-32.2	-4.4	2.5	-12.5	-34.0	1.7
2009	-19.6	-9.9	4.3	4.4	3.2	2.9	-13.5	-8.6
2010	-2.4	-0.5	3.4	-5.9	8.9	1.0	9.9	-7.4
2011	1.9	6.8	4.2	-2.7	6.0	4.7	12.6	-1.0
2012	6.3	-0.7	-6.9	4.1	8.3	1.9	7.1	1.4
2013	3.1	11.0	5.2	13.3	1.2	-4.8	9.7	31.8
Avg.	0.3 %	4.8 %	1.7 %	7.2 %	2.7 %	-2.0 %	4.9 %	14.5 %
Fq>0	50 %	67 %	71	79 %	83 %	46 %	71 %	79 %

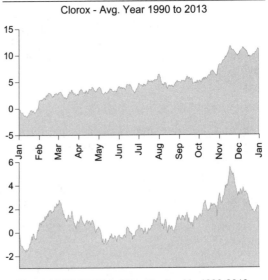

Clorox - Avg. Year 1990 to 2013

Clorox / S&P 500 Rel. Strength- Avg Yr. 1990-2013

2013-14 Strategy Performance

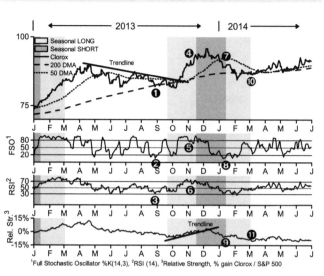

¹Full Stochastic Oscillator %K(14,3), ²RSI (14), ³Relative Strength, % gain Clorox / S&P 500

Market Indices & Rates
Weekly Values**

Stock Markets	2013	2014
Dow	13,413	16,460
S&P500	1,465	1,837
Nasdaq	3,109	4,153
TSX	12,546	13,617
FTSE	6,088	6,728
DAX	7,715	9,465
Nikkei	10,628	15,927
Hang Seng	23,256	22,805

Commodities	2013	2014
Oil	93.36	92.76
Gold	1,658.3	1,233.0

Bond Yields	2013	2014
USA 5 Yr Treasury	0.79	1.71
USA 10 Yr T	1.90	2.96
USA 20 Yr T	2.67	3.63
Moody's Aaa	3.77	4.53
Moody's Baa	4.70	5.28
CAN 5 Yr T	1.47	1.86
CAN 10 Yr T	1.93	2.67

Money Market	2013	2014
USA Fed Funds	0.25	0.25
USA 3 Mo T-B	0.07	0.05
CAN tgt overnight rate	1.00	1.00
CAN 3 Mo T-B	0.91	0.89

Foreign Exchange	2013	2014
EUR/USD	1.32	1.36
GBP/USD	1.61	1.64
USD/CAD	0.99	1.08
USD/JPY	88.14	104.54

Clorox Performance

Clorox turned down in April 2013 and started to underperform the S&P 500. It maintained a consistent downward trend, but managed to bounce off its 200 day moving average at the beginning of September.

Technical Conditions– September to March 2014

–September Long Position–

After trending downwards for most of 2013, Clorox bounced off its 200 day moving average❶. An early buy signal was triggered when the FSO crossed back over 20❷ in early September. At the time, the RSI bounced off 30❸. Although Clorox was performing well and above its 50 and 200 day moving averages❹, a sell signal was triggered when the FSO crossed below 80❺ at the beginning of November. At the time, the RSI supported an early exit crossing below 70❻.

–November Short Position–

Neither the entry or the exit dates were adjusted by technical indicators. The short position of the trade was successful.

–January Long Position–

At the start of the trade, Clorox was below its 50 day moving average❼ and although the overall trend was down the FSO triggered a buy signal as it crossed back over 20❽. At the time, Clorox was performing at market❾. Clorox lost ground and ended the trade on its 200 day moving average❿ and underperforming the S&P 500⓫. Overall, the complete trade combination of a long, short and long position was positive and outperformed the S&P 500.

JANUARY

M	T	W	T	F	S	S
			1	2	3	4
5	6	7	8	9	10	11
12	13	14	15	16	17	18
19	20	21	22	23	24	25
26	27	28	29	30	31	

FEBRUARY

M	T	W	T	F	S	S
						1
2	3	4	5	6	7	8
9	10	11	12	13	14	15
16	17	18	19	20	21	22
23	24	25	26	27	28	

MARCH

M	T	W	T	F	S	S
						1
2	3	4	5	6	7	8
9	10	11	12	13	14	15
16	17	18	19	20	21	22
23	24	25	26	27	28	29
30	31					

RETAIL – POST HOLIDAY BARGAIN
1st of II Retail Strategies for the Year
SHOP Jan 21st and RETURN Your Investment Apr 12th

When large exogenous unpredictable events take place, they can overwhelm a seasonal influence. In late 2013 and into early 2014, the north-east coast of the U.S. suffered extreme weather, keeping shoppers away from the stores. As a result, the retail sector underperformed in its seasonal period.

Historically, the retail sector has outperformed from January 21st until April 12th - the start of the next earnings season. From 1990 to 2014, during its seasonally strong period, the retail sector produced an average gain of 8.2%, compared with the S&P 500 average gain of 2.2%. Not only has the retail sector had greater gains than the broad market, but it has also outperformed it on a fairly regular basis: 80% of the time.

> ### *6% extra & 80% of the time better than the S&P 500*

Jan 21 to Apr 12	S&P 500	Positive Retail	Diff
1990	1.5 %	9.7 %	8.1 %
1991	14.5	29.9	15.4
1992	-2.9	-2.7	0.2
1993	3.5	-0.6	-4.0
1994	-5.8	2.0	7.8
1995	9.1	7.4	-1.8
1996	4.1	19.7	15.7
1997	-5.0	6.0	11.0
1998	13.5	20.1	6.6
1999	8.1	23.4	15.2
2000	1.5	5.8	4.3
2001	-11.8	-0.5	11.3
2002	-1.5	6.7	8.2
2003	-3.7	6.5	10.3
2004	0.6	6.7	6.1
2005	1.1	-1.6	-2.7
2006	2.1	3.4	1.3
2007	1.2	-0.7	-1.9
2008	0.6	3.5	3.0
2009	6.4	25.1	18.7
2010	5.1	15.5	10.4
2011	2.7	4.4	1.7
2012	5.5	12.1	6.6
2013	6.9	10.1	3.2
2014	-1.3	-7.1	-5.8
Avg.	2.2 %	8.2 %	6.0 %
Fq > 0	72 %	76 %	80 %

Caption: Retail Sector vs. S&P 500 1990 to 2014

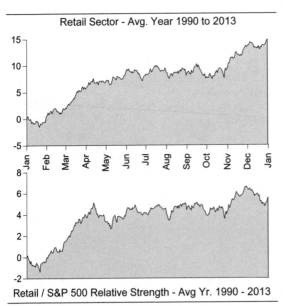

Retail Sector - Avg. Year 1990 to 2013

Retail / S&P 500 Relative Strength - Avg Yr. 1990 - 2013

not nearly as strong as the cycle from January to April.

The January retail bounce coincides with the "rosy" stock market analysts' forecasts that tend to occur at the beginning of the year. These forecasts generally rely on healthy consumer spending which makes up approximately 2/3 of the GDP. The retail sector benefits from the optimistic forecasts and tends to outperform the S&P 500.

From a seasonal basis, investors have been best served by exiting the retail sector in April and then returning to it later at the end of October (see *Retail Shop Early* strategy).

> (i) *Retail SP GIC Sector # 2550:*
> *An index designed to represent a cross section of retail companies*
> *For more information on the retail sector, see www.standardandpoors.com.*

Most investors think that the best time to invest in retail stocks is before Black Friday in November. Yes, there is a positive seasonal cycle at this time, but it is

2013-14 Strategy Performance

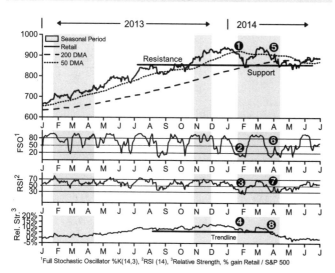

¹Full Stochastic Oscillator %K(14,3), ²RSI (14), ³Relative Strength, % gain Retail / S&P 500

Market Indices & Rates
Weekly Values**

Stock Markets	2013	2014
Dow	13,560	16,398
S&P500	1,477	1,838
Nasdaq	3,123	4,185
TSX	12,651	13,773
FTSE	6,123	6,798
DAX	7,707	9,649
Nikkei	10,751	15,678
Hang Seng	23,419	22,940

Commodities	2013	2014
Oil	94.58	93.38
Gold	1677.4	1,245.4

Bond Yields	2013	2014
USA 5 Yr Treasury	0.77	1.65
USA 10 Yr T	1.87	2.86
USA 20 Yr T	2.63	3.53
Moody's Aaa	3.76	4.48
Moody's Baa	4.69	5.19
CAN 5 Yr T	1.46	1.74
CAN 10 Yr T	1.92	2.55

Money Market	2013	2014
USA Fed Funds	0.25	0.25
USA 3 Mo T-B	0.08	0.04
CAN tgt overnight rate	1.00	1.00
CAN 3 Mo T-B	0.90	0.89

Foreign Exchange	2013	2014
EUR/USD	1.33	1.36
GBP/USD	1.60	1.64
USD/CAD	0.99	1.09
USD/JPY	89.33	104.09

Retail Sector Performance

The retail sector performed positively and outperformed the S&P 500 in its November seasonal period. At the beginning of 2014, it started to perform negatively and underperform the S&P 500 as the effects of the extremely cold weather had a chilling effect on retail sales.

Technical Conditions – January 21st to April 12th, 2014

Entry Strategy –Buy Position on Entry Date–
At the start of the January retail trade, the sector was heading down❶ as investors were concerned that the harsh winter weather was keeping shoppers out of the stores. The FSO was below 20❷, the RSI close to 30❸ and the retail sector was just starting to perform at market❹.

Exit Strategy –Sell Position Early–
Towards the end of March, the retail sector was trading just below its 50 day moving average❺, the FSO was at 50❻ and the RSI was at 50❼. At the time, the retail sector started to underperform the S&P 500❽, triggering an early sell signal. When a sector demonstrates underperformance relative to the S&P 500, it is time to exit the trade.

In the end, the *Retail- Post Holiday Bargain* was not successful. Exiting the trade early, when the retail sector started to underperform the S&P 500, helped to mitigate the losses of the trade.

JANUARY

M	T	W	T	F	S	S
			1	2	3	4
5	6	7	8	9	10	11
12	13	14	15	16	17	18
19	20	21	22	23	24	25
26	27	28	29	30	31	

FEBRUARY

M	T	W	T	F	S	S
						1
2	3	4	5	6	7	8
9	10	11	12	13	14	15
16	17	18	19	20	21	22
23	24	25	26	27	28	

MARCH

M	T	W	T	F	S	S
						1
2	3	4	5	6	7	8
9	10	11	12	13	14	15
16	17	18	19	20	21	22
23	24	25	26	27	28	29
30	31					

** Weekly avg closing values- except Fed Funds & CAN overnight tgt rate weekly closing values.

TJX COMPANIES INC.
January 22nd to March 30th

In 2014, TJX during its seasonally strong period, out-performed the retail sector, but produced a small loss. Over the long-term, TJX stock has typically outper-formed the retail sector when the sector has been pos-itive, making it an excellent complement to a retail sector investment during its seasonal period.

TJX is an off-price apparel and home fashions retailer that typically reports its fourth quarter earnings in ap-proximately the third week of February. The compa-ny, like the retail sector, benefits from investors expecting positive results from the Christmas season.

TJX's period of seasonal strength is similar to the sea-sonal period for the retail sector. The best time to in-vest in TJX has been from January 22nd to March 30th. From 1990 to 2014, investing in this period has produced an average gain of 12.7%, which is substan-tially better than the 1.8% performance of the S&P 500. It is also important to note that the stock has been positive 72% of the time during this period.

12.7% gain & positive 72% of the time

Equally impressive is the amount of times TJX has produced a large gain, versus a large loss in its sea-sonal period. In the last twenty-five years, TJX has only had one loss of 10% or greater. This compares to twelve times where the company had gains of 10% or greater.

Jan 22 to Mar 30	S&P 500	Retail	TJX
1990	0.2%	6.3%	6.7%
1991	13.3	21.7	61.9
1992	-2.3	1.7	17.0
1993	3.8	3.0	21.7
1994	-6.1	-0.1	-2.8
1995	8.1	9.7	-6.9
1996	5.5	19.7	43.6
1997	-1.1	10.4	-0.3
1998	12.6	19.7	25.4
1999	5.3	16.5	18.9
2000	3.2	5.1	35.4
2001	-13.6	1.7	16.4
2002	1.8	4.7	2.9
2003	-2.7	6.6	-6.7
2004	-1.8	5.4	3.5
2005	1.2	-0.6	-1.6
2006	3.1	4.5	3.8
2007	-0.7	-2.7	-10.2
2008	-0.8	1.4	13.1
2009	-6.3	8.1	29.0
2010	5.1	12.5	17.2
2011	3.5	3.5	6.1
2012	7.1	12.9	19.3
2013	5.6	6.2	4.5
2014	0.8	-2.7	-0.2
Avg	1.8%	7.0%	12.7%
Fq > 0	64%	84%	72%

TJX* vs. Retail vs. S&P 500 — 1990 to 2014 (Positive)

It is interesting to note that the season-ally strong period for TJX ends before one of the strongest months of the year, April. It is possible that by the end of March, after a typically strong run for TJX, that the full value of TJX's first quarter earnings report has already been priced into the stock and investors look to other companies in which to invest. This is particularly true if the economy and the stock mar-ket are in good shape.

On the other hand, in a soft economy, consumers favor off-price apparel companies such as TJX. In this sce-nario, TJX is more likely to perform strongly past the end of its seasonal period in March, allowing seasonal investors to continue to hold TJX un-til it shows signs of weakness.

TJX - Avg. Year 1990 to 2013

TJX / S&P 500 Relative Strength - Avg Yr. 1990 - 2013

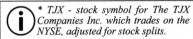

(i) * TJX - stock symbol for The TJX Companies Inc. which trades on the NYSE, adjusted for stock splits.

2013-14 Strategy Performance

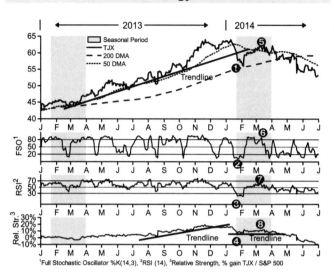

[1]Full Stochastic Oscillator %K(14,3), [2]RSI (14), [3]Relative Strength, % gain TJX / S&P 500

Market Indices & Rates
Weekly Values**

Stock Markets	2013	2014
Dow	13,803	16,216
S&P500	1,496	1,827
Nasdaq	3,144	4,204
TSX	12,811	13,916
FTSE	6,221	6,787
DAX	7,752	9,638
Nikkei	10,698	15,669
Hang Seng	23,613	22,846

Commodities	2013	2014
Oil	95.34	96.46
Gold	1679.9	1253.0

Bond Yields	2013	2014
USA 5 Yr Treasury	0.79	1.65
USA 10 Yr T	1.90	2.82
USA 20 Yr T	2.66	3.47
Moody's Aaa	3.78	4.46
Moody's Baa	4.72	5.13
CAN 5 Yr T	1.45	1.65
CAN 10 Yr T	1.91	2.46

Money Market	2013	2014
USA Fed Funds	0.25	0.25
USA 3 Mo T-B	0.08	0.04
CAN tgt overnight rate	1.00	1.00
CAN 3 Mo T-B	0.92	0.90

Foreign Exchange	2013	2014
EUR/USD	1.34	1.36
GBP/USD	1.58	1.65
USD/CAD	1.00	1.10
USD/JPY	89.63	103.71

TJX Performance

For most of 2013, TJX was in a solid uptrend and was outperforming the S&P 500. In December, TJX started to perform at market and in January, TJX started to correct along with other retail stocks as the result of the harsh weather on the U.S. north-east coast, dampening retail sales.

Technical Conditions– January 22nd to March 30th, 2014

Entry Strategy –Buy Position on Entry Date–

TJX corrected sharply before its seasonal period. At the start of its seasonal period, it broke its upward trendline❶, indicating possible further weakness ahead. At the time, the FSO was indicating an oversold condition with a reading below 20❷. In addition, the RSI was below 30❸. On a positive note, TJX broke its downward trend of underperformance relative to the S&P 500 and started to perform at market❹.

Exit Strategy –Sell Position Early–

In mid-March, TJX was trading above its 50 day moving average❺, but the FSO crossed below 80❻, indicating an early sell signal. At the time, the RSI was above 50❼ and had just started to turn down, and TJX was outperforming the S&P 500❽.

The early sell signal proved to be profitable as it produced a positive return and outperformance of the S&P 500, compared with waiting until the exit date in April, which produced a loss and underperformance of the S&P 500.

JANUARY

M	T	W	T	F	S	S
			1	2	3	4
5	6	7	8	9	10	11
12	13	14	15	16	17	18
19	20	21	22	23	24	25
26	27	28	29	30	31	

FEBRUARY

M	T	W	T	F	S	S
						1
2	3	4	5	6	7	8
9	10	11	12	13	14	15
16	17	18	19	20	21	22
23	24	25	26	27	28	

MARCH

M	T	W	T	F	S	S
						1
2	3	4	5	6	7	8
9	10	11	12	13	14	15
16	17	18	19	20	21	22
23	24	25	26	27	28	29
30	31					

** Weekly avg closing values- except Fed Funds & CAN overnight tgt rate weekly closing values.

ROYAL BANK— A TRADE TO BANK ON
①Oct 10 - Nov 28 ②Jan 23 - Apr 13

Canadians love their banks and tend to hold large amounts of the banking sector in their portfolios. Their love for the sector has remained strong, as international accolades have supported a positive viewpoint of Canadian banks. In a 2012 Bloomberg report, the Canadian banks dominated the top ten strongest banks in the world, with four banks in the top ten.

For years, Royal Bank was considered one of the most conservative banks and often attracted investors during tough times. After a few mis-steps in their expansion into the U.S., Royal Bank seems to be getting back on track.

Through its ups and downs, Royal Bank has followed the same general pattern as the banking sector: rising in autumn and then once again in the new year.

11.9% gain & positive 76% of the time

In the period from October 10th to November 28th, from 1989 to 2013, Royal Bank has produced an average gain of 5.2% and has been positive 88% of the time. The bank tends to perform well at this time, as Canadians tend to increase their bank holdings before the year-end earnings reports are released in late November. It is not a coincidence that Royal Bank's seasonally strong period ends at approximately the same time as their year-end earnings announcements. Seasonal investors benefit from buying Royal Bank before the "masses," whom are also trying to take advantage of the possibility of positive earnings.

The second seasonal period from January 23rd to April 13 is also very positive. In this time period, Canadian banks in general tend to outperform the TSX Composite, as they benefit from the typically strong economic forecasts at the beginning of the year. In addition, they "echo," or get a boost from the strong seasonal performance of the U.S banks at this time.

Royal Bank* vs. TSX Comp 1989/90 to 2013/14 Positive ☐

Year	Oct 10 to Nov 28		Jan 23 to Apr 13		Compound Growth	
	TSX Comp	RY	TSX Comp	RY	TSX Comp	RY
1989/90	-2.8 %	2.4 %	-6.3 %	-10.0 %	-8.9 %	-7.8 %
1990/91	0.2	3.5	9.8	11.6	10.0	15.5
1991/92	2.9	3.3	-6.8	-14.5	-4.1	-11.6
1992/93	1.8	5.0	10.7	17.6	12.6	23.4
1993/94	3.8	0.0	-5.6	-13.1	-2.1	-13.1
1994/95	-4.7	2.2	5.0	13.2	0.0	15.7
1995/96	4.0	3.3	3.6	0.0	7.7	3.3
1996/97	10.7	23.3	-6.2	1.3	3.9	24.9
1997/98	-8.7	7.6	19.9	24.0	9.4	33.4
1998/99	18.0	20.9	4.8	0.6	23.7	21.6
1999/00	10.9	8.6	3.8	34.5	15.1	46.0
2000/01	-14.5	5.1	-14.1	-12.0	-26.5	-7.5
2001/02	7.1	3.2	2.3	11.8	9.6	15.4
2002/03	16.4	18.1	-4.3	1.8	11.4	20.2
2003/04	3.4	0.3	2.0	1.8	5.4	2.1
2004/05	2.8	4.0	4.5	17.6	7.3	22.3
2005/06	3.1	7.3	5.5	7.0	8.8	14.8
2006/07	7.2	8.5	6.9	7.1	14.5	16.2
2007/08	-4.4	-5.1	8.2	-4.9	3.5	-9.8
2008/09	-3.4	4.3	9.4	35.0	5.7	40.8
2009/10	0.2	1.3	6.7	12.6	6.9	14.1
2010/11	2.9	0.4	4.3	12.4	7.3	12.8
2011/12	0.5	-6.3	-2.9	3.8	-2.4	-2.8
2012/13	-1.1	2.1	-3.8	-0.3	-4.8	1.9
2013/14	5.0	6.0	1.9	-0.5	7.1	5.5
Avg.	2.5 %	5.2 %	2.4 %	6.3 %	4.8 %	11.9 %
Fq > 0	72 %	88 %	68 %	68 %	76 %	76 %

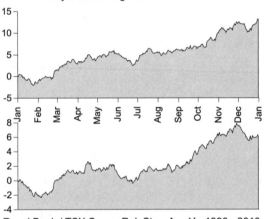

Royal Bank* Avg. Year 1990 to 2013

Royal Bank / TSX Comp. Rel. Str. - Avg Yr. 1990 - 2013

Alternate Strategy—
Investors can bridge the gap between the two positive seasonal trends for the bank sector by holding from October 10th to April 13th. Longer term investors may prefer this strategy, shorter term investors can use technical tools to determine the appropriate strategy.

ⓘ *Royal Bank of Canada (RBC) is a diversified financial services company that trades on both the Toronto and NYSE exchanges under the symbol RY. Data from TSX Exchange, includes stock splits only.*

2013-14 Strategy Performance

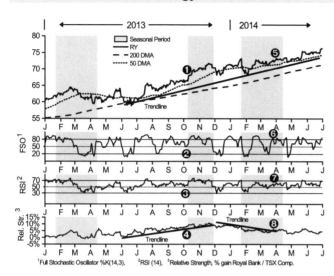

¹Full Stochastic Oscillator %K(14,3), ²RSI (14), ³Relative Strength, % gain Royal Bank / TSX Comp.

Market Indices & Rates
Weekly Values**

Stock Markets	2013	2014
Dow	13,923	15,811
S&P500	1,504	1,785
Nasdaq	3,154	4,092
TSX	12,779	13,669
FTSE	6,316	6,543
DAX	7,820	9,355
Nikkei	11,027	15,058
Hang Seng	23,720	22,028

Commodities	2013	2014
Oil	97.44	97.24
Gold	1666.3	1253.9

Bond Yields	2013	2014
USA 5 Yr Treasury	0.89	1.55
USA 10 Yr T	2.02	2.73
USA 20 Yr T	2.79	3.39
Moody's Aaa	3.91	4.45
Moody's Baa	4.85	5.10
CAN 5 Yr T	1.50	1.59
CAN 10 Yr T	2.00	2.39

Money Market	2013	2014
USA Fed Funds	0.25	0.25
USA 3 Mo T-B	0.06	0.04
CAN tgt overnight rate	1.00	1.00
CAN 3 Mo T-B	0.93	0.89

Foreign Exchange	2013	2014
EUR/USD	1.35	1.36
GBP/USD	1.58	1.65
USD/CAD	1.00	1.11
USD/JPY	91.43	102.51

Royal Bank Performance

In first half of 2013, Royal Bank's performance was fairly flat. In August of 2013, Canadian banks released strong earnings reports helping to boost the banking sector. In addition, the media was writing about the possibility that some Canadian banks might raise their dividends and split their stocks at their year-ends in October (Canadian banks generally release their earnings reports towards the last week of November).

Technical Conditions– October 10, 2012 to April 13, 2014

Entry Strategy –Buy Position on Entry Date–

After rising and outperforming the TSX Composite since August, Royal Bank was entering its seasonal period on a strong note. It was in an upwards trend, trading above its 50 day moving average❶. The FSO❷ and RSI❸ both bounced off 50 and Royal Bank was outperforming the TSX Composite❹.

Exit Strategy –Sell Position Early–

Note: The exit date being discussed is for the second seasonal period from January 23rd to April 13th. After underperforming from late in November (after releasing its year-end report) to late January, Royal Bank was able to stabilize against the TSX Composite. In late March, Royal Bank was trading above its 50 day moving average❺, but an early sell signal was triggered when the FSO crossed below 80❻. At the time, the RSI was above 50❼ and Royal Bank was performing at market❽. Overall, the combination of the October 10th to November 28th trade and the January 23rd to April 13th trade, worked well producing a gain and outperforming the TSX Composite.

JANUARY

M	T	W	T	F	S	S
		1	2	3	4	
5	6	7	8	9	10	11
12	13	14	15	16	17	18
19	20	21	22	23	24	25
26	27	28	29	30	31	

FEBRUARY

M	T	W	T	F	S	S
						1
2	3	4	5	6	7	8
9	10	11	12	13	14	15
16	17	18	19	20	21	22
23	24	25	26	27	28	

MARCH

M	T	W	T	F	S	S
						1
2	3	4	5	6	7	8
9	10	11	12	13	14	15
16	17	18	19	20	21	22
23	24	25	26	27	28	29
30	31					

FEBRUARY

	MONDAY	TUESDAY	WEDNESDAY
WEEK 06	**2** 26	**3** 25	**4** 24
WEEK 07	**9** 19	**10** 18	**11** 17
WEEK 08	**16** 12 CAN Market Closed - Family Day USA Market Closed - Presidents' Day	**17** 11	**18** 10
WEEK 09	**23** 5	**24** 4	**25** 3
WEEK 10	2	3	4

THURSDAY		FRIDAY	
5	23	**6**	22
12	16	**13**	15
19	9	**20**	8
26	2	**27**	1
5		6	

MARCH

M	T	W	T	F	S	S
						1
2	3	4	5	6	7	8
9	10	11	12	13	14	15
16	17	18	19	20	21	22
23	24	25	26	27	28	29
30	31					

APRIL

M	T	W	T	F	S	S
		1	2	3	4	5
6	7	8	9	10	11	12
13	14	15	16	17	18	19
20	21	22	23	24	25	26
27	28	29	30			

MAY

M	T	W	T	F	S	S
				1	2	3
4	5	6	7	8	9	10
11	12	13	14	15	16	17
18	19	20	21	22	23	24
25	26	27	28	29	30	31

JUNE

M	T	W	T	F	S	S
1	2	3	4	5	6	7
8	9	10	11	12	13	14
15	16	17	18	19	20	21
22	23	24	25	26	27	28
29	30					

FEBRUARY
S U M M A R Y

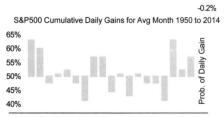

0.4%
0.2%
0.0%
-0.2%

S&P500 Cumulative Daily Gains for Avg Month 1950 to 2014

Prob. of Daily Gain

	Dow Jones	S&P 500	Nasdaq	TSX Comp
Month Rank	8	11	9	5
# Up	37	35	22	17
# Down	27	29	20	12
% Pos	58	55	52	59
% Avg. Gain	0.1	-0.1	0.4	0.9

Dow & S&P 1950-2013, Nasdaq 1972-2013, TSX 1985-2013

65%
60%
55%
50%
45%
40%

♦ Historically, February has been the second weakest month of the year. From 1950 to 2013, the S&P 500 has produced an average loss of 0.03% and has been positive 55% of the time. ♦ In the last four years (2011 to 2014), February has produced strong gains. ♦ In February 2014, the S&P 500 produced a gain of 4.3% with gains across a large number of sectors. Its strong performance was mainly the result of investors jumping back into the stock market after a weak January.

BEST / WORST FEBRUARY BROAD MKTS. 2005-2014

BEST FEBRUARY MARKETS
- ♦ Nikkei 225 (2012) 10.5%
- ♦ Nasdaq (2012) 5.4%
- ♦ Russell 2000 (2011) 5.4%

WORST FEBRUARY MARKETS
- ♦ Russell 2000 (2009) -12.3%
- ♦ Dow (2009) -11.7%
- ♦ S&P 500 (2009) -11.0%

Index Values End of Month

	2005	2006	2007	2008	2009	2010	2011	2012	2013	2014
Dow	10,766	10,993	12,269	12,266	7,063	10,325	12,226	12,952	14,054	16,322
S&P 500	1,204	1,281	1,407	1,331	735	1,104	1,327	1,366	1,515	1,859
Nasdaq	2,052	2,281	2,416	2,271	1,378	2,238	2,782	2,967	3,160	4,308
TSX Comp.	9,668	11,688	13,045	13,583	8,123	11,630	14,137	12,644	12,822	14,210
Russell 1000	1,244	1,341	1,478	1,396	768	1,168	1,415	1,454	1,617	2,002
Russell 2000	1,576	1,816	1,972	1,705	967	1,562	2,046	2,015	2,264	2,940
FTSE 100	4,969	5,792	6,172	5,884	3,830	5,355	5,994	5,872	6,361	6,810
Nikkei 225	11,741	16,205	17,604	13,603	7,568	10,126	10,624	9,723	11,559	14,841

Percent Gain for February

	2005	2006	2007	2008	2009	2010	2011	2012	2013	2014
Dow	2.6	1.2	-2.8	-3.0	-11.7	2.6	2.8	2.5	1.4	4.0
S&P 500	1.9	0.0	-2.2	-3.5	-11.0	2.9	3.2	4.1	1.1	4.3
Nasdaq	-0.5	-1.1	-1.9	-5.0	-6.7	4.2	3.0	5.4	0.6	5.0
TSX Comp.	5.0	-2.2	0.1	3.3	-6.6	4.8	4.3	1.5	1.1	3.8
Russell 1000	2.0	0.0	-1.9	-3.3	-10.7	3.1	3.3	4.1	1.1	4.5
Russell 2000	1.6	-0.3	-0.9	-3.8	-12.3	4.4	5.4	2.3	1.0	4.6
FTSE 100	2.4	0.5	-0.5	0.1	-7.7	3.2	2.2	3.3	1.3	4.6
Nikkei 225	3.1	-2.7	1.3	0.1	-5.3	-0.7	3.8	10.5	3.8	-0.5

February Market Avg. Performance 2005 to 2014[1]

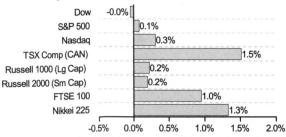

	Dow	-0.0%
	S&P 500	0.1%
	Nasdaq	0.3%
	TSX Comp (CAN)	1.5%
	Russell 1000 (Lg Cap)	0.2%
	Russell 2000 (Sm Cap)	0.2%
	FTSE 100	1.0%
	Nikkei 225	1.3%

-0.5%   0.0%   0.5%   1.0%   1.5%   2.0%

Interest Corner Feb[2]

	Fed Funds % [3]	3 Mo. T-Bill % [4]	10 Yr % [5]	20 Yr % [6]
2014	0.25	0.05	2.66	3.31
2013	0.25	0.11	1.89	2.71
2012	0.25	0.08	1.98	2.73
2011	0.25	0.15	3.42	4.25
2010	0.25	0.13	3.61	4.40

(1) Russell Data provided by Russell (2) Federal Reserve Bank of St. Louis- end of month values (3) Target rate set by FOMC (4)(5)(6) Constant yield maturities.

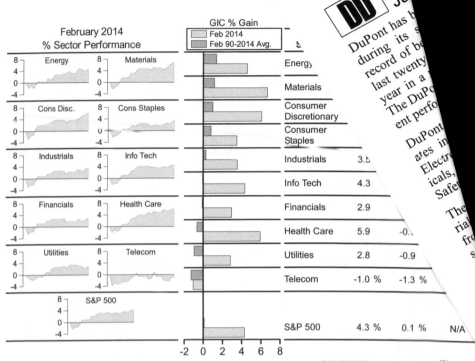

February 2014
% Sector Performance

GIC % Gain — Feb 2014 / Feb 90-2014 Avg.

Sector	Feb 2014	Feb 90-2014 Avg.	
Energy			
Materials			
Consumer Discretionary			
Consumer Staples			
Industrials	3.5		
Info Tech	4.3		
Financials	2.9		
Health Care	5.9	-0.?	
Utilities	2.8	-0.9	
Telecom	-1.0 %	-1.3 %	
S&P 500	4.3 %	0.1 %	N/A

-2 0 2 4 6 8

Sector Commentary

♦ In February 2014, the market showed its strength as all of the majors sectors except telecom, increased in value. ♦ The top performing sector in February was the materials sector, as investors were becoming more optimistic about the economy. ♦The consumer discretionary sector managed to put in a good performance as investors anticipated increasing retail sales after January's poor winter weather. ♦Health care performed well, as mergers and acquisitions in the sector continued from January.

Sub-Sector Commentary

♦ In February, silver rallied strongly past gold, benefiting from being a precious metal and an industrial metal. It gained 10.2% in the month. ♦ The retail sub-sector produced an 8.0% gain, bouncing back after a poor January. ♦The chemicals sub-sector, typically performs well in February and in 2014 it produced a solid gain of 7.8%. ♦ Pharma and Biotech benefited from investors' strong interest in the health care sector. Typically, biotech does not perform well in February and any rally that has occurred at the end of the year and into January, usually fizzles. An above average number of mergers and acquisitions helped to propel the biotech sub-sector upwards in February.

SELECTED SUB-SECTORS[3]

Sub-Sector			
Silver	10.2 %	2.7 %	52 %
SOX (1995-2014)	6.5	2.7	60
Retail	8.0	1.8	72
Chemicals	7.8	1.5	72
Metals & Mining	2.2	1.1	52
Gold (London PM)	6.0	1.0	48
Agriculture (1994-2014)	2.8	0.7	52
Transportation	1.5	0.4	56
Steel	1.8	0.3	48
Banks	2.8	0.1	56
Railroads	1.4	0.1	48
Software & Services	4.7	-0.1	48
Homebuilders	5.7	-0.2	60
Pharma	7.2	-0.7	40
Biotech (1993-2014)	5.9	-1.1	55

een positive for the last fourteen years easonally strong period, extending a ing positive twenty-four times over the five years. In 2014 and for the seventh ow, DuPont outperformed the S&P 500. nt trade is considered to be a strong consist- mer at this time of the year.

is a diversified chemicals company that oper- seven segments: Agriculture & Nutrition, nics & Communications, Performance Chem- Performance Coatings, Performance Materials, y & Protection, and Pharmaceuticals.

chemicals sector is a large part of the U.S. mate- s sector, which has a seasonally strong period m January 23rd to May 5th. DuPont has a similar asonal trend that starts a few days later on January 8th. Investors can use technical analysis to deter- mine if an earlier position in DuPont should be taken.

10.9% gain & positive 96% of the time

The DuPont seasonal trade has worked very well since 1990, producing an average gain of 10.9% with a very high 96% frequency rate of being positive.

DuPont vs. S&P 500 1990 to 2014			
			Positive
Jan 28 to May 5	S&P 500	DD	Diff
1990	3.9%	0.3%	-3.5%
1991	13.3	19.6	6.3
1992	0.5	11.2	10.7
1993	1.5	15.2	13.8
1994	-5.4	6.6	12.0
1995	10.6	21.8	11.2
1996	3.2	6.1	2.9
1997	8.5	4.4	-4.2
1998	15.1	35.2	20.0
1999	8.4	33.6	25.2
2000	2.4	-16.7	-19.1
2001	-6.5	12.8	19.3
2002	-5.3	3.2	8.4
2003	9.3	11.3	2.0
2004	-2.0	2.5	4.5
2005	-0.2	2.6	2.8
2006	3.3	13.4	10.1
2007	5.9	4.2	-1.7
2008	5.8	11.1	5.4
2009	6.9	24.9	18.1
2010	6.2	15.3	9.0
2011	2.7	7.2	4.4
2012	4.0	4.3	0.3
2013	7.4	11.6	4.2
2014	5.8	11.9	6.1
Avg	4.2%	10.9%	6.7%
Fq > 0	80%	96%	84%

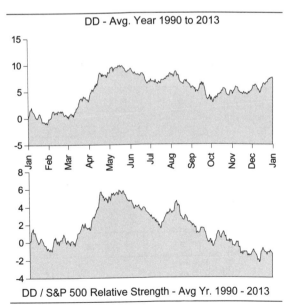

DD - Avg. Year 1990 to 2013

DD / S&P 500 Relative Strength - Avg Yr. 1990 - 2013

end of the year. In fact, during this period, from 1990 to 2013, DuPont has generated an average loss of 2.0% and has only been positive 42% of the time.

This compares to the S&P 500, which has produced an average gain of 4.2% and has been positive 71% of the time, during the same time period.

If investors are interested in purchasing DuPont on a seasonal basis, it is clear that they should concentrate their efforts from the end of January to the beginning of May.

Investors should be aware that DuPont does not perform as well as the broad market from May 6th to the

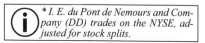

I. E. du Pont de Nemours and Company (DD) trades on the NYSE, adjusted for stock splits.

2013-14 Strategy Performance

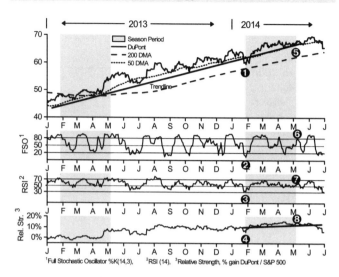

¹Full Stochastic Oscillator %K(14,3), ²RSI (14), ³Relative Strength, % gain DuPont / S&P 500

Market Indices & Rates Weekly Values**

Stock Markets	2013	2014
Dow	13,957	15,536
S&P500	1,509	1,764
Nasdaq	3,166	4,045
TSX	12,756	13,610
FTSE	6,263	6,501
DAX	7,625	9,198
Nikkei	11,256	14,285
Hang Seng	23,297	21,432
Commodities	**2013**	**2014**
Oil	96.20	97.74
Gold	1670.0	1256.5
Bond Yields	**2013**	**2014**
USA 5 Yr Treasury	0.85	1.48
USA 10 Yr T	2.00	2.68
USA 20 Yr T	2.80	3.37
Moody's Aaa	3.90	4.45
Moody's Baa	4.86	5.09
CAN 5 Yr T	1.48	1.57
CAN 10 Yr T	1.99	2.38
Money Market	**2013**	**2014**
USA Fed Funds	0.25	0.25
USA 3 Mo T-B	0.07	0.07
CAN tgt overnight rate	1.00	1.00
CAN 3 Mo T-B	0.94	0.88
Foreign Exchange	**2013**	**2014**
EUR/USD	1.35	1.36
GBP/USD	1.57	1.63
USD/CAD	1.00	1.11
USD/JPY	93.19	101.70

Dupont Performance

In 2013, DuPont performed positively during its seasonal period and outperformed the S&P 500. For the rest of 2013, DuPont continued its positive trend and just before the start of its seasonal period in 2014, it dipped below its trendline, setting up for a possible bounce as its seasonal period started.

Technical Conditions– January 28th to May 5th, 2014

Entry Strategy –Buy Position on Entry Date–

At the start of its seasonal period, DuPont was trading below its 50 day moving average❶ and the FSO was showing a short-term oversold condition with a reading below 20❷. The RSI was registering just above 30❸ and its relative strength, compared to the S&P 500 temporarily dipped❹. As a result of the technical conditions, an early entry signal was not triggered. DuPont released positive earnings at the start of its seasonal period, giving the stock a boost and helping it to start to outperform.

Exit Strategy –Sell Position on Exit Date–

After a strong start to its seasonal period, in March, DuPont started to provide flat returns which was better than the S&P 500 which was losing ground. As a result, DuPont was outperforming the S&P 500. At the end of its seasonal period, DuPont was at its trendline and touching its 50 day moving average❺. The FSO had just touched 80, but had not turned down❻ and the RSI was above 50❼. In addition, DuPont was performing at market❽. The technical conditions supported an exit at the end of the seasonal period.

** Weekly avg closing values- except Fed Funds & CAN overnight tgt rate weekly closing values.

FEBRUARY

M	T	W	T	F	S	S
						1
2	3	4	5	6	7	8
9	10	11	12	13	14	15
16	17	18	19	20	21	22
23	24	25	26	27	28	

MARCH

M	T	W	T	F	S	S
						1
2	3	4	5	6	7	8
9	10	11	12	13	14	15
16	17	18	19	20	21	22
23	24	25	26	27	28	29
30	31					

APRIL

M	T	W	T	F	S	S
	1	2	3	4	5
6	7	8	9	10	11	12
13	14	15	16	17	18	19
20	21	22	23	24	25	26
27	28	29	30			

WM DON'T WASTE THIS OPPORTUNITY
February 24th to May 14th

Waste Management Inc. tends to perform well just prior to the peak of the waste disposal season in the summer time.

This is mainly the result of increased construction and demolition at this time of the year. In addition the company undergoes increased maintenance on its equipment in the winter time during slower times, which raises expenses. Overall, investors are attracted to the stock as revenue and profits increase in the summer months.

From February 24th to May 14th, during the period from 1992 to 2014, Waste Management Inc. produced an average return of 9.2% and has been positive 70% of the time.

9.2% gain & better than the S&P 500 74% of the time

Although the frequency of positive performance is less than the S&P 500, it has beaten the S&P 500, 74% of the time. In other words, when Waste Management Inc. has produced positive performances, it has typically outperformed the S&P 500.

Feb 24 to May 14	S&P 500	WM	Positive Diff
1992	0.4%	-15.8%	-16.2%
1993	1.1	-12.1	-13.2
1994	-5.6	-5.1	0.5
1995	7.9	41.4	33.5
1996	1.0	38.3	37.3
1997	4.3	-1.4	-5.7
1998	7.6	32.2	24.5
1999	5.2	14.2	9.0
2000	4.4	19.0	14.6
2001	0.3	18.4	18.2
2002	0.7	10.0	9.3
2003	10.7	15.0	4.3
2004	-4.0	0.8	4.8
2005	-3.1	-0.5	2.6
2006	0.3	9.5	9.3
2007	3.6	12.3	8.7
2008	4.1	11.3	7.2
2009	20.1	-0.6	-20.7
2010	3.8	3.6	-0.2
2011	2.3	4.9	2.6
2012	-1.8	-7.1	-5.2
2013	8.9	14.5	5.6
2014	2.9	7.4	4.5
Avg	3.3%	9.2%	5.9%
Fq > 0	83%	70%	74%

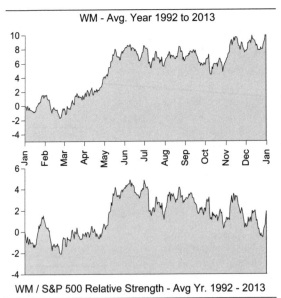

WM - Avg. Year 1992 to 2013

WM / S&P 500 Relative Strength - Avg Yr. 1992 - 2013

skewed downwards by the first two years as a public company.

From 1992/93 to 2013/14, outside of its seasonal period (unfavorable period), Waste Management Inc. has produced an average gain of 1.2% and has been positive 55% of the time.

This compares to the S&P 500 which produced an average gain of 5.5% and was positive 77% of the time.

Although historically Waste Management Inc. has produced a gain during its unfavorable period, its performance is substantially less than the S&P 500 and investors should be looking to invest in other areas of the market during Waste Management's unfavorable season.

The frequency of positive performance of Waste Management Inc. during its seasonal period is

*(i) * WM - stock symbol for Waste Management Inc. which trades on the NYSE exchange. Prices adjusted for stock splits.*

2013-14 Strategy Performance

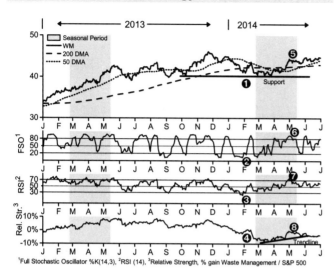

Market Indices & Rates
Weekly Values**

Stock Markets	2013	2014
Dow	13,986	15,988
S&P500	1,520	1,821
Nasdaq	3,193	4,205
TSX	12,744	13,926
FTSE	6,326	6,652
DAX	7,646	9,514
Nikkei	11,275	14,592
Hang Seng	23,429	22,058

Commodities	2013	2014
Oil	96.94	100.20
Gold	1640.6	1292.9

Bond Yields	2013	2014
USA 5 Yr Treasury	0.88	1.53
USA 10 Yr T	2.01	2.75
USA 20 Yr T	2.81	3.41
Moody's Aaa	3.91	4.50
Moody's Baa	4.86	5.13
CAN 5 Yr T	1.47	1.64
CAN 10 Yr T	2.00	2.45

Money Market	2013	2014
USA Fed Funds	0.25	0.25
USA 3 Mo T-B	0.10	0.04
CAN tgt overnight rate	1.00	1.00
CAN 3 Mo T-B	0.94	0.88

Foreign Exchange	2013	2014
EUR/USD	1.34	1.37
GBP/USD	1.56	1.66
USD/CAD	1.00	1.10
USD/JPY	93.51	102.28

¹Full Stochastic Oscillator %K(14,3), ²RSI (14), ³Relative Strength, % gain Waste Management / S&P 500

Waste Management Performance

In 2013, after increasing in value for October and most of November, Waste Management started to turn down and underperform the S&P 500 in late November.

Technical Conditions– February 24th to May 14th, 2014

Entry Strategy –Buy Position Early–
As Waste Management approached its support level❶, an early buy signal was produced as the FSO crossed back above 20❷. In addition, the RSI was below 50 and started to turn up❸. At the time, Waste Management was underperforming the S&P 500❹. Waste Management did manage a bounce before heading lower to its seasonal start date.

Exit Strategy –Sell Position Early–
In late April, Waste Management was trading above its 50 and 200 day moving averages❺. A sell signal was triggered when the FSO dropped back below 80❻. At the same time, the RSI dropped back below 70❼. From that point on, Waste Management traded down and underperformed the S&P 500❽.

Overall, the trade was positive and outperformed the S&P 500. Entering and exiting the position early produced approximately the same results as buying and selling the position on the seasonal buy and sell dates.

FEBRUARY
M	T	W	T	F	S	S
						1
2	3	4	5	6	7	8
9	10	11	12	13	14	15
16	17	18	19	20	21	22
23	24	25	26	27	28	

MARCH
M	T	W	T	F	S	S
						1
2	3	4	5	6	7	8
9	10	11	12	13	14	15
16	17	18	19	20	21	22
23	24	25	26	27	28	29
30	31					

APRIL
M	T	W	T	F	S	S
		1	2	3	4	5
6	7	8	9	10	11	12
13	14	15	16	17	18	19
20	21	22	23	24	25	26
27	28	29	30			

** Weekly avg closing values- except Fed Funds & CAN overnight tgt rate weekly closing values.

The automotive and components sector (auto sector) has its main seasonal period from February 24th to April 24. In this time period, from 1990 to 2013, the sector has produced an average gain of 8.8% and has been positive 75% of the time. The total seasonal strategy of investing in the auto sector on December 14th, exiting on January 7th, reinvesting on February 24th, exiting on April 24th and shorting the sector from September 14th to October 3rd has produced an average gain of 20.2% since 1990.

20.2% gain

The auto sector tends to rise in the spring, as investors look to benefit from being in this sector ahead of the peak in auto sales in May. After the peak, auto sales generally decline from May until November (1975-2013, source: BEA). Investors tend to lose interest in the auto sector as sales decline and investors believe that their money can be better invested elsewhere. As a result, shorting the sector from September 14th to October 3rd has proven to be profitable. The trend changes as auto sales increase in December, creating a positive seasonal period from December 14th to January 7th.

ⓘ *The SP GICS Automotive and Components Sector encompasses a wide range automotive based companies. For more information, see www.standardandpoors.com*

Automotive & Components vs. S&P 500 1990 to 2013
Negative Short ☐   Positive Long ▨

Year	Dec 14 to Jan 07 S&P 500	Auto	Feb 24 to Apr 24 S&P 500	Auto	Sep 14 to Oct 3 S&P 500	Auto	Compound Growth S&P 500	Auto
1990	-4.2 %	-4.0 %	1.9 %	4.4 %	-2.3	-7.2 %	-4.6 %	7.4 %
1991	8.0	16.7	4.7	6.9	0.2	1.0	13.9	22.5
1992	-0.7	3.6	-0.6	9.1	-2.2	-5.5	-3.4	19.2
1993	0.9	1.5	0.5	11.2	-0.2	-1.7	1.2	14.8
1994	2.3	10.9	-4.9	-11.1	-1.2	-4.5	-3.9	3.0
1995	-0.8	1.1	5.3	2.7	0.6	-2.9	5.1	6.9
1996	3.4	4.3	-1.4	11.4	1.8	0.1	3.8	16.1
1997	1.1	0.1	-3.8	-4.0	4.5	3.3	1.6	-7.1
1998	8.9	10.0	6.7	10.4	-0.6	-4.2	15.4	26.5
1999	1.9	8.5	6.7	5.8	-4.6	-6.2	3.8	21.9
2000	-4.5	8.7	5.1	22.9	-3.9	-4.0	-3.6	38.9
2001	4.1	4.6	-2.9	4.0	-1.9	-10.5	-0.8	20.3
2002	3.8	5.2	0.3	12.2	-8.0	-11.8	-4.2	32.0
2003	4.9	12.8	7.5	10.1	1.1	0.2	13.9	23.9
2004	-1.0	0.7	0.0	7.0	0.5	-0.6	-0.6	8.4
2005	1.4	0.8	-3.3	-22.4	-0.4	-4.4	-2.2	-18.4
2006	-0.3	5.1	1.6	-0.8	1.2	-2.2	2.6	6.5
2007	-4.9	-9.6	2.0	-2.5	3.8	9.4	0.7	-20.2
2008	3.1	1.0	2.6	6.1	-12.2	-22.5	-7.1	31.2
2009	3.2	16.3	16.5	102.4	-1.7	-9.8	18.2	158.6
2010	2.5	9.8	11.2	21.3	2.2	3.1	16.5	28.9
2011	4.3	10.3	2.3	2.7	-6.3	-8.8	-0.1	23.2
2012	3.0	13.6	0.6	-5.8	-0.6	-5.3	3.0	12.6
2013	3.5	-1.4	4.2	6.9	-0.6	-1.2	7.2	6.7
Avg.	1.8 %	5.4 %	2.6 %	8.8 %	-1.3 %	-4.0 %	3.2 %	20.2 %
Fq>0	71 %	88 %	71	75 %	38 %	25 %	58 %	88 %

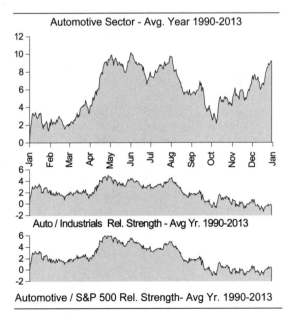

Automotive Sector - Avg. Year 1990-2013

Auto / Industrials Rel. Strength - Avg Yr. 1990-2013

Automotive / S&P 500 Rel. Strength- Avg Yr. 1990-2013

2013-14 Strategy Performance

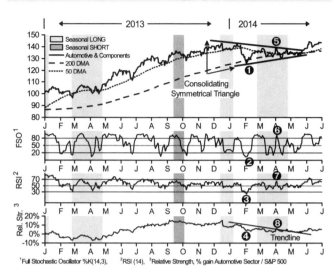

¹Full Stochastic Oscillator %K(14,3), ²RSI (14), ³Relative Strength, % gain Automotive Sector / S&P 500

Market Indices & Rates Weekly Values**		
Stock Markets	**2013**	**2014**
Dow	13,961	16,102
S&P500	1,515	1,836
Nasdaq	3,168	4,260
TSX	12,716	14,153
FTSE	6,344	6,796
DAX	7,671	9,650
Nikkei	11,389	14,664
Hang Seng	23,104	22,550
Commodities	**2013**	**2014**
Oil	94.08	102.79
Gold	1592.1	1321.7
Bond Yields	**2013**	**2014**
USA 5 Yr Treasury	0.87	1.54
USA 10 Yr T	2.00	2.73
USA 20 Yr T	2.80	3.42
Moody's Aaa	3.93	4.48
Moody's Baa	4.87	5.13
CAN 5 Yr T	1.45	1.66
CAN 10 Yr T	2.00	2.48
Money Market	**2013**	**2014**
USA Fed Funds	0.25	0.25
USA 3 Mo T-B	0.13	0.05
CAN tgt overnight rate	1.00	1.00
CAN 3 Mo T-B	0.95	0.87
Foreign Exchange	**2013**	**2014**
EUR/USD	1.33	1.37
GBP/USD	1.53	1.67
USD/CAD	1.02	1.10
USD/JPY	93.53	102.28

Automotive and Components Performance

After performing well for most of 2013, the automotive and components sector (auto sector), started to decline at the time of the year when it typically underperforms the S&P 500 in September. The auto sector continued its underperformance into 2014. Generally the cyclical sectors of the market were underperforming at the beginning of the year as investors were favoring defensive sectors in the market. In addition, the extreme cold weather dampened the auto sales as many buyers stayed indoors rather than look for new cars.

Technical Conditions– February 24th to April 24th, 2014

Entry Strategy –Buy Position Early–

After a sharp correction in January, the auto sector bounced from just below its 200 day moving average❶ and triggered an early buy signal as the FSO crossed above 20❷. At the same time, the RSI moved above 50❸ and the sector broke its trend of underperformance, and started to perform at market❹.

Exit Strategy –Sell Position Early–

After starting its seasonal period performing at market, the auto sector shortly resumed its downward trend relative to the S&P 500. On an absolute basis, it was tracing out a consolidating symmetrical triangle. At the beginning of April, the auto sector turned down❺, triggering an early sell signal as the FSO crossed below 80❻. At the same time, the RSI crossed below 50❼ and the auto sector continued its underperformance relative to the S&P 500❽.

The early exit date produced a small gain for the auto sector.

FEBRUARY

M	T	W	T	F	S	S
						1
2	3	4	5	6	7	8
9	10	11	12	13	14	15
16	17	18	19	20	21	22
23	24	25	26	27	28	

MARCH

M	T	W	T	F	S	S
						1
2	3	4	5	6	7	8
9	10	11	12	13	14	15
16	17	18	19	20	21	22
23	24	25	26	27	28	29
30	31					

APRIL

M	T	W	T	F	S	S
	1	2	3	4	5	
6	7	8	9	10	11	12
13	14	15	16	17	18	19
20	21	22	23	24	25	26
27	28	29	30			

OIL STOCKS– WINTER/SPRING STRATEGY
Ist of II Oil Stock Strategies for the Year
February 25th to May 9th

In 2014, the *Energy- Winter/Spring Strategy* got back on track by outperforming the S&P 500 during its winter-spring seasonal period. The *Energy- Winter/Spring Strategy* is a strong seasonal performer over the long-term. From 1984 to 2014, for the two and half months starting on February 25th and ending May 9th, the energy sector (XOI) has outperformed the S&P 500 by an average 4.2%.

What is even more impressive are the positive returns 26 out of 31 times, and the outperformance of the S&P 500, 24 out of 31 times.

4.2% extra and 26 out of 31 times positive, in just over two months

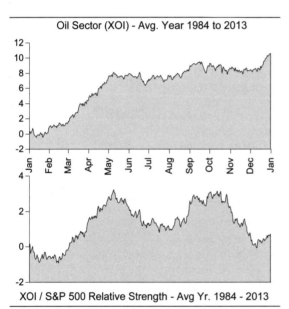

Oil Sector (XOI) - Avg. Year 1984 to 2013

XOI / S&P 500 Relative Strength - Avg Yr. 1984 - 2013

A lot of investors assume that the time to buy oil stocks is just before the winter cold sets in. The rationale is that oil will climb in price as the temperature drops.

The results in the market have not supported this assumption. The price for a barrel of oil has more to do with oil inventory. Refineries have a choice: they can produce either gasoline or heating oil. As the winter progresses, refineries start to convert their operations from heating oil to gasoline.

Feb 25 to May 9	positive S&P 500	XOI	Diff
1984	1.7 %	5.6 %	3.9 %
1985	1.4	4.9	3.5
1986	6.0	7.7	1.7
1987	3.7	25.5	21.8
1988	-3.0	5.8	0.0
1989	6.3	8.1	1.8
1990	5.8	-0.6	-6.3
1991	4.8	6.8	2.0
1992	0.9	5.8	4.9
1993	0.3	6.3	6.0
1994	-4.7	3.2	7.9
1995	7.3	10.3	3.1
1996	-2.1	2.2	4.3
1997	1.8	4.7	2.9
1998	7.5	9.8	2.3
1999	7.3	35.4	28.1
2000	4.3	22.2	17.9
2001	0.8	10.2	9.4
2002	-1.5	5.3	6.9
2003	12.1	5.7	-6.4
2004	-3.5	4.0	7.5
2005	-1.8	-1.0	0.8
2006	2.8	9.4	6.6
2007	4.2	10.1	5.8
2008	2.6	7.6	5.0
2009	20.2	15.8	-4.4
2010	0.5	-2.3	-2.8
2011	3.1	-0.6	-3.7
2012	-0.8	-13.4	-12.5
2013	7.3	3.8	-3.5
2014	1.7	9.1	7.4
Avg	3.1 %	7.3 %	4.2 %
Fq > 0	77 %	84 %	77 %

XOI vs S&P 500 1984 to 2014

In late winter and early spring, as refineries start coming off their conversion and winter maintenance programs, they increase their demand for oil putting upward pressure on its price. In addition, later in the spring, in April and early May, investors increase their holdings in the oil sector before the kick-off of the driving season (Memorial Day in May), helping to drive up the price of oil stocks.

> (i) *NYSE Arca Oil Index (XOI):*
> *An index designed to represent a cross section of widely held oil corporations involved in various phases of the oil industry.*
>
> *For more information on the XOI index, see www.cboe.com*

2013-14 Strategy Performance

Market Indices & Rates
Weekly Values**

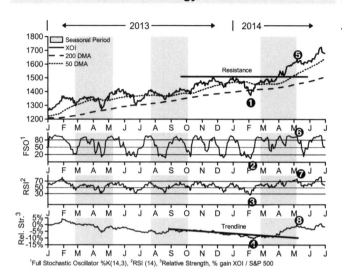

¹Full Stochastic Oscillator %K(14,3), ²RSI (14), ³Relative Strength, % gain XOI / S&P 500

Stock Markets	2013	2014
Dow	13,981	16,236
S&P500	1,507	1,850
Nasdaq	3,148	4,300
TSX	12,728	14,206
FTSE	6,338	6,823
DAX	7,699	9,670
Nikkei	11,496	14,925
Hang Seng	22,763	22,562

Commodities	2013	2014
Oil	92.18	102.58
Gold	1590.4	1332.9

Bond Yields	2013	2014
USA 5 Yr Treasury	0.77	1.52
USA 10 Yr T	1.88	2.69
USA 20 Yr T	2.70	3.35
Moody's Aaa	3.84	4.37
Moody's Baa	4.78	5.06
CAN 5 Yr T	1.32	1.65
CAN 10 Yr T	1.85	2.46

Money Market	2013	2014
USA Fed Funds	0.25	0.25
USA 3 Mo T-B	0.12	0.05
CAN tgt overnight rate	1.00	1.00
CAN 3 Mo T-B	0.96	0.85

Foreign Exchange	2013	2014
EUR/USD	1.31	1.37
GBP/USD	1.51	1.67
USD/CAD	1.03	1.11
USD/JPY	92.44	102.21

NYSE Arca Oil Index (XOI) Performance

From October 2013 to the beginning of its seasonal trade in February, XOI had flat performance and was unable to successfully break above resistance at 1500. Over this time period, it underperformed the S&P 500.

Technical Conditions– February 25th to May 9th, 2014

Entry Strategy –Buy Position Early–

In early February, XOI was trading below its 50 and 200 day moving averages❶ and an early buy signal was triggered when the FSO crossed back over 20❷. In support, the RSI also crossed back above 30❸. At the time, XOI was underperforming the S&P 500❹. The early buy signal provided extra gains going into the seasonal period as XOI continued to rise.

Exit Strategy –Sell Position on Exit Date–

After the entry date, XOI continued to perform well and broke above resistance at the beginning of April. At the end of its seasonal period, it was trading above its 50 and 200 day moving averages❺. Days after the seasonal trade finished, the FSO crossed below 80❻, the RSI dropped below 70❼, and XOI started to underperform the S&P 500❽.

Overall, the trade was successful as XOI performed positively and outperformed the S&P 500. Entering the trade early proved to be beneficial as the February low was a multi-month low.

FEBRUARY

M	T	W	T	F	S	S
						1
2	3	4	5	6	7	8
9	10	11	12	13	14	15
16	17	18	19	20	21	22
23	24	25	26	27	28	

MARCH

M	T	W	T	F	S	S
						1
2	3	4	5	6	7	8
9	10	11	12	13	14	15
16	17	18	19	20	21	22
23	24	25	26	27	28	29
30	31					

APRIL

M	T	W	T	F	S	S
	1	2	3	4	5	
6	7	8	9	10	11	12
13	14	15	16	17	18	19
20	21	22	23	24	25	26
27	28	29	30			

** Weekly avg closing values- except Fed Funds & CAN overnight tgt rate weekly closing values.

MARCH

	MONDAY	TUESDAY	WEDNESDAY
WEEK 10	**2** 29	**3** 28	**4** 27
WEEK 11	**9** 22	**10** 21	**11** 20
WEEK 12	**16** 15	**17** 14	**18** 13
WEEK 13	**23** 8	**24** 7	**25** 6
WEEK 14	**30** 1	**31**	1

THURSDAY		FRIDAY	
5	26	**6**	25
12	19	**13**	18
19	12	**20**	11
26	5	**27**	4
2		3	

APRIL

M	T	W	T	F	S	S
		1	2	3	4	5
6	7	8	9	10	11	12
13	14	15	16	17	18	19
20	21	22	23	24	25	26
27	28	29	30			

MAY

M	T	W	T	F	S	S
				1	2	3
4	5	6	7	8	9	10
11	12	13	14	15	16	17
18	19	20	21	22	23	24
25	26	27	28	29	30	31

JUNE

M	T	W	T	F	S	S
1	2	3	4	5	6	7
8	9	10	11	12	13	14
15	16	17	18	19	20	21
22	23	24	25	26	27	28
29	30					

JULY

M	T	W	T	F	S	S
		1	2	3	4	5
6	7	8	9	10	11	12
13	14	15	16	17	18	19
20	21	22	23	24	25	26
27	28	29	30	31		

MARCH
S U M M A R Y

1.6%
1.4%
1.2%
1.0%
0.8%
0.6%
0.4%
0.2%
0.0%

S&P500 Cumulative Daily Gains for Avg Month 1950 to 2013

	Dow Jones	S&P 500	Nasdaq	TSX Comp
Month Rank	6	4	6	4
# Up	42	42	27	17
# Down	22	22	15	12
% Pos	66	66	64	59
% Avg. Gain	1.1	1.2	0.8	1.1

Dow & S&P 1950-2013, Nasdaq 1972-2013, TSX 1985-2013

70%
60%
50%
40%
30%

Prob. of Daily Gain

♦ March tends to be a strong month for stocks. From 1990 to 2014, the S&P 500 has produced an average gain of 1.4%.♦ Typically, it is the cyclicals that perform well and the defensive sectors that underperform. ♦ In the last few years, the defensive sectors have performed better than average, as investors have taken a defensive stance in March ♦ Silver can perform well in March, given its industrial uses, but its success is not reflected in gold, which since 1990 has produced an average loss of 1.0% and has only beaten the S&P 500, 36% of the time.

**BEST / WORST MARCH
BROAD MKTS. 2005-2014**

BEST MARCH MARKETS
♦ Nasdaq (2009) 10.9%
♦ Nikkei 225 (2010) 9.5%
♦ Russell 2000 (2009) 8.7%

WORST MARCH MARKETS
♦ Nikkei 225 (2011) -8.2%
♦ Nikkei 225 (2008) -7.9%
♦ FTSE 100 (2014) -3.1%

Index Values End of Month

	2005	2006	2007	2008	2009	2010	2011	2012	2013	2014
Dow	10,504	11,109	12,354	12,263	7,609	10,857	12,320	13,212	14,579	16,458
S&P 500	1,181	1,295	1,421	1,323	798	1,169	1,326	1,408	1,569	1,872
Nasdaq	1,999	2,340	2,422	2,279	1,529	2,398	2,781	3,092	3,268	4,199
TSX	9,612	12,111	13,166	13,350	8,720	12,038	14,116	12,392	12,750	14,335
Russell 1000	1,222	1,359	1,492	1,385	834	1,238	1,417	1,497	1,676	2,012
Russell 2000	1,529	1,902	1,990	1,710	1,051	1,687	2,096	2,064	2,365	2,915
FTSE 100	4,894	5,965	6,308	5,702	3,926	5,680	5,909	5,768	6,412	6,598
Nikkei 225	11,669	17,060	17,288	12,526	8,110	11,090	9,755	10,084	12,398	14,828

Percent Gain for March

	2005	2006	2007	2008	2009	2010	2011	2012	2013	2014
Dow	-2.4	1.1	0.7	0.0	7.7	5.1	0.8	2.0	3.7	0.8
S&P 500	-1.9	1.1	1.0	-0.6	8.5	5.9	-0.1	3.1	3.6	0.7
Nasdaq	-2.6	2.6	0.2	0.3	10.9	7.1	0.0	4.2	3.4	-2.5
TSX	-0.6	3.6	0.9	-1.7	7.4	3.5	-0.1	-2.0	-0.6	0.9
Russell 1000	-1.7	1.3	0.9	-0.8	8.5	6.0	0.1	3.0	3.7	0.5
Russell 2000	-3.0	4.7	0.9	0.3	8.7	8.0	2.4	2.4	4.4	-0.8
FTSE 100	-1.5	3.0	2.2	-3.1	2.5	6.1	-1.4	-1.8	0.8	-3.1
Nikkei 225	-0.6	5.3	-1.8	-7.9	7.1	9.5	-8.2	3.7	7.3	-0.1

March Market Avg. Performance 2005 to 2014[1]

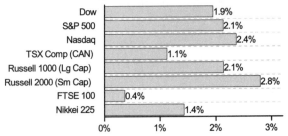

Dow 1.9%
S&P 500 2.1%
Nasdaq 2.4%
TSX Comp (CAN) 1.1%
Russell 1000 (Lg Cap) 2.1%
Russell 2000 (Sm Cap) 2.8%
FTSE 100 0.4%
Nikkei 225 1.4%

0%   1%   2%   3%

Interest Corner Mar[2]

	Fed Funds % [3]	3 Mo. T-Bill % [4]	10 Yr % [5]	20 Yr % [6]
2014	0.25	0.05	2.73	3.31
2013	0.25	0.00	1.87	2.71
2012	0.25	0.07	2.23	3.00
2011	0.25	0.09	3.47	4.29
2010	0.25	0.16	3.84	4.55

(1) Russell Data provided by Russell (2) Federal Reserve Bank of St. Louis- end of month values (3) Target rate set by FOMC (4)(5)(6) Constant yield maturities.

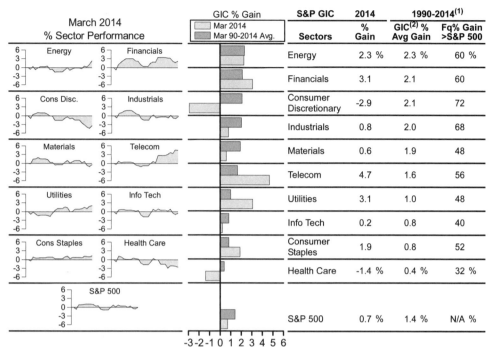

S&P GIC Sectors	2014 % Gain	1990-2014[1] GIC[2] % Avg Gain	1990-2014[1] Fq% Gain >S&P 500
Energy	2.3 %	2.3 %	60 %
Financials	3.1	2.1	60
Consumer Discretionary	-2.9	2.1	72
Industrials	0.8	2.0	68
Materials	0.6	1.9	48
Telecom	4.7	1.6	56
Utilities	3.1	1.0	48
Info Tech	0.2	0.8	40
Consumer Staples	1.9	0.8	52
Health Care	-1.4 %	0.4 %	32 %
S&P 500	0.7 %	1.4 %	N/A %

Sector Commentary

♦ In March 2014, the defensive sectors were generally the leaders in the market as investors questioned the lofty levels of the S&P 500, which was setting all time highs. ♦ Telecom led the way with a gain of 4.7% in March. ♦ The utilities sector was not far behind, producing a gain of 3.1%. ♦ Many investors look for the financial sector to be one of the top sectors in order for a market rally to be sustainable and in March 2014, with the financial sector also producing a return of 3.1%, it was pointing to higher market returns ahead.

Sub-Sector Commentary

♦ After having a strong rally in the first two months of the year, the biotech sub-sector had gotten ahead of itself and corrected sharply in March with a loss of 10.2%. ♦ The homebuilders sector typically finishes its run in February. After a strong rally at the beginning of the year, the homebuilders sub-sector corrected sharply in response to a weaker outlook for the housing market, producing a loss of 10.0%. ♦ The retail sub-sector continued its roller coaster ride and after a strong February, declined to produce a loss of 5%. ♦ The railroads and transportation sub-sectors started to improve in their seasonal periods.

SELECTED SUB-SECTORS[3]

Retail	-5.0 %	3.5 %	72 %
Steel	5.0	2.5	60
Transportation	3.3	2.4	68
Chemicals	0.5	2.3	56
Railroads	4.8	2.3	60
Banks	4.7	1.7	52
Silver	-6.1	1.7	48
Software & Services	-2.1	1.6	56
SOX (1995-2014)	4.1	1.6	45
Metals & Mining	3.6	1.2	44
Agriculture (1994-2014)	6.9	0.7	33
Homebuilders	-10.0	0.5	44
Pharma	0.4	0.5	32
Biotech (1993-2014)	-10.2	-0.2	36
Gold (London PM)	-2.6	-1.0	36

NIKE RUNS INTO EARNINGS
① Mar1- Mar20 ② Sep1-Sep25 ③ Dec 12-Dec24

Nike has had a strong run in the stock market since it went public in 1980. More recently, from 1990 to 2013, it has produced an average annual gain of 22.6%. A lot of the gains in the stock price can be accounted for in the two to three week periods leading up to its first, second and third quarters earnings reports.

Nike's year-end is May 31st, and although from year to year, the actual report dates for Nike's earnings changes, generally speaking Nike reports its earnings in the third or fourth week in the months of March, June, September and December.

It is interesting to note that Nike has strong seasonal runs at different times in the year. Stocks typically have similar seasonal patterns as the sector to which they belong. Nike belongs to the consumer discretionary sector and it would be expected that Nike would have a similar seasonal pattern.

There are large differences in Nike's pattern of seasonal strength compared with the consumer discretionary's seasonal pattern. First, Nike has a period of seasonal strength that includes September, a month that is not favorable to consumer discretionary stocks. Second, Nike's outperformance is focused on very short periods in the weeks leading up to three of its earnings periods. In contrast, the consumer discretionary sector has much more gradual transitions from its seasonal period to its unfavorable seasonal period.

From 1990 to 2013, Nike produced an average annual gain of 22.6%. In comparison, its three short seasonal periods within the year have produced an average compound gain of 16.6%. The seasonal periods in total are approximately eight weeks and yet, they have produced most of the average annual gains of Nike. Investors have been well served investing in Nike in its seasonal periods and then running to another investment during its "off-season."

Nike Inc. Seasonal Gains 1990 to 2013

Year %	Mar 1 to Mar 20	Sep 1 to Sep 25	Dec 12 to Dec 24	Positive Compound Growth
1990	51.8 %	14.7 %	1.0 %	11.7 %	29.3 %
1991	79.4	-5.7	9.3	12.7	16.2
1992	14.8	-8.3	6.2	-2.8	-5.3
1993	-44.3	5.8	-13.7	0.7	-8.0
1994	61.3	10.5	-7.0	14.7	17.9
1995	86.7	5.4	18.8	10.7	38.6
1996	72.4	22.2	13.6	13.0	56.9
1997	-34.9	-6.1	1.0	-14.1	-18.5
1998	3.8	1.0	18.0	14.8	36.8
1999	22.2	15.6	15.1	18.2	57.2
2000	12.6	16.0	1.6	16.4	37.2
2001	0.8	-2.7	-8.7	3.7	-7.9
2002	-20.9	8.7	2.7	2.0	13.9
2003	54.0	14.0	6.0	4.4	26.2
2004	32.4	5.0	5.8	5.1	16.7
2005	-4.3	-1.8	3.0	1.3	2.4
2006	14.1	-1.5	7.1	2.6	8.2
2007	29.7	4.6	3.7	4.2	13.0
2008	-20.6	11.8	7.3	0.8	20.9
2009	29.6	8.4	5.9	2.2	17.3
2010	29.3	8.8	13.5	-2.0	20.9
2011	12.8	-12.9	2.3	-0.8	-11.6
2012	7.1	3.5	-2.3	6.2	7.4
2013	52.4	0.7	9.7	1.1	11.6
Avg.	22.6 %	4.9 %	5.0 %	5.3 %	16.6 %

NKE - Avg. Year 1990 to 2013

NKE / S&P 500 Relative Strength - Avg. Yr. 1990 - 2013

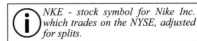

ⓘ NKE - stock symbol for Nike Inc. which trades on the NYSE, adjusted for splits.

2013-14 Strategy Performance

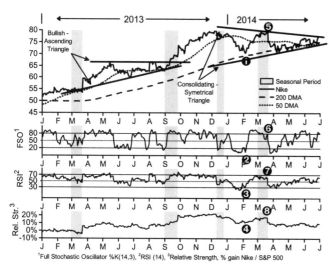

[1]Full Stochastic Oscillator %K(14,3), [2]RSI (14), [3]Relative Strength, % gain Nike / S&P 500

Market Indices & Rates Weekly Values**

Stock Markets	2013	2014
Dow	14,281	16,360
S&P500	1,540	1,870
Nasdaq	3,221	4,335
TSX	12,788	14,276
FTSE	6,426	6,762
DAX	7,882	9,477
Nikkei	11,904	14,936
Hang Seng	22,748	22,620

Commodities	2013	2014
Oil	90.98	102.77
Gold	1577.9	1340.4

Bond Yields	2013	2014
USA 5 Yr Treasury	0.82	1.55
USA 10 Yr T	1.96	2.71
USA 20 Yr T	2.78	3.37
Moody's Aaa	3.92	4.38
Moody's Baa	4.85	5.07
CAN 5 Yr T	1.33	1.68
CAN 10 Yr T	1.86	2.48

Money Market	2013	2014
USA Fed Funds	0.25	0.25
USA 3 Mo T-B	0.10	0.05
CAN tgt overnight rate	1.00	1.00
CAN 3 Mo T-B	0.96	0.83

Foreign Exchange	2013	2014
EUR/USD	1.30	1.38
GBP/USD	1.50	1.67
USD/CAD	1.03	1.11
USD/JPY	94.33	102.46

Nike Performance

In 2013, Nike performed well with the majority of its increases occurring at the end of its seasonal periods or shortly after, in March and September. Nike started to show weakness in its December seasonal period, which continued to the beginning of February.

Technical Conditions– March 9th to April 18th, 2013

Entry Strategy –Buy Position Early–

In February 2014, Nike bounced from just above its 200 day moving average❶ and triggered an early buy signal when the FSO crossed above 20❷. At the time, the RSI confirmed the buy signal by bouncing off 30❸. Nike had already started to outperform the S&P 500 earlier in January❹ and the trend continued into March.

Exit Strategy –Sell Position on Exit Date–

Although the FSO crossed below 80 in early March, triggering an early sell signal, with a short-term trade investors have the option of extending the trade. From this point, Nike started to trade sideways and perform at market. At the end of its seasonal period, Nike was performing positively❺. At the time, the FSO was trending down from 80❻, the RSI was decreasing❼, and Nike was slightly outperforming the S&P 500❽. The day after the seasonal period ended, Nike came out with earnings that disappointed the market and the stock dropped sharply.

Overall, the Nike seasonal trade was nominally successful, and the gains were increased if the early buy signal was taken into account.

MARCH
M	T	W	T	F	S	S
						1
2	3	4	5	6	7	8
9	10	11	12	13	14	15
16	17	18	19	20	21	22
23	24	25	26	27	28	29
30	31					

APRIL
M	T	W	T	F	S	S
	1	2	3	4	5	
6	7	8	9	10	11	12
13	14	15	16	17	18	19
20	21	22	23	24	25	26
27	28	29	30			

MAY
M	T	W	T	F	S	S
			1	2	3	
4	5	6	7	8	9	10
11	12	13	14	15	16	17
18	19	20	21	22	23	24
25	26	27	28	29	30	31

BA BOEING– LET YOUR PORTFOLIO FLY
March 13th to June 15th

Boeing has recently completed the production cycle and release of its 787 Dreamliner. The plane was much anticipated and after battery and fire problems were fixed, the plane was reapproved by the FAA in late April 2013.

11.6% gain & positive 80% of the time

Many investors avoid investing in airplane manufacturers when the companies are in the design stage of a new plane. They do this to avoid any detrimental effects from costs overruns and delays. Investors have an increased interest once the plane is in production, as sales and profits are more predictable.

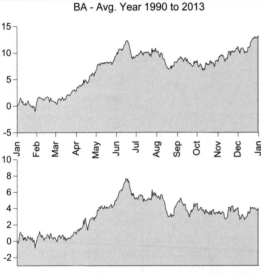

BA - Avg. Year 1990 to 2013

BA / S&P 500 Relative Strength - Avg Yr. 1990 - 2013

BA* vs. S&P 500 1990 to 2014			
Mar 13 to Jun15	S&P 500	BA	Positive Diff
1990	7.2%	34.9%	27.7%
1991	3.3	3.1	-0.2
1992	1.6	-1.7	-3.3
1993	-0.8	11.7	12.5
1994	1.3	3.7	4.9
1995	9.7	36.5	26.8
1996	4.5	2.1	-2.4
1997	11.1	7.4	-3.7
1998	0.7	-15.6	-16.3
1999	0.5	21.6	21.1
2000	6.0	23.9	17.9
2001	2.9	5.3	2.4
2002	-13.9	-15.4	-1.8
2003	22.9	40.5	17.6
2004	1.0	22.2	21.2
2005	0.5	12.0	11.5
2006	-2.0	13.4	15.4
2007	9.0	7.6	-1.4
2008	3.9	3.7	-0.2
2009	23.0	47.3	24.2
2010	-3.0	-3.4	-0.3
2011	-3.0	3.1	6.1
2012	-2.1	-2.2	-0.1
2013	4.8	21.0	16.2
2014	3.6	6.3	2.7
Avg	3.6%	11.6%	7.9%
Fq > 0	72%	80%	60%

16th to October 27th, during the period 1990 to 2013. Essentially, once the major impetus for the seasonal trend finishes, the stock tends to underperform.

There will be years when the June to October time period is positive, but on average this is not the case. Not only has Boeing produced an average loss since 1990 in this time period, but it has only been positive 33% of the time and outperformed the S&P 500, 25% of the time.

Boeing typically starts to outperform the S&P 500 in mid-March and then peaks three months later in mid-June. The driver for the seasonal trend is the annual Paris Air Show that takes place in mid-June.

This is the time of year when the major players from the airline industry get together to sign contracts for new plane orders.

Investors tend to take positions in Boeing before the Paris Air Show to take advantage of any positive announcements. Seasonal investors start taking their positions even earlier, in order to benefit from other investors pushing up the price of Boeing before the air show. Boeing has a distinct seasonal pattern and on average has produced a loss of 4.9% from June

Seasonal investors should look to take a position in Boeing from March 13th to June 15th. In this time period, from 1990 to 2014, Boeing has produced an average 11.6% gain and has been positive 80% of the time.

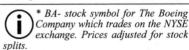

* BA- stock symbol for The Boeing Company which trades on the NYSE exchange. Prices adjusted for stock splits.

2013-14 Strategy Performance

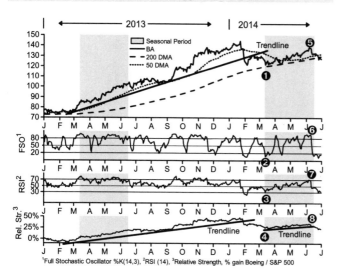

¹Full Stochastic Oscillator %K(14,3), ²RSI (14), ³Relative Strength, % gain Boeing / S&P 500

Market Indices & Rates
Weekly Values**

Stock Markets	2013	2014
Dow	14,481	16,257
S&P500	1,557	1,860
Nasdaq	3,250	4,294
TSX	12,822	14,272
FTSE	6,503	6,616
DAX	8,005	9,167
Nikkei	12,369	14,864
Hang Seng	22,738	21,946

Commodities	2013	2014
Oil	92.72	99.25
Gold	1588.8	1362.0

Bond Yields	2013	2014
USA 5 Yr Treasury	0.88	1.59
USA 10 Yr T	2.04	2.72
USA 20 Yr T	2.86	3.37
Moody's Aaa	4.00	4.41
Moody's Baa	4.91	5.10
CAN 5 Yr T	1.38	1.64
CAN 10 Yr T	1.92	2.44

Money Market	2013	2014
USA Fed Funds	0.25	0.25
USA 3 Mo T-B	0.10	0.05
CAN tgt overnight rate	1.00	1.00
CAN 3 Mo T-B	0.96	0.82

Foreign Exchange	2013	2014
EUR/USD	1.30	1.39
GBP/USD	1.50	1.66
USD/CAD	1.02	1.11
USD/JPY	95.98	102.45

Boeing Performance

After performing strongly since March 2013, Boeing corrected below its rising trendline in January 2014. It held above its 200 day moving average and bounced up before correcting just before the start of its seasonal period in March.

Technical Conditions– March 13th to June 15th, 2014

Entry Strategy –Buy on Entry Date–

At the start of its seasonal period in March, Boeing was trading just above its 200 day moving average❶. The FSO was below 20❷, indicating an oversold condition. The RSI bounced off 30❸ and at the time, Boeing was still underperforming the S&P 500❹. The correction provided a good opportunity for an entry point in the seasonal trade as Boeing started to outperform the S&P 500.

Exit Strategy –Sell Position Early–

Boeing performed well in its seasonal period, staying above its 200 day moving average. In early June, it started to turn down❺ and the FSO triggered a sell signal as it crossed below 80❻. In addition, the RSI turned down from 70❼. At the same time, Boeing started to underperform the S&P 500❽.

Overall, the seasonal trade was successful as Boeing started to outperform at the beginning of its seasonal period and underperform as the trade was finishing.

MARCH

M	T	W	T	F	S	S
						1
2	3	4	5	6	7	8
9	10	11	12	13	14	15
16	17	18	19	20	21	22
23	24	25	26	27	28	29
30	31					

APRIL

M	T	W	T	F	S	S
	1	2	3	4	5	
6	7	8	9	10	11	12
13	14	15	16	17	18	19
20	21	22	23	24	25	26
27	28	29	30			

MAY

M	T	W	T	F	S	S
			1	2	3	
4	5	6	7	8	9	10
11	12	13	14	15	16	17
18	19	20	21	22	23	24
25	26	27	28	29	30	31

** Weekly avg closing values- except Fed Funds & CAN overnight tgt rate weekly closing values.

SYY | SYSCO– "THE FOOD COMPANY"
①Apr23 to May30   ②Oct11 to Nov21

The other "Sysco," the one in the food marketing and distribution business, tends to outperform the S&P 500 in the spring and autumn.

10.9% gain & positive 83% of the time

Why does Sysco outperform at these two times of the year? There are two parts to this answer. First, Sysco is part of the consumer staples sector, which tends to be one of the top performing sectors during the transition times, to and from the favorable six month period for stocks in late October and early May. In these periods, the consumer staples sector performs well because investors are looking for stable earnings.

Second, Sysco tends to release its earnings in the first week in November and the first week in May. Investors are attracted to the stock before the earnings are released to benefit from any positive announcements.

Usually, the best time to exit a stock position that has a seasonal period driven by earnings, is just before the earnings release date. In Sysco's case, it is typically best to hold onto the stock after the earnings announcements for another two to three weeks.

It is possible that the strategy of holding past Sysco's earnings release date, is the result of Sysco's strong seasonal performance occurring during the transition times for the stock market, when the unfavorable season transitions to the favorable season, and vice versa.

(i) *SYY - stock symbol for Sysco which trades on the NYSE exchange. Prices adjusted for stock splits.*

Sysco* vs. S&P 500 1990 to 2013   Positive [ ]

Year	Apr 23 to May 30 S&P 500	SYY	Oct 11 to Nov 21 S&P 500	SYY	Compound Growth S&P 500	SYY
1990	7.7	14.8%	5.2	0.3%	13.3	15.1%
1991	1.6	16.6	-0.1	3.8	1.4	21.0
1992	1.4	2.6	6.0	8.6	7.4	11.4
1993	2.4	14.5	0.5	-1.1	3.0	13.2
1994	2.2	0.0	-0.2	5.4	2.0	5.4
1995	3.0	-4.6	3.9	15.7	7.0	10.4
1996	3.7	7.4	6.9	3.0	10.9	10.6
1997	9.5	-0.3	-0.4	16.5	9.1	16.1
1998	-3.5	-1.3	18.2	11.3	14.1	9.9
1999	-4.2	3.5	6.4	16.3	2.0	20.4
2000	-0.8	20.5	-2.9	23.8	-3.7	49.2
2001	0.4	9.0	5.2	-1.2	5.6	7.6
2002	-3.9	-6.3	16.2	10.2	11.6	3.3
2003	5.7	11.3	-0.3	5.8	5.4	17.7
2004	-1.7	-3.6	4.3	18.4	2.5	14.2
2005	4.1	7.6	5.7	3.6	10.0	11.5
2006	-3.9	-0.6	3.7	6.1	-0.4	5.4
2007	3.1	-1.6	-9.3	-6.8	-6.5	-8.3
2008	1.8	9.4	-11.0	-9.5	-9.4	-1.0
2009	9.0	8.3	1.9	8.0	11.0	16.9
2010	-9.9	-3.4	3.0	1.1	-7.2	-2.4
2011	-0.5	10.3	-0.2	4.1	-0.6	14.8
2012	-4.7	-3.5	-2.9	-2.2	-7.5	-5.6
2013	5.9	-1.8	6.1	3.8	12.3	1.9
Avg.	1.2%	4.6%	2.7%	6.1%	3.9%	10.9%
Fq>0	63%	58%	63%	79%	71%	83%

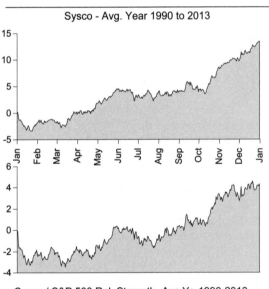

Sysco - Avg. Year 1990 to 2013

Sysco / S&P 500 Rel. Strength- Avg Yr. 1990-2013

2013-14 Strategy Performance

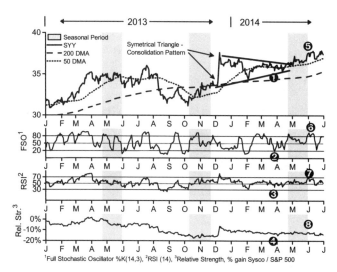

¹Full Stochastic Oscillator %K(14,3), ²RSI (14), ³Relative Strength, % gain Sysco / S&P 500

Market Indices & Rates
Weekly Values**

Stock Markets	2013	2014
Dow	14,471	16,288
S&P500	1,552	1,866
Nasdaq	3,238	4,303
TSX	12,777	14,327
FTSE	6,423	6,569
DAX	7,961	9,268
Nikkei	12,416	14,344
Hang Seng	22,145	21,449

Commodities	2013	2014
Oil	92.88	99.51
Gold	1608.7	1347.1

Bond Yields	2013	2014
USA 5 Yr Treasury	0.80	1.67
USA 10 Yr T	1.94	2.74
USA 20 Yr T	2.77	3.36
Moody's Aaa	3.93	4.42
Moody's Baa	4.85	5.11
CAN 5 Yr T	1.33	1.69
CAN 10 Yr T	1.84	2.46

Money Market	2013	2014
USA Fed Funds	0.25	0.25
USA 3 Mo T-B	0.07	0.06
CAN tgt overnight rate	1.00	1.00
CAN 3 Mo T-B	0.97	0.84

Foreign Exchange	2013	2014
EUR/USD	1.29	1.39
GBP/USD	1.51	1.66
USD/CAD	1.02	1.12
USD/JPY	95.15	102.03

Sysco Performance

As the S&P 500 advanced strongly in 2013, Sysco underperformed. In 2014, Sysco created a symmetrical triangle consolidation pattern, leading into the start of its seasonal period in April.

Technical Conditions– April 23rd to May 30th, 2014

Entry Strategy –Buy Position Early–

While Sysco was in its consolidation pattern❶, an early buy signal was triggered in late March as the FSO crossed back over 20❷. At the same time, the RSI moved above 50❸ and Sysco was performing equal to the S&P 500❹. At the start of the seasonal period, Sysco broke through its consolidation pattern to the upside.

Exit Strategy –Sell Position on Exit Date–

Just before the end of its seasonal period, Sysco was trading just above its 50 day moving average❺ and spiked to move the FSO into overbought territory, above 80❻. The RSI also increased to just under 70❼. The last spike in Sysco's price, helped to bump it up into outperformance territory relative to the S&P 500❽.

MARCH

M	T	W	T	F	S	S
						1
2	3	4	5	6	7	8
9	10	11	12	13	14	15
16	17	18	19	20	21	22
23	24	25	26	27	28	29
30	31					

APRIL

M	T	W	T	F	S	S
	1	2	3	4	5	
6	7	8	9	10	11	12
13	14	15	16	17	18	19
20	21	22	23	24	25	26
27	28	29	30			

MAY

M	T	W	T	F	S	S
			1	2	3	
4	5	6	7	8	9	10
11	12	13	14	15	16	17
18	19	20	21	22	23	24
25	26	27	28	29	30	31

** Weekly avg closing values- except Fed Funds & CAN overnight tgt rate weekly closing values.

CANADIANS GIVE 3 CHEERS FOR AMERICAN HOLIDAYS

When I used to work on the retail side of the investment business, I was always amazed at how often the Canadian market increased on American holidays, when the Canadian stock market was open and the American market was closed.

The holidays always had light volume, tended not to have large increases or decreases, but nevertheless usually ended the day with a gain.

> *1% average gain from 1977 to 2013 and 95% of the time positive*

How the trade works

For the three big holidays in the United States that do not exist in Canada (Memorial, Independence and U.S. Thanksgiving Days), buy at the end of the market day before the holiday (TSX Composite) and sell at the end of the U.S. holiday when the U.S markets are closed.

For U.S. investors to take advantage of this trade, they must have access to the TSX Composite. Unfortunately, as of the current time, SEC regulations do not allow Americans to purchase foreign ETFs.

Generally, markets perform well around most major American holidays, hence the trading strategies for American holidays included in this book. The typical U.S. holiday trade is to get into the stock market the day before the holiday and then exit the day after the holiday.

The main reason for the strong performance around these holidays is a lack of institutional involvement in the markets, allowing bullish retail investors to push up the markets.

On the actual holidays, there are no economic news releases in America and very seldom is there anything released in Canada of significance. During market hours without any influences, the market tends to float, preferring to wait until the next day before making any significant moves.

Despite this laxidasical action during the day, the TSX Composite tends to end the day on a gain. This is true for the three major holidays that are covered in this book: Memorial, Independence and U.S. Thanksgiving Day.

From a theoretical perspective, a lot of the gain that is captured on the U.S. holiday is realized on the next day when the markets are open in the United States. This does not invalidate the *Canadians Give 3 Cheers* trade – it presents more alternatives for the astute investor.

For example, an investor can allocate a portion of money to a standard American holiday trade and another portion to the *Canadian Give 3 Cheers* version. By spreading out the exit days, the overall risk in the trade is reduced.

S&P/TSX Comp
Gain 1977-2013   Positive ▢

	Memorial	Independence	Thanksgiving	Compound Growth
1977	0.10 %	-0.08 %	0.61 %	0.63 %
1978	-0.05	-0.16	0.57	0.36
1979	1.11	0.23	0.58	1.93
1980	1.64	0.76	0.89	3.32
1981	0.51	-0.15	1.03	1.40
1982	-0.18	-0.01	0.35	0.17
1983	0.29	0.53	0.15	0.97
1984	0.86	-0.11	0.73	1.48
1985	0.61	0.31	0.31	1.24
1986	0.23	-0.02	0.22	0.44
1987	-0.11	1.08	1.57	2.55
1988	0.44	0.08	0.58	1.11
1989	0.10	-0.12	-0.11	-0.13
1990	0.11	0.43	0.02	0.57
1991	0.02	0.18	-0.09	0.11
1992	-0.06	0.35	0.36	0.65
1993	0.42	-0.18	0.14	0.38
1994	-0.19	0.70	0.91	1.43
1995	0.14	0.25	0.29	0.68
1996	0.11	0.25	0.54	0.90
1997	1.08	-0.04	-0.85	0.18
1998	0.56	0.18	0.51	1.25
1999	0.57	1.63	1.14	3.39
2000	0.43	1.04	0.91	2.40
2001	-0.02	-0.23	0.70	0.45
2002	-0.01	0.08	0.38	0.45
2003	0.03	0.03	0.26	0.31
2004	0.84	-0.02	0.55	1.39
2005	0.56	0.39	1.48	2.45
2006	0.70	1.04	0.70	2.46
2007	0.35	-0.03	0.76	1.08
2008	0.24	-0.94	1.28	0.56
2009	0.76	0.36	-1.29	-0.18
2010	0.78	-0.92	0.34	0.19
2011	0.23	0.64	-0.75	0.12
2012	-0.09	0.55	0.44	0.90
2013	0.23	0.17	0.07	0.47
Avg	0.36 %	0.22 %	0.44 %	1.03 %
Fq > 0	78 %	62 %	86 %	95 %

2013-14 Strategy Performance

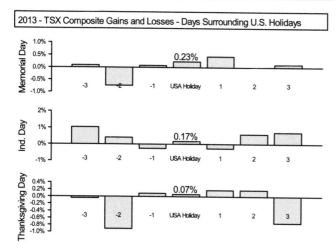

2013 - TSX Composite Gains and Losses - Days Surrounding U.S. Holidays

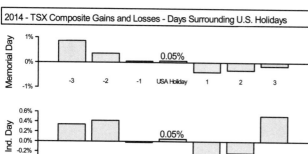

2014 - TSX Composite Gains and Losses - Days Surrounding U.S. Holidays

Market Indices & Rates
Weekly Values**

Stock Markets	2013	2014
Dow	14,528	16,300
S&P500	1,562	1,856
Nasdaq	3,253	4,188
TSX	12,709	14,240
FTSE	6,394	6,587
DAX	7,834	9,403
Nikkei	12,449	14,539
Hang Seng	22,332	21,873

Commodities	2013	2014
Oil	96.18	100.57
Gold	1599.6	1303.8

Bond Yields	2013	2014
USA 5 Yr Treasury	0.78	1.73
USA 10 Yr T	1.90	2.72
USA 20 Yr T	2.73	3.29
Moody's Aaa	3.90	4.33
Moody's Baa	4.83	5.00
CAN 5 Yr T	1.31	1.71
CAN 10 Yr T	1.83	2.45

Money Market	2013	2014
USA Fed Funds	0.25	0.25
USA 3 Mo T-B	0.08	0.05
CAN tgt overnight rate	1.00	1.00
CAN 3 Mo T-B	0.98	0.89

Foreign Exchange	2013	2014
EUR/USD	1.28	1.38
GBP/USD	1.52	1.66
USD/CAD	1.02	1.11
USD/JPY	94.29	102.31

Canadians Give 3 Cheers Performance

Overall, the *Canadians Give 3 Cheers for American Holidays* strategy proved to be successful in 2013, and so far in 2014, up to the publication date of this book.

In 2013 and 2014, gains on the American holidays on average have not been large, but they have been positive. The days on either side of the U.S. holiday have produced mixed results. Over the long-term, using the *Canadians Give 3 Cheers for American Holidays* strategy, has proven to be a successful approach to trading the U.S. holidays on its own, but it can also be used to complement seasonal strategies that take advantage of the positive trend of the days before and after the holiday.

MARCH

M	T	W	T	F	S	S
						1
2	3	4	5	6	7	8
9	10	11	12	13	14	15
16	17	18	19	20	21	22
23	24	25	26	27	28	29
30	31					

APRIL

M	T	W	T	F	S	S
	1	2	3	4	5	
	1	2	3	4	5	
6	7	8	9	10	11	12
13	14	15	16	17	18	19
20	21	22	23	24	25	26
27	28	29	30			

MAY

M	T	W	T	F	S	S
				1	2	3
4	5	6	7	8	9	10
11	12	13	14	15	16	17
18	19	20	21	22	23	24
25	26	27	28	29	30	31

** Weekly avg closing values- except Fed Funds & CAN overnight tgt rate weekly closing values.

APRIL

	MONDAY	TUESDAY	WEDNESDAY
WEEK 14	30	31	**1** 29
WEEK 15	**6** 24	**7** 23	**8** 22
WEEK 16	**13** 17	**14** 16	**15** 15
WEEK 17	**20** 10	**21** 9	**22** 8
WEEK 18	**27** 3	**28** 2	**29** 1

THURSDAY   FRIDAY

2	28	3	27

USA Market Closed- Good Friday
CAN Market Closed- Good Friday

9	21	10	20

16	14	17	13

23	7	24	6

30		1	

MAY

M	T	W	T	F	S	S
				1	2	3
4	5	6	7	8	9	10
11	12	13	14	15	16	17
18	19	20	21	22	23	24
25	26	27	28	29	30	31

JUNE

M	T	W	T	F	S	S
1	2	3	4	5	6	7
8	9	10	11	12	13	14
15	16	17	18	19	20	21
22	23	24	25	26	27	28
29	30					

JULY

M	T	W	T	F	S	S
		1	2	3	4	5
6	7	8	9	10	11	12
13	14	15	16	17	18	19
20	21	22	23	24	25	26
27	28	29	30	31		

AUGUST

M	T	W	T	F	S	S
					1	2
3	4	5	6	7	8	9
10	11	12	13	14	15	16
17	18	19	20	21	22	23
24	25	26	27	28	29	30
31						

APRIL
S U M M A R Y

	Dow Jones	S&P 500	Nasdaq	TSX Comp
Month Rank	1	3	4	8
# Up	42	44	27	16
# Down	22	20	15	13
% Pos	66	69	64	55
% Avg. Gain	2.0	1.5	1.4	0.6

Dow & S&P 1950-2013, Nasdaq 1972-2013, TSX 1985-2013

S&P500 Cumulative Daily Gains for Avg Month 1950 to 2013

◆ April, on average, has been the second strongest month for the S&P 500. From 1950 to 2014, April has produced an average gain of 1.5% and been positive 68% of the time. ◆ The first part of April tends to be the strongest (see *18 Day Earnings Month Effect strategy*). ◆ The last part of April tends to be "flat." ◆ Overall, April tends to be a volatile month with the cyclical sectors outperforming. When the defensive sectors outperform in April, it often indicates market weakness ahead.

BEST / WORST APRIL BROAD MKTS. 2005-2014

BEST APRIL MARKETS
◆ Russell 2000 (2009) 15.3%
◆ Nasdaq (2009) 12.3%
◆ Nikkei 225 (2013) 11.8%

WORST APRIL MARKETS
◆ Russell 2000 (2005) -5.8%
◆ Nikkei 225 (2005) -5.7%
◆ Nikkei 225 (2012) -5.6%

Index Values End of Month

	2005	2006	2007	2008	2009	2010	2011	2012	2013	2014
Dow	10,193	11,367	13,063	12,820	8,168	11,009	12,811	13,214	14,840	16,581
S&P 500	1,157	1,311	1,482	1,386	873	1,187	1,364	1,398	1,598	1,884
Nasdaq	1,922	2,323	2,525	2,413	1,717	2,461	2,874	3,046	3,329	4,115
TSX	9,369	12,204	13,417	13,937	9,325	12,211	13,945	12,293	12,457	14,652
Russell 1000	1,198	1,373	1,553	1,453	917	1,259	1,458	1,487	1,705	2,019
Russell 2000	1,440	1,900	2,024	1,780	1,212	1,781	2,150	2,030	2,355	2,801
FTSE 100	4,802	6,023	6,449	6,087	4,244	5,553	6,070	5,738	6,430	6,780
Nikkei 225	11,009	16,906	17,400	13,850	8,828	11,057	9,850	9,521	13,861	14,304

Percent Gain for April

	2005	2006	2007	2008	2009	2010	2011	2012	2013	2014
Dow	-3.0	2.3	5.7	4.5	7.3	1.4	4.0	0.0	1.8	0.7
S&P 500	-2.0	1.2	4.3	4.8	9.4	1.5	2.8	-0.7	1.8	0.6
Nasdaq	-3.9	-0.7	4.3	5.9	12.3	2.6	3.3	-1.5	1.9	-2.0
TSX	-2.5	0.8	1.9	4.4	6.9	1.4	-1.2	-0.8	-2.3	2.2
Russell 1000	-2.0	1.1	4.1	5.0	10.0	1.8	2.9	-0.7	1.7	0.4
Russell 2000	-5.8	-0.1	1.7	4.1	15.3	5.6	2.6	-1.6	-0.4	-3.9
FTSE 100	-1.9	1.0	2.2	6.8	8.1	-2.2	2.7	-0.5	0.3	2.8
Nikkei 225	-5.7	-0.9	0.7	10.6	8.9	-0.3	1.0	-5.6	11.8	-3.5

April Market Avg. Performance 2005 to 2014[1]

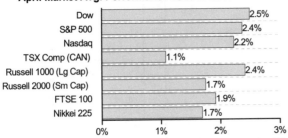

Dow	2.5%
S&P 500	2.4%
Nasdaq	2.2%
TSX Comp (CAN)	1.1%
Russell 1000 (Lg Cap)	2.4%
Russell 2000 (Sm Cap)	1.7%
FTSE 100	1.9%
Nikkei 225	1.7%

Interest Corner Apr[2]

	Fed Funds % [3]	3 Mo. T-Bill % [4]	10 Yr % [5]	20 Yr % [6]
2014	0.25	0.03	2.67	3.22
2013	0.25	0.05	1.70	2.49
2012	0.25	0.10	1.95	2.73
2011	0.25	0.04	3.32	4.15
2010	0.25	0.16	3.69	4.36

(1) Russell Data provided by Russell (2) Federal Reserve Bank of St. Louis- end of month values (3) Target rate set by FOMC (4)(5)(6) Constant yield maturities.

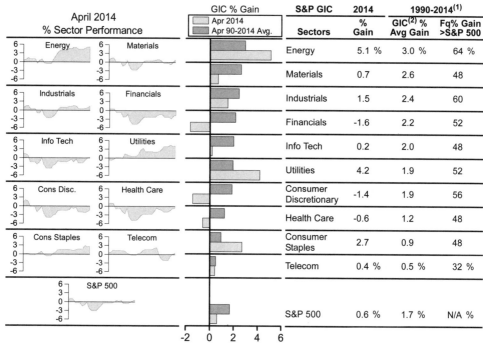

	S&P GIC Sectors	2014 % Gain	1990-2014[1] GIC[2] % Avg Gain	1990-2014[1] Fq% Gain >S&P 500
	Energy	5.1 %	3.0 %	64 %
	Materials	0.7	2.6	48
	Industrials	1.5	2.4	60
	Financials	-1.6	2.2	52
	Info Tech	0.2	2.0	48
	Utilities	4.2	1.9	52
	Consumer Discretionary	-1.4	1.9	56
	Health Care	-0.6	1.2	48
	Consumer Staples	2.7	0.9	48
	Telecom	0.4 %	0.5 %	32 %
	S&P 500	0.6 %	1.7 %	N/A %

Sector Commentary

♦ In April 2014, geopolitical tensions around the world started to increase further as the Ukraine conflict was making its way into the main stream media. The energy sector responded accordingly, producing a gain of 5.1%. ♦ Investors, questioning the lofty levels of the S&P 500, were attracted to the defensive sectors and as a result, the utilities sector produced a strong gain of 4.2%. The utilities sector also benefited from falling interest rates. ♦ The consumer discretionary sector was the worst performing sector as investors doubted whether the sector was going to improve as the consumer purchasing numbers from earlier in the year had still not shown signs of growth.

Sub-Sector Commentary

♦ The metals and mining sub-sector put in another strong month as investors were focused on an improving economy. ♦ The banks sub-sector continued the underperformance that it started in late March. ♦ Retail typically performs well in March, but analysts were having trouble proclaiming improvement in the sub-sector as the bad weather effects from earlier in the year had still not worked their way through the system.

SELECTED SUB-SECTORS[3]

	2014 % Gain	1990-2014 GIC % Avg Gain	Fq% Gain >S&P 500
SOX (1995-2013)	-1.8 %	3.9 %	55 %
Railroads	-0.3	3.3	60
Chemicals	0.1	3.2	68
Banks	-5.0	2.5	52
Transportation	1.5	2.4	60
Homebuilders	-1.4	1.9	48
Pharma	1.9	1.8	56
Software & Services	-2.2	1.5	48
Steel	1.9	1.4	44
Metals & Mining	3.7	1.1	40
Retail	-3.5	0.8	44
Biotech (1993-2013)	0.4	0.3	41
Gold (London PM)	-0.3	0.2	44
Agriculture (1994-2013)	0.8	-0.2	52
Silver	-3.5	-0.3	40

(1) Sector data provided by Standard and Poors (2) GIC is short form for Global Industry Classification (3) Sub Sector data provided by Standard and Poors, except where marked by symbol.

18 DAY EARNINGS MONTH EFFECT
Markets Outperform 1st 18 Calendar Days of Earnings Months

Earnings season occurs the first month of every quarter. At this time, public companies report their financials for the previous quarter and often give guidance on future expectations. As a result, investors tend to bid up stocks, anticipating good earnings. Earnings are a major driver of stock market prices as investors generally like to get in the stock market early in anticipation of favorable results, which helps to run up stock prices in the first half of the month.

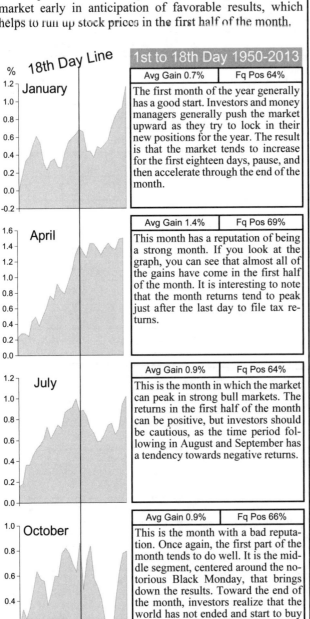

1st to 18th Day Gain S&P500			
	JAN	APR	JUL	OCT
1950	0.54 %	4.28 %	-3.56 %	2.88 %
1951	4.85	3.41	4.39	1.76
1952	2.02	-3.57	-0.44	-1.39
1953	-2.07	-2.65	0.87	3.38
1954	2.50	3.71	2.91	-1.49
1955	-3.28	4.62	3.24	-4.63
1956	-2.88	-1.53	4.96	2.18
1957	-4.36	2.95	2.45	-4.93
1958	2.78	1.45	1.17	2.80
1959	1.09	4.47	1.23	0.79
1960	-3.34	2.26	-2.14	1.55
1961	2.70	1.75	-0.36	2.22
1962	-4.42	-1.84	2.65	0.12
1963	3.30	3.49	-1.27	2.26
1964	2.05	1.99	2.84	0.77
1965	2.05	2.31	1.87	1.91
1966	1.64	2.63	2.66	2.77
1967	6.80	1.84	3.16	-1.51
1968	-0.94	7.63	1.87	2.09
1969	-1.76	-0.27	-2.82	3.37
1970	-1.24	-4.42	6.83	-0.02
1971	1.37	3.17	0.42	-1.01
1972	1.92	2.40	-1.22	-2.13
1973	0.68	0.02	2.00	1.46
1974	-2.04	0.85	-2.58	13.76
1975	3.50	3.53	-2.09	5.95
1976	7.55	-2.04	0.38	-3.58
1977	-3.85	2.15	0.47	-3.18
1978	-4.77	4.73	1.40	-2.00
1979	3.76	0.11	-1.19	-5.22
1980	2.90	-1.51	6.83	4.83
1981	-0.73	-0.96	-0.34	2.59
1982	-4.35	4.33	1.33	13.54
1983	4.10	4.43	-2.20	1.05
1984	1.59	-0.80	-1.16	1.20
1985	2.44	0.10	1.32	2.72
1986	-1.35	1.46	-5.77	3.25
1987	9.96	-1.64	3.48	-12.16
1988	1.94	0.12	-1.09	2.75
1989	3.17	3.78	4.20	-2.12
1990	-4.30	0.23	1.73	-0.10
1991	0.61	3.53	3.83	1.20
1992	0.42	3.06	1.83	-1.45
1993	0.26	-0.60	-1.06	2.07
1994	1.67	-0.74	2.46	1.07
1995	2.27	0.93	2.52	0.52
1996	-1.25	-0.29	-4.04	3.42
1997	4.78	1.22	3.41	-0.33
1998	-0.92	1.90	4.67	3.88
1999	1.14	2.54	3.36	-2.23
2000	-0.96	-3.80	2.69	-6.57
2001	2.10	6.71	-1.36	2.66
2002	-1.79	-2.00	-10.94	8.48
2003	2.50	5.35	1.93	4.35
2004	2.51	0.75	-3.46	-0.05
2005	-1.32	-2.93	2.50	-4.12
2006	2.55	1.22	0.51	3.15
2007	1.41	4.33	-3.20	1.48
2008	-9.75	5.11	-1.51	-19.36
2009	-5.88	8.99	2.29	2.89
2010	1.88	1.94	3.32	3.81
2011	2.97	-1.56	-1.15	8.30
2012	4.01	-1.66	0.78	1.16
2013	4.2	-1.76	5.17	3.74
Avg	0.68 %	1.40 %	0.87 %	0.86 %

1st to 18th Day 1950-2013

January

Avg Gain 0.7%	Fq Pos 64%

The first month of the year generally has a good start. Investors and money managers generally push the market upward as they try to lock in their new positions for the year. The result is that the market tends to increase for the first eighteen days, pause, and then accelerate through the end of the month.

April

Avg Gain 1.4%	Fq Pos 69%

This month has a reputation of being a strong month. If you look at the graph, you can see that almost all of the gains have come in the first half of the month. It is interesting to note that the month returns tend to peak just after the last day to file tax returns.

July

Avg Gain 0.9%	Fq Pos 64%

This is the month in which the market can peak in strong bull markets. The returns in the first half of the month can be positive, but investors should be cautious, as the time period following in August and September has a tendency towards negative returns.

October

Avg Gain 0.9%	Fq Pos 66%

This is the month with a bad reputation. Once again, the first part of the month tends to do well. It is the middle segment, centered around the notorious Black Monday, that brings down the results. Toward the end of the month, investors realize that the world has not ended and start to buy stocks again, providing a strong finish to the month.

18th Day Line

2013-14 Strategy Performance

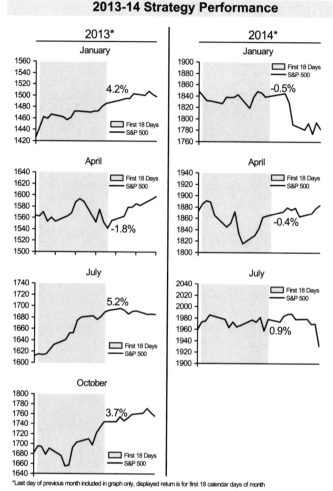

*Last day of previous month included in graph only, displayed return is for first 18 calendar days of month

Market Indices & Rates
Weekly Values**

Stock Markets	2013	2014
Dow	14,591	16,510
S&P500	1,560	1,881
Nasdaq	3,228	4,222
TSX	12,499	14,394
FTSE	6,376	6,651
DAX	7,824	9,622
Nikkei	12,394	14,940
Hang Seng	22,144	22,440

Commodities	2013	2014
Oil	94.93	100.47
Gold	1565.6	1289.8

Bond Yields	2013	2014
USA 5 Yr Treasury	0.73	1.75
USA 10 Yr T	1.81	2.77
USA 20 Yr T	2.64	3.35
Moody's Aaa	3.82	4.31
Moody's Baa	4.70	5.02
CAN 5 Yr T	1.26	1.75
CAN 10 Yr T	1.82	2.51

Money Market	2013	2014
USA Fed Funds	0.25	0.25
USA 3 Mo T-B	0.07	0.03
CAN tgt overnight rate	1.00	1.00
CAN 3 Mo T-B	0.98	0.91

Foreign Exchange	2013	2014
EUR/USD	1.29	1.38
GBP/USD	1.52	1.66
USD/CAD	1.02	1.10
USD/JPY	94.72	103.60

APRIL

M	T	W	T	F	S	S
		1	2	3	4	5
6	7	8	9	10	11	12
13	14	15	16	17	18	19
20	21	22	23	24	25	26
27	28	29	30			

MAY

M	T	W	T	F	S	S
				1	2	3
4	5	6	7	8	9	10
11	12	13	14	15	16	17
18	19	20	21	22	23	24
25	26	27	28	29	30	31

JUNE

M	T	W	T	F	S	S
1	2	3	4	5	6	7
8	9	10	11	12	13	14
15	16	17	18	19	20	21
22	23	24	25	26	27	28
29	30					

Earnings Month Effect Performance

In 2013, the first eighteen calendar days of earnings months, on average produced strong gains. July was the only earnings month where the S&P 500 ended up lower at the end of the month, compared with its level after eighteen calendar days. After producing a strong gain of 5.2% in the first eighteen calendar days, the S&P 500 had become extended and pulled back slightly in the remainder of the month. After a volatile start, October produced a strong gain of 3.7% in the first eighteen calendar days and continued to perform strongly until the end of the month.

In 2014, the results have been mixed, with both January and April producing losses and July off-setting the losses with a gain of 0.9%.

** Weekly avg closing values- except Fed Funds & CAN overnight tgt rate weekly closing values.

- 44 -

CONSUMER SWITCH
SELL CONSUMER DISCRETIONARY
BUY CONSUMER STAPLES
Consumer Staples Outperform Apr 23 to Oct 27

The *Consumer Switch* strategy has allowed investors to use a set portion of their account to switch between the two related consumer sectors. To use this strategy, investors invest in the consumer discretionary sector from October 28th to April 22nd, and then use the proceeds to invest in the consumer staples sector from April 23rd to October 27th, and then repeat the cycle.

The end result has been outperformance compared with buying and holding both consumer sectors, or buying and holding the broad market.

3060% total aggregate gain compared with 466% for the S&P 500

The basic premise of the strategy is that the consumer discretionary sector tends to outperform during the favorable six months when more money flows into the market, pushing up stock prices. On the other hand, the consumer staples sector tends to outperform when investors are looking for safety and stability of earnings in the six months when the market tends to move into a defensive mode.

Consumer Staples & Discretionary Switch Strategy*			
Investment Period	Buy @ Beginning of Period	% Gain @ End of Period	% Gain Cumulative
90 Apr23 - 90 Oct29	Staples	7.7%	8%
90 Oct29 - 91 Apr23	Discretionary	41.7	53
91 Apr23 - 91 Oct20	Staples	2.1	56
91 Oct28 - 92 Apr23	Discretionary	15.9	81
92 Apr23 - 92 Oct27	Staples	6.3	92
92 Oct27 - 93 Apr23	Discretionary	6.3	104
93 Apr23 - 93 Oct27	Staples	5.8	116
93 Oct27 - 94 Apr25	Discretionary	-3.7	108
94 Apr25 - 94 Oct27	Staples	10.2	129
94 Oct27 - 95 Apr24	Discretionary	4.4	139
95 Apr24 - 95 Oct27	Staples	15.3	176
95 Oct27 - 96 Apr23	Discretionary	17.3	227
96 Apr23 - 96 Oct27	Staples	12.6	265
96 Oct27 - 97 Apr23	Discretionary	5.1	283
97 Apr23 - 97 Oct27	Staples	2.5	293
97 Oct27 - 98 Apr23	Discretionary	35.9	434
98 Apr23 - 98 Oct27	Staples	-0.7	423
98 Oct27 - 99 Apr23	Discretionary	41.8	651
99 Apr23 - 99 Oct27	Staples	-9.7	578
99 Oct27 - 00 Apr24	Discretionary	11.9	659
00 Apr24 - 00 Oct27	Staples	16.5	785
00 Oct27 - 01 Apr23	Discretionary	9.8	872
01 Apr23 - 01 Oct29	Staples	4.0	910
01 Oct29 - 02 Apr23	Discretionary	16.1	1073
02 Apr23 - 02 Oct28	Staples	-13.9	910
02 Oct28 - 03 Apr23	Discretionary	3.0	941
03 Apr23 - 03 Oct27	Staples	8.4	1028
03 Oct27 - 04 Apr23	Discretionary	9.6	1137
04 Apr23 - 04 Oct27	Staples	-7.4	1045
04 Oct27 - 05 Apr25	Discretionary	-2.0	1021
05 Apr25 - 05 Oct27	Staples	-0.5	1016
05 Oct27 - 06 Apr24	Discretionary	9.2	1119
06 Apr24 - 06 Oct27	Staples	10.6	1249
06 Oct27 - 07 Apr23	Discretionary	6.3	1334
07 Apr23 - 07 Oct29	Staples	4.6	1400
07 Oct29 - 08 Apr23	Discretionary	-13.7	1194
08 Apr23 - 08 Oct27	Staples	-21.5	916
08 Oct27 - 09 Apr23	Discretionary	17.7	1096
09 Apr23 - 09 Oct27	Staples	20.6	1342
09 Oct27 - 10 Apr23	Discretionary	29.7	1770
10 Apr23 - 10 Oct27	Staples	2.4	1815
10 Oct27 - 11 Apr25	Discretionary	13.7	2079
11 Apr25 - 11 Oct27	Staples	2.2	2126
11 Oct27 - 12 Apr23	Discretionary	10.9	2368
12 Apr23 - 12 Oct31	Staples	4.7	2485
12 Oct31 - 13 Apr23	Discretionary	17.5	2938
13 Apr23 - 13 Oct28	Staples	2.3	3006
13 Oct28 - 14 Apr23	Discretionary	1.7	3060

* If buy date lands on weekend or holiday, then buy date used is next trading date

Total Gains From
Apr 1990 to Apr 2014

3060%

466% — S&P 500
649% — Con Disc
661% — Con Staples
3060% — Switch Strategy Con. Disc.- Con. Staples

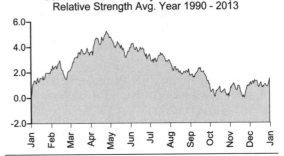

Consumer Discretionary / Consumer Staples
Relative Strength Avg. Year 1990 - 2013

2013-14 Strategy Performance

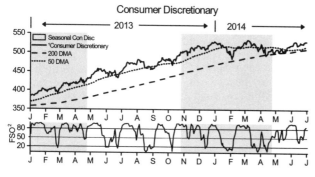

Consumer Discretionary

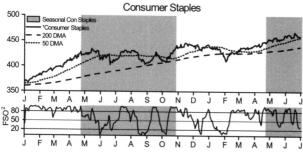

Consumer Staples

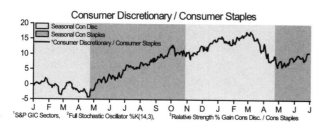

Consumer Discretionary / Consumer Staples

[1] S&P GIC Sectors, [2] Full Stochastic Oscillator %K(14,3), [3] Relative Strength % Gain Cons Disc. / Cons Staples

Market Indices & Rates
Weekly Values**

Stock Markets	2013	2014
Dow	14,764	16,227
S&P500	1,580	1,844
Nasdaq	3,270	4,086
TSX	12,436	14,329
FTSE	6,356	6,611
DAX	7,745	9,456
Nikkei	13,341	14,395
Hang Seng	21,963	22,802

Commodities	2013	2014
Oil	93.40	102.75
Gold	1565.6	1309.8

Bond Yields	2013	2014
USA 5 Yr Treasury	0.72	1.63
USA 10 Yr T	1.79	2.68
USA 20 Yr T	2.58	3.27
Moody's Aaa	3.75	4.24
Moody's Baa	4.62	4.92
CAN 5 Yr T	1.24	1.70
CAN 10 Yr T	1.77	2.45

Money Market	2013	2014
USA Fed Funds	0.25	0.25
USA 3 Mo T-B	0.07	0.04
CAN tgt overnight rate	1.00	1.00
CAN 3 Mo T-B	0.98	0.91

Foreign Exchange	2013	2014
EUR/USD	1.31	1.38
GBP/USD	1.53	1.67
USD/CAD	1.01	1.09
USD/JPY	99.24	102.01

APRIL
M	T	W	T	F	S	S
	1	2	3	4	5	
6	7	8	9	10	11	12
13	14	15	16	17	18	19
20	21	22	23	24	25	26
27	28	29	30			

MAY
M	T	W	T	F	S	S
			1	2	3	
4	5	6	7	8	9	10
11	12	13	14	15	16	17
18	19	20	21	22	23	24
25	26	27	28	29	30	31

JUNE
M	T	W	T	F	S	S
1	2	3	4	5	6	7
8	9	10	11	12	13	14
15	16	17	18	19	20	21
22	23	24	25	26	27	28
29	30					

Consumer Switch Strategy Performance

The consumer discretionary sector has been one of the top performing sectors of the market over the last few years. In 2013, the consumer discretionary sector outperformed the consumer staples sector during the period when the consumer staples sector typically outperforms, from April 23rd to October 27th.

The consumer discretionary sector continued to outperform at the start of its seasonally strong period. In March of 2014, the consumer staples started to outperform as investors were getting nervous in the markets and moving into the defensive sectors. The consumer discretionary sector was also hit hard by a faltering retail sector due to harsh winter weather conditions. At the end of its seasonal period, the consumer discretionary sector underperformed the consumer staples sector.

** Weekly avg closing values- except Fed Funds & CAN overnight tgt rate weekly closing values.

NATURAL GAS FIRES UP AND DOWN
①LONG (Mar22-Jun19) ②LONG (Sep5-Dec21)
③SHORT (Dec22-Dec31)

Note: The natural gas spring seasonal period has been added to the natural gas strategy previously published in Thackray's Investor's Guides.

There are two high consumption times for natural gas: winter and summer. The colder it gets in winter, the more natural gas is consumed to keep the furnaces going. The warmer it gets in the summer, the more natural gas is used to produce power for air conditioners.

On the supply side, weather plays a large factor in determining price. During the hurricane season in the Gulf of Mexico, the price of natural gas is affected by the forecast of the number and severity of hurricanes.

gas has on average increased 12% and has been positive 74% of the time. Natural gas tends to also rise between September 5th and December 21st, due to the demands of the heating season. In this time period, from 1995 to 2013, natural gas has produced an average gain of 46% and has been positive 84% of the time.

75% gain & positive 89% of the time

Natural gas tends to fall in price from December 22nd to December 31st. Although this is a short time period, for the years from 1995 to 2013, natural gas has produced an average loss of 7.4%, more losses than gains and has failed to generate any large gains. The poor performance of natural gas at this time is largely driven by southern U.S. refiners dumping inventory on the market to help mitigate year-end taxes on their inventory.

Applying a strategy of investing in natural gas from March 22nd to June 19th, reinvesting the proceeds from September 5th to December 21st, reinvesting the proceeds again to short natural gas from December 22nd to December 31st, has produced a compounded average return of 75% and has been positive 89% of the time.

Using the natural gas compound strategy has produced returns that are over three times greater than the average annual gain in natural gas. By using the strategy, an investor would have caught most of the large gains and missed most of the large losses.

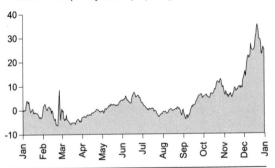

Natural Gas (Cash) Henry Hub LA
Seasonal Gains 1995 to 2013

		Pos.	Pos.	Neg. (Short)	Pos.
Year	%	Mar 22 to Jun 19	Sep 5 to Dec 21	Dec 22 to Dec 31	Compound Growth
1995	99.4	13.0 %	103.0 %	1.2 %	126.7
1996	-27.4	-6.6	170.4	-46.2	269.2
1997	-9.4	16.8	-13.1	-6.3	7.9
1998	-13.0	-2.6	20.9	-6.7	25.7
1999	18.6	28.9	5.3	-11.2	50.9
2000	356.5	57.1	121.9	0.7	246.3
2001	-74.3	-24.1	21.5	1.5	-9.2
2002	70.0	0.6	61.3	-9.1	77.1
2003	26.4	9.5	47.1	-16.3	87.4
2004	3.6	18.2	54.6	-11.6	103.9
2005	58.4	6.3	14.5	-29.6	57.7
2006	-42.2	-1.8	17.4	-9.5	26.3
2007	30.2	9.2	32.7	2.0	42.1
2008	-21.4	52.2	-21.4	-0.9	20.6
2009	3.6	1.5	208.0	0.7	210.4
2010	-27.4	28.6	10.4	2.4	38.6
2011	-29.6	10.0	-26.1	-1.7	-17.3
2012	15.4	18.7	21.7	0.6	43.7
2013	26.3	-1.4	18.2	-0.2	16.8
Avg.	24.4	12.3 %	45.7 %	-7.4 %	75.0

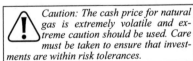

Natural Gas (Henry Hub Spot)- Avg. Year 1995 to 2013

Natural gas prices tend to rise from mid-March to mid-June ahead of the cooling season demands in the summer. From 1995 to 2013, during the time period of March 22nd to June 19th, the spot price of natural

Source: New York Mercantile Exchange. NYMX is an exchange provider of futures and options.

2013-14 Strategy Performance

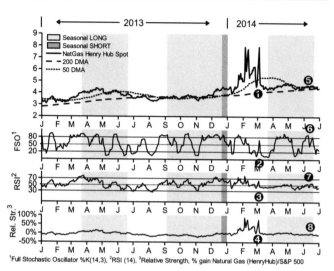

¹Full Stochastic Oscillator %K(14,3), ²RSI (14), ³Relative Strength, % gain Natural Gas (HenryHub)/S&P 500

Market Indices & Rates
Weekly Values**

Stock Markets	2013	2014
Dow	14,612	16,317
S&P500	1,555	1,850
Nasdaq	3,212	4,060
TSX	12,027	14,384
FTSE	6,285	6,584
DAX	7,566	9,310
Nikkei	13,283	14,252
Hang Seng	21,708	22,792

Commodities	2013	2014
Oil	87.97	103.97
Gold	1393.3	1306.1

Bond Yields	2013	2014
USA 5 Yr Treasury	0.71	1.67
USA 10 Yr T	1.73	2.67
USA 20 Yr T	2.51	3.23
Moody's Aaa	3.68	4.22
Moody's Baa	4.54	4.86
CAN 5 Yr T	1.18	1.68
CAN 10 Yr T	1.71	2.42

Money Market	2013	2014
USA Fed Funds	0.25	0.25
USA 3 Mo T-B	0.06	0.04
CAN tgt overnight rate	0.80	1.00
CAN 3 Mo T-B	0.98	0.93

Foreign Exchange	2013	2014
EUR/USD	1.31	1.38
GBP/USD	1.53	1.68
USD/CAD	1.03	1.10
USD/JPY	98.02	102.16

Natural Gas Performance

The extremely cold winter of 2013-2014 caused much greater levels of natural gas consumption than average.

Technical Conditions– March 22nd to June 19th, 2014

Entry Strategy –Buy Position Early–

After a sharp drop in price in late February, natural gas prices rebounded❶ and the FSO moved above 20❷ triggering an early buy signal. The RSI also moved above 50❸ and the relative performance of natural gas compared to the S&P 500 spiked❹. In the end, it proved to be another volatile spike and the start of the seasonal period proved to be a better entry point.

Exit Strategy –Sell Position Early–

Natural gas rose in early June and was just above its 50 and 200 day moving averages❺. A slight correction caused the FSO to fall below 80❻ and trigger an early sell signal. At the time, the RSI was barely above 50❼ and the fall in natural gas price pushed it below 50. Natural gas was performing equal to the S&P 500❽.

Overall, natural gas produced a gain in its seasonal period and the early exit date produced only slightly better results than selling at the end of the seasonal period.

APRIL

M	T	W	T	F	S	S
		1	2	3	4	5
6	7	8	9	10	11	12
13	14	15	16	17	18	19
20	21	22	23	24	25	26
27	28	29	30			

MAY

M	T	W	T	F	S	S
				1	2	3
4	5	6	7	8	9	10
11	12	13	14	15	16	17
18	19	20	21	22	23	24
25	26	27	28	29	30	31

JUNE

M	T	W	T	F	S	S
1	2	3	4	5	6	7
8	9	10	11	12	13	14
15	16	17	18	19	20	21
22	23	24	25	26	27	28
29	30					

** Weekly avg closing values- except Fed Funds & CAN overnight tgt rate weekly closing values.

CANADIAN DOLLAR STRONG– TWICE
①APRIL & ②AUG 20 TO SEP 25

All other things being equal, if oil increases in price, investors favor the Canadian dollar over the U.S. dollar. They do so with good reason, as Canada is a net exporter of oil and benefits from its rising price.

Oil tends to do well in the month of April as this is the heart of one of the strongest seasonal strategies – oil and oil stocks outperform from February 25th to May 9th.

April has been a strong month for the Canadian dollar relative to the U.S. dollar. The largest losses have had a tendency to occur in years when the Fed Reserve has been aggressively hiking their target rate.

At some point during the years 1987, 2000, 2004 and 2005, the Fed increased their target rate by a total of at least 1%

CAD vs USD Avg. % Gain 1971 to 2013

in each year. Since 1971, three of these years (1987, 2004 and 2005) were three of the biggest losers for the Canadian dollar in the month of April.

The Canadian dollar also has a second period of seasonality, August 20th to September 25th. It is not a coincidence that oil also has a second period of seasonal strength at this time. Although the August 20th to September 25th seasonal period is not as strong as the April seasonal period, it is still a trade worth considering.

CAD vs USD Apr & Aug 20 to Sep 25 % Gain (1971-2014) Source: Bloomberg   Positive ▢

	Apr1-Apr30	Aug20-Sep25		Apr1-Apr30	Aug20-Sep25		Apr1-Apr30	Aug20-Sep25		Apr1-Apr30	Aug20-Sep25		Apr1-Apr30	Aug20-Sep25
			1980	0.29%	-0.15%	1990	0.44%	-0.43%	2000	-1.89%	-0.96%	2010	0.44%	1.32%
1971	-0.10%	0.46%	1981	-0.74	1.08	1991	0.65	0.86	2001	2.76	-1.76	2011	2.44	-4.20
1972	0.53	0.01	1982	0.89	0.78	1992	-0.48	-3.37	2002	1.77	-0.61	2012	1.05	1.16
1973	-0.41	-0.32	1983	0.64	0.17	1993	-1.02	-0.08	2003	2.50	3.95	2013	1.01	0.39
1974	1.27	-0.40	1984	-0.62	-1.01	1994	0.14	2.22	2004	-4.46	1.57	2014	0.89	
1975	-1.56	1.33	1985	0.04	-0.32	1995	2.91	0.96	2005	-3.77	3.75			
1976	0.55	1.41	1986	1.69	0.35	1996	0.15	0.48	2006	4.17	0.64			
1977	0.91	0.31	1987	-2.38	1.41	1997	-0.97	0.79	2007	4.17	6.30			
1978	0.09	-3.22	1988	0.41	0.43	1998	-0.85	1.37	2008	1.81	2.59			
1979	1.61	0.15	1989	0.60	0.55	1999	3.53	1.36	2009	5.59	0.46			
Avg.	0.32%	-0.03%		0.06%	0.38%		0.45%	0.51%		1.62%	1.88%		1.35%	-0.88%

CAD vs. USD Avg. Year By Month By Decade (1971 to 2013)

Legend:
- 1971 to 1979
- 1980 to 1989
- 1990 to 1999
- 2000 to 2009
- 2010 to 2013

J F M A M J J A S O N D

2012-13-14 Strategy Performance

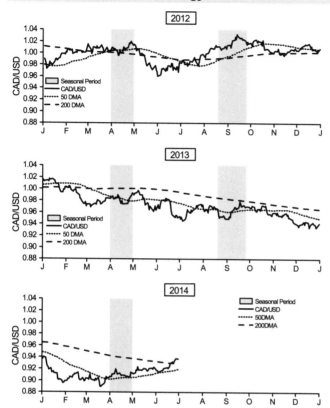

Market Indices & Rates
Weekly Values**

Stock Markets	2013	2014
Dow	14,675	16,466
S&P500	1,577	1,874
Nasdaq	3,268	4,127
TSX	12,200	14,534
FTSE	6,398	5,349
DAX	7,709	9,524
Nikkei	13,750	14,456
Hang Seng	22,197	22,507

Commodities	2013	2014
Oil	90.99	102.28
Gold	1436.7	1291.2

Bond Yields	2013	2014
USA 5 Yr Treasury	0.70	1.74
USA 10 Yr T	1.73	2.71
USA 20 Yr T	2.50	3.23
Moody's Aaa	3.70	4.22
Moody's Baa	4.53	4.86
CAN 5 Yr T	1.19	1.70
CAN 10 Yr T	1.72	2.43

Money Market	2013	2014
USA Fed Funds	0.25	0.25
USA 3 Mo T-B	0.05	0.03
CAN tgt overnight rate	1.00	1.00
CAN 3 Mo T-B	0.99	0.94

Foreign Exchange	2013	2014
EUR/USD	1.30	1.38
GBP/USD	1.53	1.68
USD/CAD	1.02	1.10
USD/JPY	99.11	102.45

APRIL

M	T	W	T	F	S	S
	1	2	3	4	5	
6	7	8	9	10	11	12
13	14	15	16	17	18	19
20	21	22	23	24	25	26
27	28	29	30			

MAY

M	T	W	T	F	S	S
			1	2	3	
4	5	6	7	8	9	10
11	12	13	14	15	16	17
18	19	20	21	22	23	24
25	26	27	28	29	30	31

JUNE

M	T	W	T	F	S	S
1	2	3	4	5	6	7
8	9	10	11	12	13	14
15	16	17	18	19	20	21
22	23	24	25	26	27	28
29	30					

Canadian Dollar Performance (CAD/USD)

The Canadian dollar was successful in both of its seasonal periods in 2012 and 2013.

In January 2014, the Canadian dollar fell sharply against a rising U.S. dollar. In February and March, it oscillated back and forth around the $0.90 level. At the start of its seasonal period, the Canadian dollar had just broken above its 50 day moving average. For most of its April seasonal period, the Canadian dollar was flat against the U.S. dollar. Towards the end of its seasonal period, the Canadian dollar bounced off its 50 day moving average to finish on a positive note against the U.S. dollar. Overall, the seasonal trade was successful once again.

** Weekly avg closing values- except Fed Funds & CAN overnight tgt rate weekly closing values.

- 50 -

MAY

	MONDAY	TUESDAY	WEDNESDAY
WEEK 18	27	28	29
WEEK 19	**4** 27	**5** 26	**6** 25
WEEK 20	**11** 20	**12** 19	**13** 18
WEEK 21	**18** 13 CAN Market Closed- Victoria Day	**19** 12	**20** 11
WEEK 22	**25** 6 USA Market Closed- Memorial Day	**26** 5	**27** 4

THURSDAY		FRIDAY	
30		**1**	30
7	24	**8**	23
14	17	**15**	16
21	10	**22**	9
28	3	**29**	2

JUNE

M	T	W	T	F	S	S
1	2	3	4	5	6	7
8	9	10	11	12	13	14
15	16	17	18	19	20	21
22	23	24	25	26	27	28
29	30					

JULY

M	T	W	T	F	S	S
		1	2	3	4	5
6	7	8	9	10	11	12
13	14	15	16	17	18	19
20	21	22	23	24	25	26
27	28	29	30	31		

AUGUST

M	T	W	T	F	S	S
					1	2
3	4	5	6	7	8	9
10	11	12	13	14	15	16
17	18	19	20	21	22	23
24	25	26	27	28	29	30
31						

SEPTEMBER

M	T	W	T	F	S	S
	1	2	3	4	5	6
7	8	9	10	11	12	13
14	15	16	17	18	19	20
21	22	23	24	25	26	27
28	29	30				

MAY SUMMARY

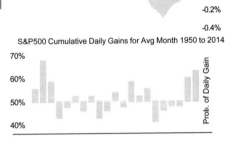

	Dow Jones	S&P 500	Nasdaq	TSX Comp
Month Rank	9	8	5	2
# Up	32	36	25	19
# Down	32	28	17	10
% Pos	50	56	60	66
% Avg. Gain	-0.1	0.2	0.9	1.6

Dow & S&P 1950-2013, Nasdaq 1972-2013, TSX 1985-2013

S&P500 Cumulative Daily Gains for Avg Month 1950 to 2014

♦ The S&P 500 often peaks in May and as a result seasonal investors should start to be more cautious with their investments. ♦ After producing a loss for three years in a row from 2010 to 2012, the S&P 500 produced a gain of 2.1% in May 2013 and then another gain of 2.1% in May 2014. ♦ The first few days and the last few days in May, tend to be strong. The period in between tends to negative. ♦ A lot of the cyclical sectors finish their seasonal periods at the beginning of May.

BEST / WORST MAY BROAD MKTS. 2005-2014

BEST MAY MARKETS
♦ TSX Comp. (2009) 11.2%
♦ Nikkei 225 (2009) 7.9%
♦ Nasdaq (2005) 7.6%

WORST MAY MARKETS
♦ Nikkei 225 (2010) -11.7%
♦ Nikkei 225 (2012) -10.3%
♦ Nikkei 225 (2006) -8.5%

Index Values End of Month

	2005	2006	2007	2008	2009	2010	2011	2012	2013	2014
Dow	10,467	11,168	13,628	12,638	8,500	10,137	12,570	12,393	15,116	16,717
S&P 500	1,192	1,270	1,531	1,400	919	1,089	1,345	1,310	1,631	1,924
Nasdaq	2,068	2,179	2,605	2,523	1,774	2,257	2,835	2,827	3,456	4,243
TSX Comp.	9,607	11,745	14,057	14,715	10,370	11,763	13,803	11,513	12,650	14,604
Russell 1000	1,239	1,330	1,605	1,477	965	1,157	1,439	1,392	1,739	2,061
Russell 2000	1,533	1,792	2,105	1,860	1,247	1,644	2,108	1,893	2,446	2,820
FTSE 100	4,964	5,724	6,621	6,054	4,418	5,188	5,990	5,321	6,583	6,845
Nikkei 225	11,277	15,467	17,876	14,339	9,523	9,769	9,694	8,543	13,775	14,632

Percent Gain for May

	2005	2006	2007	2008	2009	2010	2011	2012	2013	2014
Dow	2.7	-1.7	4.3	-1.4	4.1	-7.9	-1.9	-6.2	1.9	0.8
S&P 500	3.0	-3.1	3.3	1.1	5.3	-8.2	-1.4	-6.3	2.1	2.1
Nasdaq	7.6	-6.2	3.1	4.6	3.3	-8.3	-1.3	-7.2	3.8	3.1
TSX Comp.	2.5	-3.8	4.8	5.6	11.2	-3.7	-1.0	-6.3	1.6	-0.3
Russell 1000	3.4	-3.2	3.4	1.6	5.3	-8.1	-1.3	-6.4	2.0	2.1
Russell 2000	6.4	-5.7	4.0	4.5	2.9	-7.7	-2.0	-6.7	3.9	0.7
FTSE 100	3.4	-5.0	2.7	-0.6	4.1	-6.6	-1.3	-7.3	2.4	1.0
Nikkei 225	2.4	-8.5	2.7	3.5	7.9	-11.7	-1.6	-10.3	-0.6	2.3

May Market Avg. Performance 2005 to 2014[1]

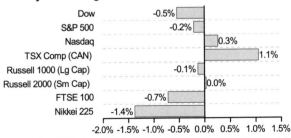

Dow	-0.5%
S&P 500	-0.2%
Nasdaq	0.3%
TSX Comp (CAN)	1.1%
Russell 1000 (Lg Cap)	-0.1%
Russell 2000 (Sm Cap)	0.0%
FTSE 100	-0.7%
Nikkei 225	-1.4%

Interest Corner May[2]

	Fed Funds % [3]	3 Mo. T-Bill % [4]	10 Yr % [5]	20 Yr % [6]
2014	0.25	0.04	2.48	3.05
2013	0.25	0.04	2.16	2.95
2012	0.25	0.07	1.59	2.27
2011	0.25	0.06	3.05	3.91
2010	0.25	0.16	3.31	4.05

(1) Russell Data provided by Russell (2) Federal Reserve Bank of St. Louis- end of month values (3) Target rate set by FOMC (4)(5)(6) Constant yield maturities.

MAY SECTOR PERFORMANCE

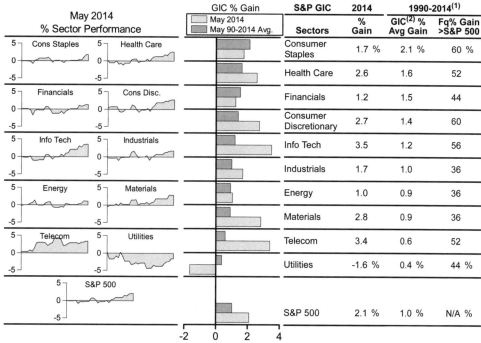

S&P GIC Sectors	2014 % Gain	1990-2014[1] GIC[2] % Avg Gain	Fq% Gain >S&P 500
Consumer Staples	1.7 %	2.1 %	60 %
Health Care	2.6	1.6	52
Financials	1.2	1.5	44
Consumer Discretionary	2.7	1.4	60
Info Tech	3.5	1.2	56
Industrials	1.7	1.0	36
Energy	1.0	0.9	36
Materials	2.8	0.9	36
Telecom	3.4	0.6	52
Utilities	-1.6 %	0.4 %	44 %
S&P 500	2.1 %	1.0 %	N/A %

Sector Commentary

♦ In May 2014, the information technology sector performed well in the last half of the month, helping to propel the S&P 500 to record highs above 1900. ♦ The telecom sector is typically one of the weaker sectors, but with the announcement of a possible $50 billion merger between DirectTV and AT&T, the sector produced a gain of 3.4%. ♦ After performing well in the first part of the year, the utilities sector took a breather, and produced a loss of 1.6%, despite interest rates moving lower at the time.

Sub-Sector Commentary

♦ The transportation and railroad sub-sectors continued their strength from April, and in May produced gains of 5.8% and 5.1% respectively. A strong transportation sub-sector generally means a favorable outlook for the overall economy. ♦ The homebuilders sector bounced with a 6.2% gain, after performing poorly in the previous months. ♦ The agriculture sub-sector has on average outperformed the S&P 500 with an average gain of 2.2% from 1994 to 2014. In May 2014, the agriculture sub-sector produced a gain of 2.8%.

SELECTED SUB-SECTORS[3]

Agriculture (1994-2014)	2.8 %	2.2 %	52 %
Banks	0.6	2.1	48
Biotech (1993-2014)	5.2	2.1	68
Retail	2.2	1.8	60
Railroads	5.1	1.8	60
Metals & Mining	-2.2	1.2	48
Pharma	-0.6	1.2	44
Chemicals	4.0	1.0	48
Steel	-3.2	0.9	52
Transportation	5.8	0.8	52
Software & Services	2.4	0.7	36
Gold (London PM)	-2.9	0.3	56
SOX (1995-2014)	4.1	0.0	50
Silver	-1.5	-0.3	48
Homebuilders	6.2	-1.1	48

1/2 'N' 1/2
First 1/2 of April – Financial Stocks
Second 1/2 of April – Information Technology Stocks

The *1/2 'N' 1/2* strategy is a short-term switch combination that takes advantage of the superior performance of financial stocks in the first part of April and information technology stocks in the second half.

The opportunity exists because technology stocks tend to start increasing at the same time financial stocks tend to start decreasing, in mid-April. This creates an ideal switch opportunity between the two sectors.

2.7% extra & 18 times out of 25 better than the S&P 500

Why do financial stocks tend to perform well in the first half of April? It is not a coincidence that the rate on the three month T-Bill tends to bottom in mid-April.

Liquidity is the common denominator that affects both the financial stocks and the money market. Investors sell-off their money market positions in the beginning of April to cover their taxes that are due to the IRS in mid-April. As a result, short-term money market rates tend to decrease.

Decreasing short-term yields are good for financial stocks, particularly banks. Banks tend to make more money with a steeper yield curve. They borrow short-term money (your savings account) and lend out long-term (mortgages). The steeper the curve, the more money banks make.

The end result is that financial stocks benefit from this trend in the first half of April.

On the flip side, investors stop selling their money market positions to cover taxes by mid-month. At this time, short-term yields tend to increase and financial stocks decrease.

Financials & Info Tech & 1/2 & 1/2 > S&P 500

Year	April 1st to April 15th S&P 500	Financials	April 16th to April 30 S&P 500	Info Tech	April Compound Growth S&P 500	1/2 & 1/2
1990	1.3%	1.0%	-3.0%	1.9%	-2.7%	-0.6%
1991	1.6	2.3	-1.5	-3.1	0.0	-0.9
1992	3.1	1.0	-0.3	-1.3	2.8	-0.3
1993	-0.7	3.5	-1.8	-2.2	-2.5	1.3
1994	0.1	4.9	1.1	3.5	1.2	8.6
1995	1.7	2.9	1.1	5.8	2.8	8.8
1996	-0.5	-2.3	1.8	8.2	1.3	5.8
1997	-0.3	0.3	6.2	11.3	5.8	11.6
1998	1.6	5.5	-0.7	4.3	0.9	10.0
1999	2.8	5.0	0.9	1.3	3.8	6.4
2000	-9.5	-7.0	7.1	14.8	-3.1	6.8
2001	2.0	0.2	5.6	8.3	7.7	8.5
2002	-3.9	-1.6	-2.3	-3.5	-6.1	-5.1
2003	5.0	9.3	2.9	5.3	8.1	15.1
2004	0.2	-3.0	-1.9	-5.0	-1.7	-7.8
2005	-3.2	-2.6	1.2	2.3	-2.0	-0.4
2006	-0.4	-0.3	1.7	-1.3	1.2	-1.6
2007	2.3	0.5	2.0	2.7	4.3	3.2
2008	0.9	-0.6	3.8	6.8	4.8	6.2
2009	6.8	23.0	2.4	5.8	9.4	30.1
2010	3.6	6.5	-2.1	-2.9	1.5	3.4
2011	-0.5	-1.6	3.3	4.6	2.9	2.9
2012	-2.7	-4.4	2.0	0.0	-0.7	-4.4
2013	-1.1	-0.8	2.9	3.4	1.8	2.6
2014	-1.6	-3.1	2.2	2.4	0.6	-0.8
Avg	0.3%	1.6%	1.4%	2.8%	1.7%	4.4%

Fortunately, information technology stocks tend to present a good opportunity in mid-April, just when financials stocks are starting to underperform. Very often at this time of the year, technology stocks have corrected after their seasonal period finished in January and have become oversold and set up for a bounce.

Alternate Strategy—
The first few days in May tend to produce gains. An alternate strategy is to hold the information technology position for the first three trading days in May.

The SP GICS Financial Sector # 40 encompasses a wide range financial based companies.
The SP GICS Information Technology Sector # 45 encompasses a wide range technology based companies. For more information on the information technology sector, see www.standardandpoors.com

2014 Strategy Performance

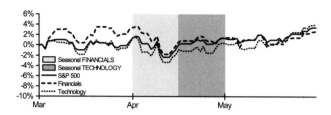

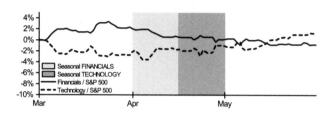

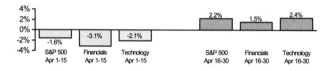

Market Indices & Rates
Weekly Values**

Stock Markets	2013	2014
Dow	14,833	16,527
S&P500	1,597	1,879
Nasdaq	3,331	4,109
TSX	12,382	14,639
FTSE	6,464	6,776
DAX	7,968	9,547
Nikkei	13,785	14,384
Hang Seng	22,669	22,245

Commodities	2013	2014
Oil	93.72	100.21
Gold	1466.0	1289.0

Bond Yields	2013	2014
USA 5 Yr Treasury	0.68	1.70
USA 10 Yr T	1.70	2.66
USA 20 Yr T	2.49	3.20
Moody's Aaa	3.69	4.19
Moody's Baa	4.52	4.81
CAN 5 Yr T	1.18	1.67
CAN 10 Yr T	1.70	2.40

Money Market	2013	2014
USA Fed Funds	0.25	0.25
USA 3 Mo T-B	0.05	0.03
CAN tgt overnight rate	1.00	1.00
CAN 3 Mo T-B	0.99	0.95

Foreign Exchange	2013	2014
EUR/USD	1.31	1.39
GBP/USD	1.55	1.69
USD/CAD	1.01	1.10
USD/JPY	97.91	102.38

1/2 and 1/2 Performance

In March 2014, the financial sector outperformed the S&P 500, mainly as a result of a sharp increase at the beginning of the month. This outperformance is not unusual as the financial sector typically performs well in March and when it does perform well, it often leads to positive broad market performance in April.

Technical Conditions–
April 1st to April 15th, 2014 –

The S&P 500 fell at the beginning of April and went on to lose 1.6% in the first half of the month. The financial sector performed poorly as investors were questioning the strength of the earnings that were about to be released in the second half of April. The technology sector also underperformed the S&P 500.

April 16th to April 30th, 2014 –

In the second half of April, the S&P 500 bounced back, producing a 2.2% gain. The financial sector underperformed as investors were not overly excited about the April earnings being released. The technology sector did manage to outperform the S&P 500, but its gain did not make up for the underperformance of the financial sector in the first half of April.

MAY

M	T	W	T	F	S	S
			1	2	3
4	5	6	7	8	9	10
11	12	13	14	15	16	17
18	19	20	21	22	23	24
25	26	27	28	29	30	31

JUNE

M	T	W	T	F	S	S
1	2	3	4	5	6	7
8	9	10	11	12	13	14
15	16	17	18	19	20	21
22	23	24	25	26	27	28
29	30					

JULY

M	T	W	T	F	S	S
	1	2	3	4	5
6	7	8	9	10	11	12
13	14	15	16	17	18	19
20	21	22	23	24	25	26
27	28	29	30	31		

SIX 'N' SIX
Take a Break for Six Months - May 6th to October 27th

In the last three years, the stock market has corrected sharply in the spring, which has prompted many pundits to release reports in the media on "Sell in May and Go Away." But most do not grasp the full value of the favorable six month period from October 28th to May 5th, compared to the other six months: the unfavorable six month period.

Not only does the favorable period on average have bigger gains more frequently and smaller losses, but the period, also on a yearly basis outperforms the unfavorable period 70% of the time (last column in the table with YES values). There is no question which six month period seasonal investors should favor.

$1,383,667 gain on $10,000

The accompanying table uses the S&P 500 to compare the returns made from Oct 28th to May 5th, to the returns made during the remainder of the year.

Starting with $10,000 and investing from October 28th to May 5th every year (October 28th, 1950, to May 5th, 2013) has produced a gain of $1,383,667. On the flip side, being invested from May 6th to October 27th, has actually lost money. An initial investment of $10,000 has lost $2,578 over the same time period.

S&P 500 Unfavorable 6 Month Avg. Gain vs Favorable 6 Month Avg. Gain (1950-2014)

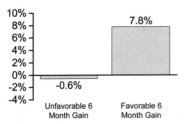

- Unfavorable 6 Month Gain: -0.6%
- Favorable 6 Month Gain: 7.8%

ⓘ *The above growth rates are geometric averages in order to represent the cumulative growth of a dollar investment over time. These figures differ from the arithmetic mean calculations used in the Six 'N' Six Take a Break Strategy, which are used to represent an average year.*

	S&P 500 % May 6 to Oct 27	$10,000 Start	S&P 500 % Oct 28 to May 5	$10,000 Start	Oct28-May5 > May6-Oct27
1950/51	8.5%	10,851	15.2%	11,517	YES
1951/52	0.2	10,870	3.7	11,947	YES
1952/53	1.8	11,067	3.9	12,413	YES
1953/54	-3.1	10,727	16.6	14,475	YES
1954/55	13.2	12,141	18.1	17,097	YES
1955/56	11.4	13,528	15.1	19,681	YES
1956/57	-4.0	12,903	0.2	19,711	YES
1957/58	-12.4	11,302	7.9	21,205	YES
1958/59	15.1	13,013	14.5	24,356	
1959/60	-0.6	12,939	-4.5	23,270	
1960/61	-2.3	12,647	24.1	28,869	YES
1961/62	2.7	12,993	-3.1	27,982	
1962/63	-17.7	10,698	28.4	35,929	YES
1963/64	5.7	11,306	9.3	39,264	YES
1964/65	5.1	11,882	5.5	41,440	YES
1965/66	3.1	12,253	-5.0	39,388	
1966/67	-8.8	11,180	17.7	46,364	YES
1967/68	0.6	11,241	3.9	48,171	YES
1968/69	5.6	11,872	0.2	48,249	
1969/70	-6.2	11,141	-19.7	38,722	
1970/71	5.8	11,782	24.9	48,346	YES
1971/72	-9.6	10,647	13.7	54,965	YES
1972/73	3.7	11,046	0.3	55,154	
1973/74	0.3	11,084	-18.0	45,205	
1974/75	-23.2	8,513	28.5	58,073	YES
1975/76	-0.4	8,480	12.4	65,290	YES
1976/77	0.9	8,554	-1.6	64,231	
1977/78	-7.8	7,890	4.5	67,146	YES
1978/79	-2.0	7,732	6.4	71,476	YES
1979/80	-0.1	7,723	5.8	75,605	YES
1980/81	20.2	9,283	1.9	77,047	
1981/82	-8.5	8,498	-1.4	76,001	YES
1982/83	15.0	9,769	21.4	92,293	YES
1983/84	0.3	9,803	-3.5	89,085	
1984/85	3.9	10,183	8.9	97,057	YES
1985/86	4.1	10,604	26.8	123,044	YES
1986/87	0.4	10,651	23.7	152,196	YES
1987/88	-21.0	8,409	11.0	168,904	YES
1988/89	7.1	9,010	10.9	187,380	YES
1989/90	8.9	9,814	1.0	189,242	
1990/91	-10.0	8,837	25.0	236,498	YES
1991/92	0.9	8,916	8.5	256,590	YES
1992/93	0.4	8,952	6.2	272,550	YES
1993/94	4.5	9,356	-2.8	264,789	
1994/95	3.2	9,656	11.6	295,636	YES
1995/96	11.5	10,762	10.7	327,219	
1996/97	9.2	11,757	18.5	387,591	YES
1997/98	5.6	12,419	27.2	493,003	YES
1998/99	-4.5	11,860	26.5	623,489	YES
1999/00	-3.8	11,415	10.5	688,842	YES
2000/01	-3.7	10,992	-8.2	632,435	
2001/02	-12.8	9,586	-2.8	614,583	YES
2002/03	-16.4	8,016	3.2	634,369	YES
2003/04	11.3	8,921	8.8	689,985	
2004/05	0.3	8,952	4.2	718,942	YES
2005/06	0.5	9,000	12.5	808,503	YES
2006/07	3.9	9,350	9.3	883,804	YES
2007/08	2.0	9,534	-8.3	810,240	
2008/09	-39.7	5,750	6.5	862,619	YES
2009/10	17.7	6,766	9.6	934,470	
2010/11	1.4	6,862	12.9	1,067,851	YES
2011/12	-3.8	6,602	6.6	1,138,103	YES
2012/13	3.1	6,809	14.3	1,301,313	YES
2013/14	9.0	7,422	7.1	1,393,667	
Total Gain (Loss)	**($2,578)**		**$1,383,667**		

2013-14 Strategy Performance

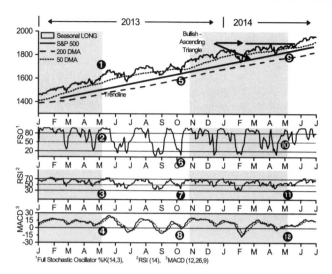

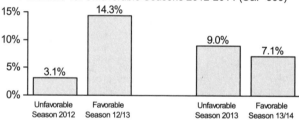

Favorable vs. Unfavorable Seasons 2012-2014 (S&P 500)

Technical Conditions– May 6th to October 27th, 2013

In mid-April, the S&P 500 bounced off its 50 day moving average and continued its ascent into May❶. In early May, the S&P 500 became overbought as the FSO was above 80❷ and the RSI was moving up close to 70❸. The MACD was also heading higher at the time❹.

Technical Conditions– October 28th to May 5th, 2014
Entry Strategy –Buy Position Early–

In early October, the S&P 500 traded below its 50 day moving average and then bounced on its trend line❺. An early buy signal was triggered when the FSO crossed above 20❻. The RSI supported the action by moving above 50❼ and the MACD bounced into positive territory❽.

Exit Strategy –Sell Position On Exit Date–

Since March of 2014, the S&P 500 had been pushing up against the 1900 level of resistance. As a pattern of higher lows was forming, a bullish ascending triangle was formed. On the exit date, the S&P 500 was just above its 50 moving average❾, the FSO had just turned down from 80❿, the RSI was just above 50⓫ and the MACD was positive⓬.

Market Indices & Rates
Weekly Values**

Stock Markets	2013	2014
Dow	15,066	16,517
S&P500	1,627	1,877
Nasdaq	3,410	4,082
TSX	12,527	14,609
FTSE	5,272	5,450
DAX	8,217	9,541
Nikkei	14,316	14,132
Hang Seng	23,148	21,856

Commodities	2013	2014
Oil	96.17	100.00
Gold	1451.1	1295.1

Bond Yields	2013	2014
USA 5 Yr Treasury	0.76	1.65
USA 10 Yr T	1.83	2.62
USA 20 Yr T	2.63	3.15
Moody's Aaa	3.81	4.17
Moody's Baa	4.65	4.79
CAN 5 Yr T	1.28	1.65
CAN 10 Yr T	1.82	2.37

Money Market	2013	2014
USA Fed Funds	0.25	0.25
USA 3 Mo T-B	0.04	0.03
CAN tgt overnight rate	1.00	1.00
CAN 3 Mo T-B	0.99	0.93

Foreign Exchange	2013	2014
EUR/USD	1.31	1.39
GBP/USD	1.55	1.69
USD/CAD	1.01	1.09
USD/JPY	99.91	101.85

MAY

M	T	W	T	F	S	S
				1	2	3
4	5	6	7	8	9	10
11	12	13	14	15	16	17
18	19	20	21	22	23	24
25	26	27	28	29	30	31

JUNE

M	T	W	T	F	S	S
1	2	3	4	5	6	7
8	9	10	11	12	13	14
15	16	17	18	19	20	21
22	23	24	25	26	27	28
29	30					

JULY

M	T	W	T	F	S	S
		1	2	3	4	5
6	7	8	9	10	11	12
13	14	15	16	17	18	19
20	21	22	23	24	25	26
27	28	29	30	31		

CANADIAN SIX 'N' SIX
Take a Break for Six Months - May 6th to October 27th

In analysing long-term trends for the broad markets such as the S&P 500 or the TSX Composite, a large data set is preferable because it incorporates various economic cycles. The daily data set for the TSX Composite starts in 1977.

Over this time period, investors have been rewarded for following the six month cycle of investing from October 28th to May 5th, versus the other unfavorable six months, May 6th to October 27th.

Starting with an investment of $10,000 in 1977, investing in the unfavorable six months has produced a loss of $3,098, versus investing in the favorable six months which has produced a gain of $202,072.

intervals, the period from October to May is far superior compared with the other half of the year.

The table below illustrates the superiority of the best six months over the worst six months. Going down the table year by year, the period from October 28 to May 5th outperforms the period from May 6th to October 27 on a regular basis.

In a strong bull market, investors always have the choice of using a stop loss or technical indicators to help extend the exit point past the May date

$202,072 gain on $10,000 since 1977

The TSX Composite Average Year 1977 to 2013 (graph below) indicates that the market tended to peak in mid-July or the end of August. In our book *Time In Time Out, Outsmart the Stock Market Using Calendar Investment Strategies*, Bruce Lindsay and I analysed a number of market trends and peaks over different decades.

What we found was that the markets tend to peak at the beginning of May or mid-July. The mid-July peak was usually the result of a strong bull market in place that had a lot of momentum.

The main reason that the TSX Composite data shows a peak occurring in July-August is that the data is primarily from the biggest bull market in history, starting in 1982.

	TSX Comp May 6 to Oct 27	$10,000 Start	TSX Comp Oct 28 to May 5	$10,000 Start
1977/78	-3.9%	9,608	13.1%	11,313
1978/79	12.1	10,775	21.3	13,728
1979/80	2.9	11,084	23.0	16,883
1980/81	22.5	13,579	-2.4	16,479
1981/82	-17.0	11,272	-18.2	13,488
1982/83	16.6	13,138	34.6	18,150
1983/84	-0.9	13,015	-1.9	17,811
1984/85	1.6	13,226	10.7	19,718
1985/86	0.5	13,299	16.5	22,978
1986/87	-1.9	13,045	24.8	28,666
1987/88	-23.4	9,992	15.3	33,050
1988/89	2.7	10,260	5.7	34,939
1989/90	7.9	11,072	-13.3	30,294
1990/91	-8.4	10,148	13.1	34,266
1991/92	-1.6	9,982	-2.0	33,571
1992/93	-2.3	9,750	15.3	38,704
1993/94	10.8	10,801	1.7	39,365
1994/95	-0.1	10,792	0.3	39,483
1995/96	1.3	10,936	18.2	46,671
1996/97	8.3	11,843	10.8	51,725
1997/98	7.3	12,707	17.0	60,510
1998/99	-22.3	9,870	17.1	70,871
1999/00	-0.2	9,853	36.9	97,009
2000/01	-2.9	9,570	-14.4	83,062
2001/02	-12.2	8,399	9.4	90,875
2002/03	-16.4	7,020	4.0	94,476
2003/04	15.1	8,079	10.3	104,252
2004/05	3.9	8,398	7.8	112,379
2005/06	8.1	9,080	19.8	134,587
2006/07	0.0	9,079	12.2	151,053
2007/08	3.8	9,426	-0.2	150,820
2008/09	-40.2	5,638	15.7	174,551
2009/10	11.9	6,307	7.4	187,526
2010/11	5.8	6,674	7.1	200,778
2011/12	-7.4	6,183	-4.8	191,207
2012/13	3.6	6,407	1.1	193,348
2013/14	7.7	6,902	9.7	212,072
Total Gain (Loss)	**($-3,098)**			**$202,072**

TSX Composite % Gain Avg. Year 1977 to 2013

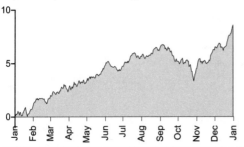

Does a later average peak in the stock market mean that the best six month cycle does not work? No. Dividing the year up into six month

2013-14 Strategy Performance

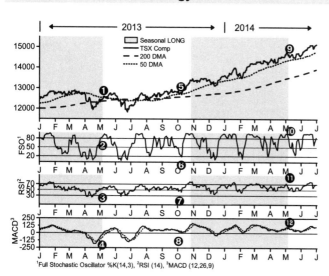

¹Full Stochastic Oscillator %K(14,3), ²RSI (14), ³MACD (12,26,9)

Favorable vs. Unfavorable Seasons 2012-2014 (TSX Composite)

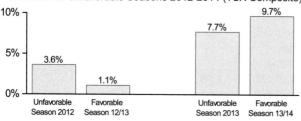

WEEK 20

Market Indices & Rates
Weekly Values**

Stock Markets	2013	2014
Dow	15,234	16,593
S&P500	1,652	1,886
Nasdaq	3,467	4,107
TSX	12,540	14,622
FTSE	6,684	6,860
DAX	8,350	9,699
Nikkei	14,962	14,275
Hang Seng	23,012	22,528

Commodities	2013	2014
Oil	94.97	101.64
Gold	1404.9	1298.2

Bond Yields	2013	2014
USA 5 Yr Treasury	0.83	1.59
USA 10 Yr T	1.93	2.57
USA 20 Yr T	2.74	3.12
Moody's Aaa	3.91	4.15
Moody's Baa	4.74	4.77
CAN 5 Yr T	1.36	1.58
CAN 10 Yr T	1.92	2.31

Money Market	2013	2014
USA Fed Funds	0.25	0.25
USA 3 Mo T-B	0.04	0.03
CAN tgt overnight rate	1.00	1.00
CAN 3 Mo T-B	1.00	0.92

Foreign Exchange	2013	2014
EUR/USD	1.29	1.37
GBP/USD	1.52	1.68
USD/CAD	1.02	1.09
USD/JPY	102.39	101.87

TSX Composite Performance– May 6th to October 27, 2013

At the start of its unfavorable season, the TSX Composite was above its 50 day moving average❶, the FSO had just entered overbought territory above 80❷ and the RSI had just risen above 50❸. The MACD was negative, but still rising❹. Despite volatility in the unfavorable season, a few months later, at the beginning of October, the TSX Composite was only marginally higher.

October 28th to May 5th, 2014
Entry Strategy –Buy Position Early–

At the beginning of October, the TSX Composite was trading above its 50 day moving average❺. An early buy signal was produced when the FSO bounced off 20❻. The RSI supported this move with a strong move above 50❼ and at the same time, the MACD started to trend higher❽.

Exit Strategy –Sell Position on Exit Date–

At the beginning of May, the TSX Composite started to turn down❾ and the FSO registered a sell signal crossing below 80❿. The RSI just turned down from 70⓫ and the MACD was just turning negative ⓬. Overall it was time to exit.

MAY

M	T	W	T	F	S	S
				1	2	3
4	5	6	7	8	9	10
11	12	13	14	15	16	17
18	19	20	21	22	23	24
25	26	27	28	29	30	31

JUNE

M	T	W	T	F	S	S
1	2	3	4	5	6	7
8	9	10	11	12	13	14
15	16	17	18	19	20	21
22	23	24	25	26	27	28
29	30					

JULY

M	T	W	T	F	S	S
		1	2	3	4	5
6	7	8	9	10	11	12
13	14	15	16	17	18	19
20	21	22	23	24	25	26
27	28	29	30	31		

COSTCO– BUY AT A DISCOUNT
①May26 to Jun30 ②Oct4 to Dec1

COST

Shoppers are attracted to Costco because of its consistently low prices. They take comfort in the fact that although the prices may not always be the lowest, they are consistently in the lower range.

Costco performs well in the late spring and early summer, and in the autumn and early winter. These two periods are considered to be transition periods where the stock market is moving to and from its unfavorable and favorable seasons. Companies such as Costco that have stable earnings are desirable at these times.

There are two times when Costco is a seasonal bargain: May 26th to June 30th and October 4th to December 1st. From 1990 to 2013, during the period of May 26th to June 30th, Costco has averaged a gain of 5.8% and has been positive 67% of the time. From October 4th to December 1st, Costco has averaged a gain of 9.9% and has been positive 79% of the time.

16.5% gain & positive 92% of the time

Putting both seasonal periods together has produced a 92% positive success rate and an average gain of 17.0%. Although the earlier strong years in the 1990's skews the data to the high-side, Costco has still maintained its strong seasonal performances in both the May to June and the October to December time periods. When investors go shopping for stocks, Costco is one consumer staples company that should be on their list. They should also remember not to bulk up with too much, even if it is selling at a discount.

ⓘ *COST - stock symbol for Costco which trades on the Nasdaq exchange. Stock data adjusted for stock splits.*

Costco* vs. S&P 500 1990 to 2013   Positive ☐

Year	May 26 to Jun 30		Oct 4 to Dec 1		Compound Growth	
	S&P 500	COST	S&P 500	COST	S&P 500	COST
1990	1.0	16.5 %	3.5	26.5 %	4.5	47.4 %
1991	-1.7	-2.1	-2.4	-3.7	-4.0	-5.7
1992	-1.4	-2.2	5.0	22.7	3.5	20.1
1993	0.4	17.2	0.1	13.4	0.5	32.9
1994	-2.6	10.7	-2.8	-0.3	5.3	3.7
1995	3.1	19.2	4.2	-2.1	7.4	16.7
1996	-1.2	9.4	9.3	15.5	8.0	26.4
1997	4.5	3.1	1.0	16.6	5.6	20.2
1998	2.1	17.6	17.2	41.1	19.7	65.9
1999	6.9	8.1	9.0	30.7	16.5	41.2
2000	5.3	10.0	-7.8	-3.6	-2.9	6.1
2001	-4.2	9.3	6.3	12.3	1.8	22.6
2002	-8.7	-0.8	14.3	4.6	4.4	3.8
2003	4.4	5.3	3.9	13.5	8.5	19.4
2004	2.5	10.3	5.3	17.3	7.9	29.4
2005	0.1	-1.5	3.1	13.9	3.2	12.2
2006	-0.2	5.0	4.7	6.0	4.5	11.3
2007	-0.8	3.8	-3.8	8.9	-4.6	12.9
2008	-7.0	-1.7	-25.8	-23.5	-30.9	-24.7
2009	3.6	-5.2	8.2	7.5	12.1	1.9
2010	-4.0	-3.0	5.2	5.0	1.0	1.9
2011	0.0	1.2	13.2	6.7	13.2	7.9
2012	3.4	12.5	-2.4	4.3	0.9	17.3
2013	-2.6	-3.3	7.6	9.6	4.7	6.0
Avg.	0.1 %	5.8 %	3.2 %	9.9 %	3.3 %	16.5 %
Fq>0	54 %	67 %	75 %	79 %	79 %	92 %

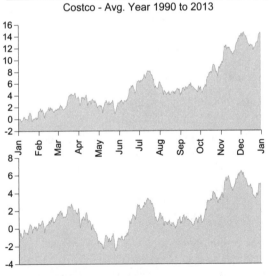

Costco - Avg. Year 1990 to 2013

Costco / S&P 500 Rel. Strength- Avg Yr. 1990-2013

2013-14 Strategy Performance

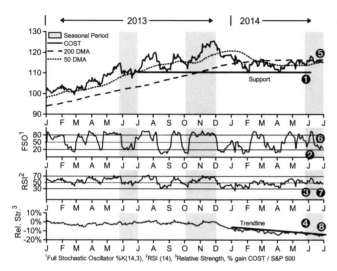

¹Full Stochastic Oscillator %K(14,3), ²RSI (14), ³Relative Strength, % gain COST / S&P 500

Costco Performance

After a positive October and November 2013 seasonal period, Costco corrected briefly and then for the first six months, Costco consolidated above its support line of $110. Typically this is a good entry pattern at the start of a seasonal period.

Technical Conditions– May 26th to June 30th, 2014

Entry Strategy – Buy Position on Entry Date–

In its consolidation phase, Costco ended up above its 50 day moving average at the start of its seasonal period❶. The FSO was turning up❷, but the RSI was still trending flat at 50❸. There was no sign that Costco's relative performance to the S&P 500 was changing its downward direction❹. Overall, the technical indicators were not strong.

Exit Strategy –Sell Position on Exit Date–

Although the FSO did fall below 80 before the seasonal exit date, with such a short-term trade, consideration should be given to holding the trade until the exit date. On the exit date, Costco was at its 50 and 200 day moving averages❺, the FSO was trending down❻, the RSI was trending flat at 50❼ and the performance relative to the S&P 500 was still negative❽. The technical indicators were not strong and there was no reason to hold Costco past its seasonal exit date.

Overall, Costco was positive in its seasonal period, but underperformed the S&P 500.

WEEK 21

Market Indices & Rates
Weekly Values**

Stock Markets	2013	2014
Dow	15,326	16,514
S&P500	1,658	1,888
Nasdaq	3,476	4,139
TSX	12,705	14,646
FTSE	6,750	6,821
DAX	8,423	9,697
Nikkei	15,093	14,185
Hang Seng	23,082	22,859

Commodities	2013	2014
Oil	94.93	103.73
Gold	1379.0	1295.0

Bond Yields	2013	2014
USA 5 Yr Treasury	0.88	1.55
USA 10 Yr T	1.99	2.54
USA 20 Yr T	2.80	3.12
Moody's Aaa	3.95	4.18
Moody's Baa	4.78	4.78
CAN 5 Yr T	1.37	1.56
CAN 10 Yr T	1.94	2.29

Money Market	2013	2014
USA Fed Funds	0.25	0.25
USA 3 Mo T-B	0.04	0.03
CAN tgt overnight rate	1.00	1.00
CAN 3 Mo T-B	1.00	0.92

Foreign Exchange	2013	2014
EUR/USD	1.29	1.37
GBP/USD	1.51	1.69
USD/CAD	1.03	1.09
USD/JPY	102.25	101.58

MAY

M	T	W	T	F	S	S
				1	2	3
4	5	6	7	8	9	10
11	12	13	14	15	16	17
18	19	20	21	22	23	24
25	26	27	28	29	30	31

JUNE

M	T	W	T	F	S	S
1	2	3	4	5	6	7
8	9	10	11	12	13	14
15	16	17	18	19	20	21
22	23	24	25	26	27	28
29	30					

JULY

M	T	W	T	F	S	S
	1	2	3	4	5
6	7	8	9	10	11	12
13	14	15	16	17	18	19
20	21	22	23	24	25	26
27	28	29	30	31		

** Weekly avg closing values- except Fed Funds & CAN overnight tgt rate weekly closing values.

MEMORIAL DAY – BE EARLY & STAY LATE
Positive 2 Market Days Before Memorial Day to 5 Market Days into June

A lot of strategies that focus on investing around holidays concentrate on the market performance the day before and the day after a holiday.

1.1% average gain and positive 64% of the time

Not all holidays were created equal. The typical Memorial Day trade is to invest the day before the holiday and sell the day after. If you invested in the stock market for just these two days, you would be missing out on a lot of gains.

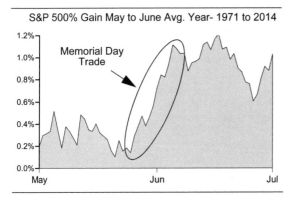

S&P 500% Gain May to June Avg. Year- 1971 to 2014

Memorial Day Trade

Historically, the best strategy has been to invest two market days before Memorial Day and hold until five market days into June.

Extending the investment into June makes sense. The first few days in June tend to be positive– so why sell early?

The graph shows the average performance of the S&P 500 on a calendar basis for the months of May and June from 1971 to 2014.

The increase from the end of May into June represents the opportunity with the *"Memorial Day - Be Early & Stay Late"* trade.

The graph clearly shows a spike in the market that occurs at the end of the month and carries on into June.

Investors using the typical Memorial Day trade, miss out on the majority of the gain. The *Memorial Day - Be Early & Stay Late* strategy has produced an average gain of 1.1% and has been positive 64% of the time (S&P 500, 1971 to 2014). Not a bad gain for being invested an average of ten market days.

The *Memorial Day - Be Early & Stay Late* trade can be extended into June primarily because the first market days of the month tend to be positive. These days are part of the end of the month effect. (see *Super Seven* strategy).

(i) *History of Memorial Day:*
Originally called Decoration Day in remembrance of those who died in the nation's service. Memorial Day was first observed on May 30th 1868 when flowers were placed on the graves of Union and Confederate soldiers at Arlington National Cemetery. The South acknowledged the day after World War I, when the holiday changed from honoring just those who died fighting in the Civil War to honoring Americans who died fighting in any war. In 1971 Congress passed the National Holiday Act recognizing Memorial Day as the last Monday in May.

2 Market Days Before Memorial Day to 5 Market Days Into June - S&P 500   Positive [ ]

			1980	5.1 %	1990	1.1 %	2000	5.2 %	2010	-1.6 %
1971	1.5 %	1981	0.2	1991	0.9	2001	-0.9	2011	-2.7
1972	-2.4	1982	-2.6	1992	-0.5	2002	-5.4	2012	-0.3
1973	1.7	1983	-2.1	1993	-1.3	2003	7.0	2013	-0.7
1974	6.3	1984	1.2	1994	0.4	2004	2.3	2014	3.3
1975	3.8	1985	4.3	1995	0.9	2005	0.6		
1976	-0.7	1986	4.3	1996	0.0	2006	-0.2		
1977	1.0	1987	5.5	1997	2.2	2007	-2.1		
1978	3.1	1988	4.5	1998	-0.5	2008	-2.2		
1979	1.9	1989	2.4	1999	2.3	2009	4.1		
Avg.	1.8 %		2.3 %		0.6 %		0.8 %		-0.4 %

2014 Strategy Performance

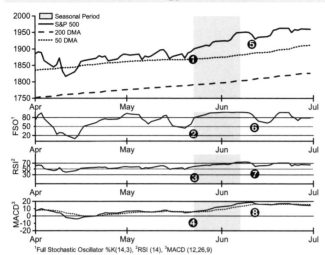

¹Full Stochastic Oscillator %K(14,3), ²RSI (14), ³MACD (12,26,9)

Market Indices & Rates
Weekly Values**

Stock Markets	2013	2014
Dow	15,288	16,681
S&P500	1,648	1,916
Nasdaq	3,476	4,238
TSX	12,715	14,636
FTSE	5,326	5,482
DAX	8,390	9,931
Nikkei	14,029	14,645
Hang Seng	22,608	23,016

Commodities	2013	2014
Oil	93.43	103.28
Gold	1391.8	1261.1

Bond Yields	2013	2014
USA 5 Yr Treasury	1.03	1.53
USA 10 Yr T	2.14	2.47
USA 20 Yr T	2.93	3.05
Moody's Aaa	4.06	4.16
Moody's Baa	4.90	4.70
CAN 5 Yr T	1.46	1.55
CAN 10 Yr T	2.05	2.27

Money Market	2013	2014
USA Fed Funds	0.25	0.25
USA 3 Mo T-B	0.05	0.04
CAN tgt overnight rate	1.00	1.00
CAN 3 Mo T-B	1.01	0.93

Foreign Exchange	2013	2014
EUR/USD	1.30	1.36
GBP/USD	1.51	1.68
USD/CAD	1.04	1.09
USD/JPY	101.13	101.87

Memorial Day Performance

Starting in mid-April 2013, the S&P 500 started to rise after touching its 50 day moving average. It continued its strong performance until mid-May and then started to turn down.

Technical Conditions– 2 Market Days Before Memorial Day to 5 Market Days into June, 2014

Entry Strategy –Buy Position on Entry Date–

The S&P 500 was flat for most of May coming into the Memorial Day trade. Just before the start of the trade, the S&P 500 bounced off its 50 day moving average❶ and the FSO crossed above 80❷. The RSI also started to trend upwards❸ as did the MACD❹.

Exit Strategy –Sell Position Late–

At the end of the trade the S&P 500 was still performing positively and as a result, investors could have held the position past its exit date. Shortly after the seasonal exit date, the S&P 500 started to turn down❺ and the FSO crossed below 80 triggering a sell signal❻. The RSI also dropped below 70❼ and the MACD turned down from 20❽.

Overall, the Memorial Day trade was positive and it would have been better to sell at the end of the seasonal period rather than wait for the FSO to turn below 80 before exiting the position.

MAY

M	T	W	T	F	S	S
				1	2	3
4	5	6	7	8	9	10
11	12	13	14	15	16	17
18	19	20	21	22	23	24
25	26	27	28	29	30	31

JUNE

M	T	W	T	F	S	S
1	2	3	4	5	6	7
8	9	10	11	12	13	14
15	16	17	18	19	20	21
22	23	24	25	26	27	28
29	30					

JULY

M	T	W	T	F	S	S
		1	2	3	4	5
6	7	8	9	10	11	12
13	14	15	16	17	18	19
20	21	22	23	24	25	26
27	28	29	30	31		

** Weekly avg closing values- except Fed Funds & CAN overnight tgt rate weekly closing values.

JUNE

	MONDAY	TUESDAY	WEDNESDAY
WEEK 23	**1** 29	**2** 28	**3** 27
WEEK 24	**8** 22	**9** 21	**10** 20
WEEK 25	**15** 15	**16** 14	**17** 13
WEEK 26	**22** 8	**23** 7	**24** 6
WEEK 27	**29** 1	**30**	1

THURSDAY		FRIDAY	
4	26	**5**	25
11	19	**12**	18
18	12	**19**	11
25	5	**26**	4
2		3	

JULY

M	T	W	T	F	S	S
		1	2	3	4	5
6	7	8	9	10	11	12
13	14	15	16	17	18	19
20	21	22	23	24	25	26
27	28	29	30	31		

AUGUST

M	T	W	T	F	S	S
					1	2
3	4	5	6	7	8	9
10	11	12	13	14	15	16
17	18	19	20	21	22	23
24	25	26	27	28	29	30
31						

SEPTEMBER

M	T	W	T	F	S	S
	1	2	3	4	5	6
7	8	9	10	11	12	13
14	15	16	17	18	19	20
21	22	23	24	25	26	27
28	29	30				

OCTOBER

M	T	W	T	F	S	S
			1	2	3	4
5	6	7	8	9	10	11
12	13	14	15	16	17	18
19	20	21	22	23	24	25
26	27	28	29	30	31	

JUNE
S U M M A R Y

	Dow Jones	S&P 500	Nasdaq	TSX Comp
Month Rank	11	9	7	11
# Up	29	32	24	13
# Down	35	32	18	16
% Pos	45	50	57	45
% Avg. Gain	-0.3	0.0	0.7	-0.4

Dow & S&P 1950-2013, Nasdaq 1972-2013, TSX 1985-2013

S&P500 Cumulative Daily Gains for Avg Month 1950 to 2014

♦ On average, June is not a strong month. From 1950 to 2013, it was the third worst month for the S&P 500, producing a flat return of 0.0%. ♦ From year to year, different sectors of the market tend to lead in June and there is not a strong consistent outperforming major sector. ♦ On average, the biotech sector starts its seasonal run in late June. ♦ The last few days of June, the start the successful *Independence Day Trade,* tend to be positive. ♦ In June 2014, the S&P 500 produced a solid gain of 1.9% after breaking above 1900 in May.

BEST / WORST JUNE BROAD MKTS. 2005-2014

BEST JUNE MARKETS
- ♦ Nikkei 225 (2012) 5.4%
- ♦ Russell 2000 (2014) 5.2%
- ♦ Russell 2000 (2012) 4.8%

WORST JUNE MARKETS
- ♦ Dow (2008) -10.2%
- ♦ Nasdaq (2008) -9.1%
- ♦ S&P 500 (2008) -8.6%

Index Values End of Month

	2005	2006	2007	2008	2009	2010	2011	2012	2013	2014
Dow	10,275	11,150	13,409	11,350	8,447	9,774	12,414	12,880	14,910	16,827
S&P 500	1,191	1,270	1,503	1,280	919	1,031	1,321	1,362	1,606	1,960
Nasdaq	2,057	2,172	2,603	2,293	1,835	2,109	2,774	2,935	3,403	4,408
TSX Comp.	9,903	11,613	13,907	14,467	10,375	11,294	13,301	11,597	12,129	15,146
Russell 1000	1,242	1,330	1,573	1,352	966	1,091	1,412	1,443	1,712	2,104
Russell 2000	1,590	1,801	2,072	1,714	1,263	1,515	2,056	1,984	2,429	2,965
FTSE 100	5,113	5,833	6,608	5,626	4,249	4,917	5,946	5,571	6,215	6,744
Nikkei 225	11,584	15,505	18,138	13,481	9,958	9,383	9,816	9,007	13,677	15,162

Percent Gain for June

	2005	2006	2007	2008	2009	2010	2011	2012	2013	2014
Dow	-1.8	-0.2	-1.6	-10.2	-0.6	-3.6	-1.2	3.9	-1.4	0.7
S&P 500	0.0	0.0	-1.8	-8.6	0.0	-5.4	-1.8	4.0	-1.5	1.9
Nasdaq	-0.5	-0.3	0.0	-9.1	3.4	-6.5	-2.2	3.8	-1.5	3.9
TSX Comp.	3.1	-1.1	-1.1	-1.7	0.0	-4.0	-3.6	0.7	-4.1	3.7
Russell 1000	0.3	0.0	-2.0	-8.5	0.1	-5.7	-1.9	3.7	-1.5	2.1
Russell 2000	3.7	0.5	-1.6	-7.8	1.3	-7.9	-2.5	4.8	-0.7	5.2
FTSE 100	3.0	1.9	-0.2	-7.1	-3.8	-5.2	-0.7	4.7	-5.6	-1.5
Nikkei 225	2.7	0.2	1.5	-6.0	4.6	-4.0	1.3	5.4	-0.7	3.6

June Market Avg. Performance 2005 to 2014[1]

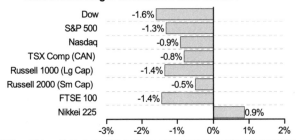

Dow	-1.6%
S&P 500	-1.3%
Nasdaq	-0.9%
TSX Comp (CAN)	-0.8%
Russell 1000 (Lg Cap)	-1.4%
Russell 2000 (Sm Cap)	-0.5%
FTSE 100	-1.4%
Nikkei 225	0.9%

Interest Corner Jun[2]

	Fed Funds % [3]	3 Mo. T-Bill % [4]	10 Yr % [5]	20 Yr % [6]
2014	0.25	0.04	2.53	3.08
2013	0.25	0.04	2.52	3.22
2012	0.25	0.09	1.67	2.38
2011	0.25	0.03	3.18	4.09
2010	0.25	0.18	2.97	3.74

(1) Russell Data provided by Russell (2) Federal Reserve Bank of St. Louis- end of month values (3) Target rate set by FOMC (4)(5)(6) Constant yield maturities.

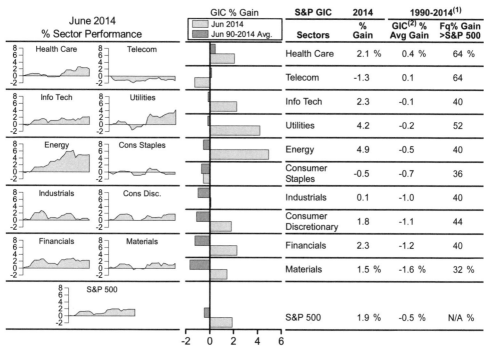

S&P GIC	2014	1990-2014[1]	
Sectors	**% Gain**	**GIC[2] % Avg Gain**	**Fq% Gain >S&P 500**
Health Care	2.1 %	0.4 %	64 %
Telecom	-1.3	0.1	64
Info Tech	2.3	-0.1	40
Utilities	4.2	-0.2	52
Energy	4.9	-0.5	40
Consumer Staples	-0.5	-0.7	36
Industrials	0.1	-1.0	40
Consumer Discretionary	1.8	-1.1	44
Financials	2.3	-1.2	40
Materials	1.5 %	-1.6 %	32 %
S&P 500	1.9 %	-0.5 %	N/A %

Sector Commentary

♦ As geopolitical tensions were on the rise in June 2014, the price of oil increased, giving a boost to the energy sector which produced a gain 4.9%. ♦ The utilities sector also put in a strong performance of 4.2%. ♦ Two other defensive sectors, consumer staples and telecom, produced losses of 0.5% and 1.3% respectively. ♦ The financial sector performed well with a 2.3% return, indicating possible strong markets ahead.

Sub-Sector Commentary

♦ Gold typically starts its seasonal rally in July, but after a pullback in late May, it was set up to start an early rally in June. By the end of June, it had produced a gain of 5.2%. ♦ The metals and mining sector produced a strong gain of 6.6% as the U.S. economic numbers were improving, providing a better outlook for the future. ♦ The semi-conductors put in a good solid performance of 6.1%. ♦ After strongly outperforming the S&P 500 in May, both the transportation and railroad sub-sectors were positive for the month, but underperformed the S&P 500. The transportation and railroad sub-sectors produced gains of 0.9% and 1.4%, respectively in June.

SELECTED SUB-SECTORS[3]		
Software & Services	1.1	2.3	72 %
Pharma	1.8 %	0.6 %	64
Gold (London PM)	5.2	-0.4	48
Retail	1.3	-0.5	56
SOX (1995-2014)	6.1	-0.6	40
Metals & Mining	6.6	-0.8	56
Biotech (1993-2014)	2.9	-0.9	45
Railroads	1.4	-1.0	40
Steel	1.8	-1.1	44
Transportation	0.9	-1.2	32
Agriculture (1994-2014)	-1.8	-1.4	33
Chemicals	0.0	-1.7	32
Homebuilders	3.2	-1.7	40
Silver	9.8	-2.2	40
Banks	2.6	-2.3	28

(1) Sector data provided by Standard and Poors (2) GIC is short form for Global Industry Classification (3) Sub Sector data provided by Standard and Poors, except where marked by symbol.

BIOTECH SUMMER SOLSTICE
June 23rd to September 13th

The *Biotech Summer Solstice* trade starts on June 23rd and lasts until September 13th. The trade is aptly named as its outperformance starts approximately on the day summer solstice starts– the longest day of the year.

There are two main drivers of the trade: biotech is a good substitute for technology stocks in the summer, and investors want to take a position in the biotech sector before the autumn conferences.

> ### 11.5% extra & 86% of the time better than the S&P 500

Biotech vs. S&P 500 1992 to 2014

Jun 23 to Sep 13	S&P 500	Biotech Positive	Diff
1992	4.0 %	17.9 %	13.8 %
1993	3.6	3.6	0.0
1994	3.2	24.2	21.0
1995	5.0	31.5	26.5
1996	2.1	7.0	4.9
1997	2.8	-18.9	-21.7
1998	-8.5	20.6	29.1
1999	0.6	64.3	63.7
2000	2.3	7.6	5.4
2001	-10.8	-3.6	7.2
2002	-10.0	8.1	18.2
2003	2.3	6.4	4.1
2004	-0.8	8.9	9.6
2005	1.4	26.0	24.5
2006	5.8	7.4	1.6
2007	-1.2	6.0	7.2
2008	-5.0	11.4	16.5
2009	16.8	7.7	-9.1
2010	2.4	2.8	0.4
2011	-8.9	-3.7	5.2
2012	9.4	15.6	6.2
2013	6.0	24.9	18.9
Avg	1.0 %	12.5 %	11.5 %
Fq>0	68 %	86 %	86 %

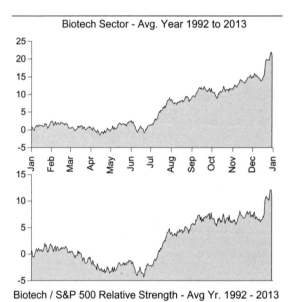

Biotech Sector - Avg. Year 1992 to 2013

Biotech / S&P 500 Relative Strength - Avg Yr. 1992 - 2013

The biotechnology sector is often considered the cousin of the technology sector, a good place for speculative investments. The sectors are similar as both include concept companies (companies without a product but with good potential).

Despite their similarity, investors view the sectors differently. The technology sector is viewed as being largely dependent on the economy and conversely, the biotech sector as being much less dependent on the economy. The end product of biotechnology companies is mainly medicine, which is not economically sensitive.

As a result, in the summer months when investors tend to be more cautious, they are more willing to commit speculative money into the biotech sector, compared with the technology sector.

The biotech sector is one of the few sectors that starts its outperformance in June. This is in part because of the biotech conferences that occur in autumn and with the possibility of positive announcements, the price of biotech companies on the stock market can increase dramatically. As a result, investors try to lock in positions early.

> (i) *Biotech SP GIC Sector # 352010: Companies primarily engaged in the research, development, manufacturing and/or marketing of products based on genetic analysis and genetic engineering. This includes companies specializing in protein-based therapeutics to treat human diseases.*

2013-14 Strategy Performance

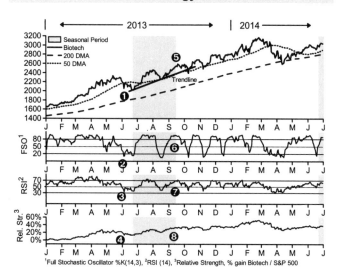

¹Full Stochastic Oscillator %K(14,3), ²RSI (14), ³Relative Strength, % gain Biotech / S&P 500

Market Indices & Rates
Weekly Values**

Stock Markets	2013	2014
Dow	15,136	16,793
S&P500	1,629	1,933
Nasdaq	3,441	4,268
TSX	12,486	14,770
FTSE	6,450	6,838
DAX	8,226	9,946
Nikkei	13,118	15,039
Hang Seng	22,010	23,126

Commodities	2013	2014
Oil	94.26	102.58
Gold	1398.4	1247.1

Bond Yields	2013	2014
USA 5 Yr Treasury	1.04	1.64
USA 10 Yr T	2.12	2.59
USA 20 Yr T	2.93	3.16
Moody's Aaa	4.10	4.27
Moody's Baa	4.99	4.82
CAN 5 Yr T	1.48	1.59
CAN 10 Yr T	2.07	2.32

Money Market	2013	2014
USA Fed Funds	0.25	0.25
USA 3 Mo T-B	0.05	0.04
CAN tgt overnight rate	1.00	1.00
CAN 3 Mo T-B	1.02	0.93

Foreign Exchange	2013	2014
EUR/USD	1.31	1.36
GBP/USD	1.54	1.68
USD/CAD	1.03	1.09
USD/JPY	98.63	102.51

Biotech Sector Performance

After outperforming the S&P 500 for the first few months of 2013, the biotech sector started to correct in March. It under-performed the S&P 500 into June before its seasonal period.

Technical Conditions– June 23rd to September 13th, 2013

Entry Strategy – Buy Position Early–
In early June, the biotech sector corrected sharply and then bounced❶, causing the FSO to cross back over 20❷, which triggered an early buy signal. At the same time, the RSI bounced off 30❸. On the negative side, the biotech sector was still in a downtrend relative to the S&P 500❹.

Exit Strategy –Sell Position on Exit Date–
The biotech sector performed well in its seasonal period on an absolute basis and relative to the S&P 500. At the end of the seasonal trade, the biotech sector was at a high point for its seasonal period and above its trend line❺. The FSO was in overbought territory above 80❻ and the RSI was just below 70❼. The biotech sector was still outperforming the S&P 500 at the end of its seasonal period❽. Although investors could hold the position past the seasonal exit date, the last half of September is on average, one of the weakest periods of the year and the biotech sector typically performs poorly at this time. As a result, it was best to exit the trade.

Overall, the biotech trade was successful, producing a gain and outperforming the S&P 500.

JUNE

M	T	W	T	F	S	S
1	2	3	4	5	6	7
8	9	10	11	12	13	14
15	16	17	18	19	20	21
22	23	24	25	26	27	28
29	30					

JULY

M	T	W	T	F	S	S
		1	2	3	4	5
6	7	8	9	10	11	12
13	14	15	16	17	18	19
20	21	22	23	24	25	26
27	28	29	30	31		

AUGUST

M	T	W	T	F	S	S
					1	2
3	4	5	6	7	8	9
10	11	12	13	14	15	16
17	18	19	20	21	22	23
24	25	26	27	28	29	30
31						

** Weekly avg closing values- except Fed Funds & CAN overnight tgt rate weekly closing values.

SUPER SEVEN DAYS
7 Best Days of the Month

The end of the month tends to be an excellent time to invest: portfolio managers "window dress" (adjust their portfolios to look good for month end reports), investors stop procrastinating and invest their extra cash, and brokers try to increase their commissions by investing their client's extra cash.

From 1950 to 2013
All 7 days better
than market average

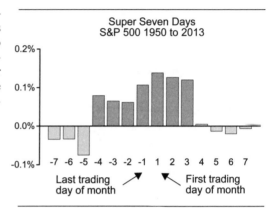

All of these factors tend to produce above average returns in the market during the days on either side of month end.

The above graph illustrates the strength of the *Super Seven* days. The *Super Seven* days are the last four trading days of the month and the first three trading days of the next month, represented by the dark columns from day -4 to day 3. All of the *Super Seven* days have daily average gains above the daily market average gain of 0.03% since 1950.

% Gain Super Seven Day Period From 2004 to 2013

	2004	2005	2006	2007	2008	2009	2010	2011	2012	2013	Avg.
Jan	-2.5 %	1.8 %	-0.1 %	1.6 %	-4.5 %	-0.5 %	0.0 %	1.2 %	1.4 %	0.6	-0.5 %
Feb	0.9	2.2	-0.4	-5.6	-2.8	4.1	1.0	1.2	0.1	1.6	-1.0
Mar	3.7	0.9	0.8	0.1	1.2	3.5	2.0	1.4	-1.2	-0.2	1.2
Apr	-1.2	1.2	0.0	1.5	1.3	4.3	-3.8	0.9	1.4	2.3	0.9
May	1.9	0.2	0.5	1.6	0.1	5.0	2.7	-1.2	-2.7	-2.5	1.1
Jun	-2.1	0.3	1.9	1.8	-3.9	-0.2	-4.2	5.6	4.1	2.7	-0.1
Jul	1.3	1.3	0.9	-5.6	2.2	2.1	1.1	-5.8	4.0	1.0	0.4
Aug	0.8	1.7	0.4	0.8	-2.4	-2.4	4.7	0.5	1.5	-0.1	0.0
Sep	2.9	-1.6	1.8	1.4	-7.3	-1.0	1.1	-1.6	-0.4	-1.1	-0.3
Oct	4.4	2.0	-1.3	-0.8	12.2	-1.9	1.0	2.6	0.3	0.2	1.7
Nov	1.2	-0.3	1.0	5.5	8.8	-0.6	3.7	8.2	0.2	-0.7	1.9
Dec	-1.8	0.4	-0.1	-5.7	7.7	0.9	1.5	1.2	2.8	-0.4	0.3
Avg.	0.8 %	0.8 %	0.0 %	0.0 %	1.1 %	0.4 %	1.1 %	1.2 %	1.0 %	0.3	0.4 %

Over the last ten years, the super seven strategy has worked very well and has produced an average gain of 0.4% per month. On an annualized basis, this return is greater than 6% per year. Given that the average month has twenty-two trading days, the *Super Seven* strategy has investors in the market for less than one third of the time. On a time-adjusted basis, adjusting returns for the amount of time in the market, the strategy has produced much greater gains than a buy and hold discipline.

If there is one time of the month that investors should be concentrating on investing, it is the last four trading days of the current month and the first three of the next month.

2013-14 Strategy Performance

Market Indices & Rates
Weekly Values**

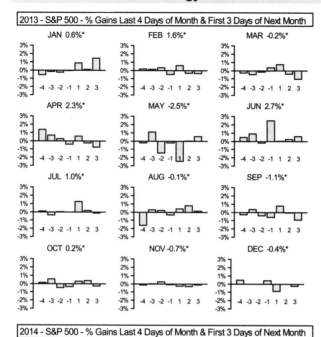

2013 - S&P 500 - % Gains Last 4 Days of Month & First 3 Days of Next Month

JAN 0.6%* FEB 1.6%* MAR -0.2%*
APR 2.3%* MAY -2.5%* JUN 2.7%*
JUL 1.0%* AUG -0.1%* SEP -1.1%*
OCT 0.2%* NOV -0.7%* DEC -0.4%*

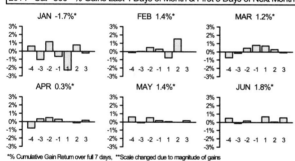

2014 - S&P 500 - % Gains Last 4 Days of Month & First 3 Days of Next Month

JAN -1.7%* FEB 1.4%* MAR 1.2%*
APR 0.3%* MAY 1.4%* JUN 1.8%*

*% Cumulative Gain Return over full 7 days, **Scale changed due to magnitude of gains

Stock Markets	2013	2014
Dow	15,120	16,849
S&P500	1,629	1,942
Nasdaq	3,436	4,323
TSX	12,236	14,916
FTSE	6,331	6,842
DAX	8,179	9,968
Nikkei	13,051	15,052
Hang Seng	21,206	23,237
Commodities	**2013**	**2014**
Oil	96.31	105.32
Gold	1383.3	1262.8
Bond Yields	**2013**	**2014**
USA 5 Yr Treasury	1.11	1.69
USA 10 Yr T	2.20	2.62
USA 20 Yr T	3.00	3.17
Moody's Aaa	4.24	4.28
Moody's Baa	5.11	4.82
CAN 5 Yr T	1.59	1.59
CAN 10 Yr T	2.17	2.33
Money Market	**2013**	**2014**
USA Fed Funds	0.25	0.25
USA 3 Mo T-B	0.05	0.04
CAN tgt overnight rate	1.00	1.00
CAN 3 Mo T-B	1.02	0.93
Foreign Exchange	**2013**	**2014**
EUR/USD	1.33	1.36
GBP/USD	1.57	1.68
USD/CAD	1.02	1.09
USD/JPY	96.10	102.14

JUNE

M	T	W	T	F	S	S
1	2	3	4	5	6	7
8	9	10	11	12	13	14
15	16	17	18	19	20	21
22	23	24	25	26	27	28
29	30					

JULY

M	T	W	T	F	S	S
		1	2	3	4	5
6	7	8	9	10	11	12
13	14	15	16	17	18	19
20	21	22	23	24	25	26
27	28	29	30	31		

AUGUST

M	T	W	T	F	S	S
					1	2
3	4	5	6	7	8	9
10	11	12	13	14	15	16
17	18	19	20	21	22	23
24	25	26	27	28	29	30
31						

Super Seven Performance

The *Super Seven* strategy continued to provide superior returns in 2013, and so far in 2014.

In 2013, the S&P 500 had six out of twelve successful *Super Seven* trades, but on average the positive results were larger than the negative results, leading to an overall gain.

In 2014, so far the *Super Seven* strategy has worked five out of six times. January produced a fairly large loss of 1.7% as the market corrected at month end, but all of the other five months have produced gains, with four of the months producing gains greater than 1%.

** Weekly avg closing values- except Fed Funds & CAN overnight tgt rate weekly closing values.

INDEPENDENCE DAY – THE FULL TRADE PROFIT BEFORE & AFTER FIREWORKS

Two Market Days Before June Month End To 5 Market Days After Independence Day

The beginning of July is a time for celebration and the markets tend to agree.

Based on previous market data, the best way to take advantage of this trend is to be invested for the two market days prior to the June month end and hold until five market days after Independence Day. This time period has produced above average returns on a fairly consistent basis.

Since 1950, 0.9% avg. gain & 72% of the time positive

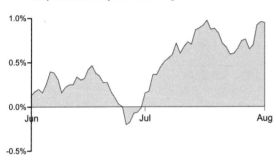

Independence Day S&P 500 Avg. Year 1950 to 2014

The typical Independence Day trade put forward by quite a few pundits has been to invest one or two days before the holiday and take profits one or two days after the holiday.

Although this strategy has produced profits, it has left a lot of money on the table. This strategy misses out on the positive days at the end of June and on the full slate of positive days after Independence Day.

The beginning part of the *Independence Day* positive trend is driven by two combining factors.

First, portfolio managers "window dress" (buying stocks that have a favorable perception in the market); thereby pushing stock prices up at the end of the month.

Second, investors have become "wise" to the *Independence Day Trade* and try to jump in before other investors.

Depending on market conditions at the time, investors should consider extending the exit date until eighteen calendar days in July. With July being an earnings month, the market can continue to rally until mid-month (see *18 Day Earnings Month Strategy*).

> (i) *History of Independence Day:*
> *Independence Day is celebrated on July 4th because that is the day when the Continental Congress adopted the final draft of the Declaration of Independence in 1776. Independence Day was made an official holiday at the end of the War of Independence in 1783. In 1941 Congress declared the 4th of July a federal holiday.*

S&P 500, 2 Market Days Before June Month End To 5 Market Days after Independence Day % Gain 1950 to 2014   Positive

1950	-4.4 %	1960	-0.1 %	1970	1.5 %	1980	1.4 %	1990	1.7 %	2000	1.8 %	2010	0.4 %
1951	1.5	1961	1.7	1971	3.2	1981	-2.4	1991	1.4	2001	-2.6	2011	1.8
1952	0.9	1962	9.8	1972	0.3	1982	-0.6	1992	2.8	2002	-4.7	2012	0.7
1953	0.8	1963	0.5	1973	2.1	1983	1.5	1993	-0.6	2003	1.2	2013	4.5
1954	2.9	1964	2.3	1974	-8.8	1984	-0.7	1994	0.4	2004	-1.7	2014	0.5
1955	4.9	1965	5.0	1975	-0.2	1985	1.5	1995	1.8	2005	1.5		
1956	3.4	1966	2.1	1976	2.4	1986	-2.6	1996	-2.8	2006	2.1		
1957	3.8	1967	1.3	1977	-0.6	1987	0.4	1997	3.7	2007	0.8		
1958	2.0	1968	2.3	1978	0.6	1988	-0.6	1998	2.7	2008	-3.4		
1959	3.3	1969	-1.5	1979	1.3	1989	0.9	1999	5.1	2009	-4.3		
Avg.	1.9 %		2.3 %		0.2 %		-0.1 %		1.8 %		-0.9 %		1.6 %

2014 Strategy Performance

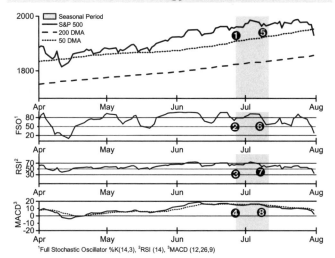

¹Full Stochastic Oscillator %K(14,3), ²RSI (14), ³MACD (12,26,9)

Market Indices & Rates
Weekly Values**

Stock Markets	2013	2014
Dow	15,034	16,873
S&P500	1,620	1,952
Nasdaq	3,420	4,350
TSX	12,178	15,085
FTSE	6,266	6,787
DAX	8,072	9,945
Nikkei	13,106	15,147
Hang Seng	20,817	23,210

Commodities	2013	2014
Oil	96.69	106.58
Gold	1342.4	1283.8

Bond Yields	2013	2014
USA 5 Yr Treasury	1.22	1.72
USA 10 Yr T	2.33	2.63
USA 20 Yr T	3.11	3.17
Moody's Aaa	4.33	4.27
Moody's Baa	5.23	4.81
CAN 5 Yr T	1.65	1.57
CAN 10 Yr T	2.27	2.28

Money Market	2013	2014
USA Fed Funds	0.25	0.25
USA 3 Mo T-B	0.05	0.03
CAN tgt overnight rate	1.00	1.00
CAN 3 Mo T-B	1.03	0.94

Foreign Exchange	2013	2014
EUR/USD	1.33	1.36
GBP/USD	1.56	1.70
USD/CAD	1.03	1.08
USD/JPY	96.29	101.98

Independence Day Performance

The S&P 500 started to perform strongly at the end of May and continued its trend into June.

Technical Conditions– Two Market Days Before June Month End to Five Market Days After Independence Day, 2014

Entry Strategy –Buy Position on Entry Date–

The S&P 500 was relatively flat for the two weeks leading into its seasonal period. On the start date of the trade, the S&P 500 was above its 50 day moving average❶, the FSO was at 80❷, the RSI was just below 70❸ and the MACD was positive, but relatively flat❹. Overall, the conditions were moderately positive for the trade.

Exit Strategy –Sell Position Early–

After a few days into June, the S&P 500 started to turn down❺ and the FSO triggered a sell signal as it crossed below 80❻. At the same time, the RSI also dropped below 70❼ and the MACD started to decline❽, although it was still in positive territory.

Overall, the trade was successful and it did not matter much if the trade was exited on the early sell signal or held until the end of the seasonal period.

JUNE

M	T	W	T	F	S	S
1	2	3	4	5	6	7
8	9	10	11	12	13	14
15	16	17	18	19	20	21
22	23	24	25	26	27	28
29	30					

JULY

M	T	W	T	F	S	S
	1	2	3	4	5	
6	7	8	9	10	11	12
13	14	15	16	17	18	19
20	21	22	23	24	25	26
27	28	29	30	31		

AUGUST

M	T	W	T	F	S	S
					1	2
3	4	5	6	7	8	9
10	11	12	13	14	15	16
17	18	19	20	21	22	23
24	25	26	27	28	29	30
31						

** Weekly avg closing values- except Fed Funds & CAN overnight tgt rate weekly closing values.

Nikkei 225- Avoid for Six Months
May 6th to November 13th

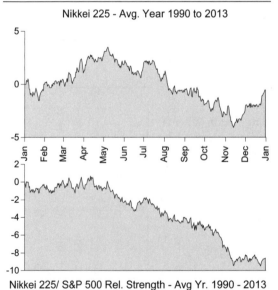

Note: Nikkei 225 Peak December 29, 1989

The Nikkei 225 hit an all time peak of 39,916 on December 29, 1989. It then went on to record its current low reading of 7,055, which occurred on March 10, 2009 for an 82% drop from its peak. It should be noted that the bulk of the data used to establish Nikkei 225's seasonal trend is from a period in which the Nikkei 225 was in a secular decline.

In the second half of the 1980's, the Nikkei 225 was climbing rapidly as Japanese businesses were increasing their exports around the world. Over-confidence and speculation developed bubbles in the stock market and real estate market. In 1990, in an attempt to control the overheated economy and speculation, the Bank of Japan tightened the money supply repeatedly and by the beginning of October, the Nikkei 225 had lost almost half its value.

Although it is possible that the Nikkei 225's secular decline has skewed its seasonal trend, historically avoiding most stock markets around the world from May to October, has generally been beneficial on a risk-reward basis. From 1990 to 2013, during the period of May 6th to November 13th, the Nikkei 225 has produced an average loss of 8.7% and has only been positive 13% of the time.

8.7% loss & positive 13% of the time

Nikkei 225 - Avg. Year 1990 to 2013

Nikkei 225/ S&P 500 Rel. Strength - Avg Yr. 1990 - 2013

The Nikkei 225's secular decline starting in the 1990's may have artificially boosted the magnitude of

May 6 to Nov 13	S&P 500	Nikkei 225	Negative Diff
1990	-6.1%	-20.6%	-14.4%
1991	4.4	-7.8	-12.2
1992	1.3	-5.6	-7.0
1993	4.7	-11.6	-16.3
1994	2.4	-1.5	-3.9
1995	13.9	4.1	-9.8
1996	14.0	-3.2	-17.1
1997	10.4	-21.0	-31.4
1998	0.9	-8.5	-9.5
1999	3.6	9.3	5.7
2000	-5.7	-20.5	-14.8
2001	-10.1	-30.5	-20.4
2002	-17.8	-27.0	-9.2
2003	14.2	30.7	16.5
2004	5.6	-6.3	-11.9
2005	5.3	28.7	23.4
2006	4.4	-6.6	-11.0
2007	-1.6	-13.0	-11.4
2008	-35.3	-41.4	-6.1
2009	21.0	8.8	-12.2
2010	2.9	-12.1	-14.9
2011	-5.3	-14.9	-9.6
2012	0.4	-7.7	-8.1
2013	10.4	6.4	-4.0
Avg	1.6%	-7.1%	-8.7%
Fq > 0	71%	25%	13%

Nikkei 225* vs. S&P 500 1990 to 2013

its underperformance during its unfavorable period from May 6th to November 13th. However, since its low in 2009, during its unfavorable period, the Nikkei 225 has still underperformed the S&P 500 every time.

After Shinza Abe was elected for a second term as Prime Minister of Japan in December 2012, he introduced expansionary policies to stimulate the economy. His "three arrows" policy of fiscal stimulus, monetary easing and structural reforms was well received by the stock market and the Nikkei 225 strongly outperformed the S&P 500 for the first few months of 2013. It is possible that as Abe's expansionary policies continue to be implemented, the direction of the Nikkei 225 will be effected, nevertheless, investors would still be wise to pay heed to the Nikkei's unfavorable period.

*ⓘ * Nikkei- Nikkei 225 Index, is a stock market index for the Tokyo Stock Exchange (TSE)*

2013-14 Strategy Performance

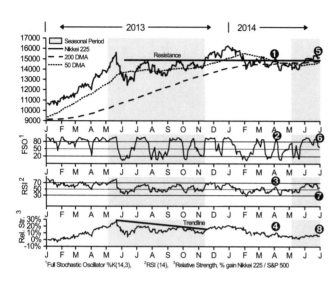

¹Full Stochastic Oscillator %K(14,3),   ²RSI (14),   ³Relative Strength, % gain Nikkei 225 / S&P 500

Market Indices & Rates
Weekly Values**

Stock Markets	2013	2014
Dow	14,853	16,864
S&P500	1,597	1,958
Nasdaq	3,370	4,375
TSX	11,986	15,034
FTSE	6,151	6,763
DAX	7,879	9,869
Nikkei	13,151	15,283
Hang Seng	20,250	22,994
Commodities	2013	2014
Oil	95.90	106.46
Gold	1245.4	1315.6
Bond Yields	2013	2014
USA 5 Yr Treasury	1.44	1.68
USA 10 Yr T	2.55	2.57
USA 20 Yr T	3.26	3.12
Moody's Aaa	4.41	4.20
Moody's Baa	5.42	4.76
CAN 5 Yr T	1.83	1.58
CAN 10 Yr T	2.48	2.28
Money Market	2013	2014
USA Fed Funds	0.25	0.25
USA 3 Mo T-B	0.06	0.03
CAN tgt overnight rate	1.00	1.00
CAN 3 Mo T-B	1.03	0.95
Foreign Exchange	2013	2014
EUR/USD	1.31	1.36
GBP/USD	1.53	1.70
USD/CAD	1.05	1.07
USD/JPY	98.15	101.78

Nikkei 225 Performance

From the beginning of 2013 to May 5th, the Nikkei 225 produced a gain of 32%. This dramatic rise was the result of Japan's expansionary policies.

Technical Conditions– May 6th to November 13th, 2013
Entry Strategy –Buy (Short) Position Early–

The Nikkei 225 was performing strongly coming into its seasonally strong short period. In late April, the Nikkei 225 had a minor correction❶, triggering an early buy signal for a short position, as the FSO turned down below 80❷. The RSI supported this position as it crossed below 70❸. At the time, the Nikkei 225 was outperforming the S&P 500❹.

Exit Strategy –Sell (Short) Position Early–

For most of its seasonal short period, the Nikkei 225 battled against a resistance level just below 15,000. In early November, the Nikkei 225 was trading just below its 50 day moving average❺. An early sell signal on the short position was triggered when the FSO bounced off 20❻. At the same time the RSI turned above 50❼ and the Nikkei 225 still maintained its downward trend❽.

Overall, in the unfavorable period for the Nikkei 225, from May 6th to November 13th 2013, the Nikkei 225 short position produced a loss of 6.4%, and underperformed the S&P 500, which produced a gain of 10.4%.

JUNE

M	T	W	T	F	S	S
						1
2	3	4	5	6	7	8
9	10	11	12	13	14	15
16	17	18	19	20	21	22
23	24	25	26	27	28	29
30						

JULY

M	T	W	T	F	S	S
	1	2	3	4	5	6
7	8	9	10	11	12	13
14	15	16	17	18	19	20
21	22	23	24	25	26	27
28	29	30	31			

AUGUST

M	T	W	T	F	S	S
				1	2	3
4	5	6	7	8	9	10
11	12	13	14	15	16	17
18	19	20	21	22	23	24
25	26	27	28	29	30	31

** Weekly avg closing values- except Fed Funds & CAN overnight tgt rate weekly closing values.

JULY

	MONDAY	TUESDAY	WEDNESDAY
	29	30	**1** 30
WEEK 27			CAN Market Closed- Canada Day
WEEK 28	**6** 25	**7** 24	**8** 23
WEEK 29	**13** 18	**14** 17	**15** 16
WEEK 30	**20** 11	**21** 10	**22** 9
WEEK 31	**27** 4	**28** 3	**29** 2

THURSDAY		FRIDAY	
2	29	**3**	28
		USA Market Closed - Independence Day	
9	22	**10**	21
16	15	**17**	14
23	8	**24**	7
30	1	**31**	

AUGUST

M	T	W	T	F	S	S
					1	2
3	4	5	6	7	8	9
10	11	12	13	14	15	16
17	18	19	20	21	22	23
24	25	26	27	28	29	30
31						

SEPTEMBER

M	T	W	T	F	S	S
	1	2	3	4	5	6
7	8	9	10	11	12	13
14	15	16	17	18	19	20
21	22	23	24	25	26	27
28	29	30				

OCTOBER

M	T	W	T	F	S	S
			1	2	3	4
5	6	7	8	9	10	11
12	13	14	15	16	17	18
19	20	21	22	23	24	25
26	27	28	29	30	31	

NOVEMBER

M	T	W	T	F	S	S
						1
2	3	4	5	6	7	8
9	10	11	12	13	14	15
16	17	18	19	20	21	22
23	24	25	26	27	28	29
30						

JULY
S U M M A R Y

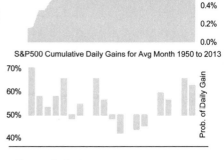

S&P500 Cumulative Daily Gains for Avg Month 1950 to 2013

	Dow Jones	S&P 500	Nasdaq	TSX Comp
Month Rank	4	6	10	6
# Up	40	35	22	19
# Down	24	20	20	10
% Pos	63	55	52	66
% Avg. Gain	1.2	1.0	0.2	0.9

Dow & S&P 1950-2012, Nasdaq 1972-2012, TSX 1985-2012

♦ When a summer rally occurs, the gains are usually made in July. ♦ Typically, it is the first part of July that produces the gains as the market rallies for Independence Day and into the first eighteen calendar days (see the 18 *Days Earning Month Effect*). In 2013, July produced a very strong gain of 5.2% during its first eighteen calendar days. ♦ Two major sector opportunities in July are gold and energy. In July 2013, both sectors started their seasonal periods with positive performances.

BEST / WORST JULY BROAD MKTS. 2004-2013

BEST JULY MARKETS
♦ Russell 2000 (2009) 9.5%
♦ Dow (2009) 8.6%
♦ FTSE 100 (2009) 8.5%

WORST JULY MARKETS
♦ Nasdaq (2004) -7.8%
♦ Russell 2000 (2007) -6.9%
♦ Russell 2000 (2004) -6.8%

Index Values End of Month

	2004	2005	2006	2007	2008	2009	2010	2011	2012	2013
Dow	10,140	10,641	11,186	13,212	11,378	9,172	10,466	12,143	13,009	15,500
S&P 500	1,102	1,234	1,277	1,455	1,267	987	1,102	1,292	1,379	1,686
Nasdaq	1,887	2,185	2,091	2,546	2,326	1,979	2,255	2,756	2,940	3,626
TSX Comp.	8,458	10,423	11,831	13,869	13,593	10,787	11,713	12,946	11,665	12,487
Russell 1000	1,129	1,288	1,331	1,523	1,334	1,038	1,165	1,380	1,458	1,802
Russell 2000	1,370	1,689	1,741	1,929	1,776	1,384	1,618	1,981	1,956	2,598
FTSE 100	4,413	5,282	5,928	6,360	5,412	4,608	5,258	5,815	5,635	6,621
Nikkei 225	11,326	11,900	15,457	17,249	13,377	10,357	9,537	9,833	8,695	13,668

Percent Gain for July

	2004	2005	2006	2007	2008	2009	2010	2011	2012	2013
Dow	-2.8	3.6	0.3	-1.5	0.2	8.6	7.1	-2.2	1.0	4.0
S&P 500	-3.4	3.6	0.5	-3.2	-1.0	7.4	6.9	-2.1	1.3	4.9
Nasdaq	-7.8	6.2	-3.7	-2.2	1.4	7.8	6.9	-0.6	0.2	6.6
TSX Comp.	-1.0	5.3	1.9	-0.3	-6.0	4.0	3.7	-2.7	0.6	2.9
Russell 1000	-3.6	3.8	0.1	-3.2	-1.3	7.5	6.8	-2.3	1.1	5.2
Russell 2000	-6.8	6.3	-3.3	-6.9	3.6	9.5	6.8	-3.7	-1.4	6.9
FTSE 100	-1.1	3.3	1.6	-3.8	-3.8	8.5	6.9	-2.2	1.2	6.5
Nikkei 225	-4.5	2.7	-0.3	-4.9	-0.8	4.0	1.6	0.2	-3.5	-0.1

July Market Avg. Performance 2004 to 2013[1]

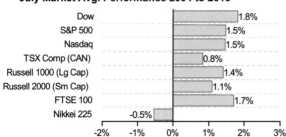

Dow 1.8%
S&P 500 1.5%
Nasdaq 1.5%
TSX Comp (CAN) 0.8%
Russell 1000 (Lg Cap) 1.4%
Russell 2000 (Sm Cap) 1.1%
FTSE 100 1.7%
Nikkei 225 -0.5%

Interest Corner Jul[2]

	Fed Funds %[3]	3 Mo. T-Bill %[4]	10 Yr %[5]	20 Yr %[6]
2013	0.25	0.04	2.60	3.34
2012	0.25	0.11	1.51	2.21
2011	0.25	0.10	2.82	3.77
2010	0.25	0.15	2.94	3.74
2009	0.25	0.18	3.52	4.29

(1) Russell Data provided by Russell (2) Federal Reserve Bank of St. Louis- end of month values (3) Target rate set by FOMC (4)(5)(6) Constant yield maturities.

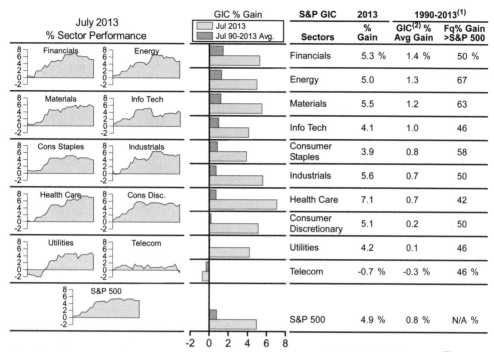

S&P GIC	2013	1990-2013[1]	
Sectors	% Gain	GIC[2] % Avg Gain	Fq% Gain >S&P 500
Financials	5.3 %	1.4 %	50 %
Energy	5.0	1.3	67
Materials	5.5	1.2	63
Info Tech	4.1	1.0	46
Consumer Staples	3.9	0.8	58
Industrials	5.6	0.7	50
Health Care	7.1	0.7	42
Consumer Discretionary	5.1	0.2	50
Utilities	4.2	0.1	46
Telecom	-0.7 %	-0.3 %	46 %
S&P 500	4.9 %	0.8 %	N/A %

Sector Commentary

♦ July is an earnings month and the stock market performed well into the start of the earnings season of July 2013. Most of the gains in the month were made in the first half of the month. Nine out of the ten S&P GIC sectors produced gains for the complete month. ♦ The only sector that produced a loss was the telecom sector as investors favored higher beta sectors. ♦ The health care sector gained a solid 7.1%, driven by the large gains in the biotech sub-sector.

Sub-Sector Commentary

♦ The biotech sub-sector gained 15.4% in July 2013, with its seasonal period starting towards the end of June. ♦ Gold also put in a solid performance for the month, producing a gain of 10.3%. ♦ Transportation and railroads, both produced gains but underperformed the S&P 500. ♦ The homebuilders sub-sector produced a substantial loss of 8.1% as investors started to question the future of the housing market. ♦ The broad agriculture sub-sector usually starts its run in August, but in 2013, it looked to be starting its seasonal run early with a gain of 7.5%. ♦Generally, commodities and commodity related companies performed well in July 2013.

SELECTED SUB-SECTORS[3]

Biotech (1993-2013)	15.4 %	6.8 %	81 %
Railroads	3.1	2.6	63
Silver	5.7	1.8	63
Chemicals	5.7	1.5	58
Banks	5.3	1.5	63
Transportation	3.3	1.2	46
Homebuilders	-8.1	1.1	46
Retail	6.1	0.8	54
Gold (London PM)	10.3	0.6	54
SOX (1995-2013)	2.0	0.4	42
Metals & Mining	3.5	0.3	46
Pharma	5.6	0.2	50
Steel	7.9	-0.5	50
Agriculture (1994-2013)	7.5	-1.4	45
Software & Services	1.5	-1.8	25

(1) Sector data provided by Standard and Poors (2) GIC is short form for Global Industry Classification (3) Sub Sector data provided by Standard and Poors, except where marked by symbol.

Volatility Index
July 3rd to October 9th

The Chicago Board Options Exchange Market Volatility Index (VIX) is often referred to as a fear index as it measures investor's expectations of market volatility over the next thirty day period. The higher the VIX value, the greater the expectation of volatility and vice versa.

The long-term average of the VIX, from 1990 to June 2014 is 20.1. In this time period, the VIX has bottomed at approximately 10 in the mid-90's, and the mid-00's. In both cases, the VIX dropped below 10 for a few days.

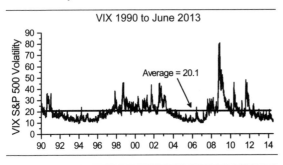

VIX 1990 to June 2013

Average = 20.1

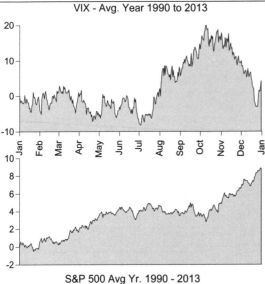

VIX - Avg. Year 1990 to 2013

S&P 500 Avg Yr. 1990 - 2013

VIX* vs. S&P 500 1990 to 2013		
		Positive
July 3 to Oct 9	S&P 500	VIX
1990	-15.1%	88.9 %
1991	-0.2	5.2
1992	-2.2	47.8
1993	3.3	6.3
1994	2.0	3.9
1995	8.2	30.5
1996	3.4	13.4
1997	7.4	13.3
1998	-14.1	138.8
1999	-4.0	9.8
2000	-3.6	22.9
2001	-14.6	85.7
2002	-18.1	45.5
2003	4.5	-1.1
2004	-0.3	-0.2
2005	0.1	28.0
2006	6.3	-10.7
2007	3.0	4.7
2008	-27.9	146.6
2009	19.5	-17.3
2010	13.9	-31.2
2011	-13.8	128.1
2012	5.6	-2.6
2013	2.6	19.2
Avg	-1.5%	32.3 %
Fq > 0	54%	75%

portunity for seasonal investors to adjust their portfolios in order to manage risk.

From 1990 to 2013, during the period of July 3rd to August 9th, the VIX has increased 75% of the time. On average the VIX tends to start increasing in July, particularly after earnings season gets underway. After mid-July, without the expectation of strong earnings ahead, investors tend to focus on the economic forecasts that often become more dire in the second half of the year. In addition, stock market analysts tend to reduce their earnings forecasts at this time. Both of these effects tend to add volatility in the markets, increasing the VIX. The VIX tends to peak in October as the stock market starts to establish a rising trend at this time.

Levels below 15 are often associated with investor complacency, as investors are expecting very little volatility. Very often when a correction occurs in this state, it can be sharp and severe as it is unexpected.

Knowing the the trends of the VIX can be useful in adjusting the amount of risk in a portfolio. Knowing the seasonal trends of the VIX provides an annual op-

(i) *VIX - ticker symbol for the Chicago Board Options Exchange Market Volatility Index, measure implied volatility of S&P 500 index options*

2013-14 Strategy Performance

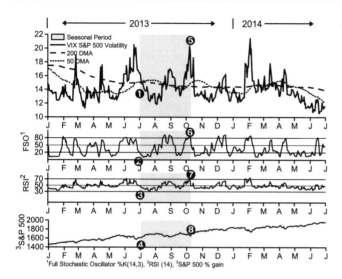

¹Full Stochastic Oscillator %K(14,3), ²RSI (14), ³S&P 500 % gain

VIX Performance

Starting in May 2013, the S&P 500 started to wane in strength, as it often does at this time of the year. At the same time the VIX started to increase from a low level of 12. The VIX eventually topped out in June at just over 20 as the stock market started to climb again.

Technical Conditions July 3rd to October 9th, 2013

Entry Strategy –Buy Position on Entry Date–

At the beginning of its seasonal period in early July 2013, the VIX crossed below its 50 and 200 day moving averages❶. At the time the FSO crossed below 20❷, the RSI crossed below 50❸ and the S&P 500 was in an uptrend❹. Technically, the conditions were not strong for the VIX to perform well.

Exit Strategy –Sell Position on Exit Date–

The VIX climbed sharply in the second half of September and peaked at the end of its seasonal period at the beginning of October❺. The FSO confirmed the exit as it fell below 80❻. In addition, the RSI turned down from 70❼. At the time the S&P 500 was falling, but as the VIX started to fall just after the seasonal period ended, it helped boost the S&P 500❽.

Overall, the VIX increased in its seasonal period, despite a volatile journey along the way. At the end of its seasonal period in the second half of October and into November, the VIX settled at a lower level than both the entry and exit dates of its seasonal period.

** Weekly avg closing values- except Fed Funds & CAN overnight tgt rate weekly closing values.

- 82 -

Market Indices & Rates
Weekly Values**

Stock Markets	2012	2013
Dow	12,871	15,008
S&P500	1,365	1,619
Nasdaq	2,960	3,448
TSX	11,810	12,156
FTSE	5,674	6,328
DAX	6,517	7,905
Nikkei	9,055	14,067
Hang Seng	19,764	20,532

Commodities	2012	2013
Oil	85.77	100.51
Gold	1602.8	1242.0

Bond Yields	2012	2013
USA 5 Yr Treasury	0.67	1.45
USA 10 Yr T	1.61	2.56
USA 20 Yr T	2.32	3.25
Moody's Aaa	3.60	4.33
Moody's Baa	5.03	5.36
CAN 5 Yr T	1.24	1.80
CAN 10 Yr T	1.72	2.45

Money Market	2012	2013
USA Fed Funds	0.25	0.25
USA 3 Mo T-B	0.08	0.04
CAN tgt overnight rate	1.00	1.00
CAN 3 Mo T-B	0.85	1.03

Foreign Exchange	2012	2013
EUR/USD	1.25	1.30
GBP/USD	1.56	1.51
USD/CAD	1.02	1.05
USD/JPY	79.75	100.29

JULY

M	T	W	T	F	S	S
	1	2	3	4	5
6	7	8	9	10	11	12
13	14	15	16	17	18	19
20	21	22	23	24	25	26
27	28	29	30	31		

AUGUST

M	T	W	T	F	S	S
					1	2
3	4	5	6	7	8	9
10	11	12	13	14	15	16
17	18	19	20	21	22	23
24	25	26	27	28	29	30
31						

SEPTEMBER

M	T	W	T	F	S	S
	1	2	3	4	5	6
7	8	9	10	11	12	13
14	15	16	17	18	19	20
21	22	23	24	25	26	27
28	29	30				

GOLD SHINES
(Metal) Gold (Metal) Outperforms – July 12th to October 9th

"Foul cankering rust the hidden treasure frets, but gold that's put to use more gold begets."

(William Shakespeare, *Venus and Adonis*)

For many years, gold was thought to be a dead investment. It was only the "gold bugs" that espoused the virtues of investing in the precious metal. Investors were mesmerized with technology stocks, and central bankers confident of their currencies, were selling gold, "left, right and center."

4.2% gain & positive 70% of the time

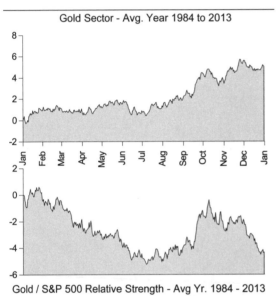

Gold Sector - Avg. Year 1984 to 2013

Gold / S&P 500 Relative Strength - Avg Yr. 1984 - 2013

Jul 12 to Oct 9th	S&P 500	Positive Gold	Diff
1984	7.4 %	0.5 %	-6.9 %
1985	-5.4	4.1	9.5
1986	-2.6	25.2	27.8
1987	0.9	3.9	3.0
1988	2.8	-7.5	-10.3
1989	9.4	-4.2	-13.6
1990	-15.5	12.1	27.6
1991	0.0	-2.9	-2.8
1992	-2.9	0.4	3.3
1993	2.7	-8.8	-11.5
1994	1.6	1.6	0.0
1995	4.3	-0.1	-4.3
1996	7.9	-0.4	-8.3
1997	5.9	4.4	-1.5
1998	-15.5	2.8	18.2
1999	-4.8	25.6	30.4
2000	-5.3	-4.5	0.8
2001	-10.5	8.4	18.8
2002	-16.2	1.7	17.9
2003	4.1	7.8	3.8
2004	0.8	3.8	2.9
2005	-1.9	11.4	13.4
2006	6.1	-8.8	-14.9
2007	3.1	11.0	8.0
2008	-26.6	-8.2	18.4
2009	21.9	15.2	- 6.7
2010	8.1	11.0	2.9
2011	-12.4	6.2	18.6
2012	7.5	12.5	5.0
2013	-1.1	1.5	2.6
Avg.	-0.9 %	4.2 %	5.1 %
Fq > 0	53 %	70 %	67 %

Gold (Metal) London PM vs S&P 500
1984 to 2013

In the early 2000's, investors started to take a shine to gold, boosting its returns. On a seasonal basis, on average from 1984 to 2013, gold has done well relative to the stock market from July 12th to October 9th. The reasons for gold's seasonal changes in price, are largely related to jewellery production and European Central banks selling cycles (see *Golden Times* strategy page).

The movement of gold stock prices, represented by the index (XAU) on the Philadelphia Exchange, coincides closely with the price of gold. Although there is a strong correlation between gold and gold stocks, there are other factors, such as company operations and hedging policies, which determine each company's price in the market. Gold has typically started its seasonal strong period a few weeks earlier than gold stocks and finished just after gold stocks have turned down.

Investors should know that gold can have a run in the month of November. Although this is a positive time for gold, producing an average gain of 1.7% and being positive 67% of the time (1984 to 2013), the trouble is in the following month. December has a history of being negative for gold, producing an average loss of 0.5% and only being positive 43% of the time, which is a lot less than the 2.0% average return of the S&P 500. The S&P 500 also has a record of being positive 83% of the time, in the same yearly period.

Source: Bank of England
London PM represents the close value of gold in afternoon trading in London.

JULY

2013-14 Strategy Performance

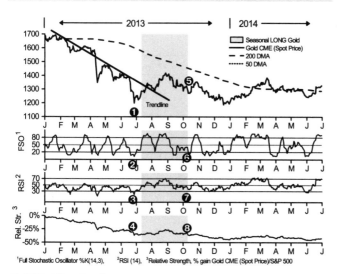

¹Full Stochastic Oscillator %K(14,3), ²RSI (14), ³Relative Strength, % gain Gold CME (Spot Price)/S&P 500

Gold Bullion Performance

As investors feared the impacts of the Federal Reserve cutting back its quantitative easing program, gold fell sharply in the first six months of 2013.

Technical Conditions– July 12th to October 9th, 2013

Entry Strategy –Buy Position Early–

In late June, a few weeks before the start of the seasonal period for gold bullion, gold suffered a correction and then bounced❶. As a result, the FSO crossed above 20❷ triggering an early buy signal. In support, the RSI crossed above 30❸. At the time, gold bullion was underperforming the S&P 500❹.

Exit Strategy – Sell on Exit Date–

At the end of its seasonal period, gold was in a downtrend❺, both the FSO and the RSI were below 50❻❼ and falling, and gold bullion was performing at market❽. There was not a reason to stay in the position past its seasonal exit date.

Overall the gold bullion seasonal trade was successful, as it produced a small gain and outperformed the S&P 500. Entering into the trade early based upon the early buy signal, was beneficial as it produced additional gains compared with the seasonal entry date.

Market Indices & Rates Weekly Values**

Stock Markets	2012	2013
Dow	12,669	15,348
S&P500	1,345	1,660
Nasdaq	2,899	3,538
TSX	11,526	12,354
FTSE	5,646	6,511
DAX	6,451	8,093
Nikkei	8,810	14,396
Hang Seng	19,272	20,977

Commodities	2012	2013
Oil	85.78	104.81
Gold	1581.8	1262.3

Bond Yields	2012	2013
USA 5 Yr Treasury	0.63	1.48
USA 10 Yr T	1.52	2.64
USA 20 Yr T	2.21	3.36
Moody's Aaa	3.44	4.37
Moody's Baa	4.90	5.41
CAN 5 Yr T	1.18	1.78
CAN 10 Yr T	1.65	2.46

Money Market	2012	2013
USA Fed Funds	0.25	0.25
USA 3 Mo T-B	0.10	0.04
CAN tgt overnight rate	1.00	1.00
CAN 3 Mo T-B	0.87	1.02

Foreign Exchange	2012	2013
EUR/USD	1.23	1.30
GBP/USD	1.55	1.50
USD/CAD	1.02	1.05
USD/JPY	79.45	100.00

JULY

M	T	W	T	F	S	S
	1	2	3	4	5	
6	7	8	9	10	11	12
13	14	15	16	17	18	19
20	21	22	23	24	25	26
27	28	29	30	31		

AUGUST

M	T	W	T	F	S	S
					1	2
3	4	5	6	7	8	9
10	11	12	13	14	15	16
17	18	19	20	21	22	23
24	25	26	27	28	29	30
31						

SEPTEMBER

M	T	W	T	F	S	S
	1	2	3	4	5	6
7	8	9	10	11	12	13
14	15	16	17	18	19	20
21	22	23	24	25	26	27
28	29	30				

** Weekly avg closing values- except Fed Funds & CAN overnight tgt rate weekly closing values.

Gold stocks were shunned for many years. It is only recently that interest in the sector has increased again. What few investors know is that even during the twenty year bear market in gold that started in 1981, it was possible to make money in gold stocks.

*6.5% gain when the S&P 500
has been negative*

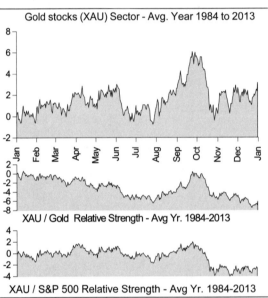

Gold stocks (XAU) Sector - Avg. Year 1984 to 2013

XAU / Gold Relative Strength - Avg Yr. 1984-2013

XAU / S&P 500 Relative Strength - Avg Yr. 1984-2013

XAU (Gold Stocks) vs S&P 500 and Gold (1984 to 2013)			
XAU>S&P 500			
XAU>Gold			
Jul 27 to Sep 25	S&P 500	Gold	XAU
1984	10.4 %	0.3 %	20.8 %
1985	-6.1	3.6	-5.5
1986	-3.5	23.0	36.9
1987	3.5	1.9	23.0
1988	1.7	-7.2	-11.9
1989	1.8	-1.3	10.5
1990	-13.4	9.5	3.8
1991	1.6	-3.1	-11.9
1992	0.7	-2.2	-3.8
1993	1.9	-8.7	-7.3
1994	1.4	2.5	18.2
1995	3.6	-0.8	-1.0
1996	7.9	-0.7	-1.0
1997	-0.1	0.2	8.7
1998	-8.4	1.2	12.0
1999	-5.2	6.5	16.9
2000	-0.9	-2.3	-2.8
2001	-15.8	7.7	3.2
2002	-1.5	6.6	29.8
2003	0.5	7.6	11.0
2004	2.4	4.4	16.5
2005	-1.3	9.3	20.5
2006	4.6	-4.8	-11.9
2007	2.3	8.7	14.0
2008	-3.9	-3.5	-18.5
2009	6.7	4.2	6.0
2010	3.0	9.6	14.7
2011	-14.7	4.7	-13.7
2012	6.0	9.5	23.4
2013	0.1	-0.6	-5.5
Avg.	-0.5 %	2.9 %	6.5 %
Fq > 0	60 %	63 %	60 %

On average from 1984 (start of the XAU index) to 2013, gold stocks as represented by the XAU index, have outperformed the S&P 500 from July 27th to September 25th. One factor that has led to a rise in the price of gold stocks in August and September is the Indian festival and wedding season that starts in October and finishes in November during Diwali. The Indian culture places a great emphasis on gold as a store of value and a lot of it is "consumed" as jewellery during the festival and wedding season. The price of gold tends to increase in the months preceding this season as the jewellery fabricators purchase gold to make their final product.

The August-September increase in gold stocks coincides with the time that a lot of investors are pulling their money out of the broad market and are looking for a place to invest. This makes gold a very attractive investment at this time of the year.

Be careful. Just as the gold stocks tend to go up in August-September, they also tend to go down in October. Historically, this negative trend has been caused by European Central banks selling some of their gold holdings in autumn when their annual allotment of possible sales is renewed yearly. In recent years, European Central banks have reduced gold sales and have even become net buyers. This has muted gold's negative trend in October. Nevertheless, gold stocks have still underperformed. From October 1st to October 27th, for the period 1984 to 2013, XAU has produced an average loss of 5.2% and has only been positive 37% of the time.

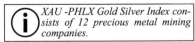
XAU -PHLX Gold Silver Index consists of 12 precious metal mining companies.

2013-14 Strategy Performance

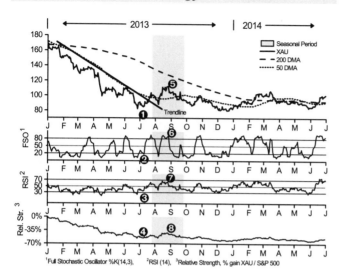

¹Full Stochastic Oscillator %K(14,3),   ²RSI (14),   ³Relative Strength, % gain XAU / S&P 500

Market Indices & Rates
Weekly Values**

Stock Markets	2012	2013
Dow	12,841	15,500
S&P500	1,366	1,684
Nasdaq	2,928	3,603
TSX	11,592	12,586
FTSE	5,669	6,596
DAX	6,643	8,272
Nikkei	8,737	14,653
Hang Seng	19,403	21,339

Commodities	2012	2013
Oil	90.32	106.98
Gold	1582.1	1290.5

Bond Yields	2012	2013
USA 5 Yr Treasury	0.61	1.35
USA 10 Yr T	1.52	2.54
USA 20 Yr T	2.20	3.28
Moody's Aaa	3.37	4.31
Moody's Baa	4.85	5.29
CAN 5 Yr T	1.17	1.69
CAN 10 Yr T	1.63	2.39

Money Market	2012	2013
USA Fed Funds	0.25	0.25
USA 3 Mo T-B	0.09	0.03
CAN tgt overnight rate	1.00	1.00
CAN 3 Mo T-B	0.91	1.01

Foreign Exchange	2012	2013
EUR/USD	1.23	1.31
GBP/USD	1.57	1.52
USD/CAD	1.01	1.04
USD/JPY	78.76	99.93

PHLX Gold Silver Index (XAU) Performance

Like gold bullion, XAU was in a downtrend for the first six months of 2013. XAU finally reached a bottom in late June.

Technical Conditions July 27th to September 25th, 2013

Entry Strategy –Buy Position Early–

After putting in a bottom in late June, XAU started to consolidate. In early July, it started to rise❶ and the FSO crossed above 20❷, triggering an early buy signal. The RSI was already rising❸ and XAU was performing at market❹. Shortly after the entry date, XAU broke through its downward trendline and then broke above its 50 day moving average.

Exit Strategy–Sell Position Early–

Towards the end of August, XAU corrected❺ and the FSO crossed below 80❻, triggering an early sell signal. At the time, the RSI was already trending down❼ and XAU had just started to underperform the S&P 500❽.

Overall, the XAU seasonal trade produced a loss and underperformed the S&P 500. If the early buy date and the early sell dates were used, then the seasonal trade would have been profitable.

JULY

M	T	W	T	F	S	S
	1	2	3	4	5
6	7	8	9	10	11	12
13	14	15	16	17	18	19
20	21	22	23	24	25	26
27	28	29	30	31

AUGUST

M	T	W	T	F	S	S
					1	2
3	4	5	6	7	8	9
10	11	12	13	14	15	16
17	18	19	20	21	22	23
24	25	26	27	28	29	30
31

SEPTEMBER

M	T	W	T	F	S	S
	1	2	3	4	5	6
7	8	9	10	11	12	13
14	15	16	17	18	19	20
21	22	23	24	25	26	27
28	29	30

** Weekly avg closing values- except Fed Funds & CAN overnight tgt rate weekly closing values.

Oil stocks tend to outperform the market from July 24th to October 3rd. Earlier in the year, there is a first wave of outperformance from late February to early May. Although the first wave has had an incredible record of outperformance, the second wave in July is still noteworthy.

While the first wave has more to do with inventories during the switch from producing heating oil to gasoline, the second wave is more related to the conversion of production from gasoline to heating oil and the effects of the hurricane season.

1.9% extra &
57% of the time better than S&P 500

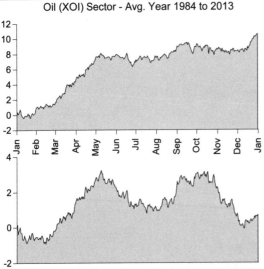

Oil (XOI) Sector - Avg. Year 1984 to 2013

Oil (XOI) / S&P 500 Relative Strength - Avg Yr. 1984 - 2013

XOI vs. S&P 500 1984 to 2013		
Jul 24 to Oct 3 S&P 500	Positive XOI	Diff
1984 9.1 %	9.0 %	-0.1 %
1985 -4.3	6.7	11.0
1986 -2.1	15.7	17.7
1987 6.6	-1.2	-7.8
1988 3.0	-3.6	-6.6
1989 5.0	6.7	0.1
1990 -12.4	-0.5	11.8
1991 1.3	0.7	-0.7
1992 -0.4	2.9	3.3
1993 3.2	7.8	4.6
1994 1.9	-3.6	-5.5
1995 5.2	-2.2	-7.4
1996 10.5	7.7	-2.8
1997 3.0	8.9	5.9
1998 -12.0	1.4	13.5
1999 -5.5	-2.1	3.3
2000 -3.6	12.2	15.8
2001 -10.0	-5.1	4.8
2002 2.7	7.3	4.6
2003 4.2	5.5	1.4
2004 4.2	10.9	6.7
2005 -0.6	14.3	14.9
2006 7.6	-8.5	-16.9
2007 -0.1	-4.2	-4.1
2008 -14.3	-18.1	-3.8
2009 5.0	3.0	-2.0
2010 4.0	8.5	4.5
2011 -18.3	-26.0	-7.7
2012 7.4	6.1	-1.3
2013 -0.8	-0.8	0.0
Avg 0.0 %	1.9 %	1.9 %
Fq > 0 57 %	60 %	57 %

First, there is a large difference between how heating oil and gasoline are stored and consumed. For individuals and businesses, gasoline is consumed in an immediate fashion. It is stored by the local distributor and the supplies are drawn upon as needed. Heating oil, on the other hand, is largely inventoried by individuals, farms and business operations in rural areas.

The inventory process starts before the cold weather arrives. The production facilities have to start switching from gasoline to heating oil, dropping their inventory levels and boosting prices. Second, the hurricane season can play havoc with the production of oil and drive up prices substantially. The official duration of the hurricane season in the Gulf of Mexico is from June 1st to November 30th, but most major hurricanes occur in September and early October.

The threat of a strong hurricane can shut down the oil platforms temporarily, interrupting production. If a strong hurricane strikes the platforms, it can do significant damage and put the them out of commission for an extended period of time.

> *NYSE Arca Oil Index (XOI):*
> *An index designed to represent a cross section of widely held oil corporations involved in various phases of the oil industry.*
>
> *For more information on the XOI index, see www.cboe.com*

2012-13-14 Sector Performance

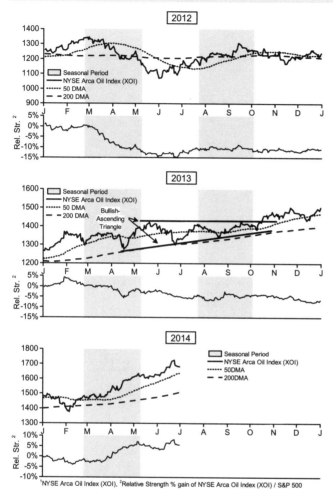

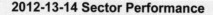

¹NYSE Arca Oil Index (XOI), ²Relative Strength % gain of NYSE Arca Oil Index (XOI) / S&P 500

Market Indices & Rates Weekly Values**

Stock Markets	2012	2013
Dow	12,796	15,554
S&P500	1,355	1,691
Nasdaq	2,892	3,596
TSX	11,582	12,699
FTSE	5,546	6,597
DAX	6,498	8,314
Nikkei	8,474	14,572
Hang Seng	19,000	21,834

Commodities	2012	2013
Oil	88.90	105.93
Gold	1598.6	1330.5

Bond Yields	2012	2013
USA 5 Yr Treasury	0.59	1.36
USA 10 Yr T	1.47	2.57
USA 20 Yr T	2.15	3.30
Moody's Aaa	3.26	4.34
Moody's Baa	4.77	5.25
CAN 5 Yr T	1.19	1.71
CAN 10 Yr T	1.63	2.43

Money Market	2012	2013
USA Fed Funds	0.25	0.25
USA 3 Mo T-B	0.11	0.03
CAN tgt overnight rate	1.00	1.00
CAN 3 Mo T-B	0.94	1.00

Foreign Exchange	2012	2013
EUR/USD	1.22	1.32
GBP/USD	1.56	1.54
USD/CAD	1.01	1.03
USD/JPY	78.28	99.37

JULY

M	T	W	T	F	S	S
	1	2	3	4	5
6	7	8	9	10	11	12
13	14	15	16	17	18	19
20	21	22	23	24	25	26
27	28	29	30	31		

AUGUST

M	T	W	T	F	S	S
					1	2
3	4	5	6	7	8	9
10	11	12	13	14	15	16
17	18	19	20	21	22	23
24	25	26	27	28	29	30
31						

SEPTEMBER

M	T	W	T	F	S	S
	1	2	3	4	5	6
7	8	9	10	11	12	13
14	15	16	17	18	19	20
21	22	23	24	25	26	27
28	29	30				

NYSE Arca Oil Index (XOI) Performance 2013

In 2013, XOI traced out a bullish ascending triangle pattern, with a level top and higher lows. While XOI was tracing out this pattern and not making much ground, the S&P 500 was moving steadily higher. Going into its July to October seasonal period of strength, XOI was underperforming the S&P 500. During its period of seasonal strength, XOI produced a loss of 0.8%, which was equal to S&P 500's loss.

Although XOI broke out to the upside once its period of seasonal strength finished, it continued its pattern of underperformance relative to the S&P 500.

** Weekly avg closing values- except Fed Funds & CAN overnight tgt rate weekly closing values.

Seasonal Investment Timeline[1]

Investment	Season	
Core Positions		
S&P 500	Oct 28 - May 5	
TSX Composite	Oct 28 - May 5	
Cash	May 6 - Oct 27	
Primary Sectors		
[4]Consumer Staples	Jan 1 - Jan 22 (S)	Apr 23 - Oct 27
Financials	Dec 15 - Apr 13	
Energy	Feb 25 - May 9	Jul 24 - Oct 3
[2]Utilities	Jul 17 - Oct 3	Jan 1 - Mar 13 (S)
Health Care	Aug 15 - Oct 18	
Information Tech	Oct 9 - Jan 17	Apr 16 - Apr 30
Consumer Disc.	Oct 28 - Apr 22	
Industrials	Oct 28 - Dec 31	Jan 23- May 5
Materials	Oct 28 - Jan 6	Jan 23 - May 5
Small Cap	Dec 19 - Mar 7	
Secondary Sectors		
Silver Bullion	Jan - Mar & Sep & Nov	
[2]Platinum	Jan 1 - May 31	
Software Jan1 - Jan19	Jun 1 - Jun 30	Oct 10 - Dec 5
Semiconductors	Jan 1 - Mar 7	Oct 28 - Nov 6
Canadian Dollar	Apr 1 - Apr 30	Aug 20 - Sep 25
Biotech	Jun 23 - Sep 13	
Gold Bullion	Jul 12 - Oct 9	
Gold Stocks (XAU)	Jul 27 - Sep 25	
Agriculture	Aug 1 - Dec 31	
Transportation Jan23-Apr16	Aug 1 - Oct 9 (S)	Oct 10 - Nov 13
Natural Gas Mar22 - Jun19	Sep 6 - Dec 21	Dec22 - Dec 31(S)
Canadian Banks	Oct 10 - Dec 31	Jan 23 - Apr 13
Retail	Oct 28 - Nov 29	Jan 21 - Apr 12
Homebuilders	Oct 28 - Feb 3	Apr 27- Jun 13(S)
Metals & Mining	Nov 19 - Jan 5	Jan 23 - May 5
Emerging Markets	Nov 24 - April 18	
Aerospace & Defense	Dec 12 - May 5	
Automotive Dec14 - Jan7	Feb 24 - Apr 24	Sep 14 - Oct 3 (S)
Nikkei 225	May 6 - Nov 19 (S)	
VIX (CBOE)	Jul 3 - Oct 9	
Fixed Income		
[3]U.S. Gov. Bonds	May 9 - Oct 3	
[3]U.S. High Yield	Nov 24 - Jan 8	
Stocks		
TJX Companies	Jan 22 - Mar 30	
Caterpillar	Jan 23 - May 5	
DuPont	Jan 28 - May 5	
[3]3M	Feb 3 - May 12	
[2]Suncor Energy	Feb 18 - May 9	
Waste Management	Feb 24 - May 14	
[3]AMD	Feb 24 - May 5	May 6 - Jul 29 (S)
[3]GE	Mar 5 - Apr 6	
[4]Harley Davidson	Mar 9- Apr 18	Jun 22 - Jul 18
Boeing	Mar 13 - Jun 15	
Sysco	Apr 23 - May 30	Oct 11 - Nov 21
Disney	Jun 5 - Sep 30 (S)	Oct 1 - Feb 15
[4]IBM Apr 14 - May 19	Jul 7 - Jul 30	Oct 28 - Nov 26
[3]Intel	May 6 - Jul 29	
Costco	May 26 - Jun 30	Oct 4 - Dec 1
[3]PotashCorp	Jun 23 - Jan 11	
[3]Johnson & Johnson	Jul 14 - Oct 21	
[4]Altria	Jul 19 - Dec 19	
Procter and Gamble	Aug 7 - Nov 19	
Archer-Daniels Midland	Aug 7 - Dec 31	
[3]Alcoa	Aug 23 - Sep 26 (S)	
Union Pacific	Oct 10 - Nov 4	Mar 11 - May 5
Royal Bank	Oct 10 - Nov 28	Jan 23 - Apr 13
Clorox Jan14-Mar2	Sep22 - Nov 17	Nov 18 - Jan 13 (S)
Nike Mar1-Mar20	Sep 1 - Sep 25	Dec 12 - Dec 24
Campbell Soup	Sep 22 - Nov 17	
UPS	Oct 10 - Dec 8	

Long Investment   Short Investment (S)

[1] Holiday, End of Month, Witches' Hangover, - et al not included. [2]Thackray's 2012 Investor's Guide [3]Thackray's 2013 Investor's Guide [4]Thackray's 2014 Investor's Guide

AUGUST

	MONDAY	TUESDAY	WEDNESDAY
WEEK 32	**3** 28 CAN Market Closed- Civic Day	**4** 27	**5** 26
WEEK 33	**10** 21	**11** 20	**12** 19
WEEK 34	**17** 14	**18** 13	**19** 12
WEEK 35	**24** 7	**25** 6	**26** 5
WEEK 36	**31**	1	2

THURSDAY		FRIDAY	
6	25	**7**	24
13	18	**14**	17
20	11	**21**	10
27	4	**28**	3
3		4	

SEPTEMBER

M	T	W	T	F	S	S
	1	2	3	4	5	6
7	8	9	10	11	12	13
14	15	16	17	18	19	20
21	22	23	24	25	26	27
28	29	30				

OCTOBER

M	T	W	T	F	S	S
			1	2	3	4
5	6	7	8	9	10	11
12	13	14	15	16	17	18
19	20	21	22	23	24	25
26	27	28	29	30	31	

NOVEMBER

M	T	W	T	F	S	S
						1
2	3	4	5	6	7	8
9	10	11	12	13	14	15
16	17	18	19	20	21	22
23	24	25	26	27	28	29
30						

DECEMBER

M	T	W	T	F	S	S
	1	2	3	4	5	6
7	8	9	10	11	12	13
14	15	16	17	18	19	20
21	22	23	24	25	26	27
28	29	30	31			

AUGUST
S U M M A R Y

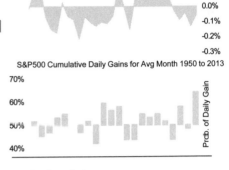

S&P500 Cumulative Daily Gains for Avg Month 1950 to 2013

	Dow Jones	S&P 500	Nasdaq	TSX Comp
Month Rank	10	10	11	10
# Up	36	35	22	16
# Down	28	29	20	13
% Pos	56	55	52	55
% Avg. Gain	-0.1	-0.1	0.1	-0.2

Dow & S&P 1950-2012, Nasdaq 1972-2012, TSX 1985-2012

♦ August is typically a marginal month and has been the fourth worst month for the S&P 500 from 1950 to 2013, producing an average loss of 0.1%. ♦ If there is a summer rally in July, it is often in jeopardy in August. ♦ In July 2013, the S&P 500's strong rally continued only for the first few days of August and then it lost ground for the rest of the month, producing a total loss of 3.1% for the month. ♦ When the S&P 500 is negative in the month of August, the Russell 2000 typically underperforms.

BEST / WORST AUGUST BROAD MKTS. 2004-2013

BEST AUGUST MARKETS
♦ FTSE 100 (2009) 6.5%
♦ Nikkei 225 (2006) 4.4%
♦ Nasdaq (2006) 4.4%

WORST AUGUST MARKETS
♦ Nikkei 225 (2011) -8.9%
♦ Russell 2000 (2011) -8.8%
♦ Russell 2000 (2010) -7.5%

Index Values End of Month

	2004	2005	2006	2007	2008	2009	2010	2011	2012	2013
Dow	10,174	10,482	11,381	13,358	11,544	9,496	10,015	11,614	13,091	14,810
S&P 500	1,104	1,220	1,304	1,474	1,283	1,021	1,049	1,219	1,407	1,633
Nasdaq	1,838	2,152	2,184	2,596	2,368	2,009	2,114	2,579	3,067	3,590
TSX Comp.	8,377	10,669	12,074	13,660	13,771	10,868	11,914	12,769	11,949	12,654
Russell 1000	1,132	1,275	1,360	1,540	1,350	1,073	1,110	1,297	1,490	1,748
Russell 2000	1,362	1,656	1,791	1,970	1,838	1,422	1,496	1,806	2,018	2,512
FTSE 100	4,459	5,297	5,906	6,303	5,637	4,909	5,225	5,395	5,711	6,413
Nikkei 225	11,082	12,414	16,141	16,569	13,073	10,493	8,824	8,955	8,840	13,389

Percent Gain for August

	2004	2005	2006	2007	2008	2009	2010	2011	2012	2013
Dow	0.3	-1.5	1.7	1.1	1.5	3.5	-4.3	-4.4	0.6	-4.4
S&P 500	0.2	-1.1	2.1	1.3	1.2	3.4	-4.7	-5.7	2.0	-3.1
Nasdaq	-2.6	-1.5	4.4	2.0	1.8	1.5	-6.2	-6.4	4.3	-1.0
TSX Comp.	-1.0	2.4	2.1	-1.5	1.3	0.8	1.7	-1.4	2.4	1.3
Russell 1000	0.3	-1.1	2.2	1.2	1.2	3.4	-4.7	-6.0	2.2	-3.0
Russell 2000	-0.6	-1.9	2.9	2.2	3.5	2.8	-7.5	-8.8	3.2	-3.3
FTSE 100	1.0	0.3	-0.4	-0.9	4.2	6.5	-0.6	-7.2	1.4	-3.1
Nikkei 225	-2.2	4.3	4.4	-3.9	-2.3	1.3	-7.5	-8.9	1.7	-2.0

August Market Avg. Performance 2004 to 2013[1]

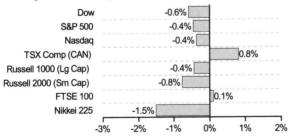

	Dow	-0.6%
	S&P 500	-0.4%
	Nasdaq	-0.4%
	TSX Comp (CAN)	0.8%
	Russell 1000 (Lg Cap)	-0.4%
	Russell 2000 (Sm Cap)	-0.8%
	FTSE 100	0.1%
	Nikkei 225	-1.5%

Interest Corner Aug[2]

	Fed Funds %[3]	3 Mo. T-Bill %[4]	10 Yr %[5]	20 Yr %[6]
2013	0.25	0.03	2.78	3.46
2012	0.25	0.09	1.57	2.29
2011	0.25	0.02	2.23	3.19
2010	0.25	0.14	2.47	3.23
2009	0.25	0.15	3.40	4.14

(1) Russell Data provided by Russell (2) Federal Reserve Bank of St. Louis- end of month values (3) Target rate set by FOMC (4)(5)(6) Constant yield maturities.

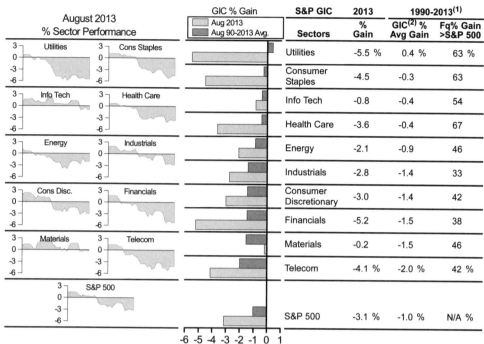

S&P GIC Sectors	2013 % Gain	1990-2013[1] GIC[2] % Avg Gain	Fq% Gain >S&P 500
Utilities	-5.5 %	0.4 %	63 %
Consumer Staples	-4.5	-0.3	63
Info Tech	-0.8	-0.4	54
Health Care	-3.6	-0.4	67
Energy	-2.1	-0.9	46
Industrials	-2.8	-1.4	33
Consumer Discretionary	-3.0	-1.4	42
Financials	-5.2	-1.5	38
Materials	-0.2	-1.5	46
Telecom	-4.1 %	-2.0 %	42 %
S&P 500	-3.1 %	-1.0 %	N/A %

Sector Commentary

♦ In August 2013, all of the major sectors lost ground as a broad based sell-off took place. The utilities sector was the biggest loser amongst the major sectors, producing a loss of 5.5%. Interest rate stocks were hit hard as investors reacted to the Federal Reserve's goal of eliminating its bond purchasing program. ♦ The materials sector had the smallest loss of 0.2%.

Sub-Sector Commentary

♦ Gold and silver both continued their seasonal run with strong positive performances. ♦ After a strong month in July, the biotech sub-sector paused its strong performance with a loss of 2.8%, but still managed to outperform the S&P 500. ♦ The homebuilders sub-sector continued to lose ground with a loss of 8.2% and the banking sector produced a loss of 5.0%. ♦ Investors were concerned with the possibility of the Federal Reserve moving closer to increasing rates and generally sectors and sub-sectors of the market with interest rate exposure risk became less attractive.

SELECTED SUB-SECTORS[3]

Gold (London PM)	6.1 %	0.7 %	50 %
Biotech (1993-2013)	-2.8	0.5	62
Agriculture (1994-2013)	-3.5	0.2	50
Homebuilders	-8.2	-0.1	54
Silver	18.6	-0.2	50
Pharma	-4.4	-0.5	63
SOX (1995-2013)	-4.2	-0.6	47
Software & Services	-1.4	-0.7	58
Retail	-3.2	-0.8	58
Metals & Mining	3.2	-1.2	50
Banks	-5.0	-1.3	38
Chemicals	-0.7	-1.7	42
Railroads	-2.3	-2.6	42
Transportation	-2.0	-3.0	29
Steel	-0.9	-3.9	46

(1) Sector data provided by Standard and Poors (2) GIC is short form for Global Industry Classification (3) Sub Sector data provided by Standard and Poors, except where marked by symbol.

ARCHER-DANIELS-MIDLAND
PLANT YOUR SEEDS FOR GROWTH
August 7th to December 31st

The agriculture sector generally performs well in the last five months of the year and ADM is no exception. If you had to choose just one part of the year in which to invest in ADM, it would have to be the last five months. From August 7th to December 31st, for the years 1990 to 2013, ADM produced an average gain of 14.0% and was positive 83% of the time.

The business of "growing" really takes place in the last part of the year. This is the harvest season for the northern hemisphere and time when cash flows in the agriculture business. As a result, investors are much more interested in committing money to the agriculture sector.

14.0% gain & positive 83% of the time positive

Aug 7 to Dec 31	S&P 500	ADM	Diff
			Positive
1990	-1.3%	0.1%	1.3%
1991	6.8	41.1	34.3
1992	3.6	3.1	-0.5
1993	4.0	1.7	-2.3
1994	0.5	31.9	31.4
1995	10.2	17.2	7.0
1996	11.8	27.5	15.6
1997	1.1	1.2	0.2
1998	12.8	9.4	-3.4
1999	13.0	-9.8	-22.8
2000	-9.8	58.5	68.2
2001	-4.4	14.6	19.0
2002	2.4	13.6	11.2
2003	15.0	16.7	1.7
2004	13.9	42.9	29.0
2005	1.8	18.7	16.9
2006	10.9	-21.9	-32.7
2007	0.1	34.5	34.5
2008	-29.9	5.4	35.3
2009	11.8	9.3	-2.6
2010	12.1	-0.3	-12.5
2011	4.9	-0.1	-5.0
2012	2.3	8.3	6.0
2013	8.9	14.5	5.7
Avg	4.3%	14.0%	9.8%
Fq > 0	83%	83%	67%

ADM vs. S&P 500 1990 to 2013

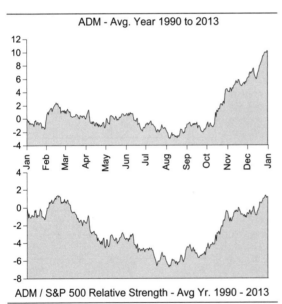

ADM - Avg. Year 1990 to 2013

ADM / S&P 500 Relative Strength - Avg Yr. 1990 - 2013

Investing in ADM for the last five months of the year has produced very strong results over the long-term. On the other hand, the first seven months leading up to the favorable season (January 1st to August 6th) has produced an average loss of 3.0% and has only been positive 42% of the time.

Investors should avoid investing in ADM for the first seven months of the year. In fact, shorting ADM during the first seven months of the year and then switching to a long position for the last five months has proven to be a profitable strategy.

Seasonal investors can take advantage of the growing interest in the agriculture sector in the second half of the year by investing at the beginning of August. The idea is to get in before everyone else and get out when interest in the sector is at a maximum, towards the end of the year.

(i) *ADM - stock symbol for Archer-Daniels-Midland which trades on the NYSE. Archer-Daniels-Midland Company engages in the manufacture and sale of protein meal, vegetable oil, corn sweeteners, flour, biodiesel, ethanol, and other value-added food and feed ingredients. Data adjusted for stock splits.*

2013-14 Strategy Performance

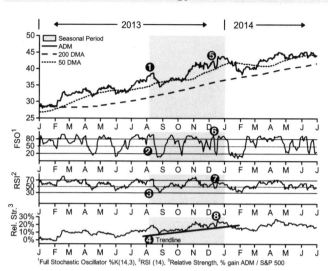

¹Full Stochastic Oscillator %K(14,3), ²RSI (14), ³Relative Strength, % gain ADM / S&P 500

Market Indices & Rates
Weekly Values**

Stock Markets	2012	2013
Dow	13,006	15,566
S&P500	1,379	1,695
Nasdaq	2,937	3,641
TSX	11,642	12,587
FTSE	5,698	6,616
DAX	6,755	8,325
Nikkei	8,636	13,934
Hang Seng	19,712	21,994

Commodities	2012	2013
Oil	89.06	105.50
Gold	1607.6	1318.5

Bond Yields	2012	2013
USA 5 Yr Treasury	0.62	1.40
USA 10 Yr T	1.54	2.64
USA 20 Yr T	2.24	3.38
Moody's Aaa	3.31	4.42
Moody's Baa	4.80	5.32
CAN 5 Yr T	1.29	1.78
CAN 10 Yr T	1.71	2.50

Money Market	2012	2013
USA Fed Funds	0.25	0.25
USA 3 Mo T-B	0.09	0.04
CAN tgt overnight rate	1.00	1.00
CAN 3 Mo T-B	0.98	1.00

Foreign Exchange	2012	2013
EUR/USD	1.23	1.33
GBP/USD	1.56	1.52
USD/CAD	1.00	1.03
USD/JPY	78.29	98.47

AUGUST

M	T	W	T	F	S	S
					1	2
3	4	5	6	7	8	9
10	11	12	13	14	15	16
17	18	19	20	21	22	23
24	25	26	27	28	29	30
31						

SEPTEMBER

M	T	W	T	F	S	S
1	2	3	4	5	6
7	8	9	10	11	12	13
14	15	16	17	18	19	20
21	22	23	24	25	26	27
28	29	30				

OCTOBER

M	T	W	T	F	S	S
		1	2	3	4
5	6	7	8	9	10	11
12	13	14	15	16	17	18
19	20	21	22	23	24	25
26	27	28	29	30	31	

ADM Performance

At the beginning of 2013, ADM was trading flat to the market. At the beginning of February, ADM announced the details of its failed bid for GrainCorp and investors reacted positively, pushing up ADM's price. After the February boost, ADM settled into a pattern of underperforming the S&P 500 until the beginning of June. At that time, ADM started to perform positively and outperform the S&P 500. It continued its strong performance up to the start of its seasonal period in August.

Technical Conditions August 7th to December 31st, 2013

Entry Strategy –Buy Position on Entry Date–

At the start of the seasonal period, ADM was trading well above its 50 day moving average❶ and both the FSO and the RSI were in overbought territory with readings above 80 and 70 respectively❷❸. At the time, ADM was outperforming the S&P 500❹.

Exit Strategy –Sell Position Early–

After initially declining at the start of its seasonal period, ADM started to perform well in September and resumed its upward trend that it had established in June. In early December, ADM turned down❺, causing the FSO to trigger an early sell signal as the FSO crossed below 80❻. At the time, the RSI crossed below 50❼ and ADM's relative strength to the S&P 500 moved back to its trendline❽.

In the end, ADM's seasonal trade was successful, producing a gain and outperforming the S&P 500.

TRANSPORTATION— ON A ROLL
①LONG (Jan23-Apr16) ②SHORT (Aug1-Oct9)
③LONG (Oct10-Nov13)

The transportation sector can provide a "hilly" ride as the seasonal trends rise and fall throughout the year.

Activity in the transportation sub-sectors in rails, airlines and freight, tends to bottom in February.

17% gain & positive 92% of the time

Increased transportation activity in the spring, coupled with a typically positive economic outlook in the first part of the year, creates a positive seasonal trend, starting January 23rd and lasting until April 16th.

The next seasonal period is a weak period, giving investors an opportunity to sell short the sector and profit from its decline. This negative seasonal period lasts from August 1st to October 9th and is largely the result of investors questioning economic growth during this time of the year.

The third seasonal period is positive and occurs from October 10th to November 13th. This trend is the result of a generally improved economic outlook at this time of the year and investors wanting to get into the sector ahead of earnings announcements.

The SP GICS Transportation Sector encompasses a wide range transportation based companies.
For more information, see www.standardandpoors.com

Transportation Sector vs. S&P 500 1990 to 2013
Negative Short ☐   Positive Long ▨

Year	Jan 23 to Apr 16 S&P 500	Jan 23 to Apr 16 Trans port	Aug 1 to Oct 9 S&P 500	Aug 1 to Oct 9 Trans port	Oct 10 to Nov 13 S&P 500	Oct 10 to Nov 13 Trans port	Compound Growth S&P 500	Compound Growth Trans port
1990	4.4 %	4.1 %	-14.3 %	-19.2 %	4.1	3.3 %	-6.9 %	28.1 %
1991	18.1	11.4	-2.8	0.5	5.5	9.0	21.0	21.6
1992	-0.5	3.7	-5.1	-9.1	4.9	14.1	-0.9	29.1
1993	2.9	9.1	2.7	-0.3	1.1	6.4	6.9	16.5
1994	-6.0	-10.7	-0.7	-9.3	1.6	0.8	-5.2	-1.6
1995	9.6	10.5	2.9	-1.3	2.4	5.0	15.5	17.6
1996	5.2	9.4	8.9	4.9	4.9	6.1	20.1	10.4
1997	-2.9	-2.0	1.7	0.9	-5.6	-5.4	-6.7	-8.2
1998	15.1	12.2	-12.2	-16.5	14.4	12.5	15.6	47.0
1999	7.7	17.7	0.6	-11.0	4.5	4.0	13.1	35.8
2000	-5.9	-2.7	-2.0	-6.0	-3.6	13.0	-11.1	16.6
2001	12.2	0.1	-12.8	-20.0	7.8	14.1	-17.4	37.0
2002	0.8	6.9	-14.8	-11.2	13.6	8.2	-2.4	28.6
2003	0.2	0.6	4.9	4.9	1.9	8.0	7.1	3.3
2004	-0.8	-2.9	1.9	6.6	5.5	11.1	6.6	0.7
2005	-2.2	-5.1	-3.1	-0.5	3.3	9.0	-2.1	3.9
2006	2.2	13.2	5.8	6.4	2.5	3.8	10.8	9.9
2007	3.2	4.8	7.6	-0.2	-5.4	-2.9	5.0	1.9
2008	4.1	19.1	-28.2	-23.5	0.2	4.0	-25.1	52.9
2009	4.6	7.2	8.5	6.7	2.1	5.9	15.8	5.9
2010	9.2	17.4	5.8	7.9	2.9	2.5	18.9	10.9
2011	2.8	2.2	-10.6	-11.8	9.4	11.4	0.6	26.9
2012	4.1	-2.0	4.5	-3.5	-4.6	-1.1	3.8	0.3
2013	5.5	3.5	-1.7	1.8	7.6	10.9	11.5	12.7
Avg.	2.9 %	5.3 %	-2.2 %	-2.2 %	3.4 %	6.4 %	3.9 %	17.0 %
Fq>0	71 %	75 %	50	38 %	83 %	88 %	63 %	92 %

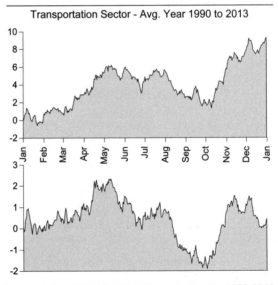

Transportation Sector - Avg. Year 1990 to 2013

Transportation / S&P 500 Rel. Strength- Avg Yr. 1990-2013

2013-14 Strategy Performance

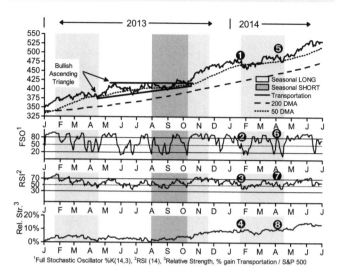

[1] Full Stochastic Oscillator %K(14,3), [2] RSI (14), [3] Relative Strength, % gain Transportation / S&P 500

Transportation Sector Performance

After performing positively in its October 10th to November 13th seasonal period in 2013, the transportation sector started to perform at market. The sector continued its market performance for December and most of January.

Technical Conditions– January 23rd to April 16th, 2014

Entry Strategy –Buy Position on Entry Date–

In the week preceding the start of its seasonal trade in January, the transportation sector turned down. At the start of its seasonal trade, the sector was above its 50 day moving average❶ and both the FSO❷ and RSI❸ were trending down. Despite these negative indicators, the sector was performing at market❹.

Exit Strategy –Sell Position Early–

After rising for most of its seasonal period, the transportation sector produced a short-term peak in early April❺ and then turned down, causing the FSO to cross below 80❻, which produced an early sell signal. At the same time, the RSI confirmed the sell signal by crossing below 70❼. The relative performance of the transportation sector to the S&P 500 was neutral❽ and did not provide an indication of possible direction.

Overall, the transportation seasonal trade was successful, producing a positive gain and outperforming the S&P 500. The early sell signal provided extra gains compared with the seasonal period sell date.

Market Indices & Rates
Weekly Values**

Stock Markets	2012	2013
Dow	13,167	15,505
S&P500	1,401	1,697
Nasdaq	3,011	3,668
TSX	11,848	12,494
FTSE	5,839	6,570
DAX	6,952	8,323
Nikkei	8,856	13,941
Hang Seng	20,108	21,840

Commodities	2012	2013
Oil	93.09	105.12
Gold	1613.6	1295.0

Bond Yields	2012	2013
USA 5 Yr Treasury	0.71	1.38
USA 10 Yr T	1.65	2.62
USA 20 Yr T	2.36	3.39
Moody's Aaa	3.45	4.44
Moody's Baa	4.89	5.34
CAN 5 Yr T	1.38	1.77
CAN 10 Yr T	1.80	2.50

Money Market	2012	2013
USA Fed Funds	0.25	0.25
USA 3 Mo T-B	0.10	0.05
CAN tgt overnight rate	1.00	1.00
CAN 3 Mo T-B	0.97	0.99

Foreign Exchange	2012	2013
EUR/USD	1.24	1.33
GBP/USD	1.56	1.54
USD/CAD	0.99	1.04
USD/JPY	78.43	97.05

AUGUST

M	T	W	T	F	S	S
					1	2
3	4	5	6	7	8	9
10	11	12	13	14	15	16
17	18	19	20	21	22	23
24	25	26	27	28	29	30
31						

SEPTEMBER

M	T	W	T	F	S	S
	1	2	3	4	5	6
7	8	9	10	11	12	13
14	15	16	17	18	19	20
21	22	23	24	25	26	27
28	29	30				

OCTOBER

M	T	W	T	F	S	S
		1	2	3	4
5	6	7	8	9	10	11
12	13	14	15	16	17	18
19	20	21	22	23	24	25
26	27	28	29	30	31	

** Weekly avg closing values- except Fed Funds & CAN overnight tgt rate weekly closing values.

AGRICULTURE MOOOVES
LAST 5 MONTHS OF THE YEAR – Aug to Dec

The agriculture sector has typically performed well during the last five months of the year (August to December).

This is the result of the major summer growing season in the northern hemisphere producing cash for the growers and subsequently, increasing sales for the farming suppliers.

70% of the time better than the S&P 500

Although this sector can represent a good opportunity, investors should be wary of the wide performance swings. Out of the twenty cycles from 1994 to 2013, during August to December, there have been six years with absolute returns greater than +25% or less than -25%, and ten years of returns greater than +10% or less than -10%. In other words, this sector is very volatile.

Agriculture* vs. S&P 500 1994 to 2013

Aug 1 to Dec 31	S&P 500	Positive Agri	Diff
1994	0.2 %	8.0 %	7.8 %
1995	9.6	31.7	22.1
1996	15.8	30.2	14.5
1997	1.7	14.7	13.0
1998	9.7	-3.4	-13.1
1999	10.6	-2.6	-13.2
2000	-7.7	68.0	75.7
2001	-5.2	12.5	17.7
2002	-3.5	6.0	9.5
2003	12.3	15.8	3.6
2004	10.0	44.6	34.6
2005	1.1	7.5	6.4
2006	11.1	-27.4	-38.5
2007	0.9	38.2	37.3
2008	-28.7	0.7	29.4
2009	12.9	4.0	-9.0
2010	14.2	9.9	-4.2
2011	-2.7	-5.9	-3.2
2012	3.4	5.0	1.6
2013	9.7	19.0	9.4
Avg.	3.8 %	13.8 %	10.1 %
Fq > 0	75 %	80 %	70 %

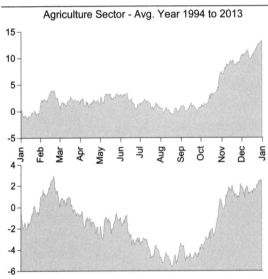

Agriculture Sector - Avg. Year 1994 to 2013

Agriculture / S&P 500 Relative Strength - Avg Yr. 1994-2013

On a year by year basis, the agriculture sector produced its biggest gain during its seasonally strong period in 2000, producing a gain of 68%. It is interesting to note that this is the same year that the technology sector's bubble burst.

After realizing that technology stocks were not going to grow to the sky, investors started to have an epiphany– that the world might be running out of food and as a result, interest in the agriculture sector started to pick up.

In the second half of 2006, the agriculture sector corrected after a strong run in the first half of the year. In 2007 and the first half of 2008, the agriculture sector once again rocketed upwards due to the increase in prices of agricultural products.

Although food prices have had some reprieve with the global slowdown, the world population is still increasing and imbalances in food supply and demand will continue to exist in the future.

Investors should consider "moooving" into the agriculture sector for the last five months of the year.

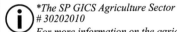

The SP GICS Agriculture Sector # 30202010
For more information on the agriculture sector, see www.standardandpoors.com

2013-14 Strategy Performance

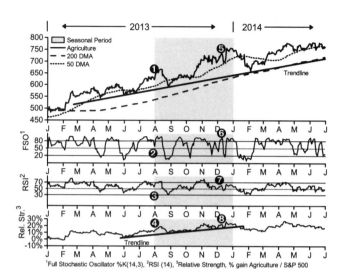

¹Full Stochastic Oscillator %K(14,3), ²RSI (14), ³Relative Strength, % gain Agriculture / S&P 500

Market Indices & Rates
Weekly Values**

Stock Markets	2012	2013
Dow	13,206	15,280
S&P500	1,409	1,677
Nasdaq	3,042	3,647
TSX	11,944	12,663
FTSE	5,843	6,551
DAX	6,974	8,396
Nikkei	8,999	13,768
Hang Seng	20,101	22,467

Commodities	2012	2013
Oil	94.42	106.92
Gold	1608.3	1339.0

Bond Yields	2012	2013
USA 5 Yr Treasury	0.78	1.50
USA 10 Yr T	1.76	2.73
USA 20 Yr T	2.49	3.50
Moody's Aaa	3.59	4.56
Moody's Baa	5.02	5.44
CAN 5 Yr T	1.47	1.89
CAN 10 Yr T	1.90	2.63

Money Market	2012	2013
USA Fed Funds	0.25	0.25
USA 3 Mo T-B	0.09	0.05
CAN tgt overnight rate	1.00	1.00
CAN 3 Mo T-B	1.00	0.99

Foreign Exchange	2012	2013
EUR/USD	1.23	1.33
GBP/USD	1.57	1.55
USD/CAD	0.99	1.03
USD/JPY	78.99	97.63

AUGUST

M	T	W	T	F	S	S
					1	2
3	4	5	6	7	8	9
10	11	12	13	14	15	16
17	18	19	20	21	22	23
24	25	26	27	28	29	30
31						

SEPTEMBER

M	T	W	T	F	S	S
	1	2	3	4	5	6
7	8	9	10	11	12	13
14	15	16	17	18	19	20
21	22	23	24	25	26	27
28	29	30				

OCTOBER

M	T	W	T	F	S	S
		1	2	3	4
5	6	7	8	9	10	11
12	13	14	15	16	17	18
19	20	21	22	23	24	25
26	27	28	29	30	31	

Agriculture Sector Performance

After starting flat for the year in January 2013, the agriculture sector produced an upward trend over the next few months. Up until the beginning of June, it was underperforming the S&P 500. In June, the sector started to gain traction and outperform the S&P 500.

Technical Conditions August 1st to December 31st, 2013

Entry Strategy –Buy Position on Start Date–

At the start of its seasonal trade, the agriculture sector was well above its 50 day moving average❶ and the FSO was close to overbought territory at 80❷. In addition, the RSI was trending down from 70❸ and the sector was performing at market❹. A few days into the trade in August 2013, the agriculture sector corrected sharply downwards to its trendline as it digested the news of the breakup between Russia's Uralkali partnership with Belarus's Belaruskali. In September, the agriculture sector started to outperform the S&P 500.

Exit Strategy –Sell Position Early–

After outperforming the S&P 500 in October, the sweet spot of the agriculture seasonal trade, the sector established a positive upwards trend. At the beginning of December, the agriculture sector turned down❺, causing the FSO to fall below 80❻ and triggering an early sell signal. At the same time, the RSI moved below 50❼. At this point, the agriculture sector had still not broken its upward trend relative to the S&P 500❽.

Overall, the agriculture seasonal trade was successful, producing a gain and outperforming the S&P 500.

PROCTER AND GAMBLE
SOMETHING FOR EVERYONE – Aug 7 to Nov 19

In investors' eyes, Procter and Gamble is a relatively defensive investment, as the company is in the consumer packaged goods business and its revenues are generated in over 180 countries. Defensive stocks have a reputation of producing sub-par performance compared with the broad market. This is not the case with PG, as on average it has outperformed the S&P 500 over the last twenty-four years during its seasonally strong period.

10.1% gain & positive 88% of the time

Interestingly, on average, the gains have been produced largely in the second half of the year. In the first half of the year, PG has been relatively flat and has underperformed the S&P 500.

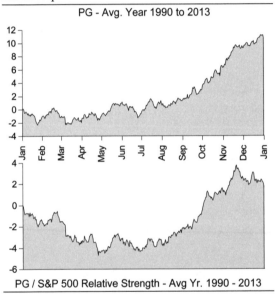

PG - Avg. Year 1990 to 2013

PG / S&P 500 Relative Strength - Avg Yr. 1990 - 2013

PG vs. S&P 500 - 1990 to 2013			
Aug 7			Positive
to Nov 19	S&P 500	PG	Diff
1990	-4.5%	8.3%	12.8%
1991	-2.9	-2.2	0.7
1992	0.7	10.1	9.4
1993	3.1	17.7	14.6
1994	1.0	19.3	18.3
1995	7.4	27.8	20.4
1996	12.0	18.6	6.5
1997	-1.6	0.2	1.9
1998	5.8	14.0	8.2
1999	9.4	18.7	9.3
2000	-6.5	31.8	38.3
2001	-4.1	11.2	15.3
2002	4.3	-0.7	-5.0
2003	7.8	8.2	0.4
2004	10.0	2.5	-7.5
2005	1.8	6.2	4.4
2006	9.5	7.4	-2.1
2007	-2.3	12.0	14.4
2008	-37.4	-8.1	29.3
2009	9.8	20.8	11.0
2010	7.0	6.7	-0.3
2011	1.4	4.4	3.0
2012	-0.5	3.2	3.7
2013	5.3	3.2	-2.2
Avg	1.5%	10.1%	8.5%
Fq > 0	67%	88%	79%

From a seasonal perspective, the best time to invest in PG has been from August 7th to November 19th. During this period, from 1990 to 2013, PG on average produced a gain of 10.1% and was positive 88% of the time. In addition, it substantially outperformed the S&P 500, generating an extra profit of 8.5% and beating its performance 79% of the time.

Investors will often seek sanctuary in defensive stocks in late summer and early autumn. Although August is not typically the worst month of the year, it does have a weak risk reward profile. With the dreaded month of September falling right after August, investors become "gun shy" and start to become more conservative in August.

This trend benefits PG as more investors switch over to defensive companies. PG's outperformance, on average, starts to occur just after it releases its fourth quarter earnings in the beginning of August.

PG continues to outperform the S&P 500 through September and October. For the S&P 500, September on average is the worst month of the year and October is the most volatile month. The outperformance of PG continues into mid-November.

PG's seasonally strong period extends past the seasonal period for the consumer staples sector. It is possible that investors wait until after PG's first quarter results are released in the beginning of November before adjusting their portfolios.

(i) * The Procter and Gamble Company is a consumer packaged goods company. Its products are sold in more than 180 countries. Data adjusted for stock splits.

2013-14 Strategy Performance

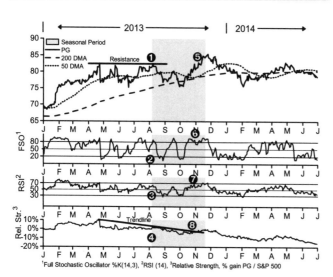

¹Full Stochastic Oscillator %K(14,3), ²RSI (14), ³Relative Strength, % gain PG / S&P 500

Procter and Gamble (PG) Performance

At the beginning of 2013, PG performed strongly and outperformed the S&P 500. At the time, the market was favoring defensive sectors, including the consumer staples sector. In late April, PG started to underperform the S&P 500, as the S&P 500 started to appreciate and PG provided flat performance.

Technical Conditions August 7th to November 19th, 2013
Entry Strategy –Buy Position on Start Date–

At the start of its seasonal period, PG was pushing up against its resistance level❶ and the FSO was just shy of indicating an overbought condition with a reading just under 80❷. The RSI was above 50❸ with a positive trend and PG was performing at market❹.

Exit Strategy – Sell Position Early–

After underperforming in August and September, PG bounced sharply in October (typically a strong month for consumer staples). Towards the end of October, PG corrected slightly❺, causing the FSO to cross below 80❻ and trigger an early sell signal. At the time, the RSI was positive and above 50❼. After the early sell signal, PG continued to perform positively and started to outperform the S&P 500❽. Just after the end of its seasonal period in November, PG started to perform negatively and resumed its underperforming trend relative to the S&P 500.

Overall, the PG trade produced a gain, but underperformed the S&P 500.

** Weekly avg closing values- except Fed Funds & CAN overnight tgt rate weekly closing values.

Market Indices & Rates Weekly Values**		
Stock Markets	**2012**	**2013**
Dow	13,173	14,977
S&P500	1,412	1,652
Nasdaq	3,068	3,620
TSX	12,091	12,654
FTSE	5,802	6,450
DAX	7,012	8,353
Nikkei	9,142	13,521
Hang Seng	20,021	22,002
Commodities	**2012**	**2013**
Oil	96.23	105.51
Gold	1645.8	1370.7
Bond Yields	**2012**	**2013**
USA 5 Yr Treasury	0.75	1.64
USA 10 Yr T	1.74	2.86
USA 20 Yr T	2.47	3.61
Moody's Aaa	3.54	4.67
Moody's Baa	4.96	5.55
CAN 5 Yr T	1.43	1.96
CAN 10 Yr T	1.87	2.72
Money Market	**2012**	**2013**
USA Fed Funds	0.25	0.25
USA 3 Mo T-B	0.10	0.04
CAN tgt overnight rate	1.00	1.00
CAN 3 Mo T-B	1.01	0.99
Foreign Exchange	**2012**	**2013**
EUR/USD	1.25	1.34
GBP/USD	1.58	1.56
USD/CAD	0.99	1.04
USD/JPY	78.89	97.99

AUGUST

M	T	W	T	F	S	S
					1	2
3	4	5	6	7	8	9
10	11	12	13	14	15	16
17	18	19	20	21	22	23
24	25	26	27	28	29	30
31						

SEPTEMBER

M	T	W	T	F	S	S
	1	2	3	4	5	6
7	8	9	10	11	12	13
14	15	16	17	18	19	20
21	22	23	24	25	26	27
28	29	30				

OCTOBER

M	T	W	T	F	S	S
		1	2	3	4	
5	6	7	8	9	10	11
12	13	14	15	16	17	18
19	20	21	22	23	24	25
26	27	28	29	30	31	

HEALTH CARE
AUGUST PRESCRIPTION RENEWAL
August 15th to October 18th

Health care stocks have traditionally been classified as defensive stocks because of their stable earnings. Pharmaceutical and other health care companies typically still perform relatively well in an economic downturn.

Even in tough times, people still need to take their medication. As a result, investors have typically found comfort in this sector starting in the late summer and riding the momentum into mid-October.

2.7% extra & 16 out of 24 times better than the S&P 500

Health Care* vs. S&P 500 Performance 1990 to 2013			
Aug 15 to Oct 18	S&P 500	Positive Health Care	Diff
1990	-9.9 %	-1.3 %	8.6 %
1991	0.7	1.3	0.6
1992	-1.9	-9.0	-7.1
1993	4.1	13.5	9.5
1994	1.2	7.2	6.0
1995	4.9	11.7	6.7
1996	7.4	9.4	2.1
1997	2.1	5.8	3.7
1998	-0.6	3.0	3.6
1999	-5.5	-0.5	5.0
2000	-10.0	6.9	16.9
2001	-10.0	-0.4	9.6
2002	-3.8	2.4	6.2
2003	4.9	-0.5	-5.4
2004	4.6	-0.8	-5.4
2005	-4.2	-3.1	1.2
2006	7.7	6.4	-1.3
2007	8.0	6.0	-2.0
2008	-27.3	-20.4	6.8
2009	8.3	5.1	-3.3
2010	9.8	8.2	-1.6
2011	4.0	3.2	-0.8
2012	3.8	6.9	3.1
2013	3.5	4.3	0.8
Avg	0.1 %	2.7 %	2.7 %
Fq > 0	63 %	67 %	67 %

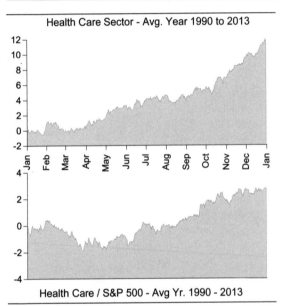

Health Care Sector - Avg. Year 1990 to 2013

Health Care / S&P 500 - Avg Yr. 1990 - 2013

From August 15th to October 18th (1990 to 2013), health care stocks have had a tendency to outperform the S&P 500 on a yearly basis.

During this time period, the broad market (S&P 500) produced an average gained 0.1%, compared with the health care stocks that produced a gain of 2.7%.

Despite competing with a runaway market in 2003 and legal problems which required drugs to be withdrawn from the market in 2004, the sector has beaten the S&P 500 sixteen out of twenty-four times from 1990 to 2013 in its seasonal period.

The real benefit of investing in the health care sector has been the positive returns that have been generated when the market has typically been negative.

Since 1950, August and September have been the worst two-month combination for gains in the broad stock market.

Having an alternative sector to invest in during the summer and early autumn is a valuable asset.

> *Alternate Strategy—As the health care sector has had a tendency to perform at par with the broad market from late October to early December, an alternative strategy is to continue holding the health care sector during this time period if the fundamentals or technicals are favorable.*

> *Health Care SP GIC Sector# 35: An index designed to represent a cross section of health care companies. For more information on the health care sector, see www.standardandpoors.com.*

2013-14 Strategy Performance

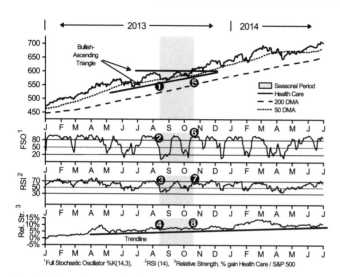

¹Full Stochastic Oscillator %K(14,3),   ²RSI (14),   ³Relative Strength, % gain Health Care / S&P 500

Health Care Sector Performance

At the beginning of 2013, the health care sector performed strongly as investors favored the defensive sectors over the cyclical sectors, which is not typical for this time of the year. The fact that the defensive sectors, such as health care, were outperforming, shows how apprehensive investors were about the market conditions at the time.

Technical Conditions August 15th to October 18th, 2013

Entry Strategy –Buy Position on Start Date–

At the start of its seasonal period, the health care sector was above its 50 day moving average, but its price action was turning down❶. At the same time, both the FSO and RSI were declining❷❸. On a positive note, the health care sector was still outperforming the S&P 500❹.

Exit Strategy –Sell Position on Exit Date–

During its seasonal period, the health care sector was trying to break through its resistance level. Its low points, bouncing off its 50 day moving average were increasing and as a result the health care sector was tracing out a bullish ascending triangle pattern. At the end of the seasonal period, the health care sector broke through the top of the ascending triangle❺. At the same time, the FSO was above 80❻ and the RSI was above 50❼ and trending upwards. In addition, the health care sector was still outperforming the S&P 500❽. All of the technical indicators were positive, and an argument could have been made to hold the sector position longer. Overall, the health care trade was positive and outperformed the S&P 500.

WEEK 35

Market Indices & Rates
Weekly Values**

Stock Markets	2012	2013
Dow	13,085	14,840
S&P500	1,407	1,639
Nasdaq	3,069	3,608
TSX	11,981	12,663
FTSE	5,738	5,153
DAX	6,985	8,227
Nikkei	9,002	13,473
Hang Seng	19,687	21,768

Commodities	2012	2013
Oil	95.68	108.30
Gold	1659.3	1410.3

Bond Yields	2012	2013
USA 5 Yr Treasury	0.67	1.60
USA 10 Yr T	1.63	2.76
USA 20 Yr T	2.35	3.48
Moody's Aaa	3.41	4.54
Moody's Baa	4.83	5.40
CAN 5 Yr T	1.37	1.92
CAN 10 Yr T	1.79	2.61

Money Market	2012	2013
USA Fed Funds	0.25	0.25
USA 3 Mo T-B	0.09	0.03
CAN tgt overnight rate	1.00	1.00
CAN 3 Mo T-B	1.03	0.99

Foreign Exchange	2012	2013
EUR/USD	1.25	1.33
GBP/USD	1.58	1.55
USD/CAD	0.99	1.05
USD/JPY	78.60	97.94

AUGUST

M	T	W	T	F	S	S
					1	2
3	4	5	6	7	8	9
10	11	12	13	14	15	16
17	18	19	20	21	22	23
24	25	26	27	28	29	30
31						

SEPTEMBER

M	T	W	T	F	S	S
	1	2	3	4	5	6
7	8	9	10	11	12	13
14	15	16	17	18	19	20
21	22	23	24	25	26	27
28	29	30				

OCTOBER

M	T	W	T	F	S	S
			1	2	3	4
5	6	7	8	9	10	11
12	13	14	15	16	17	18
19	20	21	22	23	24	25
26	27	28	29	30	31	

SEPTEMBER

	MONDAY	TUESDAY	WEDNESDAY
WEEK 36	31	**1** 29	**2** 28
WEEK 37	**7** 23 USA Market Closed- Labour Day CAN Market Closed- Labour Day	**8** 22	**9** 21
WEEK 38	**14** 16	**15** 15	**16** 14
WEEK 39	**21** 9	**22** 8	**23** 7
WEEK 40	**28** 2	**29** 1	**30**

THURSDAY	FRIDAY
3 27	**4** 26
10 20	**11** 19
17 13	**18** 12
24 6	**25** 5
1	2

OCTOBER

M	T	W	T	F	S	S
		1	2	3	4	
5	6	7	8	9	10	11
12	13	14	15	16	17	18
19	20	21	22	23	24	25
26	27	28	29	30	31	

NOVEMBER

M	T	W	T	F	S	S
						1
2	3	4	5	6	7	8
9	10	11	12	13	14	15
16	17	18	19	20	21	22
23	24	25	26	27	28	29
30						

DECEMBER

M	T	W	T	F	S	S
	1	2	3	4	5	6
7	8	9	10	11	12	13
14	15	16	17	18	19	20
21	22	23	24	25	26	27
28	29	30	31			

JANUARY

M	T	W	T	F	S	S
				1	2	3
4	5	6	7	8	9	10
11	12	13	14	15	16	17
18	19	20	21	22	23	24
26	27	28	28	29	30	31

SEPTEMBER
S U M M A R Y

	Dow Jones	S&P 500	Nasdaq	TSX Comp
Month Rank	12	12	12	12
# Up	26	29	23	12
# Down	38	35	19	17
% Pos	41	45	55	41
% Avg. Gain	-0.8	-0.5	-0.5	-1.5

Dow & S&P 1950-2013, Nasdaq 1972-2013, TSX 1985-2013

S&P500 Cumulative Daily Gains for Avg Month 1950 to 2013

♦ September has the reputation of being the worst month of the year. From 1950 to 2013, September produced an average loss of 0.5% and was only positive 44% of the time. ♦ The last part of September tends to be negative. ♦ When a rally occurs in September, it is usually the result of a large external event, such as an increase in monetary stimulus. ♦ In September 2013, the market responded positively to the U.S. Federal Reserve's decision to continue its bond purchases at the current pace rather than to start tapering as expected.

BEST / WORST SEPTEMBER BROAD MKTS. 2004-2013

BEST SEPTEMBER MARKETS
♦ Russell 2000 (2010) 12.3%
♦ Nasdaq (2010) 12.0%
♦ Nikkei 225 (2005) 9.4%

WORST SEPTEMBER MARKETS
♦ TSX Comp. (2008) -14.7%
♦ Nikkei 225 (2008) -13.9%
♦ FTSE 100 (2008) -13.0%

Index Values End of Month

	2004	2005	2006	2007	2008	2009	2010	2011	2012	2013
Dow	10,080	10,569	11,679	13,896	10,851	9,712	10,788	10,913	13,437	15,130
S&P 500	1,115	1,229	1,336	1,527	1,166	1,057	1,141	1,131	1,441	1,682
Nasdaq	1,897	2,152	2,258	2,702	2,092	2,122	2,369	2,415	3,116	3,771
TSX Comp.	8,668	11,012	11,761	14,099	11,753	11,395	12,369	11,624	12,317	12,787
Russell 1000	1,145	1,285	1,391	1,597	1,219	1,115	1,211	1,198	1,526	1,806
Russell 2000	1,424	1,660	1,803	2,002	1,689	1,502	1,680	1,601	2,081	2,669
FTSE 100	4,571	5,478	5,961	6,467	4,902	5,134	5,549	5,128	5,742	6,462
Nikkei 225	10,824	13,574	16,128	16,786	11,260	10,133	9,369	8,700	8,870	14,456

Percent Gain for September

	2004	2005	2006	2007	2008	2009	2010	2011	2012	2013
Dow	-0.9	0.8	2.6	4.0	-6.0	2.3	7.7	-6.0	2.6	2.2
S&P 500	0.9	0.7	2.5	3.6	-9.1	3.6	8.8	-7.2	2.4	3.0
Nasdaq	3.2	0.0	3.4	4.0	-11.6	5.6	12.0	-6.4	1.6	5.1
TSX Comp.	3.5	3.2	-2.6	3.2	-14.7	4.8	3.8	-9.0	3.1	1.1
Russell 1000	1.1	0.8	2.3	3.7	-9.8	3.9	9.0	-7.6	2.4	3.3
Russell 2000	4.6	0.2	0.7	1.6	-8.1	5.6	12.3	-11.4	3.1	6.2
FTSE 100	2.5	3.4	0.9	2.6	-13.0	4.6	6.2	-4.9	0.5	0.8
Nikkei 225	-2.3	9.4	-0.1	1.3	-13.9	-3.4	6.2	-2.8	0.3	8.0

September Market Avg. Performance 2004 to 2013[1]

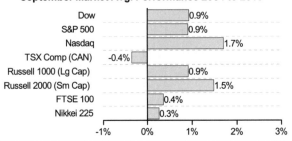

Dow	0.9%
S&P 500	0.9%
Nasdaq	1.7%
TSX Comp (CAN)	-0.4%
Russell 1000 (Lg Cap)	0.9%
Russell 2000 (Sm Cap)	1.5%
FTSE 100	0.4%
Nikkei 225	0.3%

Interest Corner Sep[2]

	Fed Funds % [3]	3 Mo. T-Bill % [4]	10 Yr % [5]	20 Yr % [6]
2013	0.25	0.02	2.64	3.41
2012	0.25	0.10	1.65	2.42
2011	0.25	0.02	1.92	2.66
2010	0.25	0.16	2.53	3.38
2009	0.25	0.14	3.31	4.02

(1) Russell Data provided by Russell (2) Federal Reserve Bank of St. Louis- end of month values (3) Target rate set by FOMC (4)(5)(6) Constant yield maturities.

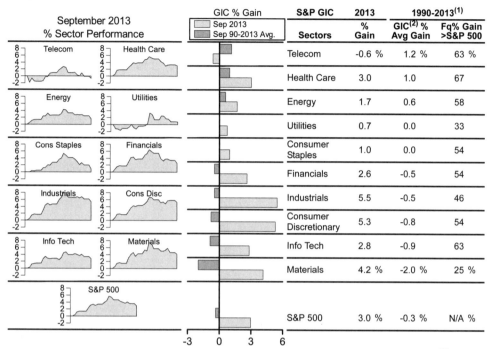

S&P GIC Sectors	2013 % Gain	1990-2013[1] GIC[2] % Avg Gain	Fq% Gain >S&P 500
Telecom	-0.6 %	1.2 %	63 %
Health Care	3.0	1.0	67
Energy	1.7	0.6	58
Utilities	0.7	0.0	33
Consumer Staples	1.0	0.0	54
Financials	2.6	-0.5	54
Industrials	5.5	-0.5	46
Consumer Discretionary	5.3	-0.8	54
Info Tech	2.8	-0.9	63
Materials	4.2 %	-2.0 %	25 %
S&P 500	3.0 %	-0.3 %	N/A %

Sector Commentary

♦ In September 2013, the Federal Reserve announced that it was going to continue the pace of its bond purchasing program instead of tapering it. As was expected, the market immediately switched to a risk-on mode.♦ The result was that the cyclical sectors of the market that typically do not perform well in September, produced strong gains in the month. ♦The industrial sector led the way with a 5.5% gain in September. ♦ The telecom sector was the only major S&P GIC sector to produce a loss. It typically is the top performing sector of the market in September.

Sub-Sector Commentary

♦ The homebuilders sub-sector benefited from the Federal Reserve's unexpected loose monetary policy, producing a gain of 9.1%. ♦ The biotech sector typically finishes its seasonal run in mid-September, but managed to keep outperforming the S&P 500 until the end of the month. ♦ After performing well in its seasonal period in earlier months, gold started to retreat at the beginning of September and ended up with a loss of 4.9%.

SELECTED SUB-SECTORS[3]			
Gold (London PM)	-4.9 %	3.0 %	67 %
Silver	-8.3	2.3	71
Biotech (1993-2013)	8.0	2.1	67
Pharma	2.2	1.0	63
Software & Services	4.1	0.8	71
Agriculture (1994-2013)	4.6	0.0	55
Home-builders	9.1	-0.5	63
Retail	4.7	-0.5	46
Transportation	5.3	-0.9	50
Banks	0.2	-0.9	54
Railroads	3.1	-1.0	33
Metals & Mining	4.4	-1.6	46
Chemicals	4.8	-1.8	29
SOX (1995-2013)	7.2	-3.1	37
Steel	8.1	-3.5	46

(1) Sector data provided by Standard and Poors (2) GIC is short form for Global Industry Classification (3) Sub Sector data provided by Standard and Poors, except where marked by symbol.

Campbell Soup for Autumn
September 22nd to November 17th

The consumer staples sector typically performs well in late September and into October. This period tends to be the most volatile period of the year for the broad stock market and investors look for companies with stable earnings in times of market volatility.

Campbell Soup, a consumer staples company, helps provide comfort to investors from September 22nd to November 17th. In this time period, from 1990 to 2013, Campbell Soup has produced an average gain of 6.2% and has been positive 83% of the time.

6.2% gain & positive 83% of the time

Campbell Soup performs well at this time of the year not only because it is part of the consumer staples sector, but also because it typically reports its full year earnings at the beginning of September (fiscal year-end is July 31st). Once the year-end earnings are reported, there is not a lot of information that can move the price of Campbell Soup.

Typically, stocks will move on the potential of good news. In the case of Campbell Soup, "boring is better." In times of market volatility, investors are attracted to dividend yield and do not want any negative surprises.

CPB* vs. S&P 500 1990 to 2013			
			Positive
Sep 22 to Nov 17	S&P 500	CPB	Diff
1990	1.9%	14.6%	12.7%
1991	-1.4	1.5	2.8
1992	-0.7	4.4	5.1
1993	2.6	13.2	10.6
1994	0.5	18.2	17.7
1995	2.9	6.8	3.9
1996	7.4	6.6	-0.8
1997	-0.5	9.0	9.5
1998	11.3	10.0	-1.2
1999	7.9	11.4	3.5
2000	-5.6	28.8	34.4
2001	17.9	12.3	-5.6
2002	7.6	2.1	-5.5
2003	0.7	-6.3	-7.0
2004	4.7	3.4	-1.3
2005	2.7	0.3	-2.4
2006	6.3	4.1	-2.2
2007	-4.4	-0.4	4.0
2008	-32.2	-2.4	29.8
2009	4.3	2.4	-1.9
2010	3.4	-5.1	-8.5
2011	4.2	8.9	4.7
2012	-6.9	4.4	11.3
2013	5.2	1.5	-3.7
Avg	1.7%	6.2%	4.6%
Fq > 0	71%	83%	54%

S&P produced a loss, Campbell Soup also produced a loss.

It is important to note that from 2001 to 2006, Campbell Soup underperformed the S&P 500 in its seasonal time period and in all cases, the S&P 500 produced a gain.

Buying Campbell Soup during its period of seasonal performance does not ensure that you will outperform the S&P 500. In fact, Campbell Soup has only outperformed the S&P 500, 54% of the time. On the other hand, during its seasonal period, Campbell Soup has provided a strong average gain, been positive 83% of the time and has not had the large drawdowns of the S&P 500. In autumn, Campbell Soup is good for the soul and the pocketbook.

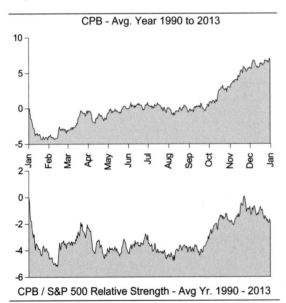

CPB - Avg. Year 1990 to 2013

CPB / S&P 500 Relative Strength - Avg Yr. 1990 - 2013

From 1990 to 2013, in the seasonal time period for Campbell Soup, every time that the S&P 500 has produced a loss, Campbell Soup has outperformed it. In fact, in only two out of the seven instances where the

 CPB - stock symbol for Campbell Soup Company, which trades on the NYSE, adjusted for splits.

2013-14 Strategy Performance

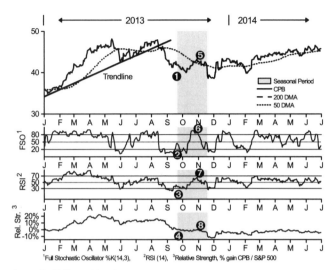

¹Full Stochastic Oscillator %K(14,3),   ²RSI (14),   ³Relative Strength, % gain CPB / S&P 500

WEEK 36

Market Indices & Rates
Weekly Values**

Stock Markets	2012	2013
Dow	13,171	14,906
S&P500	1,420	1,651
Nasdaq	3,104	3,645
TSX	12,085	12,791
FTSE	5,732	6,506
DAX	7,059	8,226
Nikkei	8,758	13,906
Hang Seng	19,429	22,423

Commodities	2012	2013
Oil	95.65	108.67
Gold	1701.5	1390.8

Bond Yields	2012	2013
USA 5 Yr Treasury	0.64	1.76
USA 10 Yr T	1.64	2.92
USA 20 Yr T	2.36	3.59
Moody's Aaa	3.43	4.67
Moody's Baa	4.82	5.49
CAN 5 Yr T	1.37	2.06
CAN 10 Yr T	1.79	2.72

Money Market	2012	2013
USA Fed Funds	0.25	0.25
USA 3 Mo T-B	0.11	0.02
CAN tgt overnight rate	1.00	1.00
CAN 3 Mo T-B	1.00	1.00

Foreign Exchange	2012	2013
EUR/USD	1.26	1.32
GBP/USD	1.59	1.56
USD/CAD	0.98	1.05
USD/JPY	78.44	99.57

Campbell Soup Performance

Campbell Soup does not typically rocket ahead of the market with substantial outperformance. In the beginning half of 2013, rumors were being spread in the market place that Campbell Soup was a potential take-over target for Warren Buffett's Berkshire Hathaway. As a result, Campbell Soup strongly outperformed the S&P 500. After Warren Buffett bought out Heinz, investors looked to Campbell Soup as a similar company that might be on Buffett's buyout list and wanted to get into the company before Buffett did.

Technical Conditions September 22nd to November 17th, 2013

Entry Strategy –Buy Position on Entry Date–

In August 2013, the rumors of Buffett buying Campbell Soup were dying down. As a result, Campbell Soup corrected and and at the start of its seasonal period, it was below its 200 day moving average❶, and both the FSO and RSI were below 50❷❸. In addition, the relative performance continued its downward trend❹.

Exit Strategy –Sell Position Early–

After a bounce in October (when consumer staples stocks tend to perform well), Campbell Soup started to correct once again❺. As a result, the FSO crossed below 80❻, triggering an early sell signal. At the same time, the RSI turned down from 70❼ and Campbell Soup resumed its underperformance relative to the S&P 500❽.

SEPTEMBER

M	T	W	T	F	S	S
	1	2	3	4	5	6
7	8	9	10	11	12	13
14	15	16	17	18	19	20
21	22	23	24	25	26	27
28	29	30				

OCTOBER

M	T	W	T	F	S	S
		1	2	3	4	
5	6	7	8	9	10	11
12	13	14	15	16	17	18
19	20	21	22	23	24	25
26	27	28	29	30	31	

NOVEMBER

M	T	W	T	F	S	S
						1
2	3	4	5	6	7	8
9	10	11	12	13	14	15
16	17	18	19	20	21	22
23	24	25	26	27	28	29
30						

SOFTWARE
POSITIVE ACTION TRIPLE PLAY
①Jan1-Jan19 ②Jun1-Jun30 ③Oct10-Dec5

The software sector starts off the year on a strong seasonal note as it echoes the outperformance of the technology sector in the first part of January.

15.6% gain & positive 83% of time

The software sector's next period of seasonal strength occurs from June 1st to June 30th. This mid-summer period of outperformance is largely the result of one company: Oracle, which is considered a bellwether for the sector.

Oracle, a software solutions based company, realizes a disproportionate amount of sales just before their year-end on May 31st. They announce their year-end earnings approximately in the third week of June. At this time of the year, the market has not started its "official" earnings season and investors gravitate to Oracle before it announces earnings in June, anticipating positive announcements.

The software sector has its biggest seasonal run starting in October as investors enter the sector to take advantage of the corporate purchases before year-end, and the positive impact on earnings as a result.

Software vs. S&P 500 1990 to 2013   Positive ☐

Year	Jan 1 to Jan 19 S&P 500	Jan 1 to Jan 19 Software	Jun 1 to Jun 30 S&P 500	Jun 1 to Jun 30 Software	Oct 10 to Dec 5 S&P 500	Oct 10 to Dec 5 Software	Compound Growth S&P 500	Compound Growth Software
1990	-4.0 %	-4.0 %	-0.9 %	1.8 %	8.1	22.7 %	2.9 %	19.8 %
1991	0.6	-0.4	-4.8	-4.2	0.2	3.0	-4.1	-1.7
1992	0.4	6.1	-1.7	-6.8	7.3	14.5	5.9	13.2
1993	-0.1	1.6	0.1	2.6	1.0	17.0	0.9	22.0
1994	1.7	6.1	-2.7	-2.8	-0.4	9.5	-1.4	12.9
1995	1.7	3.7	2.1	7.6	6.8	15.3	10.9	28.6
1996	-0.7	4.4	0.2	2.5	6.8	8.9	6.4	16.5
1997	4.8	2.0	4.4	2.0	1.4	0.9	10.8	5.0
1998	-0.9	1.4	3.9	21.4	19.5	30.3	23.1	60.4
1999	1.9	8.8	5.4	9.4	7.3	14.3	15.2	35.9
2000	-0.9	-8.8	2.4	12.5	-1.8	-4.3	-0.4	-1.8
2001	1.7	29.3	-2.5	9.2	10.8	25.8	9.8	77.5
2002	-1.8	2.6	-7.3	2.5	16.7	29.2	6.3	35.9
2003	2.5	1.3	1.1	1.4	2.2	-5.3	5.9	-2.7
2004	2.5	2.9	1.8	6.0	6.2	9.6	10.8	19.6
2005	-2.3	-4.0	0.0	-2.3	5.5	9.7	3.1	3.0
2006	2.9	1.9	0.0	2.4	4.8	6.6	7.8	11.2
2007	0.9	2.3	-1.8	-1.5	-5.1	2.9	-6.0	3.7
2008	-9.8	-10.3	-8.6	-7.5	-3.7	-9.7	-20.6	-25.1
2009	-5.9	-1.6	0.0	4.6	3.2	9.6	-2.8	12.8
2010	3.2	0.6	-5.4	-6.2	5.1	8.1	2.6	2.0
2011	1.9	3.7	-1.8	-0.7	8.8	7.0	8.9	10.2
2012	4.5	3.6	4.0	4.5	-2.2	-3.1	6.2	4.8
2013	4.2	3.0	-1.5	-2.9	7.8	10.3	10.6	10.3
Avg.	0.4 %	2.3 %	-0.6 %	2.3 %	4.8 %	9.7 %	4.7 %	15.6 %
Fq>0	63 %	75 %	50	63 %	79 %	83 %	75 %	83 %

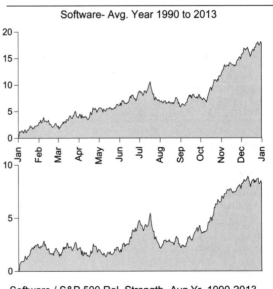

Software- Avg. Year 1990 to 2013

Software / S&P 500 Rel. Strength- Avg. Yr. 1990-2013

2013-14 Strategy Performance

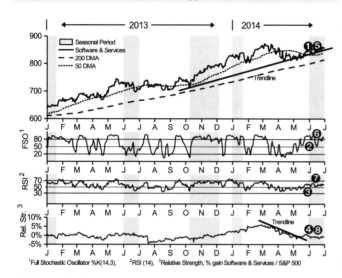

¹Full Stochastic Oscillator %K(14,3),   ²RSI (14),   ³Relative Strength, % gain Software & Services / S&P 500

Software Performance

After outperforming the S&P 500 during its seasonal periods in October to December and in January, the software & services sector (software sector), started to underperform in March of 2014. The software sector broke its downward trend relative to the S&P 500 in May, setting up well for its seasonal trade.

Technical Conditions June 1st to June 30th, 2014

Entry Strategy –Buy Position on Entry Date–

At the start of its seasonal trade, the software sector was trading above its 50 day moving average and trending upwards❶, the FSO was in overbought territory with a reading above 80❷ and the RSI was positive, with a reading above 50❸. In addition, the software sector was performing at market❹. Overall, the technical indicators pointed to a successful trade.

Exit Strategy – Sell Position Early–

Shortly after the software sector seasonal period started, the sector was above its trendline and its 50 day moving average❺. An early sell signal was triggered when the FSO turned below 80❻. At the time, the RSI was above 50❼ and turning down and the software sector was underperforming the S&P 500❽.

Overall, the June software trade was not successful, producing a loss and underperforming the S&P 500.

WEEK 37

Market Indices & Rates
Weekly Values**

Stock Markets	2012	2013
Dow	13,409	15,251
S&P500	1,445	1,683
Nasdaq	3,133	3,720
TSX	12,306	12,786
FTSE	5,821	6,575
DAX	7,318	8,444
Nikkei	8,958	14,369
Hang Seng	20,088	22,907

Commodities	2012	2013
Oil	97.61	108.26
Gold	1742.9	1351.7

Bond Yields	2012	2013
USA 5 Yr Treasury	0.68	1.73
USA 10 Yr T	1.76	2.92
USA 20 Yr T	2.52	3.61
Moody's Aaa	3.55	4.70
Moody's Baa	4.94	5.54
CAN 5 Yr T	1.43	2.13
CAN 10 Yr T	1.89	2.78

Money Market	2012	2013
USA Fed Funds	0.25	0.25
USA 3 Mo T-B	0.11	0.02
CAN tgt overnight rate	1.00	1.00
CAN 3 Mo T-B	1.00	0.99

Foreign Exchange	2012	2013
EUR/USD	1.29	1.33
GBP/USD	1.61	1.58
USD/CAD	0.97	1.03
USD/JPY	77.96	99.76

SEPTEMBER
M	T	W	T	F	S	S
	1	2	3	4	5	6
7	8	9	10	11	12	13
14	15	16	17	18	19	20
21	22	23	24	25	26	27
28	29	30				

OCTOBER
M	T	W	T	F	S	S
		1	2	3	4	
5	6	7	8	9	10	11
12	13	14	15	16	17	18
19	20	21	22	23	24	25
26	27	28	29	30	31	

NOVEMBER
M	T	W	T	F	S	S
						1
2	3	4	5	6	7	8
9	10	11	12	13	14	15
16	17	18	19	20	21	22
23	24	25	26	27	28	29
30						

INFORMATION TECHNOLOGY
USE IT OR LOSE IT
October 9th to January 17th

Information technology– the sector that investors love to love and love to hate. In recent years, most investors have made and lost money in this sector. When the sector is performing well, it can perform really well. When it is performing poorly, it can perform really poorly.

4.8% extra compared with the S&P 500

Technology stocks get bid up at the end of the year for three reasons.

First, a lot of companies operate with year end budgets and if they do not spend the money in their budget, they lose it.

In the last few months of the year, whatever money they have, they spend. Hence, the saying "use it or lose it."

The number one purchase item for this budget flush is technology equipment. An upgrade in technology equipment is something which a large number of employees in the company can benefit from and is easy to justify.

Second, consumers indirectly help push up technology stocks by purchasing electronic items during the holiday season.

Retail sales ramp up significantly on Black Friday, the Friday after Thanksgiving. Investors anticipate the upswing in sales and buy technology stocks.

Third, the "Conference Effect" helps maintain the momentum in January. This phenomenon is the result of investors increasing positions ahead of major conferences in order to benefit from positive announcements.

In the case of the information technology sector, investors increase their holdings ahead of the Las Vegas Consumer Electronics Conference that typically occurs in the second week of January.

Info Tech & Nasdaq vs S&P 500
Oct 9 to Jan 17, 1989/90-2013/14

	S&P 500	Info Tech	Nasdaq	Diff IT-S&P500	Diff Nas-S&P500
				Positive	
1989/90	-6.0 %	-6.9 %	-9.3 %	-1.0 %	-3.3 %
1990/91	4.6	13.4	8.0	8.8	3.3
1991/92	10.0	16.4	21.2	6.4	11.2
1992/93	7.2	11.2	21.5	4.0	14.3
1993/94	2.8	12.5	3.7	9.7	0.8
1994/95	3.3	16.0	3.0	12.7	-0.3
1995/96	4.1	-8.9	-1.4	-13.0	-5.5
1996/97	10.8	21.2	8.8	10.4	-2.0
1997/98	-1.3	-14.2	-10.3	-12.9	-9.0
1998/99	29.6	71.8	65.5	42.2	35.9
1999/00	9.7	29.2	40.8	19.5	31.1
2001/01	-5.6	-21.7	-20.2	-16.1	-14.5
2001/02	7.2	26.8	23.7	19.6	16.5
2002/03	12.9	30.0	21.9	17.0	8.9
2003/04	10.3	14.2	13.0	4.0	2.8
2004/05	5.6	6.8	8.7	1.2	3.2
2005/06	7.3	9.7	10.2	2.4	2.9
2006/07	6.0	7.1	7.8	1.1	1.8
2007/08	-14.1	-14.9	-15.8	-0.7	-1.7
2008/09	-13.7	-12.0	-12.1	1.6	1.6
2009/10	6.6	9.9	7.7	3.3	1.1
2010/11	11.0	13.6	14.7	2.6	3.7
2011/12	12.0	8.4	10.0	-3.6	-1.9
2012/13	1.7	-2.9	0.8	-4.7	-1.0
2013/14	11.1	15.1	13.6	4.0	2.5
Avg	5.3 %	10.1 %	9.4 %	4.8 %	4.1 %
Fq > 0	80 %	72 %	76 %	72 %	64 %

InfoTech Sector % Gain Avg. Year 1990 to 2013

Info Tech / S&P 500 - Avg Yr. 1990 - 2013

> (i) *Information Technology SP GIC Sector 45:*
> *An index designed to represent a cross section of information technology companies.*

2013-14 Strategy Performance

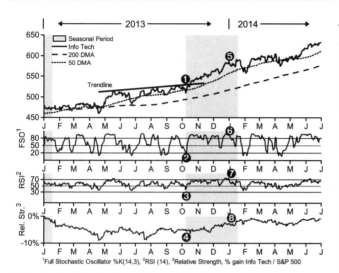

Information Technology Sector Performance

For the first seven months of 2013, the technology sector underperformed. After outperforming in August, the technology sector settled into a pattern of market performance going into its seasonal period.

Technical Conditions October 9th to January 17th, 2014

Entry Strategy –Buy on Entry Date–

Just before the start date of its seasonal period, the technology sector turned down. At the start of its seasonal period, the technology sector was at its 50 day moving average❶, with the FSO bouncing off 20❷ and the RSI crossing above 30❸. As all this was occurring, the technology sector was performing at market❹. It was not until late November that the technology sector started to outperform.

Exit Strategy – Sell Position Early–

After a brief spurt of outperformance in November and December, the technology sector pulled back❺, causing the FSO to cross below 80❻ and triggering an early sell signal and the RSI to fall below 70❼. The weak price action caused the technology sector to slightly underperform the S&P 500❽.

Overall, the trade was successful, producing a gain and outperforming the S&P 500. Staying in the trade past the early sell date proved to be more profitable as the technology sector had a spike at the end of its seasonal period.

** Weekly avg closing values- except Fed Funds & CAN overnight tgt rate weekly closing values.

WEEK 38

Market Indices & Rates
Weekly Values**

Stock Markets	2012	2013
Dow	13,574	15,558
S&P500	1,460	1,712
Nasdaq	3,179	3,762
TSX	12,420	12,863
FTSE	5,871	6,595
DAX	7,397	8,643
Nikkei	9,138	14,581
Hang Seng	20,686	23,263

Commodities	2012	2013
Oil	93.67	106.23
Gold	1769.9	1330.4

Bond Yields	2012	2013
USA 5 Yr Treasury	0.70	1.54
USA 10 Yr T	1.81	2.79
USA 20 Yr T	2.60	3.53
Moody's Aaa	3.55	4.67
Moody's Baa	4.88	5.49
CAN 5 Yr T	1.42	2.05
CAN 10 Yr T	1.89	2.73

Money Market	2012	2013
USA Fed Funds	0.25	0.25
USA 3 Mo T-B	0.11	0.01
CAN tgt overnight rate	1.00	1.00
CAN 3 Mo T-B	1.00	0.99

Foreign Exchange	2012	2013
EUR/USD	1.30	1.35
GBP/USD	1.62	1.60
USD/CAD	0.97	1.03
USD/JPY	78.46	98.99

SEPTEMBER

M	T	W	T	F	S	S
	1	2	3	4	5	6
7	8	9	10	11	12	13
14	15	16	17	18	19	20
21	22	23	24	25	26	27
28	29	30				

OCTOBER

M	T	W	T	F	S	S
			1	2	3	4
5	6	7	8	9	10	11
12	13	14	15	16	17	18
19	20	21	22	23	24	25
26	27	28	29	30	31	

NOVEMBER

M	T	W	T	F	S	S
						1
2	3	4	5	6	7	8
9	10	11	12	13	14	15
16	17	18	19	20	21	22
23	24	25	26	27	28	29
30						

CANADIAN BANKS — IN-OUT-IN AGAIN
①Oct 10-Dec 31 ②Jan 23-Apr 13

During the financial crisis of 2007/08, the Canadian banks were touted as being the best in the world. Canadians love to invest in their banks because the banks operate in a regulated environment and for long periods of time, have grown their earnings and dividends. Although a lot of sectors in the Canadian market have very similar seasonally strong periods as the U.S., the seasonality for Canadian banks starts earlier than the US banks.

The difference in seasonally strong periods is driven by the difference in fiscal year-ends. The US banks have their year-end on December 31st and the Canadian banks on October 31st. Why does this make a difference? Typically, banks clean up their "books" at their year-end, by announcing any bad news. In addition, this is often the time period when the banks announce their positive news, including increases in dividends.

11.5% gain & positive 80% of the time

The Canadian bank sector, from October 10th to December 31st for the years 1989 to 2013, has been positive 84% of the time and has produced an average gain of 5.6%. From January 23rd to April 13th, the sector has been positive 84% of the time and has produced an average gain of 5.8%. On a compounded basis, the strategy has been positive 80% of the time and produced an average gain of 11.5%.

Investors have a choice to either invest in each seasonal strategy separately and avoid the short time period between the strategies, or to hold the Canadian banking sector from October 10th to April 13th. Investors should consider that from January 1st to the 22nd, from 1990 to 2013, the sector has produced an average loss of 1.6% and has only been positive 48% of the time.

CDN Banks* vs. S&P/TSX Comp 1989/90 to 2013/14   Positive ▢

Year	Oct 10 to Dec 31		Jan 23 to Apr 13		Compound Growth	
	TSX Comp	CDN Banks	TSX Comp	CDN Banks	TSX Comp	CDN Banks
1989/90	-1.7 %	-1.8 %	-6.3 %	-9.1 %	-7.9 %	-10.8 %
1990/91	3.7	8.9	9.8	14.6	13.9	24.8
1991/92	5.2	10.2	-6.8	-11.6	-2.0	-2.6
1992/93	4.1	2.5	10.7	14.4	15.2	17.3
1993/94	6.3	6.8	-5.6	-13.3	0.3	-7.4
1994/95	-1.8	3.4	5.0	10.0	3.1	13.8
1995/96	4.9	3.5	3.6	-3.2	8.6	0.1
1996/97	9.0	15.1	-6.2	0.7	2.3	15.9
1997/98	-6.1	7.6	19.9	38.8	12.6	49.4
1998/99	18.3	28.0	4.8	13.0	24.0	44.6
1999/00	18.2	5.1	3.8	22.1	22.8	28.3
2000/01	-14.4	1.7	-14.1	-6.7	-26.4	-5.1
2001/02	11.9	6.5	2.3	8.2	14.5	15.1
2002/03	16.1	21.3	-4.3	2.6	11.1	24.4
2003/04	8.1	5.1	2.0	2.1	10.3	7.4
2004/05	4.9	6.2	4.5	6.9	9.6	13.5
2005/06	6.2	8.4	5.5	2.7	12.1	11.3
2006/07	10.4	8.4	6.9	3.2	18.0	11.8
2007/08	-3.0	-10.4	8.2	-3.5	5.0	-13.5
2008/09	-6.4	-14.8	9.4	24.4	2.4	6.1
2009/10	2.7	2.4	6.7	15.2	9.6	18.0
2010/11	7.2	-0.2	4.3	9.1	11.9	8.9
2011/12	3.2	3.1	-2.9	1.1	0.2	4.2
2012/13	1.3	4.4	-3.8	-2.0	-2.5	2.3
2013/14	7.0	9.0	1.9	1.6	9.1	10.7
Avg.	4.6 %	5.6 %	2.4 %	5.6 %	7.1 %	11.5 %
Fq > 0	76 %	84 %	76 %	84 %	84 %	80 %

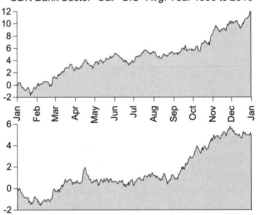

CDN Bank Sector* S&P GIC- Avg. Year 1990 to 2013

CDN Banks/S&P/TSX Rel. Strength - Avg Yr. 1990 - 2013

> Ⓨ *Alternate Strategy—*
> *Investors can bridge the gap between the two positive seasonal trends for the bank sector by holding from October 10th to April 13th. Longer term investors may prefer this strategy, shorter term investors can use technical tools to determine the appropriate strategy.*

> ⓘ ** Banks SP GIC Canadian Sector Level 2*
> *An index designed to represent a cross section of Canadian banking companies. For more information on the bank sector, see www.standardandpoors.com.*

2013-14 Strategy Performance

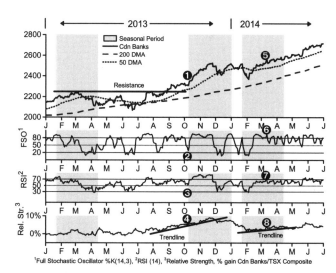

¹Full Stochastic Oscillator %K(14,3), ²RSI (14), ³Relative Strength, % gain Cdn Banks/TSX Composite

Market Indices & Rates
Weekly Values**

Stock Markets	2012	2013
Dow	13,471	15,319
S&P500	1,444	1,696
Nasdaq	3,125	3,773
TSX	12,292	12,836
FTSE	5,798	6,552
DAX	7,324	8,658
Nikkei	8,978	14,728
Hang Seng	20,705	23,218

Commodities	2012	2013
Oil	91.33	103.10
Gold	1763.6	1326.8

Bond Yields	2012	2013
USA 5 Yr Treasury	0.65	1.43
USA 10 Yr T	1.68	2.66
USA 20 Yr T	2.45	3.41
Moody's Aaa	3.40	4.54
Moody's Baa	4.72	5.37
CAN 5 Yr T	1.33	1.92
CAN 10 Yr T	1.77	2.59

Money Market	2012	2013
USA Fed Funds	0.25	0.25
USA 3 Mo T-B	0.10	0.02
CAN tgt overnight rate	1.00	1.00
CAN 3 Mo T-B	0.97	0.98

Foreign Exchange	2012	2013
EUR/USD	1.29	1.35
GBP/USD	1.62	1.61
USD/CAD	0.98	1.03
USD/JPY	77.79	98.65

Canadian Bank Sector Performance

The Canadian banking sector performed at market (TSX Composite) for the first seven months of 2013. Investors pushed up the price of bank stocks in August as they anticipated strong earnings from the sector in late August. Investors were more than pleased with the earnings results and continued to push up the price of bank stocks in September and into the beginning of October.

Technical Conditions– October 10th to April 13th, 2014

Entry Strategy –Buy Position on Entry Date–

At the start of its seasonal period, the Canadian banking sector had been trading above its resistance level for over a month❶, the FSO had bottomed at 30❷ and the RSI had bottomed just above 50❸. At the same time, the Canadian banking sector was still in its uptrend relative to the TSX Composite❹.

The sector continued its outperformance up until the banks started to release their earnings in late November. Once the earnings were published, after a strong run, there was little to push the stocks higher.

Exit Strategy –Sell Position Early–

After correcting in November, the Canadian banking sector finally bottomed in February. In February and March, the sector established a solid trend of outperformance relative to the TSX Composite. In mid-March, the sector had a small correction❺ and as a result, the FSO crossed below 80❻, triggering an early sell signal. The RSI also turned down from 70❼. The Canadian banking sector maintained its outperformance❽.

SEPTEMBER

M	T	W	T	F	S	S
	1	2	3	4	5	6
7	8	9	10	11	12	13
14	15	16	17	18	19	20
21	22	23	24	25	26	27
28	29	30				

OCTOBER

M	T	W	T	F	S	S
		1	2	3	4
5	6	7	8	9	10	11
12	13	14	15	16	17	18
19	20	21	22	23	24	25
26	27	28	29	30	31	

NOVEMBER

M	T	W	T	F	S	S
						1
2	3	4	5	6	7	8
9	10	11	12	13	14	15
16	17	18	19	20	21	22
23	24	25	26	27	28	29
30						

OCTOBER

	MONDAY	TUESDAY	WEDNESDAY
WEEK 40	28	29	30
WEEK 41	**5** 26	**6** 25	**7** 24

WEEK 42	**12** 19
	
	USA Bond Market Closed-
	       Columbus Day
	
	CAN Market Closed-
	       Thanksgiving Day
		13 18	**14** 17

WEEK 43	**19** 12	**20** 11	**21** 10
WEEK 44	**26** 5	**27** 4	**28** 3

THURSDAY	FRIDAY
1 30	**2** 29
8 22	**9** 21
15 16	**16** 15
22 9	**23** 8
29 2	**30** 1

NOVEMBER

M	T	W	T	F	S	S
						1
2	3	4	5	6	7	8
9	10	11	12	13	14	15
16	17	18	19	20	21	22
23	24	25	26	27	28	29
30						

DECEMBER

M	T	W	T	F	S	S
	1	2	3	4	5	6
7	8	9	10	11	12	13
14	15	16	17	18	19	20
21	22	23	24	25	26	27
28	29	30	31			

JANUARY

M	T	W	T	F	S	S
				1	2	3
4	5	6	7	8	9	10
11	12	13	14	15	16	17
18	19	20	21	22	23	24
25	26	27	28	29	30	31

FEBRUARY

M	T	W	T	F	S	S
1	2	3	4	5	6	7
8	9	10	11	12	13	14
15	16	17	18	19	20	21
22	23	24	25	26	27	28
29						

OCTOBER
S U M M A R Y

1.0%
0.8%
0.6%
0.4%
0.2%
0.0%

S&P500 Cumulative Daily Gains for Avg Month 1950 to 2013

	Dow Jones	S&P 500	Nasdaq	TSX Comp
Month Rank	7	7	8	9
# Up	38	38	23	19
# Down	26	20	19	10
% Pos	59	59	55	66
% Avg. Gain	0.5	0.8	0.7	0.1

Dow & S&P 1950-2012, Nasdaq 1972-2013, TSX 1985-2013

70%
60%
50%
40%
30%

Prob. of Daily Gain

♦ October, on average, is the most volatile month of the year and often provides opportunities for short-term traders. The first half of October tends to be positive. ♦ The second half of the month, leading up to the last four days, tends to be negative, and prone to large drops. ♦ Seasonal opportunities in mid-October include Canadian banks, technology and transportation. ♦ In late October, a lot of sectors start their seasonal period, including the materials, industrials, consumer discretionary and retail sectors.

BEST / WORST OCTOBER BROAD MKTS. 2004-2013

BEST OCTOBER MARKETS
♦ Russell 2000 (2011) 15.0%
♦ Nasdaq (2011) 11.1%
♦ Russell 1000 (2011) 11.1%

WORST OCTOBER MARKETS
♦ Nikkei 225 (2008) -23.8%
♦ Russell 2000 (2008) -20.9%
♦ Nasdaq (2008) -17.7%

Index Values End of Month

	2004	2005	2006	2007	2008	2009	2010	2011	2012	2013
Dow	10,027	10,440	12,081	13,930	9,325	9,713	11,118	11,955	13,096	15,546
S&P 500	1,130	1,207	1,378	1,549	969	1,036	1,183	1,253	1,412	1,757
Nasdaq	1,975	2,120	2,367	2,859	1,721	2,045	2,507	2,684	2,977	3,920
TSX Comp.	8,871	10,383	12,345	14,625	9,763	10,911	12,676	12,252	12,423	13,361
Russell 1000	1,162	1,261	1,437	1,623	1,004	1,089	1,256	1,331	1,498	1,883
Russell 2000	1,451	1,607	1,906	2,058	1,336	1,399	1,748	1,842	2,035	2,734
FTSE 100	4,624	5,317	6,129	6,722	4,377	5,045	5,675	5,544	5,783	6,731
Nikkei 225	10,771	13,607	16,399	16,738	8,577	10,035	9,202	8,988	8,928	14,328

Percent Gain for October

	2004	2005	2006	2007	2008	2009	2010	2011	2012	2013
Dow	-0.5	-1.2	3.4	0.2	-14.1	0.0	3.1	9.5	-2.5	2.8
S&P 500	1.4	-1.8	3.2	1.5	-16.9	-2.0	3.7	10.8	-2.0	4.5
Nasdaq	4.1	-1.5	4.8	5.8	-17.7	-3.6	5.9	11.1	-4.5	3.9
TSX Comp.	2.3	-5.7	5.0	3.7	-16.9	-4.2	2.5	5.4	0.9	4.5
Russell 1000	1.5	-1.9	3.3	1.6	-17.5	-2.3	3.8	11.1	-1.8	4.3
Russell 2000	1.9	-3.2	5.7	2.8	-20.9	-6.9	4.0	15.0	-2.2	2.5
FTSE 100	1.2	-2.9	2.8	3.9	-10.7	-1.7	2.3	8.1	0.7	4.2
Nikkei 225	-0.5	0.2	1.7	-0.3	-23.8	-1.0	-1.8	3.3	0.7	-0.9

October Market Avg. Performance 2004 to 2013[(1)]

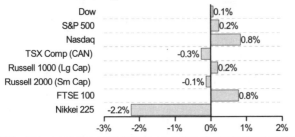

Dow 0.1%
S&P 500 0.2%
Nasdaq 0.8%
TSX Comp (CAN) -0.3%
Russell 1000 (Lg Cap) 0.2%
Russell 2000 (Sm Cap) -0.1%
FTSE 100 0.8%
Nikkei 225 -2.2%

-3%   -2%   -1%   0%   1%   2%

Interest Corner Oct[(2)]

	Fed Funds % [(3)]	3 Mo. T-Bill % [(4)]	10 Yr % [(5)]	20 Yr % [(6)]
2013	0.25	0.04	2.57	3.33
2012	0.25	0.11	1.72	2.46
2011	0.25	0.01	2.17	2.89
2010	0.25	0.12	2.63	3.64
2009	0.25	0.05	3.41	4.19

(1) Russell Data provided by Russell (2) Federal Reserve Bank of St. Louis- end of month values (3) Target rate set by FOMC (4)(5)(6) Constant yield maturities.

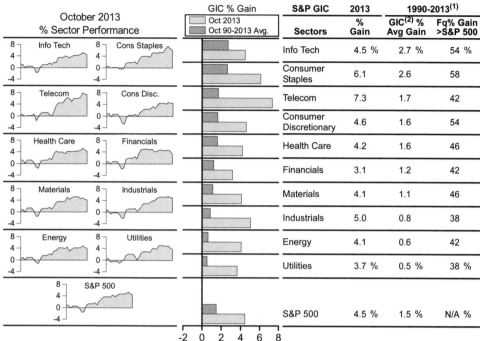

S&P GIC Sectors	2013 % Gain	1990-2013[1] GIC[2] % Avg Gain	1990-2013[1] Fq% Gain >S&P 500
Info Tech	4.5 %	2.7 %	54 %
Consumer Staples	6.1	2.6	58
Telecom	7.3	1.7	42
Consumer Discretionary	4.6	1.6	54
Health Care	4.2	1.6	46
Financials	3.1	1.2	42
Materials	4.1	1.1	46
Industrials	5.0	0.8	38
Energy	4.1	0.6	42
Utilities	3.7 %	0.5 %	38 %
S&P 500	4.5 %	1.5 %	N/A %

SELECTED SUB-SECTORS[3]

	2013 % Gain	Avg Gain	Fq% Gain >S&P 500
Agriculture (1994-2013)	11.0 %	6.6 %	80 %
Railroads	1.9	4.3	71
Software & Services	4.1	4.3	63
Transportation	6.1	4.0	75
Steel	10.3	2.3	42
Pharma	4.8	2.2	58
Chemicals	3.4	2.0	54
SOX (1995-2013)	3.3	1.9	42
Retail	5.6	1.7	54
Biotech (1993-2013)	3.4	1.4	43
Banks	3.1	0.8	38
Homebuilders	1.7	0.7	38
Metals & Mining	8.8	0.3	38
Gold (London PM)	-0.2	-1.0	25
Silver	2.4	-1.4	33

Sector Commentary

♦ Bernanke gave the green light to the stock market in September 2013, by stating that the Federal Reserve was going to continue purchasing bonds at the same rate rather than tapering as expected. As a result, all of the sectors in the market responded with gains in October. ♦ The telecom sector, in its seasonally strong period, produced a strong gain of 7.3%. ♦ The consumer staples sector, also in its seasonally strong period produced a gain of 6.1%. ♦ The weakest sector in the market was the financial sector with a gain of 3.1%.

Sub-Sector Commentary

♦ The cyclical sub-sectors performed well in October with metals and mining steel sub-sectors producing gains of 8.8% and 10.3%, respectively. ♦ The agriculture sub-sector, in its seasonally strong period, produced a gain of 11.0%. ♦ The homebuilders sub-sector produced a relatively small gain of 1.7%, compared to the S&P 500's gain of 4.5%. Homebuilders typically start their seasonal run on October 28th. The weakness coming into the seasonal trade, set up homebuilders to perform well in the next month.

UNION PACIFIC – JUMP ON BOARD
①Oct10-Nov4 ②Mar11-May5

Union Pacific follows the general seasonal pattern of the transportation sector: a strong spring, weak summer and a strong autumn.

The success of this trade can be seen in the frequency of how often the compound gains of Union Pacific, across both of its seasonal periods, outperforms the S&P 500. The seasonal period from October 10th to November 4th, for the years 1989 to 2013, has a positive success rate of 76%, and it has produced a large average gain of 4.7%. The period from March 11th to May 5th, for the years 1990 to 2014, has a positive success rate of 76%, and more than double the average gain (8.7% vs. 3.3%) compared with the S&P 500.

14.1% gain & positive 92% of the time

Both of these seasonal trades are strong trades by themselves. In addition, Union Pacific's frequency of positive performance over both seasonal periods is a very strong 92%, which is better than the S&P 500's success rate of 84%. It should also be noted that the only losing compound trade took place twenty-four years ago. Not only has this trade produced large returns, with a high frequency, but the drawdowns have also been small.

Investors should note that Union Pacific typically has a weak summer period, and if it is held past the end of its seasonal period in May, a sell criteria should be established for when the stock starts to weaken.

(i) *UNP - stock symbol for Union Pacific which trades on the NYSE exchange. Data adjusted for stock splits.*

Union Pacific vs. S&P 500 1989/90 to 2013/14   Positive ☐

Year	Oct10 to Nov4 S&P 500	UNP	Mar11 to May5 S&P 500	UNP	Compound Growth S&P 500	UNP
1989/90	-6.2	-7.0 %	0.1	-5.1 %	-6.0	-11.8 %
1990/91	2.2	-3.4	1.6	9.3	3.8	5.6
1991/92	3.6	7.9	2.5	14.0	6.1	23.1
1992/93	3.6	9.6	-2.6	6.3	0.9	16.5
1993/94	-0.6	2.1	-2.7	-0.4	3.3	1.6
1994/95	1.6	0.5	6.2	7.6	7.9	8.1
1995/96	2.1	4.0	1.3	1.1	3.4	5.1
1996/97	1.4	13.3	2.1	5.9	3.5	19.9
1997/98	-3.1	-3.8	4.8	9.1	1.6	4.9
1998/99	13.6	10.8	4.7	26.6	19.0	40.3
1999/00	2.0	6.8	2.7	20.7	4.7	28.9
2000/01	1.8	19.7	2.7	-1.6	4.5	17.8
2001/02	2.9	16.5	-7.8	-4.4	-5.2	11.3
2002/03	16.9	9.9	14.8	13.9	34.2	25.2
2003/04	1.4	8.6	-0.2	-4.5	1.2	3.7
2004/05	3.5	5.8	-3.0	-2.5	0.4	3.2
2005/06	2.0	-0.9	3.5	8.7	5.6	7.7
2006/07	1.0	1.0	7.3	18.1	8.4	19.3
2007/08	-3.6	6.7	10.5	23.6	6.6	31.9
2008/09	10.5	22.1	25.6	45.5	38.8	77.6
2009/10	-2.3	-1.1	1.8	3.8	-0.6	2.6
2010/11	4.8	8.1	3.1	8.1	8.0	16.9
2011/12	8.5	14.0	-0.1	5.5	8.3	20.3
2012/13	-1.9	2.3	4.1	7.7	2.1	10.2
2013/14	6.7	0.9	0.4	0.8	7.2	1.7
Avg.	2.9 %	4.7 %	3.3 %	8.7 %	6.4 %	14.1 %
Fq>0	76 %	76 %	76 %	76 %	84 %	92 %

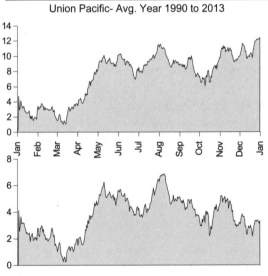

Union Pacific- Avg. Year 1990 to 2013

Union Pacific / S&P 500 Rel. Strength- Avg Yr. 1990-2013

2013-14 Strategy Performance

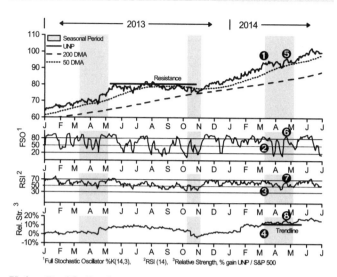

¹Full Stochastic Oscillator %K(14,3),   ²RSI (14),   ³Relative Strength, % gain UNP / S&P 500

Market Indices & Rates
Weekly Values**

Stock Markets	2012	2013
Dow	13,536	15,105
S&P500	1,453	1,688
Nasdaq	3,131	3,797
TSX	12,398	12,793
FTSE	5,831	6,453
DAX	7,332	8,627
Nikkei	8,803	14,259
Hang Seng	20,936	23,049

Commodities	2012	2013
Oil	90.82	103.12
Gold	1782.7	1309.9

Bond Yields	2012	2013
USA 5 Yr Treasury	0.63	1.39
USA 10 Yr T	1.67	2.64
USA 20 Yr T	2.45	3.42
Moody's Aaa	3.44	4.58
Moody's Baa	4.69	5.41
CAN 5 Yr T	1.31	1.87
CAN 10 Yr T	1.75	2.55

Money Market	2012	2013
USA Fed Funds	0.25	0.25
USA 3 Mo T-B	0.11	0.02
CAN tgt overnight rate	1.00	1.00
CAN 3 Mo T-B	0.96	0.97

Foreign Exchange	2012	2013
EUR/USD	1.30	1.36
GBP/USD	1.61	1.62
USD/CAD	0.98	1.03
USD/JPY	78.36	97.68

Union Pacific Performance

After a successful first seasonal period at the beginning of 2013, UNP's performance went flat from May until October. While it was consolidating into its next seasonal period in October, it was underperforming the S&P 500. During its October seasonal period, it underperformed. For the rest of 2013 and the first part of 2014, UNP marched higher and outperformed the S&P 500.

Technical Conditions– March 11th to May 5th, 2014

Entry Strategy –Buy Position on Entry Date–

At the beginning of its seasonal period, UNP was in a solid uptrend and was trading above its 50 day moving average❶. UNP was in an overbought condition, with the FSO trading above 80❷ and the RSI just under 70❸. After performing at market for February and then a small spike of outperformance at the beginning of March, UNP looked poised to perform well in its seasonal period❹.

Exit Strategy –Sell Position Early–

For most of its March/April seasonal period, UNP traded flat and performed at market. In mid-April, UNP bounced off its 50 day moving average, produced a short-term peak❺ and then started to fall in value. As a result, the FSO crossed below 80❻ and triggered an early sell signal. At this point, the RSI also started to turn down❼ and UNP's relative performance started to correct back to its flat trendline❽.

Overall, the March/April seasonal produced a nominal gain and outperformed the S&P 500.

** Weekly avg closing values- except Fed Funds & CAN overnight tgt rate weekly closing values.

OCTOBER

M	T	W	T	F	S	S
			1	2	3	4
5	6	7	8	9	10	11
12	13	14	15	16	17	18
19	20	21	22	23	24	25
26	27	28	29	30	31	

NOVEMBER

M	T	W	T	F	S	S
						1
2	3	4	5	6	7	8
9	10	11	12	13	14	15
16	17	18	19	20	21	22
23	24	25	26	27	28	29
30						

DECEMBER

M	T	W	T	F	S	S
	1	2	3	4	5	6
7	8	9	10	11	12	13
14	15	16	17	18	19	20
21	22	23	24	25	26	27
28	29	30	31			

HOMEBUILDERS—
TIME TO BREAK & TIME TO BUILD
①SELL SHORT (Apr27-Jun13) & ②LONG (Oct28-Feb3)

The homebuilders sector has been in the spotlight for the last few years: first when the mortgage meltdown occurred in 2007 and 2008, and more recently as the housing market has bounced back giving the homebuilders sector a boost.

18.8% extra & positive 19 times out of 24

Historically, the best time to be in the homebuilders sector has been from October 28th to February 3rd. In this time period, during the years 1990/91 to 2013/14, the homebuilders sector has produced an average gain of 18.4% and have been positive 92% of the time.

In the three years where losses occurred, the drawdowns were relatively small, at least compared to the large gains that the homebuilders sector has produced during its strong seasonal time period.

Generally the rest of the year, other than the strong seasonal period, is a time that seasonal investors should avoid the homebuilders sector, as not only has the average performance relative to the S&P 500 been negative, but the sector has produced both large gains and losses. In other words, the risk is substantially higher that a large drawdown will occur.

This is particularly true for the time period from April 27th to June 13th. In this time period from 1990 to 2013, the homebuilders sector produced an average loss of 4.0% and was only positive 29% of the time.

ⓘ *Homebuilders: SP GIC Sector: An index designed to represent a cross section of homebuilding companies.* For more information, see www.standardandpoors.com.

Homebuilders (HB) vs. S&P 500 1990 to 2013

Negative Short ☐ Positive Long ☐

	SHORT Apr 27 to Jun 13		LONG Oct 28 to Feb 3		Compound Growth	
Year	S&P 500	HB	S&P 500	HB	S&P 500	HB
1990/91	9.6 %	7.9 %	12.6 %	58.0 %	1.8 %	45.5 %
1991/92	-0.4	-4.8	6.0	41.2	7.0	48.0
1992/93	0.2	-11.5	6.9	26.7	6.7	41.2
1993/94	3.2	12.6	3.5	8.6	0.2	-5.1
1994/95	1.6	-4.0	2.8	-4.0	1.1	-0.2
1995/96	4.6	11.1	9.7	16.7	4.7	3.7
1996/97	2.2	10.6	12.2	6.3	9.8	-4.9
1997/98	16.7	22.6	14.7	24.8	-4.5	-3.4
1998/99	-0.8	-10.6	19.4	12.4	20.4	24.2
1999/00	-4.9	-7.1	9.9	-3.9	15.3	2.9
2000/01	0.6	-3.8	-2.2	18.6	-2.7	23.1
2001/02	0.6	-17.5	1.6	43.1	1.0	68.1
2002/03	-6.2	-5.3	-4.2	6.7	1.8	12.3
2003/04	10.0	31.5	10.2	7.6	-0.8	-26.3
2004/05	0.1	-2.6	5.7	23.7	5.6	26.9
2005/06	4.3	11.9	7.2	14.8	2.7	1.1
2006/07	-6.3	-27.1	5.2	16.8	11.7	48.4
2007/08	1.4	-7.9	-9.1	8.8	-10.4	17.4
2008/09	-2.7	-25.3	-1.2	27.7	1.4	60.0
2009/10	9.2	-25.1	3.2	15.5	-6.3	44.4
2010/11	-9.9	-22.9	10.5	12.9	21.5	38.7
2011/12	-5.6	-11.2	4.7	35.0	10.6	50.1
2012/13	-6.1	-9.3	7.2	13.7	13.7	24.3
2013/14	3.4	-7.2	-1.0	10.1	-4.4	18.1
Avg.	1.0 %	-4.0 %	5.7 %	18.4 %	4.5 %	23.3 %
Fq>0	63 %	29 %	79 %	92 %	75 %	79 %

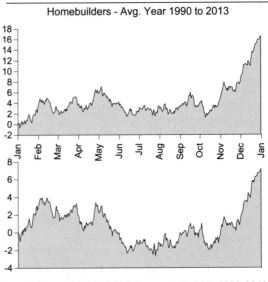

Homebuilders - Avg. Year 1990 to 2013

Homebuilders / S&P 500 Rel. Strength- Avg Yr. 1990-2013

2013-14 Strategy Performance

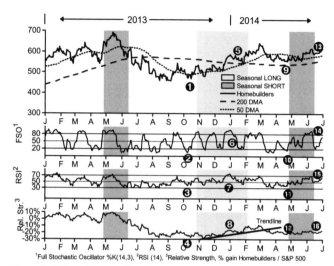

¹Full Stochastic Oscillator %K(14,3), ²RSI (14), ³Relative Strength, % gain Homebuilders / S&P 500

Homebuilders Sector Performance

In March 2013, the homebuilders sector started to correct during its seasonally weak period in May. It bottomed in September, setting up well for its October seasonal period.

Technical Conditions– October 28 to February 3 (LONG)

Entry Strategy –Buy Position Early–

At the beginning of October, the homebuilders sector bounced from below its 50 day moving average❶, causing the FSO to cross above 20❷ and produce an early buy signal. At the time, the RSI was below 70❸ but still rising. On a relative basis compared to the S&P 500, the homebuilders sector was at September's support level❹.

Exit Strategy –Exit Position Early–

The homebuilders sector rose above its 50 day moving average in late December❺ and then corrected, causing the FSO to fall below 80❻ and trigger an early sell signal. The RSI followed suit by falling below 70❼ and the relative strength compared to the S&P 500 started to weaken❽.

Technical Conditions– April 27 to June 13 (SHORT)

Entry Strategy –Buy Short Position on Entry Date–

At the start of its seasonal period in April, the homebuilders sector was trading sideways❾ with both the FSO❿ and RSI⓫ at 50 and rising. The sector was performing at market ⓬.

Exit Strategy –Sell Short Position on Exit Date–

At the end of its seasonal trade, the homebuilders sector was above its 50 day moving average⓭, the FSO⓮ and the RSI⓯ were correcting and the sector was performing at market⓰. Overall, the seasonal trade was a success.

WEEK 41

Market Indices & Rates
Weekly Values**

Stock Markets	2012	2013
Dow	13,411	14,976
S&P500	1,438	1,677
Nasdaq	3,065	3,739
TSX	12,230	12,800
FTSE	5,810	6,412
DAX	7,249	8,615
Nikkei	8,612	14,077
Hang Seng	20,963	23,071

Commodities	2012	2013
Oil	91.38	102.63
Gold	1768.9	1304.2

Bond Yields	2012	2013
USA 5 Yr Treasury	0.67	1.43
USA 10 Yr T	1.71	2.68
USA 20 Yr T	2.47	3.43
Moody's Aaa	3.44	4.58
Moody's Baa	4.60	5.38
CAN 5 Yr T	1.37	1.89
CAN 10 Yr T	1.80	2.58

Money Market	2012	2013
USA Fed Funds	0.25	0.25
USA 3 Mo T-B	0.11	0.05
CAN tgt overnight rate	1.00	1.00
CAN 3 Mo T-B	0.98	0.93

Foreign Exchange	2012	2013
EUR/USD	1.29	1.35
GBP/USD	1.60	1.60
USD/CAD	0.98	1.04
USD/JPY	78.31	97.53

OCTOBER

M	T	W	T	F	S	S
		1	2	3	4	
5	6	7	8	9	10	11
12	13	14	15	16	17	18
19	20	21	22	23	24	25
26	27	28	29	30	31	

NOVEMBER

M	T	W	T	F	S	S
						1
2	3	4	5	6	7	8
9	10	11	12	13	14	15
16	17	18	19	20	21	22
23	24	25	26	27	28	29
30						

DECEMBER

M	T	W	T	F	S	S
1	2	3	4	5	6	
7	8	9	10	11	12	13
14	15	16	17	18	19	20
21	22	23	24	25	26	27
28	29	30	31			

United Parcel Service Delivering Returns
October 10th to December 8th

Investors tend to look at UPS as a company that benefits from the retail sector as it transitions from a bricks and mortar business to an internet business. As internet transactions are increasing, demand for courier companies is increasing with their busiest time towards the end of the year during the holiday season.

United Parcel Services has been delivering returns towards the end of the year fairly consistently since the year 2000, shortly after UPS became a public company. There has only been one year (2007) that the UPS stock price has declined during its seasonally strong period from October 10th to December 8th.

UPS tends to perform well in its seasonally strong period because this is the busiest time for the company and investors anticipate strong earnings and a rising stock price. Investors are much more interested investing in the company during its busy time period than when it is in its slow season.

UPS* vs. S&P 500 2000 to 2013			
Oct 10 to Dec 8	S&P 500	UPS	Positive Diff
2000	-2.3%	12.1%	14.4%
2001	9.6	12.1	2.5
2002	17.4	6.5	-11.0
2003	2.9	11.1	8.2
2004	5.4	14.5	9.1
2005	5.0	9.6	4.6
2006	4.4	5.6	1.2
2007	-3.9	-3.5	0.3
2008	0.0	10.6	10.6
2009	1.9	3.2	1.3
2010	5.4	6.6	1.2
2011	6.8	8.7	1.9
2012	-1.6	0.2	1.8
2013	9.0	15.5	6.5
Avg	4.3%	8.1%	3.8%
Fq > 0	71%	93%	93%

8.1% gain & positive 93% of the time

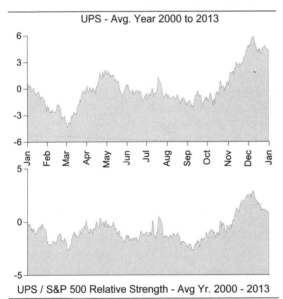

UPS - Avg. Year 2000 to 2013

UPS / S&P 500 Relative Strength - Avg Yr. 2000 - 2013

In its seasonally strong period, UPS has produced strong absolute returns with an average gain of 8.1% and a 93% frequency of being positive. What makes the UPS trade so attractive is the strength of its returns relative to the S&P 500, producing an extra 3.8% average return and outperformance 93% of the time.

Investors should note that UPS tends to start underperforming the S&P 500 at the end of its seasonal period in December. In the time period from 2000 to 2013, from December 9th to March 2nd, UPS has produced an average loss of 4.9% and has only been positive 36% of the time. It has also only beaten the S&P 500, 29% of the time in this period. The reason the UPS stock price tends to falter at this time is that this is a slower time for the business and investors are quick to look elsewhere for other opportunities. From a seasonal perspective, it is best to avoid UPS in its "unseasonal" period from December 9th to March 2nd.

The good news is that UPS starts to perform well at the beginning of March and into April when it reports its quarterly earnings. UPS benefits from retail sales starting to increase after a typically slow January and February. From 2000 to 2013, during the period of March 3rd to April 30th, UPS has produced an average gain of 6.1% and has been positive 87% of the time. Although these are good numbers, it has only beaten the S&P 500, 53% of the time in this period.

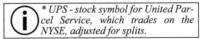

* UPS - stock symbol for United Parcel Service, which trades on the NYSE, adjusted for splits.

2013-14 Strategy Performance

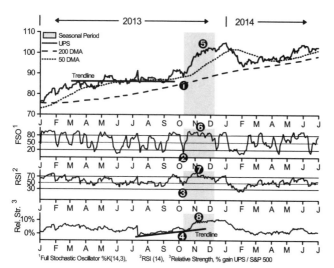

¹Full Stochastic Oscillator %K(14,3),   ²RSI (14),   ³Relative Strength, % gain UPS / S&P 500

Market Indices & Rates
Weekly Values**

Stock Markets	2012	2013
Dow	13,485	15,323
S&P500	1,449	1,721
Nasdaq	3,070	3,845
TSX	12,396	13,015
FTSE	5,880	6,565
DAX	7,370	8,810
Nikkei	8,814	14,514
Hang Seng	21,368	23,250

Commodities	2012	2013
Oil	91.64	101.48
Gold	1742.3	1293.1

Bond Yields	2012	2013
USA 5 Yr Treasury	0.74	1.39
USA 10 Yr T	1.79	2.66
USA 20 Yr T	2.55	3.41
Moody's Aaa	3.50	4.55
Moody's Baa	4.55	5.32
CAN 5 Yr T	1.38	1.88
CAN 10 Yr T	1.86	2.59

Money Market	2012	2013
USA Fed Funds	0.25	0.25
USA 3 Mo T-B	0.10	0.08
CAN tgt overnight rate	1.00	1.00
CAN 3 Mo T-B	0.96	0.92

Foreign Exchange	2012	2013
EUR/USD	1.30	1.36
GBP/USD	1.61	1.61
USD/CAD	0.98	1.03
USD/JPY	79.01	98.23

United Parcel Service Performance

For most of 2013, UPS traded flat and underperformed the S&P 500. Heading into its seasonal period, UPS started to perform positively and outperform the S&P 500.

Technical Conditions– October 10th to December 8th, 2014

Entry Strategy –Buy Position on Entry Date–

At the beginning of September, UPS spiked in price and then corrected towards the end of the month. At the start of its seasonal period, UPS had declined back to its 50 day moving average❶ and the FSO confirmed the entry at the start of the seasonal period by crossing above 20❷. The RSI also crossed back over 50❸. At the time, UPS was still in an uptrend relative to the S&P 500❹.

Exit Strategy– Exit Position Early–

UPS spiked in price right at the beginning of its seasonal period and continued its strong trend into November, trading well above its 50 day moving average❺. An early sell signal was triggered when the FSO crossed below 80❻ in mid-November. The signal was confirmed by the RSI crossing below 70❼. As a result, UPS started to perform at market❽.

Overall, the trade was very successful, producing a large gain and strongly outperforming the S&P 500. It is interesting to note that UPS started to underperform the S&P 500 shortly after its seasonal period ended.

OCTOBER

M	T	W	T	F	S	S
			1	2	3	4
5	6	7	8	9	10	11
12	13	14	15	16	17	18
19	20	21	22	23	24	25
26	27	28	29	30	31	

NOVEMBER

M	T	W	T	F	S	S
						1
2	3	4	5	6	7	8
9	10	11	12	13	14	15
16	17	18	19	20	21	22
23	24	25	26	27	28	29
30						

DECEMBER

M	T	W	T	F	S	S
	1	2	3	4	5	6
7	8	9	10	11	12	13
14	15	16	17	18	19	20
21	22	23	24	25	26	27
28	29	30	31			

** Weekly avg closing values- except Fed Funds & CAN overnight tgt rate weekly closing values.

RETAIL – SHOP EARLY
IInd of II Retail Strategies for the Year
October 28th to November 29th

The *Retail – Shop Early* strategy is the second retail sector strategy of the year and it occurs before the biggest shopping season of the year – the Christmas holiday season.

3.0% extra & 79% of the time better than S&P 500

The time to go shopping for retail stocks is at the end of October, which is about one month before Thanksgiving. It is the time when two favorable influences happen at the same time.

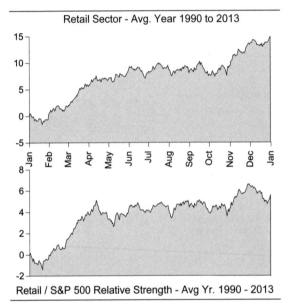

Retail Sector - Avg. Year 1990 to 2013

Retail / S&P 500 Relative Strength - Avg Yr. 1990 - 2013

First, historically, the three best months in a row for the stock market have been November, December and January. The end of October usually represents an excellent buying opportunity, not only for the next three months, but the next six months. A rising stock market is generally favorable for the stock market.

Second, investors tend to buy retail stocks in anticipation of a strong holiday sales season. At the same time that the market tends to increase, investors are attracted back into the retail sector.

Retail sales tend to be lower in the summer and a lot of investors view investing in retail stocks at this time as dead money. During the summertime, investors

prefer not to invest in this sector until it comes back into favor towards the end of October.

The trick to investing is not to be too early, but early. If an investor gets into a sector too early, they can suffer from the frustration of having dead money– having an investment that goes nowhere, while the rest of the market increases.

If an investor moves into a sector too late, there is very little upside potential. In fact, this can be a dangerous strategy because if the sales or earnings numbers disappoint the analysts, the sector can severely correct.

For the *Retail – Shop Early* strategy, the time to enter is approximately one month before Black Friday.

The end of October is also typically a good time to enter the broad market.

Retail Sector vs. S&P 500 1990 to 2013

Oct 28 to Nov 29	S&P 500	Positive Retail	Diff
1990	3.8 %	9.9 %	6.0 %
1991	-2.3	2.7	5.0
1992	2.8	5.5	2.8
1993	-0.6	6.3	6.9
1994	-2.3	0.4	2.7
1995	4.8	9.5	4.7
1996	8.0	0.4	-7.6
1997	8.9	16.9	7.9
1998	11.9	20.4	8.4
1999	8.6	14.1	5.5
2000	-2.7	9.9	12.6
2001	3.2	7.9	4.7
2002	4.3	-1.7	-6.0
2003	2.6	2.5	-0.1
2004	4.7	7.0	2.3
2005	6.7	9.9	3.2
2006	1.6	0.2	-1.4
2007	-4.3	-7.5	-3.2
2008	5.6	7.5	1.9
2009	2.6	3.6	1.0
2010	0.5	5.2	4.7
2011	-7.0	-4.5	2.5
2012	0.3	5.1	4.8
2013	2.6	5.0	2.4
Avg.	2.7 %	5.7 %	3.0 %
Fq > 0	75 %	88 %	79 %

2012-13-14 Strategy Performance

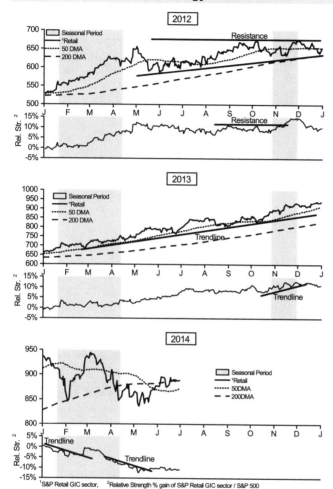

¹S&P Retail GIC sector, ²Relative Strength % gain of S&P Retail GIC sector / S&P 500

Market Indices & Rates
Weekly Values**

Stock Markets	2012	2013
Dow	13,147	15,471
S&P500	1,416	1,752
Nasdaq	2,993	3,926
TSX	12,285	13,280
FTSE	5,819	6,692
DAX	7,225	8,940
Nikkei	8,994	14,481
Hang Seng	21,704	23,058

Commodities	2012	2013
Oil	86.47	97.53
Gold	1715.2	1334.9

Bond Yields	2012	2013
USA 5 Yr Treasury	0.78	1.32
USA 10 Yr T	1.81	2.55
USA 20 Yr T	2.56	3.32
Moody's Aaa	3.50	4.46
Moody's Baa	4.54	5.21
CAN 5 Yr T	1.40	1.76
CAN 10 Yr T	1.86	2.46

Money Market	2012	2013
USA Fed Funds	0.25	0.25
USA 3 Mo T-B	0.12	0.04
CAN tgt overnight rate	1.00	1.00
CAN 3 Mo T-B	1.00	0.91

Foreign Exchange	2012	2013
EUR/USD	1.30	1.38
GBP/USD	1.60	1.62
USD/CAD	0.99	1.04
USD/JPY	79.91	97.68

OCTOBER

M	T	W	T	F	S	S
			1	2	3	4
5	6	7	8	9	10	11
12	13	14	15	16	17	18
19	20	21	22	23	24	25
26	27	28	29	30	31	

NOVEMBER

M	T	W	T	F	S	S
						1
2	3	4	5	6	7	8
9	10	11	12	13	14	15
16	17	18	19	20	21	22
23	24	25	26	27	28	29
30						

DECEMBER

M	T	W	T	F	S	S
	1	2	3	4	5	6
7	8	9	10	11	12	13
14	15	16	17	18	19	20
21	22	23	24	25	26	27
28	29	30	31			

Retail Sector Performance– October to November 2013

The retail sector in its autumn leg of its seasonal strategy in October, started flat but was showing signs of outperformance compared with the S&P 500. Over the next few weeks, the retail sector continued on its positive trend and outperformed the S&P 500.

Overall, the trade was successful during its seasonal period. It is interesting to note that shortly after its seasonal period, the retail sector once again started to underperform the S&P 500.

** Weekly avg closing values- except Fed Funds & CAN overnight tgt rate weekly closing values.

The industrial sector's seasonal trends are largely the same as the broad market, such as the S&P 500. Although the trends are similar, there still exists an opportunity to take advantage of the time period when the industrial sector tends to outperform.

12.2% gain & positive 92% of the time

Industrials tend to outperform in the favorable six months, but there is an opportunity to temporarily get out of the sector to avoid a time period when the sector has, on average, decreased before turning positive again.

The overall strategy is to be invested in the industrial sector from October 28th to December 31st, sell at the end of the day on the 31st, and re-enter the sector to be invested from January 23rd to May 5th.

Using the complete *Industrial Strength* strategy from 1989/90 to 2013/14, the industrial sector has produced a total compounded average annual gain of 12.2%.

In addition, it has been positive 92% of the time and has outperformed the S&P 500, 80% of the time.

During the time period from January 1st to January 22nd, the industrial sector has on average lost 0.7% and has only been positive 54% of the time.

It should be noted that longer term investors may decide to be invested during the whole time period from October 28th to May 5th.

Shorter term investors may decide to use technical analysis to determine, if and when, they should temporarily sell the industrials sector during its weak period from January 1st to January 22nd.

Industrials* vs. S&P 500 1989/90 to 2013/14 Positive ▢

	Oct 28 to Dec 31		Jan 23 to May 5		Compound Growth	
Year	S&P 500	Ind.	S&P 500	Ind.	S&P 500	Ind.
1989/90	5.5%	6.9%	2.4%	5.5%	8.0%	12.7%
1990/91	8.4	10.7	16.0	15.2	25.7	27.5
1991/92	8.6	7.2	-0.3	-1.0	8.2	6.1
1002/93	4 1	6.3	1.9	5.4	6.1	12.0
1993/94	0.4	5.1	-4.9	-6.7	-4.5	2.0
1994/95	-1.4	-0.5	11.9	12.4	10.3	11.8
1995/96	6.3	10.7	4.6	7.6	11.1	19.1
1996/97	5.7	4.5	5.6	5.2	11.6	9.9
1997/98	10.7	10.5	15.8	11.5	28.2	23.2
1998/99	15.4	10.5	10.0	19.5	26.9	32.1
1999/00	13.3	10.8	-0.6	4.5	12.6	15.8
2000/01	-4.3	1.8	-5.7	4.7	-9.7	6.6
2001/02	3.9	8.1	-4.1	-5.3	-0.3	2.4
2002/03	-2.0	-1.3	5.5	8.6	3.4	7.1
2003/04	7.8	11.6	-2.0	-3.3	5.7	7.9
2004/05	7.7	8.7	0.4	0.2	8.1	8.9
2005/06	5.9	7.6	5.1	14.3	11.3	23.0
2006/07	3.0	3.1	5.8	6.8	9.0	10.1
2007/08	-4.4	-3.4	7.4	9.7	2.7	6.0
2008/09	6.4	7.1	9.2	6.1	16.2	13.7
2009/10	4.9	6.4	6.8	13.4	12.0	20.6
2010/11	6.4	8.1	4.0	4.9	10.6	13.5
2011/12	-2.1	-1.0	4.1	0.3	1.9	-0.7
2012/13	1.0	4.1	8.2	4.9	9.3	9.2
2013/14	5.0	7.3	2.2	1.6	7.3	9.0
Avg.	4.6%	6.0%	4.4%	5.8%	9.3%	12.2%
Fq > 0	80%	84%	76%	84%	88%	92%

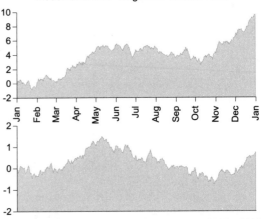

Industrial Sector - Avg. Year 1990 to 2013

Industrial / S&P 500 Rel. Strength - Avg Yr. 1990 - 2013

 Alternate Strategy—
Investors can bridge the gap between the two positive seasonal trends for the industrials sector by holding from October 28th to May 5th. Longer term investors may prefer this strategy, shorter term investors can use technical tools to determine the appropriate strategy.

ⓘ *The SP GICS Industrial Sector. For more information on the industrials sector, see www.standardandpoors.com*

2013-14 Strategy Performance

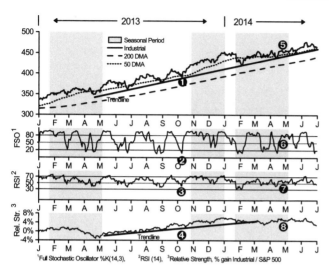

¹Full Stochastic Oscillator %K(14,3), ²RSI (14), ³Relative Strength, % gain Industrial / S&P 500

Industrial Sector Performance

The industrial sector started to outperform the S&P 500 in May 2013. It maintained this trend in the summer months when the industrial sector typically does not perform well.

Technical Conditions– October 28th to May 5th, 2014

Entry Strategy –Buy Position Early–

In its uptrend of outperformance in October, the industrial sector corrected down to its 50 day moving average and bounced❶. This triggered an early buy signal as the FSO crossed above 20❷. In support, the RSI crossed back above 50❸. The bounce also kept the sector on its trendline of outperforming the S&P 500❹.

Entry Strategy –Exit Position Early–

After performing positively and outperforming the S&P 500 for its first seasonal leg that finished at the end of the year, the industrial sector corrected up until its second seasonal leg that started in late January. At the beginning of its second seasonal leg in January, the industrial sector corrected, but was still able to manage to keep its long-term upward trend intact. In late April, close to the end of its seasonal trade, the industrial sector had a small correction❺, triggering an early sell signal as the FSO crossed below 80❻. At the same time, the RSI started trending down❼ and the industrial sector managed to continue to perform at market❽.

Overall, the complete industrial seasonal trade was successful as the strong outperformance in its first seasonal leg, more than made up for the small underperformance in the second seasonal leg.

Market Indices & Rates
Weekly Values**

Stock Markets	2012	2013
Dow	13,141	15,606
S&P500	1,418	1,763
Nasdaq	2,993	3,933
TSX	12,399	13,393
FTSE	5,832	6,749
DAX	7,290	9,011
Nikkei	8,940	14,351
Hang Seng	21,703	23,083

Commodities	2012	2013
Oil	85.86	96.93
Gold	1707.5	1339.2

Bond Yields	2012	2013
USA 5 Yr Treasury	0.73	1.32
USA 10 Yr T	1.74	2.57
USA 20 Yr T	2.49	3.34
Moody's Aaa	3.44	4.48
Moody's Baa	4.49	5.23
CAN 5 Yr T	1.35	1.73
CAN 10 Yr T	1.79	2.44

Money Market	2012	2013
USA Fed Funds	0.25	0.25
USA 3 Mo T-B	0.09	0.04
CAN tgt overnight rate	1.00	1.00
CAN 3 Mo T-B	0.99	0.90

Foreign Exchange	2012	2013
EUR/USD	1.29	1.37
GBP/USD	1.61	1.60
USD/CAD	1.00	1.04
USD/JPY	79.95	98.28

OCTOBER

M	T	W	T	F	S	S
			1	2	3	4
5	6	7	8	9	10	11
12	13	14	15	16	17	18
19	20	21	22	23	24	25
26	27	28	29	30	31	

NOVEMBER

M	T	W	T	F	S	S
						1
2	3	4	5	6	7	8
9	10	11	12	13	14	15
16	17	18	19	20	21	22
23	24	25	26	27	28	29
30						

DECEMBER

M	T	W	T	F	S	S
	1	2	3	4	5	6
7	8	9	10	11	12	13
14	15	16	17	18	19	20
21	22	23	24	25	26	27
28	29	30	31			

NOVEMBER

	MONDAY	TUESDAY	WEDNESDAY
WEEK 45	**2** 28	**3** 27	**4** 26
WEEK 46	**9** 21	**10** 20	**11** 19
WEEK 47	**16** 14	**17** 13	**18** 12
WEEK 48	**23** 7	**24** 6	**25** 5
WEEK 49	**30**	1	2

THURSDAY	FRIDAY
5 25	**6** 24
12 18	**13** 17
19 11	**20** 10
26 4	**27** 3
USA Market Closed- Thanksgiving Day	USA Early Market Close Thanksgiving
3	4

DECEMBER

M	T	W	T	F	S	S
	1	2	3	4	5	6
7	8	9	10	11	12	13
14	15	16	17	18	19	20
21	22	23	24	25	26	27
28	29	30	31			

JANUARY

M	T	W	T	F	S	S
				1	2	3
4	5	6	7	8	9	10
11	12	13	14	15	16	17
18	19	20	21	22	23	24
25	26	27	28	29	30	31

FEBRUARY

M	T	W	T	F	S	S
1	2	3	4	5	6	7
8	9	10	11	12	13	14
15	16	17	18	19	20	21
22	23	24	25	26	27	28
29						

MARCH

M	T	W	T	F	S	S
	1	2	3	4	5	6
7	8	9	10	11	12	13
14	15	16	17	18	19	20
21	22	23	24	25	26	27
28	29	30	31			

NOVEMBER
S U M M A R Y

	Dow Jones	S&P 500	Nasdaq	TSX Comp
Month Rank	3	2	3	7
# Up	42	42	28	17
# Down	22	22	14	12
% Pos	66	66	67	59
% Avg. Gain	1.5	1.5	1.6	0.6

Dow & S&P 1950-2013, Nasdaq 1972-2013, TSX 1985-2013

S&P500 Cumulative Daily Gains for Avg Month 1950 to 2013

Prob. of Daily Gain

♦ November, on average, is one of the better months of the year and from 1950 to 2013, the S&P 500 produced an average gain of 1.5% and has been positive 65% of the time. ♦ In November, the cyclical sectors start to increase their relative performance to the S&P 500, with the metals and mining sector starting its period of seasonal strength on November 16th. ♦ For investors looking for a short-term investment, the day before and the day after Thanksgiving are on average, the two strongest days of the year.

BEST / WORST NOVEMBER BROAD MKTS. 2004-2013

BEST NOVEMBER MARKETS
- ♦ Nikkei 225 (2013) 9.3%
- ♦ Nikkei 225 (2005) 9.3%
- ♦ Russell 2000 (2004) 8.6%

WORST NOVEMBER MARKETS
- ♦ Russell 2000 (2008) -12.0%
- ♦ Nasdaq (2008) -10.8%
- ♦ Russell 1000 (2008) -7.9%

Index Values End of Month

	2004	2005	2006	2007	2008	2009	2010	2011	2012	2013
Dow	10,428	10,806	12,222	13,372	8,829	10,345	11,006	12,046	13,026	16,086
S&P 500	1,174	1,249	1,401	1,481	896	1,096	1,181	1,247	1,416	1,806
Nasdaq	2,097	2,233	2,432	2,661	1,536	2,145	2,498	2,620	3,010	4,060
TSX Comp.	9,030	10,824	12,752	13,689	9,271	11,447	12,953	12,204	12,239	13,395
Russell 1000	1,210	1,306	1,464	1,550	925	1,150	1,258	1,324	1,506	1,932
Russell 2000	1,575	1,683	1,954	1,908	1,176	1,441	1,807	1,833	2,043	2,840
FTSE 100	4,703	5,423	6,049	6,433	4,288	5,191	5,528	5,505	5,867	6,651
Nikkei 225	10,899	14,872	16,274	15,681	8,512	9,346	9,937	8,435	9,446	15,662

Percent Gain for November

	2004	2005	2006	2007	2008	2009	2010	2011	2012	2013
Dow	4.0	3.5	1.2	-4.0	-5.3	6.5	-1.0	0.8	-0.5	3.5
S&P 500	3.9	3.5	1.6	-4.4	-7.5	5.7	-0.2	-0.5	0.3	2.8
Nasdaq	6.2	5.3	2.7	-6.9	-10.8	4.9	-0.4	-2.4	1.1	3.6
TSX Comp.	1.8	4.2	3.3	-6.4	-5.0	4.9	2.2	-0.4	-1.5	0.3
Russell 1000	4.1	3.5	1.9	-4.5	-7.9	5.6	0.1	-0.5	0.5	2.6
Russell 2000	8.6	4.7	2.5	-7.3	-12.0	3.0	3.4	-0.5	0.4	3.9
FTSE 100	1.7	2.0	-1.3	-4.3	-2.0	2.9	-2.6	-0.7	1.5	-1.2
Nikkei 225	1.2	9.3	-0.8	-6.3	-0.8	-6.9	8.0	-6.2	5.8	9.3

November Market Avg. Performance 2004 to 2013[1]

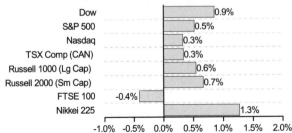

Dow	0.9%
S&P 500	0.5%
Nasdaq	0.3%
TSX Comp (CAN)	0.3%
Russell 1000 (Lg Cap)	0.6%
Russell 2000 (Sm Cap)	0.7%
FTSE 100	-0.4%
Nikkei 225	1.3%

Interest Corner Nov[2]

	Fed Funds % [3]	3 Mo. T-Bill % [4]	10 Yr % [5]	20 Yr % [6]
2013	0.25	0.06	2.75	3.54
2012	0.25	0.08	1.62	2.37
2011	0.25	0.01	2.08	2.77
2010	0.25	0.17	2.81	3.80
2009	0.25	0.06	3.21	4.07

(1) Russell Data provided by Russell (2) Federal Reserve Bank of St. Louis- end of month values (3) Target rate set by FOMC (4)(5)(6) Constant yield maturities.

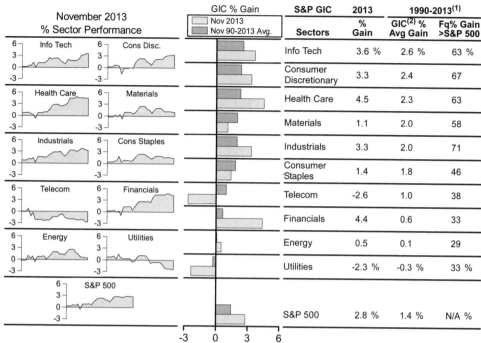

S&P GIC	2013	1990-2013[1]	
Sectors	% Gain	GIC[2] % Avg Gain	Fq% Gain >S&P 500
Info Tech	3.6 %	2.6 %	63 %
Consumer Discretionary	3.3	2.4	67
Health Care	4.5	2.3	63
Materials	1.1	2.0	58
Industrials	3.3	2.0	71
Consumer Staples	1.4	1.8	46
Telecom	-2.6	1.0	38
Financials	4.4	0.6	33
Energy	0.5	0.1	29
Utilities	-2.3 %	-0.3 %	33 %
S&P 500	2.8 %	1.4 %	N/A %

Sector Commentary

♦ In November 2013, the S&P 500 started off slowly but ended up producing a gain of 2.8%. ♦ November proved to be a very well behaved seasonal month, with the sectors that typically outperform, performing well and the sectors that tend to be weaker, underperforming the S&P 500. The exception was the financial sector that produced a very strong gain of 4.4%, when it is typically one of the weaker sectors of the month. ♦ The second largest sector gain in the month was produced by the technology sector, which gained 3.6%. The technology sector typically performs well in November after starting its seasonal run in October.

Sub-Sector Commentary

♦ The transportation and railroad sub-sectors produced strong gains of 4.9% and 4.8% respectively, as their seasonal periods ended in November. ♦ The homebuilders sub-sector started its seasonal period off on a solid foundation, producing a gain of 3.9%. ♦ After underperforming the S&P 500 in September and October, gold and silver continued their weak performance, producing losses of 5.4% and 10.2%, respectively.

SELECTED SUB-SECTORS[3]

Agriculture (1994-2013)	-1.6 %	3.9 %	45 %
Retail	4.3	3.4	67
SOX (1995-2013)	0.6	3.1	53
Steel	-0.1	3.1	54
Homebuilders	3.9	2.4	50
Software & Services	4.0	2.3	67
Pharma	3.6	2.1	58
Biotech (1993-2013)	5.6	2.0	48
Transportation	4.9	2.0	46
Chemicals	1.7	1.8	50
Gold (London PM)	-5.4	1.7	58
Metals & Mining	-3.4	1.7	54
Silver	-10.2	1.5	54
Railroads	4.8	1.0	54
Banks	3.8	0.7	46

(1) Sector data provided by Standard and Poors (2) GIC is short form for Global Industry Classification (3) Sub Sector data provided by Standard and Poors, except where marked by symbol.

MATERIAL STOCKS — MATERIAL GAINS
①Oct 28-Jan 6   ②Jan 23-May 5

Materials Composition – CAUTION

The U.S. materials sector is substantially different from the Canadian materials sector. The U.S. sector has over a 60% weight in chemical companies, versus the Canadian sector which has over a 60% weight in gold companies.

The materials sector (U.S.) generally does well during the favorable six months of the year, from the end of October to the beginning of May. The sector is economically sensitive and is leveraged to the economic forecasts. Generally, if the economy is expected to slow, the materials sector tends to decline and vice versa.

Positive 96% of the time

The materials sector has two seasonal periods. The first is from October 28th to January 6th and second period is from January 23rd to May 5th.

In the first seasonal period, the materials sector has produced an average gain of 7.3% in the years from 1990 to 2013 and has been positive 88% of the time.

The second seasonal period from January 23rd to May 5th, has produced an average gain of 7.4% (almost double the S&P 500) and has been positive 76% of the time.

The time period in between the two seasonal periods, from January 7th to January 22nd, has had an average loss of 27% and only been positive 36% of the time (1989/90 to 2013/14). Investors may decide to bridge the gap between the two seasonal periods if the materials sector has strong momentum at the beginning of January.

The complete materials strategy is to be invested from October 28th to January 6th, out from January 7th to the 22nd, and back in from January 23rd to May 5th. This strategy has produced an average gain of 15.3% and has been positive 96% of the time.

Materials vs. S&P 500 1989/90 to 2013/14   Positive ☐

Year	Oct 28 to Jan6		Jan 23 to May 5		Compound Growth	
	S&P 500	Mat.	S&P 500	Mat.	S&P 500	Mat.
1989/90	5.1 %	9.1 %	2.4 %	-3.1 %	7.7 %	5.7 %
1990/91	5.4	9.2	16.0	15.3	22.2	26.0
1991/92	8.8	1.5	-0.3	5.5	8.5	7.1
1992/93	3.8	5.6	1.9	4.3	5.8	10.2
1993/94	0.5	9.4	-4.9	-5.3	-4.4	3.6
1994/95	-1.1	-3.5	11.9	6.1	10.7	2.4
1995/96	6.4	7.6	4.6	11.1	11.3	19.5
1996/97	6.7	2.3	5.6	2.3	12.6	4.6
1997/98	10.2	1.4	15.8	20.9	27.7	22.6
1998/99	19.4	6.1	10.0	31.5	31.3	39.6
1999/00	8.2	15.7	-0.6	-7.1	7.6	7.5
2000/01	-5.9	19.2	-5.7	15.1	-11.2	37.2
2001/02	6.2	8.5	-4.1	14.9	1.8	24.7
2002/03	3.5	9.2	5.5	2.7	9.2	12.1
2003/04	9.0	16.6	-2.0	-3.0	6.8	13.1
2004/05	5.6	5.4	0.4	0.3	6.0	5.8
2005/06	9.0	16.3	5.1	14.7	14.6	33.5
2006/07	2.4	3.2	5.8	10.7	8.3	14.2
2007/08	-8.1	-5.1	7.4	16.7	-1.2	10.8
2008/09	10.1	12.0	9.2	23.3	20.3	38.1
2009/10	6.9	13.8	6.8	3.0	14.2	17.2
2010/11	7.7	11.7	4.0	4.2	12.1	16.4
2011/12	-0.5	-2.3	4.1	-2.7	3.5	-4.9
2012/13	3.9	7.2	8.2	0.0	12.3	7.2
2013/14	3.8	3.1	2.2	4.3	6.1	7.5
Avg.	5.1 %	7.3 %	4.4 %	7.4 %	9.7 %	15.3 %
Fq > 0	84 %	88 %	76 %	76 %	88 %	96 %

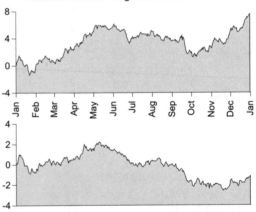

Materials Sector - Avg. Year 1990 to 2013

Materials / S&P 500 Rel. Strength - Avg. Yr. 1990 - 2013

> *Alternate Strategy—*
> *Investors can bridge the gap between the two positive seasonal trends for the materials sector by holding from October 28th to May 5th. Longer term investors may prefer this strategy. Shorter term investors can use technical tools to determine the appropriate strategy.*

> The SP GICS Materials Sector encompasses a wide range of materials based companies. For more information on the materials sector, see www.standardandpoors.com

2013-14 Strategy Performance

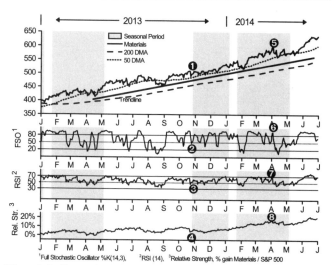

¹Full Stochastic Oscillator %K(14,3), ²RSI (14), ³Relative Strength, % gain Materials / S&P 500

Market Indices & Rates
Weekly Values**

Stock Markets	2012	2013
Dow	12,984	15,672
S&P500	1,400	1,764
Nasdaq	2,950	3,917
TSX	12,266	13,355
FTSE	5,812	6,732
DAX	7,261	9,049
Nikkei	8,910	14,219
Hang Seng	21,800	22,978

Commodities	2012	2013
Oil	85.99	94.32
Gold	1709.0	1307.9

Bond Yields	2012	2013
USA 5 Yr Treasury	0.68	1.36
USA 10 Yr T	1.68	2.68
USA 20 Yr T	2.42	3.46
Moody's Aaa	3.42	4.60
Moody's Baa	4.46	5.36
CAN 5 Yr T	1.32	1.79
CAN 10 Yr T	1.75	2.54

Money Market	2012	2013
USA Fed Funds	0.25	0.25
USA 3 Mo T-B	0.09	0.05
CAN tgt overnight rate	1.00	1.00
CAN 3 Mo T-B	0.98	0.90

Foreign Exchange	2012	2013
EUR/USD	1.28	1.35
GBP/USD	1.60	1.60
USD/CAD	1.00	1.04
USD/JPY	79.92	98.58

Materials Sector Performance

From May 2013 into October, the materials sector was in an uptrend, but was performing at market. The sector dipped just before the start of its seasonal period in late October, setting up the seasonal trade to perform well.

Technical Conditions– October 28th to May 5th, 2014

Entry Strategy –Buy Position on Entry Date–

At the start of its seasonal period, the materials sector was in an uptrend❶, with the FSO and the RSI both sitting at 50❷❸. On the negative side, the materials sector was underperforming the S&P 500❹. Overall, the timing of the trade was neutral.

Exit Strategy –Sell Position Early–

At the end of March 2014, the materials sector was performing well, trading above its trendline and well above its 50 day moving average❺. At the beginning of April, the sector started to turn down, causing the FSO to cross below 80❻ and trigger an early sell signal. At the same time, the RSI turned back from 70❼ and the sector started to underperform the S&P 500❽.

Overall, the materials seasonal trade worked well, producing a strong gain and outperforming the S&P 500. Exiting early proved to be advantageous as the materials sector continued to trend downwards and underperform the S&P 500.

NOVEMBER

M	T	W	T	F	S	S
						1
2	3	4	5	6	7	8
9	10	11	12	13	14	15
16	17	18	19	20	21	22
23	24	25	26	27	28	29
30						

DECEMBER

M	T	W	T	F	S	S
	1	2	3	4	5	6
7	8	9	10	11	12	13
14	15	16	17	18	19	20
21	22	23	24	25	26	27
28	29	30	31			

JANUARY

M	T	W	T	F	S	S
				1	2	3
4	5	6	7	8	9	10
11	12	13	14	15	16	17
18	19	20	21	22	23	24
25	26	27	28	29	30	31

** Weekly avg closing values- except Fed Funds & CAN overnight tgt rate weekly closing values.

SOX (SEMICONDUCTOR)
TIME TO PUT ON YOUR SOX TRADE
①Oct 28- Nov 6 ②Jan 1- Feb 15

Many investors think of the semiconductor sector as the technology sector on steroids, but there are some differences.

The seasonal trends in the semiconductor sector are largely driven by the ordering cycle of semiconductors and economic expectations.

15.0% gain & positive 85% of the time

Demand for semiconductors tends to reach a low in the second quarter and the beginning of the third quarter. It tends to reach a peak towards the end of the third quarter and into the forth quarter. Most of the major semiconductor companies report their third quarter earnings in mid-October. Although this quarter realizes some of the seasonal earnings peak, the market tends to be volatile in this month and investors defer their entry into the sector until the market shows consistent strength, typically towards the end of October.

The first quarter of the year tends to be positive for semiconductor companies as the sector tends to perform well into mid-February.

As a result of the cyclical demand for semiconductors, the semiconductor sector has two periods of seasonal strength, with a short period of market performance in between.

The first period of seasonal strength is very short, starting on October 28th and finishing on November 6th, and has produced an average gain of 6.1% and has been positive 90% of the time, from 1994 to 2013. Although the remainder of the year, from November 7th to December 31st, can be positive, previous returns in this time period have been very volatile and on average, the sector has underperformed the S&P 500.

SOX Semiconductor vs. S&P 500   Positive [ ]
1994/95 to 2013/14

Year	Oct 28 to Nov 6 S&P 500	SOX	Jan 1 to Feb 15 S&P 500	SOX	Compound Growth S&P 500	SOX
1994/95	-0.8 %	1.4 %	5.5 %	13.9 %	4.7 %	15.5 %
1995/96	1.5	1.5	5.8	-4.5	7.3	-3.1
1996/97	3.4	7.6	9.1	19.5	12.0	28.6
1997/98	7.0	9.9	5.1	16.4	12.4	27.9
1998/99	7.1	11.1	0.1	11.8	7.2	24.2
1999/00	5.7	25.9	-4.6	35.4	0.8	70.5
2000/01	3.8	8.8	0.5	23.4	4.3	34.2
2001/02	1.3	8.2	-3.8	6.2	-2.6	14.9
2002/03	2.9	12.8	-5.1	-3.1	-2.3	9.2
2003/04	2.6	13.8	3.1	0.5	5.7	14.3
2004/05	3.6	1.7	-0.2	1.4	3.5	3.1
2005/06	3.5	5.7	2.5	12.3	6.1	18.6
2006/07	0.2	1.1	2.7	1.3	2.9	2.4
2007/08	-1.0	0.8	-8.1	-14.8	-9.0	-14.2
2008/09	6.6	3.2	-8.5	4.0	-2.4	7.3
2009/10	0.6	-2.5	-3.6	-7.5	-3.0	-9.8
2010/11	3.7	5.8	5.6	12.0	9.5	18.6
2011/12	-2.4	-1.1	6.8	16.8	4.2	15.5
2012/13	1.2	4.5	6.6	11.6	7.8	16.5
2013/14	0.6	1.7	-0.5	4.5	0.1	6.3
Avg.	2.5 %	6.1 %	1.0 %	8.0 %	3.5 %	15.0 %
Fq > 0	85 %	90 %	60 %	80 %	75 %	85 %

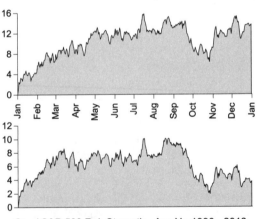

SOX PHLX Semiconductor - Avg. Year 1995 to 2013

Sox / S&P 500 Rel. Strength - Avg Yr. 1990 - 2013

> *Alternate Strategy—*
> *Investors can bridge the gap between the two positive seasonal trends for the semiconductor sector by holding from October 28th to March 1st. Longer term investors may prefer this strategy, shorter term investors can use technical tools to determine the appropriate strategy.*

> *PHLX Semiconductor Index (SOX):*
> *For more information on the PHLX Semiconductor Index (SOX), see www.nasdaq.com.*

2013-14 Strategy Performance

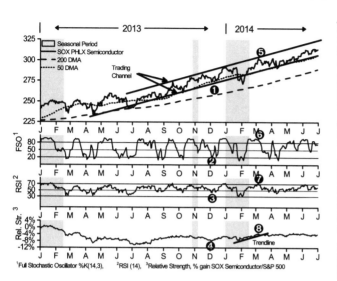

¹Full Stochastic Oscillator %K(14,3),   ²RSI (14),   ³Relative Strength, % gain SOX Semiconductor/S&P 500

Market Indices & Rates Weekly Values**

Stock Markets	2012	2013
Dow	12,655	15,839
S&P500	1,365	1,782
Nasdaq	2,865	3,953
TSX	11,989	13,394
FTSE	5,712	6,689
DAX	7,087	9,112
Nikkei	8,771	14,694
Hang Seng	21,266	22,823

Commodities	2012	2013
Oil	85.88	93.93
Gold	1722.2	1281.9

Bond Yields	2012	2013
USA 5 Yr Treasury	0.63	1.40
USA 10 Yr T	1.59	2.74
USA 20 Yr T	2.31	3.53
Moody's Aaa	3.46	4.67
Moody's Baa	4.47	5.43
CAN 5 Yr T	1.30	1.81
CAN 10 Yr T	1.71	2.59

Money Market	2012	2013
USA Fed Funds	0.25	0.25
USA 3 Mo T-B	0.06	0.08
CAN tgt overnight rate	1.00	1.00
CAN 3 Mo T-B	0.97	0.93

Foreign Exchange	2012	2013
EUR/USD	1.27	1.35
GBP/USD	1.59	1.60
USD/CAD	1.00	1.05
USD/JPY	80.32	99.65

NOVEMBER

M	T	W	T	F	S	S
						1
2	3	4	5	6	7	8
9	10	11	12	13	14	15
16	17	18	19	20	21	22
23	24	25	26	27	28	29
30						

DECEMBER

M	T	W	T	F	S	S
	1	2	3	4	5	6
7	8	9	10	11	12	13
14	15	16	17	18	19	20
21	22	23	24	25	26	27
28	29	30	31			

JANUARY

M	T	W	T	F	S	S
				1	2	3
4	5	6	7	8	9	10
11	12	13	14	15	16	17
18	19	20	21	22	23	24
25	26	27	28	29	30	31

SOX (PHLX Semiconductor) Performance

Semiconductor sector (SOX) started a solid uptrend in the summer of 2013. It wasn't until August that the sector started to outperform the S&P 500. Over the next few months, the semiconductor sector started to rise in a trading channel.

Technical Conditions– January 1st to February 15th, 2014

Entry Strategy –Buy Position on Entry Date–

In early December, the semiconductor sector declined, bringing it to the bottom of its trading channel❶. When the sector bounced, the FSO crossed above 20❷ and triggered an early buy signal. The RSI moved above 50❸ supporting the buy signal. The early entry point proved to be an inflection point for the semiconductor's performance relative to the S&P 500❹, as it started to move upwards.

Exit Strategy– Exit Position Late–

At the end of the seasonal trade, the semiconductor sector was still rising, outperforming the S&P 500 and the FSO was above 80. As a result, it was best to take advantage of the positive momentum and stay in the position.

At the beginning of March, the semiconductor sector was at the upper level of its trading channel❺ with the FSO in overbought territory. When the semiconductor sector started to decline, the FSO dropped below 80❻, triggering a sell signal. In support, the RSI dropped below 70❼. This action was the start of the sector starting to perform at market❽.

** Weekly avg closing values- except Fed Funds & CAN overnight tgt rate weekly closing values.

At the macro level, the metals and mining (M&M) sector is driven by future economic growth expectations. When worldwide growth expectations are increasing, there is a greater need for raw materials– when growth expectations are decreasing, the need is less.

Within the macro trend, the M&M sector has traditionally followed the overall market cycle of performing well from autumn until spring. This is the time of year that investors have a positive outlook on the economy and as a result, the cyclical sectors tend to outperform, including the metals and mining sector.

13.2% gain and positive 72% of the time

The metals and mining sector has two seasonal "sweet spots" – the first from November 19th to January 5th and the second from January 23rd to May 5th.

Investors have the option to hold and "bridge the gap" across the two sweet spots, but over the long-term, nimble traders have been able to capture extra value by being out of the sector from January 6th to the 22nd. During this period, from 1990 to 2014, the metals and mining sector has produced an average loss of 2.8% and has only been positive 48% of the time.

From a portfolio perspective, it is important to consider reducing exposure at the beginning of May. The danger of holding on too long is that the sector tends not to do well in the late summer, particularly in September.

(i) *For more information on the metals and mining sector, see www.standardandpoors.com*

Metals & Mining Sector vs. S&P 500 1989/90 to 2013/14

Positive [   ]

Year	Nov 19 to Jan 5 S&P 500	Nov 19 to Jan 5 M&M	Jan 23 to May 5 S&P 500	Jan 23 to May 5 M&M	Compound Growth S&P 500	Compound Growth M&M
1989/90	3.1 %	6.3 %	2.4 %	-4.6 %	5.6 %	1.4 %
1990/91	1.2	6.4	16.0	7.1	17.4	13.9
1991/92	8.9	1.0	-0.3	-1.7	0.5	0.7
1992/93	2.7	12.5	1.9	3.2	4.7	16.1
1993/94	0.9	9.0	-4.9	-11.1	-4.1	-3.1
1994/95	-0.2	-1.2	11.9	-3.0	11.6	-4.1
1995/96	2.8	8.3	4.6	5.8	7.5	14.6
1996/97	1.5	-1.9	5.6	-1.2	7.2	-3.0
1997/98	4.1	-4.5	15.8	19.3	20.6	13.9
1998/99	8.8	-7.9	10.0	31.0	19.6	20.6
1999/00	-1.6	21.7	-0.6	-10.4	-2.2	9.1
2000/01	-5.1	17.0	-5.7	19.6	-10.5	40.0
2001/02	3.0	5.5	-4.1	12.8	-1.3	19.0
2002/03	0.9	9.3	5.5	3.2	6.4	12.8
2003/04	8.5	18.2	-2.0	-12.1	6.4	3.9
2004/05	0.0	-8.4	0.4	-4.0	0.4	-12.0
2005/06	2.0	17.3	5.1	27.3	7.2	49.4
2006/07	0.6	3.0	5.8	17.2	6.5	20.8
2007/08	-3.2	0.9	7.4	27.4	3.9	28.5
2008/09	8.0	43.8	9.2	30.6	17.9	87.8
2009/10	2.4	6.3	6.8	4.8	9.4	11.3
2010/11	6.7	15.0	4.0	-1.6	11.0	13.1
2011/12	5.4	1.2	4.1	-16.0	9.7	-15.0
2012/13	7.8	3.9	8.2	-16.8	16.6	-13.6
2013/14	2.2	1.2	4.5	5.3	6.8	6.6
Avg.	2.9 %	7.4 %	4.5 %	5.3 %	7.5 %	13.2 %
Fq > 0	84 %	80 %	50 %	50 %	84 %	72 %

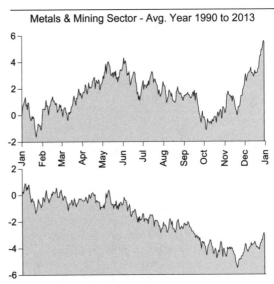

Metals & Mining Sector - Avg. Year 1990 to 2013

Metals & Mining / S&P 500 Rel. Strength- Avg Yr. 1990-2013

2013-14 Strategy Performance

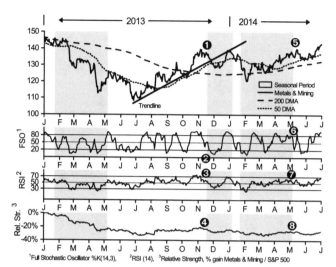

¹Full Stochastic Oscillator %K(14,3),   ²RSI (14),   ³Relative Strength, % gain Metals & Mining / S&P 500

Market Indices & Rates
Weekly Values**

Stock Markets	2012	2013
Dow	12,858	15,984
S&P500	1,394	1,792
Nasdaq	2,932	3,953
TSX	12,111	13,457
FTSE	5,770	6,692
DAX	7,207	9,207
Nikkei	9,221	15,223
Hang Seng	21,534	23,659

Commodities	2012	2013
Oil	87.64	93.86
Gold	1730.5	1260.5

Bond Yields	2012	2013
USA 5 Yr Treasury	0.68	1.37
USA 10 Yr T	1.67	2.74
USA 20 Yr T	2.40	3.54
Moody's Aaa	3.58	4.65
Moody's Baa	4.56	5.40
CAN 5 Yr T	1.35	1.77
CAN 10 Yr T	1.76	2.58

Money Market	2012	2013
USA Fed Funds	0.25	0.25
USA 3 Mo T-B	0.10	0.08
CAN tgt overnight rate	1.00	1.00
CAN 3 Mo T-B	0.96	0.94

Foreign Exchange	2012	2013
EUR/USD	1.29	1.35
GBP/USD	1.60	1.62
USD/CAD	1.00	1.05
USD/JPY	82.10	100.52

Metals and Mining Sector Performance

The metals and mining sector started to perform positively in July 2013, and formed a rising trading channel over the next few months, heading into November.

Technical Conditions– November 19th to May 5th, 2013

Entry Strategy –Buy Position on Entry Date–

Just before its entry date at the beginning of November, the metals and mining sector was at the top of its trading channel. It turned down and was at the mid-point of its channel on the buy date❶. Both the FSO and RSI were at 50❷❸ and falling. In addition, the metals and mining sector was underperforming the S&P 500 at the time❹. Given the weakness of the technical signals, a delayed entry could have been considered.

Exit Strategy –Sell Position Early–

In the second seasonal leg, from January 23rd to May 5th, the metals and mining sector started poorly, but improved its performance in March. At the beginning of April, the sector turned down❺, causing the FSO to cross below 80❻ and trigger an early sell signal. At the same time, the RSI turned down, but remained above 50❼. Also, the metal and mining sector's relative performance to the S&P 500 started to flatten out❽.

Overall, the metals and mining seasonal trade was successful as it produced a gain and outperformed the S&P 500. The early sell date did not provide additional value as the sector moved higher in absolute terms and performed at market for the rest of the seasonal trade.

** Weekly avg closing values- except Fed Funds & CAN overnight tgt rate weekly closing values.

NOVEMBER

M	T	W	T	F	S	S
						1
2	3	4	5	6	7	8
9	10	11	12	13	14	15
16	17	18	19	20	21	22
23	24	25	26	27	28	29
30						

DECEMBER

M	T	W	T	F	S	S
	1	2	3	4	5	6
7	8	9	10	11	12	13
14	15	16	17	18	19	20
21	22	23	24	25	26	27
28	29	30	31			

JANUARY

M	T	W	T	F	S	S
				1	2	3
4	5	6	7	8	9	10
11	12	13	14	15	16	17
18	19	20	21	22	23	24
25	26	27	28	29	30	31

THANKSGIVING
GIVE THANKS & TAKE RETURNS
Day Before and After – Two of the Best Days

We have a lot to be thankful for on Thanksgiving Day. As a bonus, the market day before and the market day after Thanksgiving, on average, have been two of the best days of the year in the stock market.

Each day, by itself, has produced spectacular results. From 1950 to 2013, the S&P 500 has had an average gain of 0.4% on the days before and after Thanksgiving.

The day before Thanksgiving and the day after have had an average cumulative return of 0.7% and together have been positive 84% of the time

To put the performance of these two days in perspective, the average daily return of the S&P 500 over the same time period is 0.03%.

The gains the day before Thanksgiving and the day after are almost ten times better than the average market and have a much greater frequency of being positive.

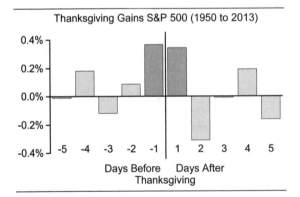

Thanksgiving Gains S&P 500 (1950 to 2013)

Days Before   Days After
Thanksgiving

Alternate Strategy — Although the focus has been on the performance of two specific days, the day before and the day after Thanksgiving, the holiday occurs at the end of November which tends to be a strong month. December, the next month is also strong. Investors have an option of expanding their trade to include the "Santa Arrives Early & Stays Late" Strategy.

History of Thanksgiving:
It was originally a "thanksgiving feast" by the pilgrims for surviving their first winter. Initially it was celebrated sporadically and the holiday, when it was granted, had its date changed several times. It was not until 1941 that it was proclaimed to be the 4th Thursday in November.

S&P500	Day Before	Day After
	Positive	
1950	1.4	0.8
1951	-0.2	-1.1
1952	0.6	0.5
1953	0.1	0.6
1954	0.6	1.0
1955	0.1	-0.1
1956	-0.5	1.1
1957	2.9	1.1
1958	1.7	1.1
1959	0.2	0.5
1960	0.1	0.6
1961	-0.1	0.2
1962	0.6	1.2
1963	-0.2	1.4
1964	-0.3	-0.3
1965	0.2	0.1
1966	0.7	0.8
1967	0.6	0.3
1968	0.5	0.6
1969	0.4	0.6
1970	0.4	1.0
1971	0.2	1.8
1972	0.6	0.3
1973	1.1	-0.3
1974	0.7	0.0
1975	0.3	0.3
1976	0.4	0.7
1977	0.4	0.2
1978	0.5	0.3
1979	0.2	0.8
1980	0.6	0.2
1981	0.4	0.8
1982	0.7	0.7
1983	0.1	0.1
1984	0.2	1.5
1985	0.9	-0.2
1986	0.2	0.2
1987	-0.9	-1.5
1988	0.7	-0.7
1989	0.7	0.6
1990	0.2	-0.3
1991	-0.4	-0.4
1992	0.4	0.2
1993	0.3	0.2
1994	0.0	0.5
1995	-0.3	0.3
1996	-0.1	0.3
1997	0.1	0.4
1998	0.3	0.5
1999	0.9	0.0
2000	-1.9	1.5
2001	-0.5	1.2
2002	2.8	-0.3
2003	0.4	0.0
2004	0.4	0.1
2005	0.3	0.2
2006	0.2	-0.4
2007	-1.6	1.7
2008	3.5	1.0
2009	0.5	-1.7
2010	1.5	-0.7
2011	-2.2	-0.3
2012	0.2	1.3
2013	0.2	-0.1
Total Avg %	0.4%	0.4%
Fq > 0	78%	75%

THANKSGIVING DAY

2011-12-13 Strategy Performance

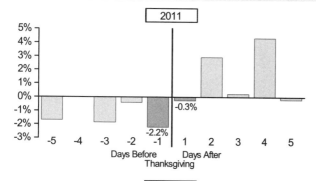

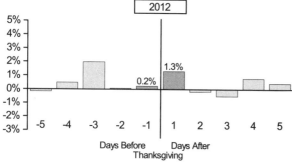

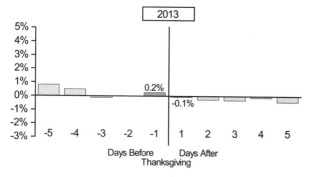

Market Indices & Rates
Weekly Values**

Stock Markets	2012	2013
Dow	12,976	16,082
S&P500	1,409	1,805
Nasdaq	2,992	4,029
TSX	12,176	13,390
FTSE	5,825	6,657
DAX	7,355	9,347
Nikkei	9,393	15,595
Hang Seng	21,874	23,768

Commodities	2012	2013
Oil	87.68	93.16
Gold	1731.2	1246.8

Bond Yields	2012	2013
USA 5 Yr Treasury	0.64	1.36
USA 10 Yr T	1.63	2.74
USA 20 Yr T	2.37	3.52
Moody's Aaa	3.56	4.62
Moody's Baa	4.56	5.37
CAN 5 Yr T	1.31	1.73
CAN 10 Yr T	1.72	2.54

Money Market	2012	2013
USA Fed Funds	0.25	0.25
USA 3 Mo T-B	0.08	0.07
CAN tgt overnight rate	1.00	1.00
CAN 3 Mo T-B	0.96	0.94

Foreign Exchange	2012	2013
EUR/USD	1.30	1.36
GBP/USD	1.60	1.63
USD/CAD	0.99	1.06
USD/JPY	82.18	101.98

NOVEMBER

M	T	W	T	F	S	S
						1
2	3	4	5	6	7	8
9	10	11	12	13	14	15
16	17	18	19	20	21	22
23	24	25	26	27	28	29
30						

DECEMBER

M	T	W	T	F	S	S
	1	2	3	4	5	6
7	8	9	10	11	12	13
14	15	16	17	18	19	20
21	22	23	24	25	26	27
28	29	30	31			

JANUARY

M	T	W	T	F	S	S
				1	2	3
4	5	6	7	8	9	10
11	12	13	14	15	16	17
18	19	20	21	22	23	24
25	26	27	28	29	30	31

Thanksgiving Strategy Performance 2013

Although the *Thanksgiving– Give Thanks and Take Returns* trade was successful in 2013, the net returns from the day before and the day after Thanksgiving were small. In fact, the days surrounding Thanksgiving were unusually quiet, producing either small gains or losses.

** Weekly avg closing values- except Fed Funds & CAN overnight tgt rate weekly closing values.

DECEMBER

	MONDAY	TUESDAY	WEDNESDAY
WEEK 49	30	**1** 30	**2** 29
WEEK 50	**7** 24	**8** 23	**9** 22
WEEK 51	**14** 17	**15** 16	**16** 15
WEEK 52	**21** 10	**22** 9	**23** 8
WEEK 01	**28** 3	**29** 2	**30** 1

THURSDAY		FRIDAY	
3	28	**4**	27
10	21	**11**	20
17	14	**18**	13
24	7	**25**	6
USA Early Market Close		CAN Market Closed-Christmas Day	
		USA Market Closed-Christmas Day	
31		1	

JANUARY

M	T	W	T	F	S	S
				1	2	3
4	5	6	7	8	9	10
11	12	13	14	15	16	17
18	19	20	21	22	23	24
25	26	27	28	29	30	31

FEBRUARY

M	T	W	T	F	S	S
1	2	3	4	5	6	7
8	9	10	11	12	13	14
15	16	17	18	19	20	21
22	23	24	25	26	27	28
29						

MARCH

M	T	W	T	F	S	S
	1	2	3	4	5	6
7	8	9	10	11	12	13
14	15	16	17	18	19	20
21	22	23	24	25	26	27
28	29	30	31			

APRIL

M	T	W	T	F	S	S
				1	2	3
4	5	6	7	8	9	10
11	12	13	14	15	16	17
18	19	20	21	22	23	24
25	26	27	28	29	30	

DECEMBER
S U M M A R Y

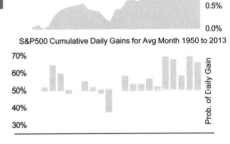

S&P500 Cumulative Daily Gains for Avg Month 1950 to 2013

	Dow Jones	S&P 500	Nasdaq	TSX Comp
Month Rank	2	1	2	1
# Up	46	50	25	26
# Down	18	14	17	3
% Pos	72	78	60	90
% Avg. Gain	1.7	1.7	1.8	2.3

Dow & S&P 1950-2013, Nasdaq 1972-2013, TSX 1985-2013

◆ December is typically one of the strongest months of the year for the S&P 500. From 1950 to 2013, the S&P 500 produced an average gain of 1.7% and was positive 78% of the time. In the last six years in a row, the S&P 500 has been positive in December. ◆ Most of the gains for the S&P 500 are in the second half of the month. ◆ The Nasdaq tends to outperform the S&P 500 starting mid-December. ◆ The small cap sector also starts to outperform mid-month.

BEST / WORST DECEMBER BROAD MKTS. 2004-2013

BEST DECEMBER MARKETS
- ◆ Nikkei 225 (2009) 12.8%
- ◆ Nikkei 225 (2012) 10.0%
- ◆ Nikkei 225 (2005) 8.3%

WORST DECEMBER MARKETS
- ◆ TSX Comp. (2008) -3.1%
- ◆ Nikkei 225 (2007) -2.4%
- ◆ TSX Comp. (2011) -2.0%

Index Values End of Month

	2004	2005	2006	2007	2008	2009	2010	2011	2012	2013
Dow	10,783	10,718	12,463	13,265	8,776	10,428	11,578	12,218	13,104	16,577
S&P 500	1,212	1,248	1,418	1,468	903	1,115	1,258	1,258	1,426	1,848
Nasdaq	2,175	2,205	2,415	2,652	1,577	2,269	2,653	2,605	3,020	4,177
TSX Comp.	9,247	11,272	12,908	13,833	8,988	11,746	13,443	11,955	12,434	13,622
Russell 1000	1,251	1,306	1,480	1,538	938	1,176	1,340	1,333	1,518	1,981
Russell 2000	1,619	1,673	1,958	1,904	1,241	1,554	1,948	1,841	2,111	2,892
FTSE 100	4,814	5,619	6,221	6,457	4,434	5,413	5,900	5,572	5,898	6,749
Nikkei 225	11,489	16,111	17,226	15,308	8,860	10,546	10,229	8,455	10,395	16,291

Percent Gain for December

	2004	2005	2006	2007	2008	2009	2010	2011	2012	2013
Dow	3.4	-0.8	2.0	-0.8	-0.6	0.8	5.2	1.4	0.6	3.0
S&P 500	3.2	-0.1	1.3	-0.9	0.8	1.8	6.5	0.9	0.7	2.4
Nasdaq	3.7	-1.2	-0.7	-0.3	2.7	5.8	6.2	-0.6	0.3	2.9
TSX Comp.	2.4	4.1	1.2	1.1	-3.1	2.6	3.8	-2.0	1.6	1.7
Russell 1000	3.5	0.0	1.1	-0.8	1.3	2.3	6.5	0.7	0.8	2.5
Russell 2000	2.8	-0.6	0.2	-0.2	5.6	7.9	7.8	0.5	3.3	1.8
FTSE 100	2.4	3.6	2.8	0.4	3.4	4.3	6.7	1.2	0.5	1.5
Nikkei 225	5.4	8.3	5.8	-2.4	4.1	12.8	2.9	0.2	10.0	4.0

December Market Avg. Performance 2004 to 2013[1]

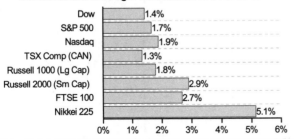

Dow	1.4%
S&P 500	1.7%
Nasdaq	1.9%
TSX Comp (CAN)	1.3%
Russell 1000 (Lg Cap)	1.8%
Russell 2000 (Sm Cap)	2.9%
FTSE 100	2.7%
Nikkei 225	5.1%

Interest Corner Dec[2]

	Fed Funds %[3]	3 Mo. T-Bill %[4]	10 Yr %[5]	20 Yr %[6]
2013	0.25	0.07	3.04	3.72
2012	0.25	0.05	1.78	2.54
2011	0.25	0.02	1.89	2.57
2010	0.25	0.12	3.30	4.13
2009	0.25	0.06	3.85	4.58

(1) Russell Data provided by Russell (2) Federal Reserve Bank of St. Louis- end of month values (3) Target rate set by FOMC (4)(5)(6) Constant yield maturities.

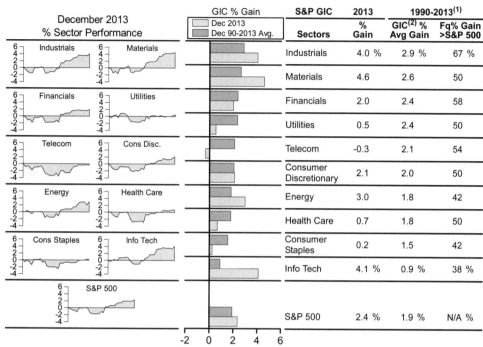

S&P GIC Sectors	2013 % Gain	1990-2013[1] GIC[2] % Avg Gain	Fq% Gain >S&P 500
Industrials	4.0 %	2.9 %	67 %
Materials	4.6	2.6	50
Financials	2.0	2.4	58
Utilities	0.5	2.4	50
Telecom	-0.3	2.1	54
Consumer Discretionary	2.1	2.0	50
Energy	3.0	1.8	42
Health Care	0.7	1.8	50
Consumer Staples	0.2	1.5	42
Info Tech	4.1 %	0.9 %	38 %
S&P 500	2.4 %	1.9 %	N/A %

Sector Commentary

♦ In December 2013, the S&P 500 performed above average, with a gain of 2.4% compared to its average 1.9% performance since 1990. ♦ After a negative first half of the month, the S&P 500 climbed steadily to the end of the year. ♦ All of the major sectors of the stock market were positive in December, except for telecom. ♦ The information technology sector had a strong gain of 4.1%, compared to its average performance of 0.9% since 1990.

Sub-Sector Commentary

♦ The homebuilders sub-sector typically performs well in December. Since 1990, it has produced an average gain of 8.4% and has been positive 92% of the time. In December 2013, homebuilders gained 10.4%, more than quadrupling the gain of the S&P 500 for the month. ♦ Agriculture also performed well with a 7.8% gain. ♦ Gold typically does not perform well in December and in 2013, it lived up to its reputation, producing a loss of 3.9% for the month. ♦ The retail sub-sector had a relatively small gain of 0.8%, underperforming the S&P 500.

SELECTED SUB-SECTORS[3]

Homebuilders	10.4 %	8.4 %	92 %
Steel	5.7	5.6	71
Biotech (1993-2013)	0.6	4.6	52
Metals & Mining	5.7	3.5	58
Agriculture (1994-2013)	7.8	2.4	55
Chemicals	4.2	2.2	58
Banks	3.0	2.1	58
Railroads	4.3	1.9	50
Software & Services	4.8	1.8	46
Pharma	0.3	1.4	42
Silver	-2.2	1.3	46
Transportation	2.8	1.2	38
SOX (1995-2013)	4.9	1.2	42
Retail	0.8	1.0	29
Gold (London PM)	-3.9	-0.1	29

EMERGING MARKETS(USD)–
TRUNCATED SIX MONTH SEASONAL
November 24th to April 18th

Emerging markets become popular periodically, mainly after they have had a strong run, or if they have suffered a major correction and investors perceive them to have a lot of value.

Markets around the world tend to have the same broad seasonal trends, including the emerging markets. Typically, emerging markets will outperform when the U.S. market is increasing and underperform when it is decreasing.

The exceptions to this usually occurs if there is a global economic contraction underway, or economic growth is in question, and investors seek the "safety" of the U.S. market. In this case the emerging markets can underperform the U.S. market.

11% gain & positive 83% of the time positive

Seasonal investors have benefited from concentrating their emerging market exposure in a truncated, or shorter version, of the favorable six month seasonal period.

Emerging Markets (USD) vs. S&P 500 1990/91 to 2013/14			
		Positive	
Nov 24 to Apr 18	S&P 500	Em. Mkts.	Diff
1990/91	23.8%	33.8%	10.5%
1991/92	10.6	37.5	26.8
1992/93	5.0	11.0	6.2
1993/94	-4.0	3.7	7.8
1994/95	12.3	-16.4	-28.7
1995/96	7.6	14.7	7.1
1996/97	2.4	7.1	4.7
1997/98	16.6	6.7	-9.9
1998/99	11.0	18.1	7.1
1999/00	2.6	3.5	0.8
2000/01	-6.4	-4.6	1.8
2001/02	-2.3	22.3	24.5
2002/03	-4.0	0.0	4.0
2003/04	9.6	19.5	9.9
2004/05	-2.6	4.3	7.0
2005/06	3.3	24.7	21.4
2006/07	4.7	13.2	8.5
2007/08	-3.5	-0.9	2.6
2008/09	8.7	37.6	28.9
2009/10	7.8	5.6	-2.2
2010/11	10.5	6.6	-3.9
2011/12	19.2	15.6	-3.6
2012/13	9.4	0.1	-9.3
2013/14	3.3	0.3	-3.1
Avg	6.1%	11.0%	5.0%
Fq > 0	75%	83%	71%

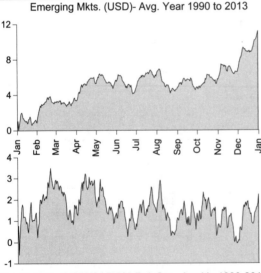

Emerging Mkts. (USD)- Avg. Year 1990 to 2013

Emerg. Mkts. (USD)/S&P 500 Rel. Str. - Avg Yr. 1990-2013

ing markets sector (USD) produced an average rate of return of 11.0% and has been positive 83% of the time.

As the world has grappled with the sub-prime crisis and then the EU crisis in the last few years, investors have sought the safety of the U.S. markets and as a result, emerging markets have underperformed.

As worldwide economic growth gains traction in the future, seasonal investors should consider adding emerging markets to their portfolio from November 24th to April 18th.

The seasonally strong period for the emerging markets sector is from November 24th to April 18th. In this time period, from 1990/91 to 2013/14, the emerg-

(i) *Emerging Markets (USD)- For more information on the emerging markets, see www.standardandpoors.com*

2013-14 Strategy Performance

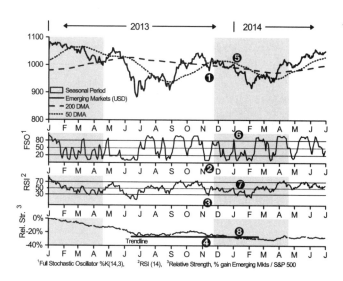

[1]Full Stochastic Oscillator %K(14,3),   [2]RSI (14),   [3]Relative Strength, % gain Emerging Mkts / S&P 500

Market Indices & Rates
Weekly Values**

Stock Markets	2012	2013
Dow	13,036	15,931
S&P500	1,412	1,796
Nasdaq	2,988	4,043
TSX	12,155	13,305
FTSE	5,890	6,538
DAX	7,475	9,205
Nikkei	9,486	15,458
Hang Seng	22,056	23,827

Commodities	2012	2013
Oil	87.53	96.42
Gold	1701.5	1226.0

Bond Yields	2012	2013
USA 5 Yr Treasury	0.62	1.46
USA 10 Yr T	1.62	2.84
USA 20 Yr T	2.36	3.61
Moody's Aaa	3.57	4.69
Moody's Baa	4.57	5.44
CAN 5 Yr T	1.27	1.79
CAN 10 Yr T	1.70	2.64

Money Market	2012	2013
USA Fed Funds	0.25	0.25
USA 3 Mo T-B	0.09	0.06
CAN tgt overnight rate	1.00	1.00
CAN 3 Mo T-B	0.96	0.93

Foreign Exchange	2012	2013
EUR/USD	1.30	1.36
GBP/USD	1.61	1.64
USD/CAD	0.99	1.07
USD/JPY	82.30	102.50

DECEMBER

M	T	W	T	F	S	S
	1	2	3	4	5	6
7	8	9	10	11	12	13
14	15	16	17	18	19	20
21	22	23	24	25	26	27
28	29	30	31			

JANUARY

M	T	W	T	F	S	S
					1	2	3
4	5	6	7	8	9	10
11	12	13	14	15	16	17
18	19	20	21	22	23	24
25	26	27	28	29	30	31

FEBRUARY

M	T	W	T	F	S	S
1	2	3	4	5	6	7
8	9	10	11	12	13	14
15	16	17	18	19	20	21
22	23	24	25	26	27	28
29						

Emerging Markets Performance

Emerging markets underperformed the S&P 500 in 2013, as investors were generally conservative in their investments and sought the stable earnings of American large blue chip companies. The emerging markets also suffered because a few of the constituents had trouble funding their current account deficits with foreign investments.

Technical Conditions– November 24th to April 18th, 2014

Entry Strategy –Buy Position Early–

After underperforming for the first half of the year, the emerging markets started to perform at market in July. In November, the emerging markets corrected and then bounced from just below its 50 day moving average❶, triggering an early buy signal as the FSO crossed above 20❷. At the same time, the RSI also supported the early buy signal by bouncing off 30❸. At the time, the emerging markets were underperforming the S&P 500❹.

Exit Strategy –Sell Position Early–

At the end of December, the emerging markets were trading just below its 50 day moving average❺. In addition, the FSO broke below 80❻ and the RSI turned down from 50❼. Both of these events occurred too far away from the end of the seasonal period to trigger a sell signal, but the breakdown of the relative performance to the S&P 500❽ did indicate a broken trade. The emerging markets broke their long-term market performance line, triggering a sell signal in the middle of their seasonal period.

Aerospace & Defense Sector Flying High
December 12th to May 5th

The aerospace and defense sector is highly dependent on government purchases and as a result is subject not only to economic cycles, but also the political environment. Despite the fact that outside variables have a large impact on aerospace and defense orders, the sector has a seasonal trend.

The aerospace and defense sector has a seasonal trend that is similar to the overall broad market's seasonal trend. There are some differences. First, although the aerospace and defense sector on average performs positively in October, November and December, it performs flat to the market in this time period up until mid-December. Second, it has a track record of strongly outperforming the S&P 500 up until the beginning of May.

10.1% gain & positive 88% of the time

The difference in the sector's seasonal trend compared with the S&P 500's trend is largely the result of the U.S. governments procurement cycle, which has a year-end of September 30th. The first quarter of the government's fiscal year (October, November and December) tends to be the weakest for orders, as typically major purchases are made towards the end of the last fiscal quarter and the new fiscal quarter is slow to get off the ground. Government procurement tends to pick up at the start of the new calendar year, helping to boost aerospace and defense stocks up until the beginning of May.

Aerospace & Defense* vs. S&P 500 1989/90 to 2013/14			
Dec 12 to May 5	S&P 500	Aero & Def.	Positive Diff
1989/90	-2.9%	6.1%	9.0%
1990/91	16.7	11.6	-5.1
1991/92	10.4	10.1	-0.3
1992/93	2.5	14.3	11.9
1993/94	-2.7	2.7	5.4
1994/95	16.4	26.0	9.7
1995/96	3.6	11.6	8.0
1996/97	12.1	8.0	-4.1
1997/98	16.8	11.5	-5.3
1998/99	15.5	29.1	13.6
1999/00	1.1	3.6	2.5
2000/01	-8.2	-0.9	7.4
2001/02	-5.6	23.3	28.9
2002/03	2.4	-7.4	-9.8
2003/04	4.7	5.6	0.9
2004/05	-1.3	4.1	5.4
2005/06	5.3	21.0	15.8
2006/07	6.6	9.0	2.5
2007/08	-4.8	-2.5	2.3
2008/09	3.5	8.5	5.1
2009/10	5.4	12.8	7.4
2010/11	7.6	13.0	5.4
2011/12	9.1	7.4	-1.7
2012/13	13.1	14.7	1.7
2013/14	5.8	8.9	3.1
Avg	5.3%	10.1%	4.8%
Fq > 0	76%	88%	76%

From 1989/90 to 2013/14, during its seasonal period, December 12th to May 5th, the aerospace and defense sector has produced an average gain of 10.1% and has been positive 88% of the time. Compared to the S&P 500, it has produced an extra 4.8% and outperformed it 76% of the time.

In the other seven months of the year, from May 6th to December 11th, the aerospace and defense sector has underperformed the market with an average 2.2% gain, and has only outperformed the S&P 500, 42% of the time. In this time period, there have been eight years of gains and five years of losses greater than 10%. In other words, the results in the unfavorable period for the sector tend to be volatile.

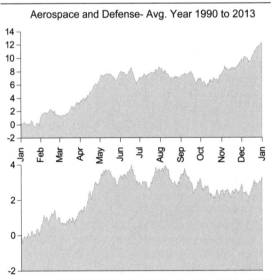

Aerospace and Defense- Avg. Year 1990 to 2013

Aerospace & Def./ S&P 500 Rel. Str. - Avg Yr. 1990 - 2013

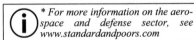

(i) * For more information on the aerospace and defense sector, see www.standardandpoors.com

2013-14 Strategy Performance

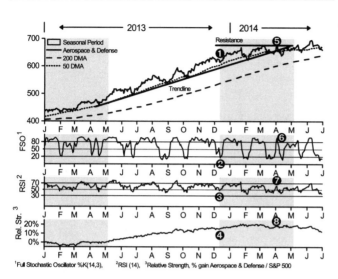

^{1}Full Stochastic Oscillator %K(14,3), ^{2}RSI (14), ^{3}Relative Strength, % gain Aerospace & Defense / S&P 500

Market Indices & Rates
Weekly Values**

Stock Markets	2012	2013
Dow	13,194	15,867
S&P500	1,422	1,789
Nasdaq	2,997	4,026
TSX	12,290	13,202
FTSE	5,929	6,495
DAX	7,583	9,082
Nikkei	9,624	15,504
Hang Seng	22,431	23,472

Commodities	2012	2013
Oil	86.15	97.48
Gold	1705.6	1244.3

Bond Yields	2012	2013
USA 5 Yr Treasury	0.66	1.51
USA 10 Yr T	1.69	2.86
USA 20 Yr T	2.44	3.60
Moody's Aaa	3.65	4.66
Moody's Baa	4.63	5.40
CAN 5 Yr T	1.33	1.81
CAN 10 Yr T	1.76	2.65

Money Market	2012	2013
USA Fed Funds	0.25	0.25
USA 3 Mo T-B	0.04	0.07
CAN tgt overnight rate	1.00	1.00
CAN 3 Mo T-B	0.96	0.93

Foreign Exchange	2012	2013
EUR/USD	1.31	1.38
GBP/USD	1.61	1.64
USD/CAD	0.99	1.06
USD/JPY	83.06	103.03

Aerospace and Defense Performance

After performing flat to the market for January and February in 2013, the aerospace and defense sector started a steady run of outperformance relative to the S&P 500 that lasted until September. In October and November, the sector performed at market heading into its seasonal period.

Technical Conditions– December 12th to May 5th, 2014

Entry Strategy –Buy Position on Entry Date–

At the start of its seasonal period, the aerospace and defense sector was falling in value, but still above its 50 day moving average❶. In addition, the FSO was in the process of bouncing off 20❷ and the RSI was bouncing off 30❸ and the sector was also performing at market❹. After the buy date, the sector turned up and started outperforming the S&P 500.

Exit Strategy –Sell Position on Exit Date–

The aerospace and defense sector turned down at resistance in early April❺, causing the FSO to cross below 80❻ and trigger an early sell signal. At the same time, the RSI crossed back below 50❼. On a relative basis, the sector had been underperforming in March, but at the beginning of April it resumed its market performance❽.

Overall, the seasonal trade was successful, as it produced a gain and outperformed the S&P 500.

DECEMBER

M	T	W	T	F	S	S
	1	2	3	4	5	6
7	8	9	10	11	12	13
14	15	16	17	18	19	20
21	22	23	24	25	26	27
28	29	30	31			

JANUARY

M	T	W	T	F	S	S
				1	2	3
4	5	6	7	8	9	10
11	12	13	14	15	16	17
18	19	20	21	22	23	24
25	26	27	28	29	30	31

FEBRUARY

M	T	W	T	F	S	S
1	2	3	4	5	6	7
8	9	10	11	12	13	14
15	16	17	18	19	20	21
22	23	24	25	26	27	28
29						

** Weekly avg closing values- except Fed Funds & CAN overnight tgt rate weekly closing values.

DO THE "NAZ" WITH SANTA
Nasdaq Gives More at Christmas – Dec 15th to Jan 23rd

One of the best times to invest in the major markets is Christmas time. What few investors know is that this seasonally strong time favors the Nasdaq market.

From December 15th to January 23rd, starting in 1972 and ending in 2014, the Nasdaq has outperformed the S&P 500 by an average 2.2% per year.

This rate of return is considered to be very high given that the length of the favorable period is just over one month.

> ## 2.2% extra &
> ## 84% of time
> ## better than S&P 500

Interestingly, the Nasdaq starts to outperform at the same time as small companies in December (see *Small Company Effect* strategy). As investors move into the market to scoop up bargains that have been sold for tax losses, smaller companies and stocks with greater volatility tend to outperform.

Compared with the S&P 500 and Dow Jones, the Nasdaq market tends to be a much greater recipient of the upward move created by investors picking up cheap stocks at this time of the year.

Nasdaq vs. S&P 500 Dec 15th to Jan 23rd 1971/72 To 2013/14

Dec 15 to Jan 23	S&P 500	Nasdaq	Diff
		Positive	
1971/72	6.1 %	7.5 %	1.3 %
1972/73	0.0	-0.7	-0.7
1973/74	4.1	6.8	2.8
1974/75	7.5	8.9	1.4
1975/76	13.0	13.8	0.9
1976/77	-1.7	2.8	4.5
1977/78	-5.1	-3.5	1.6
1978/79	4.7	6.2	1.4
1979/80	4.1	5.6	1.5
1980/81	0.8	3.3	2.5
1981/82	-6.0	-5.0	1.0
1982/83	4.7	5.5	0.8
1983/84	0.9	1.4	0.4
1984/85	9.0	13.3	4.3
1985/86	-2.7	0.8	3.5
1986/87	9.2	10.2	1.0
1987/88	1.8	9.1	7.3
1988/89	3.3	4.6	1.3
1989/90	-5.5	-3.8	1.7
1990/91	1.0	4.1	3.1
1991/92	7.9	15.2	7.2
1992/93	0.8	7.2	6.4
1993/94	2.5	5.7	3.2
1994/95	2.4	4.7	2.3
1995/96	-0.7	-1.0	-0.3
1996/97	6.7	7.3	0.6
1997/98	0.4	2.6	2.1
1998/99	7.4	18.9	11.6
1999/00	2.7	18.6	15.9
2000/01	1.5	4.1	2.6
2001/02	0.5	-1.6	-2.0
2002/03	-0.2	1.9	2.1
2003/04	6.3	9.0	2.7
2004/05	-3.0	-5.8	-2.9
2005/06	-0.7	-0.6	0.1
2006/07	0.2	-0.9	-1.1
2007/08	-8.8	-12.1	-3.3
2008/09	-5.4	-4.1	1.3
2009/10	-2.0	-0.3	1.7
2010/11	3.4	2.4	-1.0
2011/12	8.6	9.6	1.1
2012/13	5.8	6.1	0.4
2013/14	3.0	5.5	2.5
Avg	2.1 %	4.3 %	2.2 %
Fq > 0	70 %	72 %	84 %

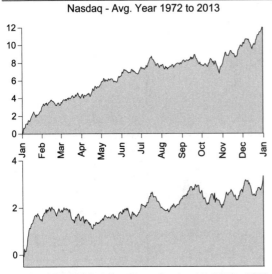

Nasdaq - Avg. Year 1972 to 2013

Nasdaq / SP 500 Relative Strength - Avg Yr. 1972 - 2013

> **Y** *Alternate Strategy — For those investors who favor the Nasdaq, an alternative strategy is to invest in the Nasdaq at an earlier date: October 28th. Historically, on average the Nasdaq has started its outperformance at this time. The "Do the Naz with Santa" strategy focuses on the sweet spot of the Nasdaq's outperformance.*

> **i** *Nasdaq is a market with a number of sectors. It is more focused on technology and is typically more volatile than the S&P 500.*

2013-14 Strategy Performance

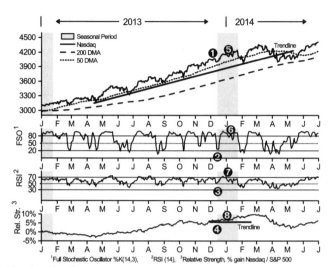

[1]Full Stochastic Oscillator %K(14,3),   [2]RSI (14),   [3]Relative Strength, % gain Nasdaq / S&P 500

Market Indices & Rates
Weekly Values**

Stock Markets	2012	2013
Dow	13,268	16,066
S&P500	1,437	1,801
Nasdaq	3,036	4,057
TSX	12,359	13,298
FTSE	5,942	6,538
DAX	7,647	9,233
Nikkei	9,978	15,550
Hang Seng	22,560	23,006

Commodities	2012	2013
Oil	88.53	98.04
Gold	1671.4	1217.7

Bond Yields	2012	2013
USA 5 Yr Treasury	0.76	1.58
USA 10 Yr T	1.80	2.89
USA 20 Yr T	2.56	3.61
Moody's Aaa	3.73	4.59
Moody's Baa	4.70	5.35
CAN 5 Yr T	1.39	1.83
CAN 10 Yr T	1.83	2.68

Money Market	2012	2013
USA Fed Funds	0.25	0.25
USA 3 Mo T-B	0.06	0.07
CAN tgt overnight rate	1.00	1.00
CAN 3 Mo T-B	0.92	0.91

Foreign Exchange	2012	2013
EUR/USD	1.32	1.37
GBP/USD	1.62	1.63
USD/CAD	0.99	1.06
USD/JPY	84.23	103.67

Nasdaq Performance

The Nasdaq started to outperform the S&P 500 in April 2013 and maintained a solid upward trend with a pattern of higher highs and higher lows coming into its seasonally strong period in December. In October, the Nasdaq started to perform equal to the S&P 500 and maintained this trend up until the start of its seasonal period in mid-December.

Technical Conditions– December 15 to January 23, 2014

Entry Strategy –Buy Position on Entry Date–

At the start of the seasonal period, the Nasdaq was in an up-trend and trading above its 50 and 200 day moving averages❶. The FSO turned up just after the start of the seasonal period❷, to follow the RSI which had already turned up and was rising❸. At the time, the Nasdaq was performing equal to the S&P 500❹.

Exit Strategy –Sell Position Early–

In early January, the Nasdaq had a slight correction❺, which caused the FSO to cross below 80❻ and trigger an early sell signal and the RSI to fall below 70❼. At the time, the Nasdaq was performing equal to the S&P 500❽.

In the end, the Nasdaq trade was successful, producing a gain and outperforming the S&P 500. Staying in the trade until the end of the seasonal period would have been more beneficial than exiting on the early sell signal.

DECEMBER

M	T	W	T	F	S	S
	1	2	3	4	5	6
7	8	9	10	11	12	13
14	15	16	17	18	19	20
21	22	23	24	25	26	27
28	29	30	31			

JANUARY

M	T	W	T	F	S	S
					1	2	3
4	5	6	7	8	9	10
11	12	13	14	15	16	17
18	19	20	21	22	23	24
25	26	27	28	29	30	31

FEBRUARY

M	T	W	T	F	S	S
1	2	3	4	5	6	7
8	9	10	11	12	13	14
15	16	17	18	19	20	21
22	23	24	25	26	27	28
29						

** Weekly avg closing values- except Fed Funds & CAN overnight tgt rate weekly closing values.

SMALL CAP (SMALL COMPANY) EFFECT
Small Companies Outperform - Dec 19th to Mar 7th

At different stages of the business cycle, small capitalization companies (small caps represented by Russell 2000), perform better than large capitalization companies (large caps represented by Russell 1000).

Evidence shows that the small caps relative outperformance also has a seasonal component as they typically outperform large caps from December 19th to March 7th.

25 times out of 35 better than the Russell 1000

Russell 2000 - Avg. Year 1979 to 2013

Russell 2000 / Russell 1000 - Avg Yr. 1979 - 2013

Russell 2000 vs. Russell 1000 Gains 19th Dec to Mar 7th 1979/80 to 2013/14

Dec 19 - Mar7	Russell 1000	Russell 2000	Diff
1979/80	-1.3 %	-0.4 %	0.9 %
1980/81	-2.8	4.0	6.8
1981/82	-12.4	-12.1	0.3
1982/83	11.8	19.8	8.0
1983/84	-6.4	-7.5	-1.1
1984/85	7.7	17.1	9.4
1985/86	8.2	11.7	3.5
1986/87	17.2	21.3	4.1
1987/88	8.3	16.4	8.0
1988/89	6.9	9.1	2.5
1989/90	-2.0	-1.9	0.2
1990/91	14.6	29.0	14.4
1991/92	6.0	16.8	10.8
1992/93	1.4	5.0	3.5
1993/94	0.5	5.7	5.3
1994/95	5.3	5.5	0.2
1995/96	8.3	7.8	-0.5
1996/97	9.5	3.5	-6.0
1997/98	10.2	10.3	0.1
1998 99	7.3	0.2	-7.2
1999/00	-1.7	27.7	29.4
2000/01	-5.2	4.7	9.8
2001/02	1.6	1.9	0.4
2002/03	-6.7	-7.8	-1.0
2003/04	6.4	9.6	3.3
2004/05	2.8	0.3	-2.5
2005/06	0.8	5.6	4.7
2006/07	-1.6	-0.8	0.9
2007/08	-10.9	-12.5	-1.5
2008/09	-22.2	-26.7	-4.5
2009/10	3.6	9.1	5.5
2010/11	5.5	4.2	-1.3
2011/12	11.3	10.2	-1.1
2012/13	7.1	10.3	3.1
2013/14	4.2	6.1	2.0
Avg.	2.7 %	5.8 %	3.1 %
Fq > 0	69 %	77 %	69 %

The core part of the small cap seasonal strategy occurs in January and includes what has been described as the January Effect (Wachtel 1942, 184).

This well documented anomaly of superior performance of stocks in the month of January is based upon the tenet that investors sell stocks in December for tax loss reasons, artificially driving down prices, and creating a great opportunity for astute investors.

In recent times, the January Effect start date has shifted to mid-December and is more pronounced for small caps as their prices are more volatile than large caps. At the beginning of the year, small cap stocks benefit from a phenomenon that I have coined, "beta out of the gate, and coast." If small cap stocks are outperforming at the beginning of the year, money man-

agers will gravitate to the sector in order to produce returns that are above their index benchmark. Once above average returns have been "locked in," the managers then rotate from their small cap overweight positions back to index large cap positions and coast for the rest of the year with above average returns. The overall process boosts small cap stocks at the beginning of the year.

(i) *Russell 2000 (small cap index): The 2000 smallest companies in the Russell 3000 stock index (a broad market index). Russell 1000 (large cap index): The 1000 largest companies in the Russell 3000 stock index*

For more information on the Russell indexes, see www.Russell.com

Wachtel, S.B. 1942. Certain observations on seasonal movements in stock prices. The Journal of Business and Economics (Winter): 184.

2013-14 Strategy Performance

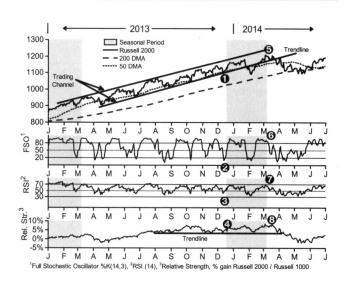

[1] Full Stochastic Oscillator %K(14,3), [2] RSI (14), [3] Relative Strength, % gain Russell 2000 / Russell 1000

Small Cap Sector Russell 2000 Performance

The Russell 2000 (small cap sector) started an uptrend in April 2013. In the uptrend, it initially outperformed the Russell 1000 (large cap sector). In August, the small cap sector settled into a pattern of equal performance to the large cap sector.

Technical Conditions– December 19th to March 7th, 2014

Entry Strategy –Buy Position on Entry Date–

At the start of its seasonal period, the small cap sector was at the bottom of its trading channel❶ and the FSO had just crossed above 20❷, and the RSI above 30❸, both supporting an entry into the small cap sector on its seasonal entry date. At the time the small cap sector had just started to outperform the large cap sector❹.

Exit Strategy –Sell Position on Exit Date–

After breaking below its trading channel in February, the small cap sector managed to climb back into its trading channel towards the end of its seasonal period❺. On the seasonal exit date, the small cap sector started to turn down, causing the FSO to drop below 80❻ and the RSI to turn down from 70❼. At the same time, the relative performance of the small cap sector compared to the large cap sector, changed from outperformance to equal performance❽.

In the end, the small cap sector seasonal trade was positive and outperformed the large cap sector. Shortly after its seasonal period, the small cap sector declined sharply.

Market Indices & Rates
Weekly Values**

Stock Markets	2012	2013
Dow	13,072	16,403
S&P500	1,417	1,836
Nasdaq	2,987	4,157
TSX	12,354	13,518
FTSE	5,945	6,708
DAX	7,634	9,539
Nikkei	10,257	16,063
Hang Seng	22,609	23,115

Commodities	2012	2013
Oil	90.23	99.38
Gold	1656.5	1206.8

Bond Yields	2012	2013
USA 5 Yr Treasury	0.74	1.72
USA 10 Yr T	1.76	2.99
USA 20 Yr T	2.50	3.66
Moody's Aaa	3.65	4.56
Moody's Baa	4.61	5.35
CAN 5 Yr T	1.37	1.91
CAN 10 Yr T	1.80	2.72

Money Market	2012	2013
USA Fed Funds	0.25	0.25
USA 3 Mo T-B	0.01	0.07
CAN tgt overnight rate	1.00	1.00
CAN 3 Mo T-B	0.92	0.90

Foreign Exchange	2012	2013
EUR/USD	1.32	1.37
GBP/USD	1.61	1.64
USD/CAD	0.99	1.06
USD/JPY	85.48	104.54

DECEMBER

M	T	W	T	F	S	S
	1	2	3	4	5	6
7	8	9	10	11	12	13
14	15	16	17	18	19	20
21	22	23	24	25	26	27
28	29	30	31			

JANUARY

M	T	W	T	F	S	S
			1	2	3
4	5	6	7	8	9	10
11	12	13	14	15	16	17
18	19	20	21	22	23	24
25	26	27	28	29	30	31

FEBRUARY

M	T	W	T	F	S	S
1	2	3	4	5	6	7
8	9	10	11	12	13	14
15	16	17	18	19	20	21
22	23	24	25	26	27	28
29						

FINANCIALS (U.S.) YEAR END CLEAN UP
Outperform December 15th to April 13th

Note: The U.S. financial sector seasonal period start date has been adjusted to December 15th to better reflect the opportunity for the month leading up to mid-January when the large U.S. banks tend to release their earnings.

The U.S. financial sector often starts its strong performance in October, steps up its performance in mid-December and then strongly outperforms the S&P 500 starting in mid-January.

Extra 2.4% & 68% of the time better than the S&P 500

In the 1990s and early 2000s, financial stocks benefited from the tailwind of falling interest rates. During this period, with a few exceptions, this sector has participated in both the rallies and the declines.

Financials Sector vs. S&P 500
1989/90 to 2013/14

Dec 15 to Apr 13	S&P 500	Positive Financials	Diff
1989/90	-1.9 %	-9.9 %	-8.0 %
1990/91	16.4	29.2	12.8
1991/92	5.6	9.2	3.5
1992/93	3.8	17.9	14.1
1993/04	3.6	0.1	3.2
1994/95	11.9	14.0	2.1
1995/96	3.2	5.5	2.3
1996/97	1.2	4.7	3.4
19/9798	16.4	19.7	3.3
1998/99	18.3	24.9	6.6
1999/00	2.7	4.0	1.3
2000/01	-11.7	-4.8	6.9
2001/02	-1.1	6.5	7.6
2002/03	-2.4	-1.8	0.6
2003/04	5.2	6.7	1.5
2004/05	-2.5	-6.2	-3.7
2005/06	1.3	1.1	-0.2
2006/07	1.9	-2.2	-4.1
2007/08	-9.2	-14.1	-4.9
2008/09	-2.4	-7.0	-4.6
2009/10	7.5	15.2	7.8
2010/11	5.9	4.6	-1.3
2011/12	13.1	20.7	7.7
2012/13	12.4	16.0	3.6
2013/14	2.3	1.0	-1.3
Avg.	3.8 %	6.2 %	2.4 %
Fq > 0	68 %	68 %	68 %

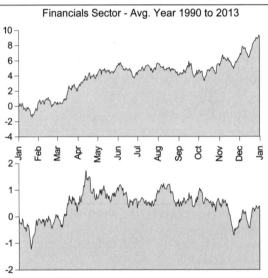

Financials Sector - Avg. Year 1990 to 2013

Financials / S&P 500 Relative Strength - Avg Yr. 1990-2013

The main driver for the strong seasonal performance of the financial sector has been the year-end earnings of the banks that start to report in mid-January. A strong performance from mid-December has been the result of investors getting into the market early to take advantage of positive year-end earnings.

Interest rates are at historic lows and although they may move lower over the next few years, it is not possible for them to have the same decline that they have had since the 1980s. The Federal Reserve, through its quantitative easing policies, has been pushing down interest rates on the long part of the yield curve and as a result, flattening the curve and making it difficult for banks to increase profits. Banks profit from borrowing at the short end of the curve and lending at the long end. With the Federal Reserve finishing its quantitative easing program, the downward pressure flattening the yield curve should be reduced, which will help increase bank profits. On the other hand, less monetary stimulation will slow the economy and reduce bank profits. Given this volatile situation, investors should concentrate their financial investments during the sector's strong seasonal period.

It should be noted that Canadian banks have their year-ends at the end of October (reporting in November) and as such, their seasonally strong period starts in October.

(i) *Financial SP GIC Sector # 40:*
For more information on the financial sector, see www.standardand-poors.com

2013-14 Strategy Performance

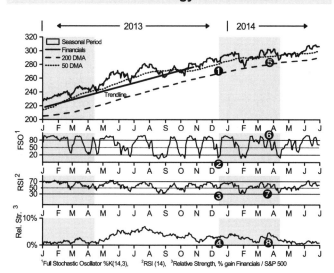

[1]Full Stochastic Oscillator %K(14,3),   [2]RSI (14),   [3]Relative Strength, % gain Financials / S&P 500

Financial Sector Performance

For the first few months in 2013, the financial sector was in an uptrend and mostly traded above its 50 day moving average. Up until mid-April, the financial sector was performing at market. From May until July, the financial sector outperformed the S&P 500 and from August to November, the sector erased all of its gains relative to the S&P 500.

Technical Conditions– December 15th to April 13th, 2014

Entry Strategy –Buy Position on Entry Date–

At the beginning of its seasonal period, in mid-December, the financial sector corrected to its 50 day moving average❶, the FSO crossed above 50❷ and the RSI bounced off 30❸. At the time, the financial sector was performing at market❹. After underperforming in the first part of the trade in January and February, the financial sector started to outperform the S&P 500 in March.

Exit Strategy– Sell Position Early–

The financial sector started to outperform the S&P 500 in March, but corrected on an absolute performance basis❺, causing the FSO to cross below 80❻ and trigger an early sell signal. The RSI had already started to fall from 70❼. At the time, the financial sector was outperforming the S&P 500❽, but its outperformance was erratic.

In the end, the financial seasonal trade produced a gain, but underperformed the S&P 500. If the early exit was implemented, then the financial sector would have both performed positively and outperformed the S&P 500.

** Weekly avg closing values- except Fed Funds & CAN overnight tgt rate weekly closing values.

JANUARY

M	T	W	T	F	S	S
				1	2	3
4	5	6	7	8	9	10
11	12	13	14	15	16	17
18	19	20	21	22	23	24
25	26	27	28	29	30	31

FEBRUARY

M	T	W	T	F	S	S
1	2	3	4	5	6	7
8	9	10	11	12	13	14
15	16	17	18	19	20	21
22	23	24	25	26	27	28
29						

MARCH

M	T	W	T	F	S	S
	1	2	3	4	5	6
7	8	9	10	11	12	13
14	15	16	17	18	19	20
21	22	23	24	25	26	27
28	29	30	31			

APRIL

M	T	W	T	F	S	S
				1	2	3
4	5	6	7	8	9	10
11	12	13	14	15	16	17
18	19	20	21	22	23	24
25	26	27	28	29	30	

MAY

M	T	W	T	F	S	S
						1
2	3	4	5	6	7	8
9	10	11	12	13	14	15
16	17	18	19	20	21	22
23	24	25	26	27	28	29
30	31					

JUNE

M	T	W	T	F	S	S
		1	2	3	4	5
6	7	8	9	10	11	12
13	14	15	16	17	18	19
20	21	22	23	24	25	26
27	28	29	30			

APPENDIX

STOCK MARKET RETURNS

S&P 500
PERCENT CHANGES

	JAN	FEB	MAR	APR	MAY	JUN
1950	1.7 %	1.0 %	0.4 %	4.5 %	3.9 %	− 5.8 %
1951	6.1	0.6	− 1.8	4.8	− 4.1	− 2.6
1952	1.6	− 3.6	4.8	− 4.3	2.3	4.6
1953	− 0.7	− 1.8	− 2.4	− 2.6	− 0.3	− 1.6
1954	5.1	0.3	3.0	4.9	3.3	0.1
1955	1.8	0.4	− 0.5	3.8	− 0.1	8.2
1956	− 3.6	3.5	6.9	− 0.2	− 6.6	3.9
1957	− 4.2	− 3.3	2.0	3.7	3.7	− 0.1
1958	4.3	2.1	3.1	3.2	1.5	2.6
1959	0.4	0.1	0.1	3.9	1.9	− 0.4
1960	− 7.1	0.9	− 1.4	− 1.8	2.7	2.0
1961	6.3	2.7	2.6	0.4	1.9	− 2.9
1962	− 3.8	1.6	− 0.6	− 6.2	− 8.6	− 8.2
1963	4.9	− 2.9	3.5	4.9	1.4	− 2.0
1964	2.7	1.0	1.5	0.6	1.1	1.6
1965	3.3	− 0.1	− 1.5	3.4	− 0.8	− 4.9
1966	0.5	− 1.8	− 2.2	2.1	− 5.4	− 1.6
1967	7.8	0.2	3.9	4.2	− 5.2	1.8
1968	− 4.4	− 3.1	0.9	8.0	1.3	0.9
1969	− 0.8	− 4.7	3.4	2.1	− 0.2	− 5.6
1970	− 7.6	5.3	0.1	− 9.0	− 6.1	− 5.0
1971	4.0	0.9	3.7	3.6	− 4.2	− 0.9
1972	1.8	2.5	0.6	0.4	1.7	− 2.2
1973	− 1.7	− 3.7	− 0.1	− 4.1	− 1.9	− 0.7
1974	− 1.0	− 0.4	− 2.3	− 3.9	− 3.4	− 1.5
1975	12.3	6.0	2.2	4.7	4.4	4.4
1976	11.8	− 1.1	3.1	− 1.1	− 1.4	4.1
1977	− 5.1	− 2.2	− 1.4	0.0	− 2.4	4.5
1978	− 6.2	− 2.5	2.5	8.5	0.4	− 1.8
1979	4.0	− 3.7	5.5	0.2	− 2.6	3.9
1980	5.8	− 0.4	− 10.2	4.1	4.7	2.7
1981	− 4.6	1.3	3.6	− 2.3	− 0.2	− 1.0
1982	− 1.8	− 6.1	− 1.0	4.0	− 3.9	− 2.0
1983	3.3	1.9	3.3	7.5	− 1.2	3.2
1984	− 0.9	− 3.9	1.3	0.5	− 5.9	1.7
1985	7.4	0.9	− 0.3	− 0.5	5.4	1.2
1986	0.2	7.1	5.3	− 1.4	5.0	1.4
1987	13.2	3.7	2.6	− 1.1	0.6	4.8
1988	4.0	4.2	− 3.3	0.9	0.3	4.3
1989	7.1	− 2.9	2.1	5.0	3.5	− 0.8
1990	− 6.9	0.9	2.4	− 2.7	9.2	− 0.9
1991	4.2	6.7	2.2	0.0	3.9	− 4.8
1992	− 2.0	1.0	− 2.2	2.8	0.1	− 1.7
1993	0.7	1.0	1.9	− 2.5	2.3	0.1
1994	3.3	− 3.0	− 4.6	1.2	1.2	− 2.7
1995	2.4	3.6	2.7	2.8	3.6	2.1
1996	3.3	0.7	0.8	1.3	2.3	0.2
1997	6.1	0.6	− 4.3	5.8	5.9	4.3
1998	1.0	7.0	5.0	0.9	− 1.9	3.9
1999	4.1	− 3.2	3.9	3.8	− 2.5	5.4
2000	− 5.1	− 2.0	9.7	− 3.1	− 2.2	2.4
2001	3.5	− 9.2	− 6.4	7.7	0.5	− 2.5
2002	− 1.6	− 2.1	3.7	− 6.1	− 0.9	− 7.2
2003	− 2.7	− 1.7	0.8	8.1	5.1	1.1
2004	1.7	1.2	− 1.6	− 1.7	1.2	1.8
2005	− 2.5	1.9	− 1.9	− 2.0	3.0	0.0
2006	2.5	0.0	1.1	1.2	− 3.1	0.0
2007	1.4	− 2.2	1.0	4.3	3.3	− 1.8
2008	− 6.1	− 3.5	− 0.6	4.8	1.1	− 8.6
2009	− 8.6	− 11.0	8.5	9.4	5.3	0.0
2010	− 3.7	2.9	5.9	1.5	− 8.2	− 5.4
2011	2.3	3.2	− 0.1	2.8	− 1.4	− 1.8
2012	4.4	4.1	3.1	− 0.7	− 6.3	4.0
2013	5.0	1.1	3.6	1.8	2.1	− 1.5
FQ POS*	40/ 64	35 / 64	42 / 64	44 / 64	36 / 64	32 / 64
% FQ POS*	63 %	55 %	66 %	69 %	56 %	50 %
AVG GAIN*	1.2 %	-0.1 %	1.2 %	1.5 %	0.2 %	0.0 %
RANK GAIN*	5	11	4	3	8	9

S&P 500 PERCENT CHANGES — STOCK MKT

JUL	AUG	SEP	OCT	NOV	DEC		YEAR
0.8 %	3.3 %	5.6 %	0.4 %	− 0.1 %	4.6 %	**1950**	21.8 %
6.9	3.9	− 0.1	− 1.4	− 0.3	3.9	**1951**	16.5
1.8	− 1.5	− 2.0	− 0.1	4.6	3.5	**1952**	11.8
2.5	− 5.8	0.1	5.1	0.9	0.2	**1953**	− 6.6
5.7	− 3.4	8.3	− 1.9	8.1	5.1	**1954**	45.0
6.1	− 0.8	1.1	− 3.0	7.5	− 0.1	**1955**	26.4
5.2	− 3.8	− 4.5	0.5	− 1.1	3.5	**1956**	2.6
1.1	− 5.6	− 6.2	− 3.2	1.6	− 4.1	**1957**	− 14.3
4.3	1.2	4.8	2.5	2.2	5.2	**1958**	38.1
3.5	− 1.5	− 4.6	1.1	1.3	2.8	**1959**	8.5
− 2.5	2.6	− 6.0	− 0.2	4.0	4.6	**1960**	− 3.0
3.3	2.0	− 2.0	2.8	3.9	0.3	**1961**	23.1
6.4	1.5	− 4.8	0.4	10.2	1.3	**1962**	− 11.8
− 0.3	4.9	− 1.1	3.2	− 1.1	2.4	**1963**	18.9
1.8	− 1.6	2.9	0.8	− 0.5	0.4	**1964**	13.0
1.3	2.3	3.2	2.7	− 0.9	0.9	**1965**	9.1
− 1.3	− 7.8	− 0.7	4.8	0.3	− 0.1	**1966**	− 13.1
4.5	− 1.2	3.3	− 3.5	0.8	2.6	**1967**	20.1
− 1.8	1.1	3.9	0.7	4.8	− 4.2	**1968**	7.7
− 6.0	4.0	− 2.5	4.3	− 3.4	− 1.9	**1969**	− 11.4
7.3	4.4	3.4	− 1.2	4.7	5.7	**1970**	0.1
− 3.2	3.6	− 0.7	− 4.2	− 0.3	8.6	**1971**	10.8
0.2	3.4	− 0.5	0.9	4.6	1.2	**1972**	15.6
3.8	− 3.7	4.0	− 0.1	− 11.4	1.7	**1973**	− 17.4
− 7.8	− 9.0	− 11.9	16.3	− 5.3	− 2.0	**1974**	− 29.7
− 6.8	− 2.1	− 3.5	6.2	2.5	− 1.2	**1975**	31.5
− 0.8	− 0.5	2.3	− 2.2	− 0.8	5.2	**1976**	19.1
− 1.6	− 2.1	− 0.2	− 4.3	2.7	0.3	**1977**	− 11.5
5.4	2.6	− 0.7	− 9.2	1.7	1.5	**1978**	1.1
0.9	5.3	0.0	− 6.9	4.3	1.7	**1979**	12.3
6.5	0.6	2.5	1.6	10.2	− 3.4	**1980**	25.8
− 0.2	− 6.2	− 5.4	4.9	3.7	− 3.0	**1981**	− 9.7
− 2.3	11.6	0.8	11.0	3.6	1.5	**1982**	14.8
− 3.0	1.1	1.0	− 1.5	1.7	− 0.9	**1983**	17.3
− 1.6	10.6	− 0.3	0.0	− 1.5	2.2	**1984**	1.4
− 0.5	− 1.2	− 3.5	4.3	6.5	4.5	**1985**	26.3
− 5.9	7.1	− 8.5	5.5	2.1	− 2.8	**1986**	14.6
4.8	3.5	− 2.4	− 21.8	− 8.5	7.3	**1987**	2.0
− 0.5	− 3.9	4.0	2.6	− 1.9	1.5	**1988**	12.4
8.8	1.6	− 0.7	− 2.5	1.7	2.1	**1989**	27.3
− 0.5	− 9.4	− 5.1	− 0.7	6.0	2.5	**1990**	− 6.6
4.5	2.0	− 1.9	1.2	− 4.4	11.2	**1991**	26.3
3.9	− 2.4	0.9	0.2	3.0	1.0	**1992**	4.5
− 0.5	3.4	− 1.0	1.9	− 1.3	1.0	**1993**	7.1
3.1	3.8	− 2.7	2.1	− 4.0	1.2	**1994**	− 1.5
3.2	0.0	4.0	− 0.5	4.1	1.7	**1995**	34.1
− 4.6	1.9	5.4	2.6	7.3	− 2.2	**1996**	20.3
7.8	− 5.7	5.3	− 3.4	4.5	1.6	**1997**	31.0
− 1.2	− 14.6	6.2	8.0	5.9	5.6	**1998**	26.7
− 3.2	− 0.6	− 2.9	6.3	1.9	5.8	**1999**	19.5
− 1.6	6.1	− 5.3	− 0.5	− 8.0	0.4	**2000**	− 10.1
− 1.1	− 6.4	− 8.2	1.8	7.5	0.8	**2001**	− 13.0
− 7.9	0.5	− 11.0	8.6	5.7	− 6.0	**2002**	− 23.4
1.6	1.8	− 1.2	5.5	0.7	5.1	**2003**	26.4
-3.4	0.2	0.9	1.4	3.9	3.2	**2004**	9.0
3.6	− 1.1	0.7	− 1.8	3.5	− 0.1	**2005**	3.0
0.5	2.1	2.5	3.2	1.6	1.3	**2006**	13.6
− 3.2	1.3	3.6	1.5	− 4.4	− 0.9	**2007**	3.5
− 1.0	1.2	− 9.2	− 16.8	− 7.5	0.8	**2008**	-38.5
7.4	3.4	3.6	− 2.0	5.7	1.8	**2009**	23.5
6.9	− 4.7	8.8	3.7	− 0.2	6.5	**2010**	12.8
− 2.1	− 5.7	− 7.2	10.8	− 0.5	0.9	**2011**	0.0
1.3	2.0	2.4	− 2.0	0.3	0.7	**2012**	13.4
4.9	− 3.1	3.0	4.5	2.8	2.4	**2013**	29.6
35 / 64	35 / 64	29 / 64	38 / 64	42/ 64	50 / 64		46 / 64
55 %	55 %	45 %	59 %	66 %	78 %		73 %
1.0 %	− 0.1 %	− 0.5 %	0.8 %	1.5 %	1.7 %		9.0 %
6	10	12	7	2	1		

S&P 500 MONTH CLOSING VALUES

	JAN	FEB	MAR	APR	MAY	JUN
1950	17	17	17	18	19	18
1951	22	22	21	22	22	21
1952	24	23	24	23	24	25
1953	26	26	25	25	25	24
1954	26	26	27	28	29	29
1955	37	37	37	38	38	41
1956	44	45	48	48	45	47
1957	45	43	44	46	47	47
1958	42	41	42	43	44	45
1959	55	55	55	58	59	50
1960	56	56	55	54	56	57
1961	62	63	65	65	67	65
1962	69	70	70	65	60	55
1963	66	64	67	70	71	69
1964	77	78	79	79	80	82
1965	88	87	86	89	88	84
1966	93	91	89	91	86	85
1967	87	87	90	94	89	91
1968	92	89	90	97	99	100
1969	103	98	102	104	103	98
1970	85	90	90	82	77	73
1971	96	97	100	104	100	99
1972	104	107	107	108	110	107
1973	116	112	112	107	105	104
1974	97	96	94	90	87	86
1975	77	82	83	87	91	95
1976	101	100	103	102	100	104
1977	102	100	98	98	96	100
1978	89	87	89	97	97	96
1979	100	96	102	102	99	103
1980	114	114	102	106	111	114
1981	130	131	136	133	133	131
1982	120	113	112	116	112	110
1983	145	148	153	164	162	168
1984	163	157	159	160	151	153
1985	180	181	181	180	190	192
1986	212	227	239	236	247	251
1987	274	284	292	288	290	304
1988	257	268	259	261	262	274
1989	297	289	295	310	321	318
1990	329	332	340	331	361	358
1991	344	367	375	375	390	371
1992	409	413	404	415	415	408
1993	439	443	452	440	450	451
1994	482	467	446	451	457	444
1995	470	487	501	515	533	545
1996	636	640	646	654	669	671
1997	786	791	757	801	848	885
1998	980	1049	1102	1112	1091	1134
1999	1280	1238	1286	1335	1302	1373
2000	1394	1366	1499	1452	1421	1455
2001	1366	1240	1160	1249	1256	1224
2002	1130	1107	1147	1077	1067	990
2003	856	841	848	917	964	975
2004	1131	1145	1126	1107	1121	1141
2005	1181	1204	1181	1157	1192	1191
2006	1280	1281	1295	1311	1270	1270
2007	1438	1407	1421	1482	1531	1503
2008	1379	1331	1323	1386	1400	1280
2009	826	735	798	873	919	919
2010	1074	1104	1169	1187	1089	1031
2011	1286	1327	1326	1364	1345	1321
2012	1312	1366	1408	1398	1310	1362
2013	1498	1515	1569	1598	1631	1606

JUL	AUG	SEP	OCT	NOV	DEC	
18	18	19	20	20	20	**1950**
22	23	23	23	23	24	**1951**
25	25	25	25	26	27	**1952**
25	23	23	25	25	25	**1953**
31	30	32	32	34	36	**1954**
44	43	44	42	46	45	**1955**
49	48	45	46	45	47	**1956**
48	45	42	41	42	40	**1957**
47	48	50	51	52	55	**1958**
61	60	57	58	58	60	**1959**
56	57	54	53	56	58	**1960**
67	68	67	69	71	72	**1961**
58	59	56	57	62	63	**1962**
69	73	72	74	73	75	**1963**
83	82	84	85	84	85	**1964**
85	87	90	92	92	92	**1965**
84	77	77	80	80	80	**1966**
95	94	97	93	94	96	**1967**
98	99	103	103	108	104	**1968**
92	96	93	97	94	92	**1969**
78	82	84	83	87	92	**1970**
96	99	98	94	94	102	**1971**
107	111	111	112	117	118	**1972**
108	104	108	108	96	98	**1973**
79	72	64	74	70	69	**1974**
89	87	84	89	91	90	**1975**
103	103	105	103	102	107	**1976**
99	97	97	92	95	95	**1977**
101	103	103	93	95	96	**1978**
104	109	109	102	106	108	**1979**
122	122	125	127	141	136	**1980**
131	123	116	122	126	123	**1981**
107	120	120	134	139	141	**1982**
163	164	166	164	166	165	**1983**
151	167	166	166	164	167	**1984**
191	189	182	190	202	211	**1985**
236	253	231	244	249	242	**1986**
319	330	322	252	230	247	**1987**
272	262	272	279	274	278	**1988**
346	351	349	340	346	353	**1989**
356	323	306	304	322	330	**1990**
388	395	388	392	375	417	**1991**
424	414	418	419	431	436	**1992**
448	464	459	468	462	466	**1993**
458	475	463	472	454	459	**1994**
562	562	584	582	605	616	**1995**
640	652	687	705	757	741	**1996**
954	899	947	915	955	970	**1997**
1121	957	1017	1099	1164	1229	**1998**
1329	1320	1283	1363	1389	1469	**1999**
1431	1518	1437	1429	1315	1320	**2000**
1211	1134	1041	1060	1139	1148	**2001**
912	916	815	886	936	880	**2002**
990	1008	996	1051	1058	1112	**2003**
1102	1104	1115	1130	1174	1212	**2004**
1234	1220	1229	1207	1249	1248	**2005**
1277	1304	1336	1378	1401	1418	**2006**
1455	1474	1527	1549	1481	1468	**2007**
1267	1283	1165	969	896	903	**2008**
987	1021	1057	1036	1096	1115	**2009**
1102	1049	1141	1183	1181	1258	**2010**
1292	1219	1131	1253	1247	1258	**2011**
1379	1407	1441	1412	1416	1426	**2012**
1686	1633	1682	1757	1806	1848	**2013**

DOW JONES PERCENT
MONTH CHANGES

	JAN	FEB	MAR	APR	MAY	JUN
1950	0.8 %	0.8 %	1.3 %	4.0 %	4.2 %	− 6.4 %
1951	5.7	1.3	− 1.7	4.5	− 3.6	− 2.8
1952	0.6	− 3.9	3.6	− 4.4	2.1	4.3
1953	− 0.7	− 2.0	− 1.5	− 1.8	− 0.9	− 1.5
1954	4.1	0.7	3.1	5.2	2.6	1.8
1955	1.1	0.8	− 0.5	3.9	− 0.2	6.2
1956	− 3.6	2.8	5.8	0.8	− 7.4	3.1
1957	− 4.1	− 3.0	2.2	4.1	2.1	− 0.3
1958	3.3	− 2.2	1.6	2.0	1.5	3.3
1959	1.8	1.6	− 0.3	3.7	3.2	0.0
1960	− 8.4	1.2	− 2.1	− 2.4	4.0	2.4
1961	5.2	2.1	2.2	0.3	2.7	− 1.8
1962	− 4.3	1.2	− 0.2	− 5.9	− 7.8	− 8.5
1963	4.7	− 2.9	3.0	5.2	1.3	− 2.8
1964	2.9	1.9	1.6	− 0.3	1.2	1.3
1965	3.3	0.1	− 1.6	3.7	− 0.5	− 5.4
1966	1.5	− 3.2	− 2.8	1.0	− 5.3	− 1.6
1967	8.2	− 1.2	3.2	3.6	− 5.0	0.9
1968	− 5.5	− 1.8	0.0	8.5	− 1.4	− 0.1
1969	0.2	− 4.3	3.3	1.6	− 1.3	− 6.9
1970	− 7.0	4.5	1.0	− 6.3	− 4.8	− 2.4
1971	3.5	1.2	2.9	4.1	− 3.6	− 1.8
1972	1.3	2.9	1.4	1.4	0.7	− 3.3
1973	− 2.1	− 4.4	− 0.4	− 3.1	− 2.2	− 1.1
1974	0.6	0.6	− 1.6	− 1.2	− 4.1	0.0
1975	14.2	5.0	3.9	6.9	1.3	5.6
1976	14.4	− 0.3	2.8	− 0.3	− 2.2	2.8
1977	− 5.0	− 1.9	− 1.8	0.8	− 3.0	2.0
1978	− 7.4	− 3.6	2.1	10.5	0.4	− 2.6
1979	4.2	− 3.6	6.6	− 0.8	− 3.8	2.4
1980	4.4	− 1.5	− 9.0	4.0	4.1	2.0
1981	− 1.7	2.9	3.0	− 0.6	− 0.6	− 1.5
1982	− 0.4	− 5.4	− 0.2	3.1	− 3.4	− 0.9
1983	2.8	3.4	1.6	8.5	− 2.1	1.8
1984	− 3.0	− 5.4	0.9	0.5	− 5.6	2.5
1985	6.2	− 0.2	− 1.3	− 0.7	4.6	1.5
1986	1.6	8.8	6.4	− 1.9	5.2	0.9
1987	13.8	3.1	3.6	− 0.8	0.2	5.5
1988	1.0	5.8	− 4.0	2.2	− 0.1	5.4
1989	8.0	− 3.6	1.6	5.5	2.5	− 1.6
1990	− 5.9	1.4	3.0	− 1.9	8.3	0.1
1991	3.9	5.3	1.1	− 0.9	4.8	− 4.0
1992	1.7	1.4	− 1.0	3.8	1.1	− 2.3
1993	0.3	1.8	1.9	− 0.2	2.9	− 0.3
1994	6.0	− 3.7	− 5.1	1.3	2.1	− 3.5
1995	0.2	4.3	3.7	3.9	3.3	2.0
1996	5.4	1.7	1.9	− 0.3	1.3	0.2
1997	5.7	0.9	− 4.3	6.5	4.6	4.7
1998	0.0	8.1	3.0	3.0	− 1.8	0.6
1999	1.9	− 0.6	5.2	10.2	− 2.1	3.9
2000	− 4.5	− 7.4	7.8	− 1.7	− 2.0	− 0.7
2001	0.9	− 3.6	− 5.9	8.7	1.6	− 3.8
2002	− 1.0	1.9	2.9	− 4.4	− 0.2	− 6.9
2003	− 3.5	− 2.0	1.3	6.1	4.4	1.5
2004	0.3	0.9	− 2.1	− 1.3	− 0.4	2.4
2005	− 2.7	2.6	− 2.4	− 3.0	2.7	− 1.8
2006	1.4	1.2	1.1	2.3	− 1.7	− 0.2
2007	1.3	− 2.8	0.7	5.7	4.3	− 1.6
2008	− 4.6	− 3.0	0.0	4.5	− 1.4	− 10.2
2009	− 8.8	− 11.7	7.7	7.3	4.1	− 0.6
2010	− 3.5	2.6	5.1	1.4	− 7.9	− 3.6
2011	2.7	2.8	0.8	4.0	− 1.9	− 1.2
2012	3.4	3.8	2.0	0.0	− 6.2	3.9
2013	5.8	4.8	3.7	1.8	1.9	− 1.4
FQ POS	42 / 64	37 / 64	42 / 64	42 / 64	32 / 64	29 / 64
% FQ POS	66 %	58 %	66 %	66 %	50 %	45 %
AVG GAIN	1.1 %	0.1 %	1.1 %	2.0 %	− 0.1 %	− 0.3 %
RANK GAIN	5	8	6	1	9	11

DOW JONES PERCENT MONTH CHANGES — STOCK MKT

JUL	AUG	SEP	OCT	NOV	DEC		YEAR
0.1 %	3.6 %	4.4 %	— 0.6 %	1.2 %	3.4 %	1950	17.6 %
6.3	4.8	0.3	— 3.2	— 0.4	3.0	1951	14.4
1.9	— 1.6	— 1.6	— 0.5	5.4	2.9	1952	8.4
2.6	— 5.2	1.1	4.5	2.0	— 0.2	1953	— 3.8
4.3	— 3.5	7.4	— 2.3	9.9	4.6	1954	44.0
3.2	0.5	— 0.3	— 2.5	6.2	1.1	1955	20.8
5.1	— 3.1	— 5.3	1.0	— 1.5	5.6	1956	2.3
1.0	— 4.7	— 5.8	— 3.4	2.0	— 3.2	1957	— 12.8
5.2	1.1	4.6	2.1	2.6	4.7	1958	34.0
4.9	— 1.6	— 4.9	2.4	1.9	3.1	1959	16.4
— 3.7	1.5	— 7.3	0.1	2.9	3.1	1960	— 9.3
3.1	2.1	— 2.6	0.4	2.5	1.3	1961	18.7
6.5	1.9	— 5.0	1.9	10.1	0.4	1962	— 10.8
— 1.6	4.9	0.5	3.1	— 0.6	1.7	1963	17.0
1.2	— 0.3	4.4	— 0.3	0.3	— 0.1	1964	14.6
1.6	1.3	4.2	3.2	— 1.5	2.4	1965	10.9
— 2.6	— 7.0	— 1.8	4.2	— 1.9	— 0.7	1966	— 18.9
5.1	— 0.3	2.8	— 5.1	— 0.4	3.3	1967	15.2
— 1.6	1.5	4.4	1.8	3.4	— 4.2	1968	4.3
— 6.6	2.6	— 2.8	5.3	— 5.1	— 1.5	1969	— 15.2
7.4	4.2	— 0.5	— 0.7	5.1	5.6	1970	4.8
— 3.7	4.6	— 1.2	— 5.4	— 0.9	7.1	1971	6.1
— 0.5	4.2	— 1.1	0.2	6.6	0.2	1972	14.6
3.9	— 4.2	6.7	1.0	— 14.0	3.5	1973	— 16.6
— 5.6	— 10.4	— 10.4	9.5	— 7.0	— 0.4	1974	— 27.6
— 5.4	0.5	— 5.0	5.3	3.0	— 1.0	1975	38.3
— 1.8	— 1.1	1.7	— 2.6	— 1.8	6.1	1976	17.9
— 2.9	— 3.2	— 1.7	— 3.4	1.4	0.2	1977	— 17.3
5.3	1.7	— 1.3	— 8.5	0.8	0.8	1978	3.2
0.5	4.9	— 1.0	— 7.2	0.8	2.0	1979	4.2
7.8	— 0.3	0.0	— 0.8	7.4	— 2.9	1980	14.9
— 2.5	— 7.4	— 3.6	0.3	4.3	— 1.6	1981	— 9.2
— 0.4	11.5	— 0.6	10.6	4.8	0.7	1982	19.6
— 1.9	1.4	1.4	— 0.6	4.1	— 1.4	1983	20.3
— 1.5	9.8	— 1.4	0.1	— 1.5	1.9	1984	— 3.7
0.9	— 1.0	— 0.4	3.4	7.1	5.1	1985	27.7
— 6.2	6.9	— 6.9	6.2	1.9	— 1.0	1986	22.6
6.4	3.5	— 2.5	— 23.2	— 8.0	5.7	1987	2.3
— 0.6	— 4.6	4.0	1.7	— 1.6	2.6	1988	11.9
9.0	2.9	— 1.6	— 1.8	2.3	1.7	1989	27.0
0.9	— 10.0	— 6.2	— 0.4	4.8	2.9	1990	— 4.3
4.1	0.6	— 0.9	1.7	— 5.7	9.5	1991	20.3
2.3	— 4.0	0.4	— 1.4	2.4	— 0.1	1992	4.2
0.7	3.2	— 2.6	3.5	0.1	1.9	1993	13.7
3.8	4.0	— 1.8	1.7	— 4.3	2.5	1994	2.1
3.3	— 2.1	3.9	— 0.7	6.7	0.8	1995	33.5
— 2.2	1.6	4.7	2.5	8.2	— 1.1	1996	26.0
7.2	— 7.3	4.2	— 6.3	5.1	1.1	1997	22.6
— 0.8	— 15.1	4.0	9.6	6.1	0.7	1998	16.1
— 2.9	1.6	— 4.5	3.8	1.4	5.3	1999	24.7
0.7	6.6	— 5.0	3.0	— 5.1	3.6	2000	— 5.8
0.2	— 5.4	— 11.1	2.6	8.6	1.7	2001	— 7.1
— 5.5	— 0.8	— 12.4	10.6	5.9	— 6.2	2002	16.8
2.8	2.0	— 1.5	5.7	— 0.2	6.9	2003	25.3
— 2.8	0.3	— 0.9	— 0.5	4.0	3.4	2004	3.1
3.6	— 1.5	0.8	— 1.2	3.5	— 0.8	2005	— 0.6
0.3	1.7	2.6	3.4	1.2	2.0	2006	16.3
— 1.5	1.1	4.0	0.2	— 4.0	— 0.8	2007	6.4
0.2	1.5	— 6.0	— 14.1	— 5.3	— 0.6	2008	— 33.8
8.6	3.5	2.3	0.0	6.5	0.8	2009	18.8
7.1	— 4.3	7.7	3.1	— 1.0	5.2	2010	11.0
— 2.2	— 4.4	— 6.0	9.5	0.8	1.4	2011	5.5
1.0	0.6	2.6	— 2.5	— 0.5	0.6	2012	7.3
4.0	— 4.4	2.2	2.8	3.5	3.0	2013	26.5
40 / 64	36 / 64	26 / 64	38/ 64	42/ 64	46 / 64		46 / 64
63 %	56 %	41 %	59 %	66 %	72 %		72 %
1.2 %	— 0.1 %	— 0.8 %	0.5 %	1.5 %	1.7 %		8.4 %
4	10	12	7	3	2		

DOW JONES
MONTH CLOSING VALUES

	JAN	FEB	MAR	APR	MAY	JUN
1950	202	203	206	214	223	209
1951	249	252	248	259	250	243
1952	271	260	270	258	263	274
1953	290	284	280	275	272	268
1954	292	295	304	319	328	334
1955	409	412	410	426	425	451
1956	471	484	512	516	478	493
1957	479	465	475	494	505	503
1068	450	440	447	456	463	478
1959	594	604	602	624	644	644
1960	623	630	617	602	626	641
1961	648	662	677	679	697	684
1962	700	708	707	665	613	561
1963	683	663	683	718	727	707
1964	785	800	813	811	821	832
1965	903	904	889	922	918	868
1966	984	952	925	934	884	870
1967	850	839	866	897	853	860
1968	856	841	841	912	899	898
1969	946	905	936	950	938	873
1970	744	778	786	736	700	684
1971	869	879	904	942	908	891
1972	902	928	941	954	961	929
1973	999	955	951	921	901	892
1974	856	861	847	837	802	802
1975	704	739	768	821	832	879
1976	975	973	1000	997	975	1003
1977	954	936	919	927	899	916
1978	770	742	757	837	841	819
1979	839	809	862	855	822	842
1980	876	863	786	817	851	868
1981	947	975	1004	998	992	977
1982	871	824	823	848	820	812
1983	1076	1113	1130	1226	1200	1222
1984	1221	1155	1165	1171	1105	1132
1985	1287	1284	1267	1258	1315	1336
1986	1571	1709	1819	1784	1877	1893
1987	2158	2224	2305	2286	2292	2419
1988	1958	2072	1988	2032	2031	2142
1989	2342	2258	2294	2419	2480	2440
1990	2591	2627	2707	2657	2877	2881
1991	2736	2882	2914	2888	3028	2907
1992	3223	3268	3236	3359	3397	3319
1993	3310	3371	3435	3428	3527	3516
1994	3978	3832	3636	3682	3758	3625
1995	3844	4011	4158	4321	4465	4556
1996	5395	5486	5587	5569	5643	5655
1997	6813	6878	6584	7009	7331	7673
1998	7907	8546	8800	9063	8900	8952
1999	9359	9307	9786	10789	10560	10971
2000	10941	10128	10922	10734	10522	10448
2001	10887	10495	9879	10735	10912	10502
2002	9920	10106	10404	9946	9925	9243
2003	8054	7891	7992	8480	8850	8985
2004	10488	10584	10358	10226	10188	10435
2005	10490	10766	10504	10193	10467	10275
2006	10865	10993	11109	11367	11168	11150
2007	12622	12269	12354	13063	13628	13409
2008	12650	12266	12263	12820	12638	11350
2009	8001	7063	7609	8168	8500	8447
2010	10067	10325	10857	11009	10137	9774
2011	11892	12226	12320	12811	12570	12414
2012	12633	12952	13212	13214	12393	12880
2013	13861	14054	14579	14840	15116	14910

DOW JONES
MONTH CLOSING VALUES

STOCK MKT

JUL	AUG	SEP	OCT	NOV	DEC	
209	217	226	225	228	235	**1950**
258	270	271	262	261	269	**1951**
280	275	271	269	284	292	**1952**
275	261	264	276	281	281	**1953**
348	336	361	352	387	404	**1954**
466	468	467	455	483	488	**1955**
518	502	475	480	473	500	**1956**
509	484	456	441	450	436	**1957**
503	509	532	543	558	584	**1958**
675	664	632	647	659	679	**1959**
617	626	580	580	597	616	**1960**
705	720	701	704	722	731	**1961**
598	609	579	590	649	652	**1962**
695	729	733	755	751	763	**1963**
841	839	875	873	875	874	**1964**
882	893	931	961	947	969	**1965**
847	788	774	807	792	786	**1966**
904	901	927	880	876	905	**1967**
883	896	936	952	985	944	**1968**
816	837	813	856	812	800	**1969**
734	765	761	756	794	839	**1970**
858	898	887	839	831	890	**1971**
925	964	953	956	1018	1020	**1972**
926	888	947	957	822	851	**1973**
757	679	608	666	619	616	**1974**
832	835	794	836	861	852	**1975**
985	974	990	965	947	1005	**1976**
890	862	847	818	830	831	**1977**
862	877	866	793	799	805	**1978**
846	888	879	816	822	839	**1979**
935	933	932	925	993	964	**1980**
952	882	850	853	889	875	**1981**
809	901	896	992	1039	1047	**1982**
1199	1216	1233	1225	1276	1259	**1983**
1115	1224	1207	1207	1189	1212	**1984**
1348	1334	1329	1374	1472	1547	**1985**
1775	1898	1768	1878	1914	1896	**1986**
2572	2663	2596	1994	1834	1939	**1987**
2129	2032	2113	2149	2115	2169	**1988**
2661	2737	2693	2645	2706	2753	**1989**
2905	2614	2453	2442	2560	2634	**1990**
3025	3044	3017	3069	2895	3169	**1991**
3394	3257	3272	3226	3305	3301	**1992**
3540	3651	3555	3681	3684	3754	**1993**
3765	3913	3843	3908	3739	3834	**1994**
4709	4611	4789	4756	5075	5117	**1995**
5529	5616	5882	6029	6522	6448	**1996**
8223	7622	7945	7442	7823	7908	**1997**
8883	7539	7843	8592	9117	9181	**1998**
10655	10829	10337	10730	10878	11453	**1999**
10522	11215	10651	10971	10415	10788	**2000**
10523	9950	8848	9075	9852	10022	**2001**
8737	8664	7592	8397	8896	8342	**2002**
9234	9416	9275	9801	9782	10454	**2003**
10140	10174	10080	10027	10428	10783	**2004**
10641	10482	10569	10440	10806	10718	**2005**
11186	11381	11679	12801	12222	12463	**2006**
13212	13358	13896	13930	13372	13265	**2007**
11378	11544	10851	9325	8829	8776	**2008**
9172	9496	9712	9713	10345	10428	**2009**
10466	10015	10788	11118	11006	11578	**2010**
12143	11614	10913	11955	12046	12218	**2011**
13009	13091	13437	13096	13026	13104	**2012**
15500	14810	15130	15546	16086	16577	**2013**

NASDAQ PERCENT MONTH CHANGES

	JAN	FEB	MAR	APR	MAY	JUN
1972	4.2	5.5	2.2	2.5	0.9	− 1.8
1973	− 4.0	− 6.2	− 2.4	− 8.2	− 4.8	− 1.6
1974	3.0	− 0.6	− 2.2	− 5.9	− 7.7	− 5.3
1975	16.6	4.6	3.6	3.8	5.8	4.7
1976	12.1	3.7	0.4	− 0.6	− 2.3	2.6
1977	− 2.4	− 1.0	− 0.5	1.4	0.1	4.3
1978	− 4.0	0.0	4.7	8.5	4.4	0.0
1979	6.6	− 2.6	7.5	1.6	− 1.8	5.1
1980	7.0	− 2.3	− 17.1	6.9	7.5	4.9
1981	− 2.2	0.1	6.1	3.1	3.1	− 3.5
1982	− 3.8	− 4.8	− 2.1	5.2	− 3.3	− 4.1
1983	6.9	5.0	3.9	8.2	5.3	3.2
1984	− 3.7	− 5.9	− 0.7	− 1.3	− 5.9	2.9
1985	12.8	2.0	− 1.8	0.5	3.6	1.9
1986	3.4	7.1	4.2	2.3	4.4	1.3
1987	12.4	8.4	1.2	− 2.9	− 0.3	2.0
1988	4.3	6.5	2.1	1.2	− 2.3	6.6
1989	5.2	− 0.4	1.8	5.1	4.3	− 2.4
1990	− 8.6	2.4	2.3	− 3.5	9.3	0.7
1991	10.8	9.4	6.4	0.5	4.4	− 6.0
1992	5.8	2.1	− 4.7	− 4.2	1.1	− 3.7
1993	2.9	− 3.7	2.9	− 4.2	5.9	0.5
1994	3.0	− 1.0	− 6.2	− 1.3	0.2	− 4.0
1995	0.4	5.1	3.0	3.3	2.4	8.0
1996	0.7	3.8	0.1	8.1	4.4	− 4.7
1997	6.9	− 5.1	− 6.7	3.2	11.1	3.0
1998	3.1	9.3	3.7	1.8	− 4.8	6.5
1999	14.3	− 8.7	7.6	3.3	− 2.8	8.7
2000	− 3.2	19.2	− 2.6	− 15.6	− 11.9	16.6
2001	12.2	− 22.4	− 14.5	15.0	− 0.3	2.4
2002	− 0.8	− 10.5	6.6	− 8.5	− 4.3	− 9.4
2003	− 1.1	1.3	0.3	9.2	9.0	1.7
2004	3.1	− 1.8	− 1.8	− 3.7	3.5	3.1
2005	− 5.2	− 0.5	− 2.6	− 3.9	7.6	− 0.5
2006	4.6	− 1.1	2.6	− 0.7	− 6.2	− 0.3
2007	2.0	− 1.9	0.2	4.3	3.1	0.0
2008	− 9.9	− 5.0	0.3	5.9	4.6	− 9.1
2009	− 6.4	− 6.7	10.9	12.3	3.3	3.4
2010	− 5.4	4.2	7.1	2.6	− 8.3	− 6.5
2011	1.8	3.0	0.0	3.3	− 1.3	− 2.2
2012	8.0	5.4	4.2	− 1.5	− 7.2	3.8
2013	4.1	0.6	3.4	1.9	3.8	− 1.5
FQ POS	28/42	22/42	27/42	27/42	25/42	24/42
% FQ POS	67 %	52 %	64 %	64 %	60 %	57 %
AVG GAIN	2.8 %	0.4 %	0.8 %	1.4 %	0.9 %	0.7 %
RANK GAIN	1	9	6	4	5	7

JUL	AUG	SEP	OCT	NOV	DEC		YEAR
— 1.8	1.7	— 0.3	0.5	2.1	0.6	**1972**	17.2
7.6	— 3.5	6.0	— 0.9	— 15.1	— 1.4	**1973**	— 31.1
— 7.9	— 10.9	— 10.7	17.2	— 3.5	— 5.0	**1974**	— 35.1
— 4.4	— 5.0	— 5.9	3.6	2.4	— 1.5	**1975**	29.8
1.1	— 1.7	1.7	— 1.0	0.9	7.4	**1976**	26.1
0.9	— 0.5	0.7	— 3.3	5.8	1.8	**1977**	7.3
5.0	6.9	— 1.6	— 16.4	3.2	2.9	**1978**	12.3
2.3	6.4	— 0.3	— 9.6	6.4	4.8	**1979**	28.1
8.9	5.7	3.4	2.7	8.0	— 2.8	**1980**	33.9
— 1.9	— 7.5	— 8.0	8.4	3.1	— 2.7	**1981**	— 3.2
— 2.3	6.2	5.6	13.3	9.3	0.0	**1982**	18.7
— 4.6	— 3.8	1.4	— 7.4	4.1	— 2.5	**1983**	19.9
— 4.2	10.9	— 1.8	— 1.2	— 1.9	1.9	**1984**	— 11.3
1.7	— 1.2	— 5.8	4.4	7.4	3.5	**1985**	31.5
— 8.4	3.1	— 8.4	2.9	— 0.3	— 3.0	**1986**	7.4
2.4	4.6	— 2.4	— 27.2	— 5.6	8.3	**1987**	— 5.2
— 1.9	— 2.8	2.9	— 1.3	— 2.9	2.7	**1988**	15.4
4.2	3.4	0.8	— 3.7	0.1	— 0.3	**1989**	19.2
— 5.2	— 13.0	— 9.6	— 4.3	8.9	4.1	**1990**	— 17.8
5.5	4.7	0.2	3.1	— 3.5	11.9	**1991**	56.9
3.1	— 3.0	3.6	3.8	7.9	3.7	**1992**	15.5
0.1	5.4	2.7	2.2	— 3.2	3.0	**1993**	14.7
2.3	6.0	— 0.2	1.7	— 3.5	0.2	**1994**	— 3.2
7.3	1.9	2.3	— 0.7	2.2	— 0.7	**1995**	39.9
— 8.8	5.6	7.5	— 0.4	5.8	— 0.1	**1996**	22.7
10.5	— 0.4	6.2	— -5.5	0.4	— 1.9	**1997**	21.6
— 1.2	— 19.9	13.0	4.6	10.1	12.5	**1998**	39.6
— 1.8	3.8	0.2	8.0	12.5	22.0	**1999**	85.6
— 5.0	11.7	— 12.7	— 8.3	— 22.9	— 4.9	**2000**	— 39.3
— 6.2	— 10.9	— 17.0	12.8	14.2	1.0	**2001**	— 21.1
— 9.2	— 1.0	— 10.9	13.5	11.2	— 9.7	**2002**	— 31.5
6.9	4.3	— 1.3	8.1	1.5	2.2	**2003**	50.0
— 7.8	— 2.6	3.2	4.1	6.2	3.7	**2004**	8.6
6.2	— 1.5	0.0	— 1.5	5.3	— 1.2	**2005**	1.4
— 3.7	4.4	3.4	4.8	2.7	— 0.7	**2006**	9.5
— 2.2	2.0	4.0	5.8	— 6.9	— 0.3	**2007**	9.8
1.4	1.8	— 11.6	— 17.7	— 10.8	2.7	**2008**	— 40.5
7.8	1.5	5.6	— 3.6	4.9	5.8	**2009**	43.9
6.9	— 6.2	12.0	5.9	— 0.4	6.2	**2010**	16.9
— 0.6	— 6.4	— 6.4	11.1	— 2.4	— 0.6	**2011**	— 1.8
0.2	4.3	1.6	— 4.5	1.1	0.3	**2012**	15.9
6.6	— 1.0	5.1	3.9	3.6	2.9	**2013**	38.3
22/42	22/42	23/42	23/42	28/42	25/42		30/42
52 %	52 %	55 %	55 %	67 %	60 %		71 %
0.2 %	0.1 %	— 0.5 %	0.7 %	1.6 %	1.8 %		12.3 %
10	11	12	8	3	2		

NASDAQ MONTH
CLOSING VALUES

	JAN	FEB	MAR	APR	MAY	JUN
1972	119	125	128	131	133	130
1973	128	120	117	108	103	101
1974	95	94	92	87	80	76
1975	70	73	76	79	83	87
1976	87	90	91	90	88	90
1977	96	06	94	95	96	100
1978	101	101	106	115	120	120
1979	126	123	132	134	131	138
1980	162	158	131	140	150	158
1981	198	198	210	217	223	216
1982	188	179	176	185	179	171
1983	248	261	271	293	309	319
1984	268	253	251	247	233	240
1985	279	284	279	281	291	296
1986	336	360	375	383	400	406
1987	392	425	430	418	417	425
1988	345	367	375	379	370	395
1989	401	400	407	428	446	435
1990	416	426	436	420	459	462
1991	414	453	482	485	506	476
1992	620	633	604	579	585	564
1993	696	671	690	661	701	704
1994	800	793	743	734	735	706
1995	755	794	817	844	865	933
1996	1060	1100	1101	1191	1243	1185
1997	1380	1309	1222	1261	1400	1442
1998	1619	1771	1836	1868	1779	1895
1999	2506	2288	2461	2543	2471	2686
2000	3940	4697	4573	3861	3401	3966
2001	2773	2152	1840	2116	2110	2161
2002	1934	1731	1845	1688	1616	1463
2003	1321	1338	1341	1464	1596	1623
2004	2066	2030	1994	1920	1987	2048
2005	2062	2052	1999	1922	2068	2057
2006	2306	2281	2340	2323	2179	2172
2007	2464	2416	2422	2525	2605	2603
2008	2390	2271	2279	2413	2523	2293
2009	1476	1378	1529	1717	1774	1835
2010	2147	2238	2398	2461	2257	2109
2011	2700	2782	2781	2874	2835	2774
2012	2814	2967	3092	3046	2827	2935
2013	3142	3160	3268	3329	3456	3403

NASDAQ MONTH CLOSING VALUES 🇺🇸 STOCK MKT

JUL	AUG	SEP	OCT	NOV	DEC	
128	130	130	130	133	134	**1972**
109	105	111	110	94	92	**1973**
70	62	56	65	63	60	**1974**
83	79	74	77	79	78	**1975**
91	90	91	90	91	98	**1976**
101	100	101	98	103	105	**1977**
126	135	133	111	115	118	**1978**
141	150	150	136	144	151	**1979**
172	182	188	193	208	202	**1980**
212	196	180	195	201	196	**1981**
167	178	188	213	232	232	**1982**
304	292	297	275	286	279	**1983**
230	255	250	247	242	247	**1984**
301	298	280	293	314	325	**1985**
371	383	351	361	360	349	**1986**
435	455	444	323	305	331	**1987**
387	377	388	383	372	381	**1988**
454	469	473	456	456	455	**1989**
438	381	345	330	359	374	**1990**
502	526	527	543	524	586	**1991**
581	563	583	605	653	677	**1992**
705	743	763	779	754	777	**1993**
722	766	764	777	750	752	**1994**
1001	1020	1044	1036	1059	1052	**1995**
1081	1142	1227	1222	1293	1291	**1996**
1594	1587	1686	1594	1601	1570	**1997**
1872	1499	1694	1771	1950	2193	**1998**
2638	2739	2746	2966	3336	4069	**1999**
3767	4206	3673	3370	2598	2471	**2000**
2027	1805	1499	1690	1931	1950	**2001**
1328	1315	1172	1330	1479	1336	**2002**
1735	1810	1787	1932	1960	2003	**2003**
1887	1838	1897	1975	2097	2175	**2004**
2185	2152	2152	2120	2233	2205	**2005**
2091	2184	2258	2367	2432	2415	**2006**
2546	2596	2702	2859	2661	2652	**2007**
2326	2368	2092	1721	1536	1577	**2008**
1979	2009	2122	2045	2145	2269	**2009**
2255	2114	2369	2507	2498	2653	**2010**
2756	2579	2415	2684	2620	2605	**2011**
2940	3067	3116	2977	3010	3020	**2012**
3626	3590	3771	3920	4060	4177	**2013**

S&P/TSX MONTH PERCENT CHANGES

	JAN	FEB	MAR	APR	MAY	JUN
1985	8.1	0.0	0.7	0.8	3.8	— 0.8
1986	— 1.7	0.5	6.7	1.1	1.4	— 1.2
1987	9.2	4.5	6.9	— 0.6	— 0.9	1.5
1988	— 3.3	4.8	3.4	0.8	— 2.7	5.9
1989	6.7	— 1.2	0.2	1 4	2.2	1.5
1990	— 6.7	— 0.5	— 1.3	— 8.2	6.7	— 0.6
1991	0.5	5.8	1.0	-0.8	2.2	— 2.3
1992	2.4	— 0.4	— 4.7	— 1.7	1.0	0.0
1993	— 1.3	4.4	4.4	5.2	2.5	2.2
1994	5.4	— 2.9	— 2.1	— 1.4	1.4	— 7.0
1995	— 4.7	2.7	4.6	— -0.8	4.0	1.8
1996	5.4	— 0.7	0.8	3.5	1.9	— 3.9
1997	3.1	0.8	— 5.0	2.2	6.8	0.9
1998	0.0	5.9	6.6	1.4	— 1.0	— 2.9
1999	3.8	— 6.2	4.5	6.3	— 2.5	2.5
2000	0.8	7.6	3.7	— 1.2	— 1.0	10.2
2001	4.3	— 13.3	— 5.8	4.5	2.7	— 5.2
2002	— 0.5	— 0.1	2.8	— 2.4	— 0.1	— 6.7
2003	— 0.7	— 0.2	— 3.2	3.8	4.2	1.8
2004	3.7	3.1	— 2.3	— 4.0	2.1	1.5
2005	— 0.5	5.0	— 0.6	— 3.5	3.6	3.1
2006	6.0	— 2.2	3.6	0.8	— 3.8	— 1.1
2007	1.0	0.1	0.9	1.9	4.8	— 1.1
2008	— 4.9	3.3	— 1.7	4.4	5.6	— 1.7
2009	— 3.3	— 6.6	7.4	6.9	11.2	0.0
2010	— 5.5	4.8	3.5	1.4	— 3.7	— 4.0
2011	0.8	4.3	— 0.1	— 1.2	— 1.0	— 3.6
2012	4.2	1.5	— 2.0	— 0.8	— 6.3	0.7
2013	2.0	1.1	— 0.6	— 2.3	1.6	— 4.1
FQ POS	18/29	17/29	17/29	16/29	19/29	13/29
% FQ POS	62 %	59 %	59 %	55 %	66 %	45 %
AVG GAIN	1.2 %	0.9 %	1.1 %	0.6 %	1.6 %	-0.4 %
RANK GAIN	3	5	4	8	2	11

JUL	AUG	SEP	OCT	NOV	DEC		YEAR
2.4	1.5	— 6.7	1.6	6.8	1.3	**1985**	20.5
— 4.9	3.2	— 1.6	1.6	0.7	0.6	**1986**	6.0
7.8	— 0.9	— 2.3	— 22.6	— 1.4	6.1	**1987**	3.1
— 1.9	— 2.7	— 0.1	3.4	— 3.0	2.9	**1988**	7.3
5.6	1.0	— 1.7	— 0.6	0.6	0.7	**1989**	17.1
0.5	— 6.0	— 5.6	— 2.5	2.3	3.4	**1990**	— 18.0
2.1	— 0.6	— 3.7	3.8	— 1.9	1.9	**1991**	7.8
1.6	— 1.2	— 3.1	1.2	— 1.6	2.1	**1992**	— 4.6
0.0	4.3	— 3.6	6.6	— 1.8	3.4	**1993**	29.0
3.8	4.1	0.1	— 1.4	— 4.6	2.9	**1994**	— 2.5
1.9	— 2.1	0.3	— 1.6	4.5	1.1	**1995**	11.9
— 2.3	4.3	2.9	5.8	7.5	— 1.5	**1996**	25.7
6.8	— 3.9	6.5	— 2.8	— 4.8	2.9	**1997**	13.0
— 5.9	— 20.2	1.5	10.6	2.2	2.2	**1998**	— 3.2
1.0	— 1.6	— 0.2	4.3	3.6	11.9	**1999**	29.7
2.1	8.1	— 7.7	— 7.1	— 8.5	1.3	**2000**	6.2
— 0.6	— 3.8	— 7.6	0.7	7.8	3.5	**2001**	— 13.9
— 7.6	0.1	— 6.5	1.1	5.1	0.7	**2002**	— 14.0
3.9	3.6	— 1.3	4.7	1.1	4.6	**2003**	24.3
— 1.0	— 1.0	3.5	2.3	1.8	2.4	**2004**	12.5
5.3	2.4	3.2	— 5.7	4.2	4.1	**2005**	21.9
1.9	2.1	— 2.6	5.0	3.3	1.2	**2006**	14.5
— 0.3	— 1.5	3.2	3.7	— 6.4	1.1	**2007**	7.2
— 6.0	1.3	— 14.7	— 16.9	— 5.0	— 3.1	**2008**	— 35.0
4.0	0.8	4.8	— 4.2	4.9	2.6	**2009**	30.7
3.7	1.7	3.8	2.5	2.2	3.8	**2010**	14.4
— 2.7	— 1.4	— 9.0	5.4	— 0.4	— 2.0	**2011**	— 11.1
0.6	2.4	3.1	0.9	— 1.5	1.6	**2012**	4.0
2.9	1.3	1.1	4.5	0.3	1.7	**2013**	9.6
19/29	16/29	12/29	19/29	17/29	26/29		21/29
66 %	55 %	41 %	66 %	59 %	90 %		72 %
0.9 %	— 0.2 %	— 1.5 %	0.1 %	0.6 %	2.3 %		7.4 %
6	10	12	9	7	1		

S&P/TSX MONTH CLOSING VALUES

	JAN	FEB	MAR	APR	MAY	JUN
1985	2595	2595	2613	2635	2736	2713
1986	2843	2856	3047	3079	3122	3086
1987	3349	3499	3739	3717	3685	3740
1988	3057	3205	3314	3340	3249	3441
1989	3617	3572	3578	3628	3707	3761
1990	3704	3687	3640	3341	3565	3544
1991	3273	3462	3496	3469	3546	3466
1992	3596	3582	3412	3356	3388	3388
1993	3305	3452	3602	3789	3883	3966
1994	4555	4424	4330	4267	4327	4025
1995	4018	4125	4314	4280	4449	4527
1996	4968	4934	4971	5147	5246	5044
1997	6110	6158	5850	5977	6382	6438
1998	6700	7093	7559	7665	7590	7367
1999	6730	6313	6598	7015	6842	7010
2000	8481	9129	9462	9348	9252	10196
2001	9322	8079	7608	7947	8162	7736
2002	7649	7638	7852	7663	7656	7146
2003	6570	6555	6343	6586	6860	6983
2004	8521	8789	8586	8244	8417	8546
2005	9204	9668	9612	9275	9607	9903
2006	11946	11688	12111	12204	11745	11613
2007	13034	13045	13166	13417	14057	13907
2008	13155	13583	13350	13937	14715	14467
2009	8695	8123	8720	9325	10370	10375
2010	11094	11630	12038	12211	11763	11294
2011	13552	14137	14116	13945	13803	13301
2012	12452	12644	12392	12293	11513	11597
2013	12685	12822	12750	12457	12650	12129

S&P/TSX PERCENT CLOSING VALUES — STOCK MKT

JUL	AUG	SEP	OCT	NOV	DEC	
2779	2820	2632	2675	2857	2893	**1985**
2935	3028	2979	3027	3047	3066	**1986**
4030	3994	3902	3019	2978	3160	**1987**
3377	3286	3284	3396	3295	3390	**1988**
3971	4010	3943	3919	3943	3970	**1989**
3561	3346	3159	3081	3151	3257	**1990**
3540	3518	3388	3516	3449	3512	**1991**
3443	3403	3298	3336	3283	3350	**1992**
3967	4138	3991	4256	4180	4321	**1993**
4179	4350	4354	4292	4093	4214	**1994**
4615	4517	4530	4459	4661	4714	**1995**
4929	5143	5291	5599	6017	5927	**1996**
6878	6612	7040	6842	6513	6699	**1997**
6931	5531	5614	6208	6344	6486	**1998**
7081	6971	6958	7256	7520	8414	**1999**
10406	11248	10378	9640	8820	8934	**2000**
7690	7399	6839	6886	7426	7688	**2001**
6605	6612	6180	6249	6570	6615	**2002**
7258	7517	7421	7773	7859	8221	**2003**
8458	8377	8668	8871	9030	9247	**2004**
10423	10669	11012	10383	10824	11272	**2005**
11831	12074	11761	12345	12752	12908	**2006**
13869	13660	14099	14625	13689	13833	**2007**
13593	13771	11753	9763	9271	8988	**2008**
10787	10868	11935	10911	11447	11746	**2009**
11713	11914	12369	12676	12953	13443	**2010**
12946	12769	11624	12252	12204	11955	**2011**
11665	11949	12317	12423	12239	12434	**2012**
12487	12654	12787	13361	13395	13622	**2013**

10 BEST

10 WORST

YEARS

	Close	Change	Change
1954	36	11 pt	45.0 %
1958	55	15	38.1
1995	616	157	34.1
1975	90	22	31.5
1997	970	230	31.0
2013	1848	422	29.6
1989	353	76	27.3
1998	1229	259	26.7
1955	45	10	26.4
2003	1112	232	26.4

YEARS

	Close	Change	Change
2008	903	– 566 pt	– 38.5 %
1974	69	– 29	– 29.7
2002	880	– 268	– 23.4
1973	98	– 21	– 17.4
1957	40	– 7	– 14.3
1966	80	– 12	– 13.1
2001	1148	– 172	– 13.0
1962	63	– 8	– 11.8
1977	95	– 12	– 11.5
1969	92	– 12	– 11.4

MONTHS

	Close	Change	Change
Oct 1974	74	10 pt	16.3 %
Aug 1982	120	12	11.6
Dec 1991	417	42	11.2
Oct 1982	134	13	11.0
Oct 2011	1253	122	10.8
Aug 1984	167	16	10.6
Nov 1980	141	13	10.2
Nov 1962	62	6	10.2
Mar 2000	1499	132	9.7
Apr 2009	798	75	9.4

MONTHS

	Close	Change	Change
Oct 1987	252	– 70 pt	– 21.8 %
Oct 2008	969	– 196	– 16.8
Aug 1998	957	– 163	– 14.6
Sep 1974	64	– 9	– 11.9
Nov 1973	96	– 12	– 11.4
Sep 2002	815	– 101	– 11.0
Feb 2009	735	– 91	– 11.0
Mar 1980	102	– 12	– 10.2
Aug 1990	323	– 34	– 9.4
Feb 2001	1240	– 126	– 9.2

DAYS

		Close	Change	Change
Mon	2008 Oct 13	1003	104 pt	11.6 %
Tue	2008 Oct 28	941	92	10.8
Wed	1987 Oct 21	258	22	9.1
Mon	2009 Mar 23	883	54	7.1
Thu	2008 Nov 13	911	59	6.9
Mon	2008 Nov 24	852	52	6.5
Tues	2009 Mar 10	720	43	6.4
Fri	2008 Nov 21	800	48	6.3
Wed	2002 Jul 24	843	46	5.7
Tue	2008 Sep 30	1166	60	5.4

DAYS

		Close	Change	Change
Mon	1987 Oct 19	225	– 58 pt	– 20.5 %
Wed	2008 Oct 15	908	– 90	– 9.0
Mon	2008 Dec 01	816	– 80	– 8.9
Mon	2008 Sep 29	1106	– 107	– 8.8
Mon	1987 Oct 26	228	– 21	– 8.3
Thu	2008 Oct 09	910	– 75	– 7.6
Mon	1997 Oct 27	877	– 65	– 6.9
Mon	1998 Aug 31	957	– 70	– 6.8
Fri	1988 Jan 8	243	– 18	– 6.8
Thu	2008 Nov 20	752	– 54	– 6.7

10 BEST

YEARS

	Close	Change	Change
1954	404	124 pt	44.0 %
1975	852	236	38.3
1958	584	148	34.0
1995	5117	1283	33.5
1985	1547	335	27.7
1989	2753	585	27.0
2013	16577	3473	26.5
1996	6448	1331	26.0
2003	10454	2112	25.3
1999	11453	2272	25.2

MONTHS

	Close	Change	Change
Aug 1982	901	93 pt	11.5 %
Oct 1982	992	95	10.6
Oct 2002	8397	805	10.6
Apr 1978	837	80	10.5
Apr 1999	10789	1003	10.2
Nov 1962	649	60	10.1
Nov 1954	387	35	9.9
Aug 1984	1224	109	9.8
Oct 1998	8592	750	9.6
Oct 2011	11955	1042	9.5

DAYS

		Close	Change	Change
Mon	2008 Oct 13	9388	936 pt	11.1 %
Tue	2008 Oct 28	9065	889	10.9
Wed	1987 Oct 21	2028	187	10.2
Mon	2009 Mar 23	7776	497	6.8
Thu	2008 Nov 13	8835	553	6.7
Fri	2008 Nov 21	8046	494	6.5
Wed	2002 Jul 24	8191	489	6.3
Tue	1987 Oct 20	1841	102	5.9
Tue	2009 Mar 10	6926	379	5.8
Mon	2002 Jul 29	8712	448	5.4

10 WORST

YEARS

	Close	Change	Change
2008	8776	− 4488 pt	− 33.8 %
1974	616	− 235	− 27.6
1966	786	− 184	− 18.9
1977	831	− 174	− 17.3
2002	8342	− 1680	− 16.8
1973	851	− 169	− 16.6
1969	800	− 143	− 15.2
1957	436	− 64	− 12.8
1962	652	− 79	− 10.8
1960	616	− 64	− 9.3

MONTHS

	Close	Change	Change
Oct 1987	1994	− 603 pt	− 23.2 %
Aug 1998	7539	− 1344	− 15.1
Oct 2008	9325	− 1526	− 14.1
Nov 1973	822	− 134	− 14.0
Sep 2002	7592	− 1072	− 12.4
Feb 2009	7063	− 938	− 11.7
Sep 2001	8848	− 1102	− 11.1
Sep 1974	608	− 71	− 10.4
Aug 1974	679	− 79	− 10.4
Jun 2008	11350	− 1288	− 10.2

DAYS

		Close	Change	Change
Mon	1987 Oct 19	1739	− 508 pt	− 22.6 %
Mon	1987 Oct 26	1794	− 157	− 8.0
Wed	2008 Oct 15	8578	− 733	− 7.9
Mon	2008 Dec 01	8149	− 680	− 7.7
Thu	2008 Oct 09	8579	− 679	− 7.3
Mon	1997 Oct 27	8366	− 554	− 7.2
Mon	2001 Sep 17	8921	− 685	− 7.1
Mon	2008 Sep 29	10365	− 778	− 7.0
Fri	1989 Oct 13	2569	− 191	− 6.9
Fri	1988 Jan 8	1911	− 141	− 6.9

10 BEST

10 WORST

YEARS

	Close	Change	Change
1999	4069	1877 pt	85.6 %
1991	586	213	56.9
2003	2003	668	50.0
2009	2269	692	43.9
1995	1052	300	39.9
1998	2193	622	39.6
2013	4161	1157	38.3
1980	202	51	33.9
1985	325	78	31.5
1975	78	18	29.8

YEARS

	Close	Change	Change
2008	1577	– 1075 pt	– 40.5 %
2000	2471	– 1599	– 39.3
1974	60	– 32	– 35.1
2002	1336	– 615	– 31.5
1973	92	– 42	– 31.1
2001	1950	– 520	– 21.1
1990	374	– 81	– 17.8
1984	247	– 32	– 11.3
1987	331	– 18	– 5.2
1981	196	– 7	– 3.2

MONTHS

	Close	Change	Change
Dec 1999	4069	733 pt	22.0 %
Feb 2000	4697	756	19.2
Oct 1974	65	10	17.2
Jun 2000	3966	565	16.6
Apr 2001	2116	276	15.0
Nov 2001	1931	240	14.2
Oct 2002	1330	158	13.5
Oct 1982	1771	25	13.3
Sep 1998	1694	195	13.0
Oct 2001	1690	191	12.8

MONTHS

	Close	Change	Change
Oct 1987	323	– 121 pt	– 27.2 %
Nov 2000	2598	– 772	– 22.9
Feb 2001	2152	– 621	– 22.4
Aug 1998	1499	– 373	– 19.9
Oct 2008	1721	– 371	– 17.7
Mar 1980	131	– 27	– 17.1
Sep 2001	1499	– 307	– 17.0
Oct 1978	111	– 22	– 16.4
Apr 2000	3861	– 712	– 15.6
Nov 1973	94	– 17	– 15.1

DAYS

		Close	Change	Change
Wed	2001 Jan 3	2617	325 pt	14.2 %
Mon	2008 Oct 13	1844	195	11.8
Tue	2000 Dec 5	2890	274	10.5
Tue	2008 Oct 28	1649	144	9.5
Thu	2001 Apr 5	1785	146	8.9
Wed	2001 Apr 18	2079	156	8.1
Tue	2000 May 30	3459	254	7.9
Fri	2000 Oct 13	3317	242	7.9
Thu	2000 Oct 19	3419	247	7.8
Wed	2002 May 8	1696	122	7.8

DAYS

		Close	Change	Change
Mon	1987 Oct 19	360	– 46 pt	– 11.3 %
Fri	2000 Apr 14	3321	– 355	– 9.7
Mon	2008 Sep 29	1984	– 200	– 9.1
Mon	1987 Oct 26	299	– 30	– 9.0
Tue	1987 Oct 20	328	– 32	– 9.0
Mon	2008 Dec 01	1398	– 138	– 9.0
Mon	1998 Aug 31	1499	– 140	– 8.6
Wed	2008 Oct 15	1628	– 151	– 8.5
Mon	2000 Apr 03	4224	– 349	– 7.6
Tue	2001 Jan 02	2292	– 179	– 7.2

10 BEST

10 WORST

YEARS

	Close	Change	Change
2009	8414	2758 pt	30.7 %
1999	4321	1928	29.7
1993	5927	971	29.0
1996	8221	1213	25.7
2003	11272	1606	24.3
2005	2893	2026	21.9
1985	3970	500	20.8
1989	12908	580	17.1
2006	6699	1636	14.5
2010	13433	1697	14.4

YEARS

	Close	Change	Change
2008	8988	− 4845 pt	− 35.0 %
1990	3257	− 713	− 18.0
2002	6615	− 1074	− 14.0
2001	7688	− 1245	− 13.9
2011	11955	− 1488	− 11.1
1992	3350	− 162	− 4.6
1998	6486	− 214	− 3.2
1994	4214	− 108	− 2.5
1987	3160	94	3.1
2012	12434	479	4.0

MONTHS

	Close	Change	Change
Dec 1999	8414	891 pt	11.8 %
May 2009	8500	1045	11.2
Oct 1998	6208	594	10.6
Jun 2000	10196	943	10.2
Jan 1985	2595	195	8.1
Aug 2000	11248	842	8.1
Nov 2001	7426	540	7.8
Jul 1987	4030	290	7.8
Feb 2000	9129	648	7.6
Nov 1996	6017	418	7.5

MONTHS

	Close	Change	Change
Oct 1987	3019	− 883 pt	− 22.6 %
Aug 1998	5531	− 1401	− 20.2
Oct 2008	9763	− 1990	− 16.9
Sep 2008	11753	− 2018	− 14.7
Feb 2001	8079	− 1243	− 13.3
Sep 2011	11624	− 1145	− 9.0
Nov 2000	8820	− 820	− 8.5
Apr 1990	3341	− 299	− 8.2
Sep 2000	10378	− 870	− 7.7
Sep 2001	6839	− 561	− 7.6

DAYS

		Close	Change	Change
Tue	2008 Oct 14	9956	891 pt	9.8 %
Wed	1987 Oct 21	3246	269	9.0
Mon	2008 Oct 20	10251	689	7.2
Tue	2008 Oct 28	9152	614	7.2
Fri	2008 Sep 19	12913	848	7.0
Fri	2008 Nov 28	9271	517	5.9
Fri	2008 Nov 21	8155	431	5.6
Mon	2008 Dec 08	8567	450	5.5
Mon	2009 Mar 23	8959	452	5.3
Fri	1987 Oct 30	3019	147	5.1

DAYS

		Close	Change	Change
Mon	1987 Oct 19	3192	− 407 pt	− 11.3 %
Mon	2008 Dec 01	8406	− 864	− 9.3
Thu	2008 Nov 20	7725	− 766	− 9.0
Mon	2008 Oct 27	8537	− 757	− 8.1
Wed	2000 Oct 25	9512	− 840	− 8.1
Mon	1987 Oct 26	2846	− 233	− 7.6
Thu	2008 Oct 02	10901	− 814	− 6.9
Mon	2008 Sep 29	11285	− 841	− 6.9
Tue	1987 Oct 20	2977	− 215	− 6.7
Fri	2001 Feb 16	8393	− 574	− 6.4

BOND YIELDS

	JAN	FEB	MAR	APR	MAY	JUN
1954	2.48	2.47	2.37	2.29	2.37	2.38
1955	2.61	2.65	2.68	2.75	2.76	2.78
1956	2.9	2.84	2.96	3.18	3.07	3
1957	3.46	3.34	3.41	3.48	3.6	3.8
1958	3.09	3.05	2.98	2.88	2.92	2.97
1959	4.02	3.96	3.99	4.12	4.31	4.34
1960	4.72	4.49	4.25	4.28	4.35	4.15
1961	3.84	3.78	3.74	3.78	3.71	3.88
1962	4.08	4.04	3.93	3.84	3.87	3.91
1963	3.83	3.92	3.93	3.97	3.93	3.99
1964	4.17	4.15	4.22	4.23	4.2	4.17
1965	4.19	4.21	4.21	4.2	4.21	4.21
1966	4.61	4.83	4.87	4.75	4.78	4.81
1967	4.58	4.63	4.54	4.59	4.85	5.02
1968	5.53	5.56	5.74	5.64	5.87	5.72
1969	6.04	6.19	6.3	6.17	6.32	6.57
1970	7.79	7.24	7.07	7.39	7.91	7.84
1971	6.24	6.11	5.7	5.83	6.39	6.52
1972	5.95	6.08	6.07	6.19	6.13	6.11
1973	6.46	6.64	6.71	6.67	6.85	6.9
1974	6.99	6.96	7.21	7.51	7.58	7.54
1975	7.5	7.39	7.73	8.23	8.06	7.86
1976	7.74	7.79	7.73	7.56	7.9	7.86
1977	7.21	7.39	7.46	7.37	7.46	7.28
1978	7.96	8.03	8.04	8.15	8.35	8.46
1979	9.1	9.1	9.12	9.18	9.25	8.91
1980	10.8	12.41	12.75	11.47	10.18	9.78
1981	12.57	13.19	13.12	13.68	14.1	13.47
1982	14.59	14.43	13.86	13.87	13.62	14.3
1983	10.46	10.72	10.51	10.4	10.38	10.85
1984	11.67	11.84	12.32	12.63	13.41	13.56
1985	11.38	11.51	11.86	11.43	10.85	10.16
1986	9.19	8.7	7.78	7.3	7.71	7.8
1987	7.08	7.25	7.25	8.02	8.61	8.4
1988	8.67	8.21	8.37	8.72	9.09	8.92
1989	9.09	9.17	9.36	9.18	8.86	8.28
1990	8.21	8.47	8.59	8.79	8.76	8.48
1991	8.09	7.85	8.11	8.04	8.07	8.28
1992	7.03	7.34	7.54	7.48	7.39	7.26
1993	6.6	6.26	5.98	5.97	6.04	5.96
1994	5.75	5.97	6.48	6.97	7.18	7.1
1995	7.78	7.47	7.2	7.06	6.63	6.17
1996	5.65	5.81	6.27	6.51	6.74	6.91
1997	6.58	6.42	6.69	6.89	6.71	6.49
1998	5.54	5.57	5.65	5.64	5.65	5.5
1999	4.72	5	5.23	5.18	5.54	5.9
2000	6.66	6.52	6.26	5.99	6.44	6.1
2001	5.16	5.1	4.89	5.14	5.39	5.28
2002	5.04	4.91	5.28	5.21	5.16	4.93
2003	4.05	3.9	3.81	3.96	3.57	3.33
2004	4.15	4.08	3.83	4.35	4.72	4.73
2005	4.22	4.17	4.5	4.34	4.14	4.00
2006	4.42	4.57	4.72	4.99	5.11	5.11
2007	4.76	4.72	4.56	4.69	4.75	5.10
2008	3.74	3.74	3.51	3.68	3.88	4.10
2009	2.52	2.87	2.82	2.93	3.29	3.72
2010	3.73	3.69	3.73	3.85	3.42	3.20
2011	3.39	3.58	3.41	3.46	3.17	3.00
2012	1.97	1.97	2.17	2.05	1.80	1.62
2013	1.91	1.98	1.96	1.76	1.93	2.30

* Source: Federal Reserve Bank of St. Louis, monthly data calculated as average of business days

10 YEAR TREASURY BOND YIELDS

JUL	AUG	SEP	OCT	NOV	DEC	
2.3	2.36	2.38	2.43	2.48	2.51	**1954**
2.9	2.97	2.97	2.88	2.89	2.96	**1955**
3.11	3.33	3.38	3.34	3.49	3.59	**1956**
3.93	3.93	3.92	3.97	3.72	3.21	**1957**
3.2	3.54	3.76	3.8	3.74	3.86	**1958**
4.4	4.43	4.68	4.53	4.53	4.69	**1959**
3.9	3.8	3.8	3.89	3.93	3.84	**1960**
3.92	4.04	3.98	3.92	3.94	4.06	**1961**
4.01	3.98	3.98	3.93	3.92	3.86	**1962**
4.02	4	4.08	4.11	4.12	4.13	**1963**
4.19	4.19	4.2	4.19	4.15	4.18	**1964**
4.2	4.25	4.29	4.35	4.45	4.62	**1965**
5.02	5.22	5.18	5.01	5.16	4.84	**1966**
5.16	5.28	5.3	5.48	5.75	5.7	**1967**
5.5	5.42	5.46	5.58	5.7	6.03	**1968**
6.72	6.69	7.16	7.1	7.14	7.65	**1969**
7.46	7.53	7.39	7.33	6.84	6.39	**1970**
6.73	6.58	6.14	5.93	5.81	5.93	**1971**
6.11	6.21	6.55	6.48	6.28	6.36	**1972**
7.13	7.4	7.09	6.79	6.73	6.74	**1973**
7.81	8.04	8.04	7.9	7.68	7.43	**1974**
8.06	8.4	8.43	8.14	8.05	8	**1975**
7.83	7.77	7.59	7.41	7.29	6.87	**1976**
7.33	7.4	7.34	7.52	7.58	7.69	**1977**
8.64	8.41	8.42	8.64	8.81	9.01	**1978**
8.95	9.03	9.33	10.3	10.65	10.39	**1979**
10.25	11.1	11.51	11.75	12.68	12.84	**1980**
14.28	14.94	15.32	15.15	13.39	13.72	**1981**
13.95	13.06	12.34	10.91	10.55	10.54	**1982**
11.38	11.85	11.65	11.54	11.69	11.83	**1983**
13.36	12.72	12.52	12.16	11.57	11.5	**1984**
10.31	10.33	10.37	10.24	9.78	9.26	**1985**
7.3	7.17	7.45	7.43	7.25	7.11	**1986**
8.45	8.76	9.42	9.52	8.86	8.99	**1987**
9.06	9.26	8.98	8.8	8.96	9.11	**1988**
8.02	8.11	8.19	8.01	7.87	7.84	**1989**
8.47	8.75	8.89	8.72	8.39	8.08	**1990**
8.27	7.9	7.65	7.53	7.42	7.09	**1991**
6.84	6.59	6.42	6.59	6.87	6.77	**1992**
5.81	5.68	5.36	5.33	5.72	5.77	**1993**
7.3	7.24	7.46	7.74	7.96	7.81	**1994**
6.28	6.49	6.2	6.04	5.93	5.71	**1995**
6.87	6.64	6.83	6.53	6.2	6.3	**1996**
6.22	6.3	6.21	6.03	5.88	5.81	**1997**
5.46	5.34	4.81	4.53	4.83	4.65	**1998**
5.79	5.94	5.92	6.11	6.03	6.28	**1999**
6.05	5.83	5.8	5.74	5.72	5.24	**2000**
5.24	4.97	4.73	4.57	4.65	5.09	**2001**
4.65	4.26	3.87	3.94	4.05	4.03	**2002**
3.98	4.45	4.27	4.29	4.3	4.27	**2003**
4.5	4.28	4.13	4.1	4.19	4.23	**2004**
4.18	4.26	4.20	4.46	4.54	4.47	**2005**
5.09	4.88	4.72	4.73	4.60	4.56	**2006**
5.00	4.67	4.52	4.53	4.15	4.10	**2007**
4.01	3.89	3.69	3.81	3.53	2.42	**2008**
3.56	3.59	3.40	3.39	3.40	3.59	**2009**
3.01	2.70	2.65	2.54	2.76	3.29	**2010**
3.00	2.30	1.98	2.15	2.01	1.98	**2011**
1.53	1.68	1.72	1.75	1.65	1.72	**2012**
2.58	2.74	2.81	2.62	2.72	2.90	**2013**

BOND YIELDS 5 YEAR TREASURY*

	JAN	FEB	MAR	APR	MAY	JUN
1954	2.17	2.04	1.93	1.87	1.92	1.92
1955	2.32	2.38	2.48	2.55	2.56	2.59
1956	2.84	2.74	2.93	3.20	3.08	2.97
1957	3.47	3.39	3.46	3.53	3.64	3.83
1958	2.88	2.78	2.64	2.46	2.41	2.46
1959	4.01	3.96	3.99	4.12	4.35	4.50
1960	4.92	4.69	4.31	4.29	4.49	4.12
1961	3.67	3.66	3.60	3.57	3.47	3.81
1962	3.94	3.89	3.68	3.60	3.66	3.64
1963	3.58	3.66	3.68	3.74	3.72	3.81
1964	4.07	4.03	4.14	4.15	4.05	4.02
1965	4.10	4.15	4.15	4.15	4.15	4.15
1966	4.86	4.98	4.92	4.83	4.89	4.97
1967	4.70	4.74	4.54	4.51	4.75	5.01
1968	5.54	5.59	5.76	5.69	6.04	5.85
1969	6.25	6.34	6.41	6.30	6.54	6.75
1970	8.17	7.82	7.21	7.50	7.97	7.85
1971	5.89	5.56	5.00	5.65	6.28	6.53
1972	5.59	5.69	5.87	6.17	5.85	5.91
1973	6.34	6.60	6.80	6.67	6.80	6.69
1974	6.95	6.82	7.31	7.92	8.18	8.10
1975	7.41	7.11	7.30	7.99	7.72	7.51
1976	7.46	7.45	7.49	7.25	7.59	7.61
1977	6.58	6.83	6.93	6.79	6.94	6.76
1978	7.77	7.83	7.86	7.98	8.18	8.36
1979	9.20	9.13	9.20	9.25	9.24	8.85
1980	10.74	12.60	13.47	11.84	9.95	9.21
1981	12.77	13.41	13.41	13.99	14.63	13.95
1982	14.65	14.54	13.98	14.00	13.75	14.43
1983	10.03	10.26	10.08	10.02	10.03	10.63
1984	11.37	11.54	12.02	12.37	13.17	13.48
1985	10.93	11.13	11.52	11.01	10.34	9.60
1986	8.68	8.34	7.46	7.05	7.52	7.64
1987	6.64	6.79	6.79	7.57	8.26	8.02
1988	8.18	7.71	7.83	8.19	8.58	8.49
1989	9.15	9.27	9.51	9.30	8.91	8.29
1990	8.12	8.42	8.60	8.77	8.74	8.43
1991	7.70	7.47	7.77	7.70	7.70	7.94
1992	6.24	6.58	6.95	6.78	6.69	6.48
1993	5.83	5.43	5.19	5.13	5.20	5.22
1994	5.09	5.40	5.94	6.52	6.78	6.70
1995	7.76	7.37	7.05	6.86	6.41	5.93
1996	5.36	5.38	5.97	6.30	6.48	6.69
1997	6.33	6.20	6.54	6.76	6.57	6.38
1998	5.42	5.49	5.61	5.61	5.63	5.52
1999	4.60	4.91	5.14	5.08	5.44	5.81
2000	6.58	6.68	6.50	6.26	6.69	6.30
2001	4.86	4.89	4.64	4.76	4.93	4.81
2002	4.34	4.30	4.74	4.65	4.49	4.19
2003	3.05	2.90	2.78	2.93	2.52	2.27
2004	3.12	3.07	2.79	3.39	3.85	3.93
2005	3.71	3.77	4.17	4.00	3.85	3.77
2006	4.35	4.57	4.72	4.90	5.00	5.07
2007	4.75	4.71	4.48	4.59	4.67	5.03
2008	2.98	2.78	2.48	2.84	3.15	3.49
2009	1.60	1.87	1.82	1.86	2.13	2.71
2010	2.48	2.36	2.43	2.58	2.18	2.00
2011	1.99	2.26	2.11	2.17	1.84	1.58
2012	0.84	0.83	1.02	0.89	0.76	0.71
2013	0.81	0.85	0.82	0.71	0.84	1.20

* Source: Federal Reserve Bank of St. Louis, monthly data calculated as average of business days

5 YEAR TREASURY BOND YIELDS

JUL	AUG	SEP	OCT	NOV	DEC	
1.85	1.90	1.96	2.02	2.09	2.16	1954
2.72	2.86	2.85	2.76	2.81	2.93	1955
3.12	3.41	3.47	3.40	3.56	3.70	1956
4.00	4.00	4.03	4.08	3.72	3.08	1957
2.77	3.29	3.69	3.78	3.70	3.82	1958
4.58	4.57	4.90	4.72	4.75	5.01	1959
3.79	3.62	3.61	3.76	3.81	3.67	1960
3.84	3.96	3.90	3.80	3.82	3.91	1961
3.80	3.71	3.70	3.64	3.60	3.56	1962
3.89	3.89	3.96	3.97	4.01	4.04	1963
4.03	4.05	4.08	4.07	4.04	4.09	1964
4.15	4.20	4.25	4.34	4.46	4.72	1965
5.17	5.50	5.50	5.27	5.36	5.00	1966
5.23	5.31	5.40	5.57	5.78	5.75	1967
5.60	5.50	5.48	5.55	5.66	6.12	1968
7.01	7.03	7.57	7.51	7.53	7.96	1969
7.59	7.57	7.29	7.12	6.47	5.95	1970
6.85	6.55	6.14	5.93	5.78	5.69	1971
5.97	6.02	6.25	6.18	6.12	6.16	1972
7.33	7.63	7.05	6.77	6.92	6.80	1973
8.38	8.63	8.37	7.97	7.68	7.31	1974
7.92	8.33	8.37	7.97	7.80	7.76	1975
7.49	7.31	7.13	6.75	6.52	6.10	1976
6.84	7.03	7.04	7.32	7.34	7.48	1977
8.54	8.33	8.43	8.61	8.84	9.08	1978
8.90	9.06	9.41	10.63	10.93	10.42	1979
9.53	10.84	11.62	11.86	12.83	13.25	1980
14.79	15.56	15.93	15.41	13.38	13.60	1981
14.07	13.00	12.25	10.80	10.38	10.22	1982
11.21	11.63	11.43	11.28	11.41	11.54	1983
13.27	12.68	12.53	12.06	11.33	11.07	1984
9.70	9.81	9.81	9.69	9.28	8.73	1985
7.06	6.80	6.92	6.83	6.76	6.67	1986
8.01	8.32	8.94	9.08	8.35	8.45	1987
8.66	8.94	8.69	8.51	8.79	9.09	1988
7.83	8.09	8.17	7.97	7.81	7.75	1989
8.33	8.44	8.51	8.33	8.02	7.73	1990
7.91	7.43	7.14	6.87	6.62	6.19	1991
5.84	5.60	5.38	5.60	6.04	6.08	1992
5.09	5.03	4.73	4.71	5.06	5.15	1993
6.91	6.88	7.08	7.40	7.72	7.78	1994
6.01	6.24	6.00	5.86	5.69	5.51	1995
6.64	6.39	6.60	6.27	5.97	6.07	1996
6.12	6.16	6.11	5.93	5.80	5.77	1997
5.46	5.27	4.62	4.18	4.54	4.45	1998
5.68	5.84	5.80	6.03	5.97	6.19	1999
6.18	6.06	5.93	5.78	5.70	5.17	2000
4.76	4.57	4.12	3.91	3.97	4.39	2001
3.81	3.29	2.94	2.95	3.05	3.03	2002
2.87	3.37	3.18	3.19	3.29	3.27	2003
3.69	3.47	3.36	3.35	3.53	3.60	2004
3.98	4.12	4.01	4.33	4.45	4.39	2005
5.04	4.82	4.67	4.69	4.58	4.53	2006
4.88	4.43	4.20	4.20	3.67	3.49	2007
3.30	3.14	2.88	2.73	2.29	1.52	2008
2.46	2.57	2.37	2.33	2.23	2.34	2009
1.76	1.47	1.41	1.18	1.35	1.93	2010
1.54	1.02	0.90	1.06	0.91	0.89	2011
0.62	0.71	0.67	0.71	0.67	0.70	2012
1.40	1.52	1.60	1.37	1.37	1.58	2013

BOND YIELDS 3 MONTH TREASURY

	JAN	FEB	MAR	APR	MAY	JUN
1982	12.92	14.28	13.31	13.34	12.71	13.08
1983	8.12	8.39	8.66	8.51	8.50	9.14
1984	9.26	9.46	9.89	10.07	10.22	10.26
1985	8.02	8.56	8.83	8.22	7.73	7.18
1986	7.30	7.29	6.76	6.24	6.33	6.40
1987	5.58	5.75	5.77	5.82	5.85	5.85
1988	6.00	5.84	5.87	6.08	6.45	6.66
1999	8.56	8.84	9.14	8.96	8.74	8.43
1990	7.90	8.00	8.17	8.04	8.01	7.99
1991	6.41	6.12	6.09	5.83	5.63	5.75
1992	3.91	3.95	4.14	3.84	3.72	3.75
1993	3.07	2.99	3.01	2.93	3.03	3.14
1994	3.04	3.33	3.59	3.78	4.27	4.25
1995	5.90	5.94	5.91	5.84	5.85	5.64
1996	5.15	4.96	5.10	5.09	5.15	5.23
1997	5.17	5.14	5.28	5.30	5.20	5.07
1998	5.18	5.23	5.16	5.08	5.14	5.12
1999	4.45	4.56	4.57	4.41	4.63	4.72
2000	5.50	5.73	5.86	5.82	5.99	5.86
2001	5.29	5.01	4.54	3.97	3.70	3.57
2002	1.68	1.76	1.83	1.75	1.76	1.73
2003	1.19	1.19	1.15	1.15	1.09	0.94
2004	0.90	0.94	0.95	0.96	1.04	1.29
2005	2.37	2.58	2.80	2.84	2.90	3.04
2006	4.34	4.54	4.63	4.72	4.84	4.92
2007	5.11	5.16	5.08	5.01	4.87	4.74
2008	2.82	2.17	1.28	1.31	1.76	1.89
2009	0.13	0.30	0.22	0.16	0.18	0.18
2010	0.06	0.11	0.15	0.16	0.16	0.12
2011	0.15	0.13	0.10	0.06	0.04	0.04
2012	0.03	0.09	0.08	0.08	0.09	0.09
2013	0.07	0.10	0.09	0.06	0.04	0.05

* Source: Federal Reserve Bank of St. Louis, monthly data calculated as average of business days

3 MONTH TREASURY  BOND YIELDS

JUL	AUG	SEP	OCT	NOV	DEC	
11.86	9.00	8.19	7.97	8.35	8.20	**1982**
9.45	9.74	9.36	8.99	9.11	9.36	**1983**
10.53	10.90	10.80	10.12	8.92	8.34	**1984**
7.32	7.37	7.33	7.40	7.48	7.33	**1985**
6.00	5.69	5.35	5.32	5.50	5.68	**1986**
5.88	6.23	6.62	6.35	5.89	5.96	**1987**
6.95	7.30	7.48	7.60	8.03	8.35	**1988**
8.15	8.17	8.01	7.90	7.94	7.88	**1999**
7.87	7.69	7.60	7.40	7.29	6.95	**1990**
5.75	5.50	5.37	5.14	4.69	4.18	**1991**
3.28	3.20	2.97	2.93	3.21	3.29	**1992**
3.11	3.09	3.01	3.09	3.18	3.13	**1993**
4.46	4.61	4.75	5.10	5.45	5.76	**1994**
5.59	5.57	5.43	5.44	5.52	5.29	**1995**
5.30	5.19	5.24	5.12	5.17	5.04	**1996**
5.19	5.28	5.08	5.11	5.28	5.30	**1997**
5.09	5.04	4.74	4.07	4.53	4.50	**1998**
4.69	4.87	4.82	5.02	5.23	5.36	**1999**
6.14	6.28	6.18	6.29	6.36	5.94	**2000**
3.59	3.44	2.69	2.20	1.91	1.72	**2001**
1.71	1.65	1.66	1.61	1.25	1.21	**2002**
0.92	0.97	0.96	0.94	0.95	0.91	**2003**
1.36	1.50	1.68	1.79	2.11	2.22	**2004**
3.29	3.52	3.49	3.79	3.97	3.97	**2005**
5.08	5.09	4.93	5.05	5.07	4.97	**2006**
4.96	4.32	3.99	4.00	3.35	3.07	**2007**
1.66	1.75	1.15	0.69	0.19	0.03	**2008**
0.18	0.17	0.12	0.07	0.05	0.05	**2009**
0.16	0.16	0.15	0.13	0.14	0.14	**2010**
0.04	0.02	0.01	0.02	0.01	0.01	**2011**
0.10	0.10	0.11	0.10	0.09	0.07	**2012**
0.04	0.04	0.02	0.05	0.07	0.07	**2013**

MOODY'S SEASONED
CORPORATE Aaa*

	JAN	FEB	MAR	APR	MAY	JUN
1950	2.57	2.58	2.58	2.60	2.61	2.62
1951	2.66	2.66	2.78	2.87	2.89	2.94
1952	2.98	2.93	2.96	2.93	2.93	2.94
1953	3.02	3.07	3.12	3.23	3.34	3.40
1954	3.06	2.95	2.86	2.85	2.88	2.90
1955	2.93	2.93	3.02	3.01	3.04	3.05
1956	3.11	3.08	3.10	3.24	3.28	3.26
1957	3.77	3.67	3.66	3.67	3.74	3.91
1958	3.60	3.59	3.63	3.60	3.57	3.57
1959	4.12	4.14	4.13	4.23	4.37	4.46
1960	4.61	4.56	4.49	4.45	4.46	4.45
1961	4.32	4.27	4.22	4.25	4.27	4.33
1962	4.42	4.42	4.39	4.33	4.28	4.28
1963	4.21	4.19	4.19	4.21	4.22	4.23
1964	4.39	4.36	4.38	4.40	4.41	4.41
1965	4.43	4.41	4.42	4.43	4.44	4.46
1966	4.74	4.78	4.92	4.96	4.98	5.07
1967	5.20	5.03	5.13	5.11	5.24	5.44
1968	6.17	6.10	6.11	6.21	6.27	6.28
1969	6.59	6.66	6.85	6.89	6.79	6.98
1970	7.91	7.93	7.84	7.83	8.11	8.48
1971	7.36	7.08	7.21	7.25	7.53	7.64
1972	7.19	7.27	7.24	7.30	7.30	7.23
1973	7.15	7.22	7.29	7.26	7.29	7.37
1974	7.83	7.85	8.01	8.25	8.37	8.47
1975	8.83	8.62	8.67	8.95	8.90	8.77
1976	8.60	8.55	8.52	8.40	8.58	8.62
1977	7.96	8.04	8.10	8.04	8.05	7.95
1978	8.41	8.47	8.47	8.56	8.69	8.76
1979	9.25	9.26	9.37	9.38	9.50	9.29
1980	11.09	12.38	12.96	12.04	10.99	10.58
1981	12.81	13.35	13.33	13.88	14.32	13.75
1982	15.18	15.27	14.58	14.46	14.26	14.81
1983	11.79	12.01	11.73	11.51	11.46	11.74
1984	12.20	12.08	12.57	12.81	13.28	13.55
1985	12.08	12.13	12.56	12.23	11.72	10.94
1986	10.05	9.67	9.00	8.79	9.09	9.13
1987	8.36	8.38	8.36	8.85	9.33	9.32
1988	9.88	9.40	9.39	9.67	9.90	9.86
1989	9.62	9.64	9.80	9.79	9.57	9.10
1990	8.99	9.22	9.37	9.46	9.47	9.26
1991	9.04	8.83	8.93	8.86	8.86	9.01
1992	8.20	8.29	8.35	8.33	8.28	8.22
1993	7.91	7.71	7.58	7.46	7.43	7.33
1994	6.92	7.08	7.48	7.88	7.99	7.97
1995	8.46	8.26	8.12	8.03	7.65	7.30
1996	6.81	6.99	7.35	7.50	7.62	7.71
1997	7.42	7.31	7.55	7.73	7.58	7.41
1998	6.61	6.67	6.72	6.69	6.69	6.53
1999	6.24	6.40	6.62	6.64	6.93	7.23
2000	7.78	7.68	7.68	7.64	7.99	7.67
2001	7.15	7.10	6.98	7.20	7.29	7.18
2002	6.55	6.51	6.81	6.76	6.75	6.63
2003	6.17	5.95	5.89	5.74	5.22	4.97
2004	5.54	5.50	5.33	5.73	6.04	6.01
2005	5.36	5.20	5.40	5.33	5.15	4.96
2006	5.29	5.35	5.53	5.84	5.95	5.89
2007	5.40	5.39	5.30	5.47	5.47	5.79
2008	5.33	5.53	5.51	5.55	5.57	5.68
2009	5.05	5.27	5.50	5.39	5.54	5.61
2010	5.26	5.35	5.27	5.29	4.96	4.88
2011	5.04	5.22	5.13	5.16	4.96	4.99
2012	3.85	3.85	3.99	3.96	3.80	3.64
2013	3.80	3.90	3.93	3.73	3.89	4.27

* Source: Federal Reserve Bank of St. Louis, monthly data calculated as average of business days

MOODY'S SEASONED CORPORATE Aaa BOND YIELDS

JUL	AUG	SEP	OCT	NOV	DEC	
2.65	2.61	2.64	2.67	2.67	2.67	**1950**
2.94	2.88	2.84	2.89	2.96	3.01	**1951**
2.95	2.94	2.95	3.01	2.98	2.97	**1952**
3.28	3.24	3.29	3.16	3.11	3.13	**1953**
2.89	2.87	2.89	2.87	2.89	2.90	**1954**
3.06	3.11	3.13	3.10	3.10	3.15	**1955**
3.28	3.43	3.56	3.59	3.69	3.75	**1956**
3.99	4.10	4.12	4.10	4.08	3.81	**1957**
3.67	3.85	4.09	4.11	4.09	4.08	**1958**
4.47	4.43	4.52	4.57	4.56	4.58	**1959**
4.41	4.28	4.25	4.30	4.31	4.35	**1960**
4.41	4.45	4.45	4.42	4.39	4.42	**1961**
4.34	4.35	4.32	4.28	4.25	4.24	**1962**
4.26	4.29	4.31	4.32	4.33	4.35	**1963**
4.40	4.41	4.42	4.42	4.43	4.44	**1964**
4.48	4.49	4.52	4.56	4.60	4.68	**1965**
5.16	5.31	5.49	5.41	5.35	5.39	**1966**
5.58	5.62	5.65	5.82	6.07	6.19	**1967**
6.24	6.02	5.97	6.09	6.19	6.45	**1968**
7.08	6.97	7.14	7.33	7.35	7.72	**1969**
8.44	8.13	8.09	8.03	8.05	7.64	**1970**
7.64	7.59	7.44	7.39	7.26	7.25	**1971**
7.21	7.19	7.22	7.21	7.12	7.08	**1972**
7.45	7.68	7.63	7.60	7.67	7.68	**1973**
8.72	9.00	9.24	9.27	8.89	8.89	**1974**
8.84	8.95	8.95	8.86	8.78	8.79	**1975**
8.56	8.45	8.38	8.32	8.25	7.98	**1976**
7.94	7.98	7.92	8.04	8.08	8.19	**1977**
8.88	8.69	8.69	8.89	9.03	9.16	**1978**
9.20	9.23	9.44	10.13	10.76	10.74	**1979**
11.07	11.64	12.02	12.31	12.97	13.21	**1980**
14.38	14.89	15.49	15.40	14.22	14.23	**1981**
14.61	13.71	12.94	12.12	11.68	11.83	**1982**
12.15	12.51	12.37	12.25	12.41	12.57	**1983**
13.44	12.87	12.66	12.63	12.29	12.13	**1984**
10.97	11.05	11.07	11.02	10.55	10.16	**1985**
8.88	8.72	8.89	8.86	8.68	8.49	**1986**
9.42	9.67	10.18	10.52	10.01	10.11	**1987**
9.96	10.11	9.82	9.51	9.45	9.57	**1988**
8.93	8.96	9.01	8.92	8.89	8.86	**1989**
9.24	9.41	9.56	9.53	9.30	9.05	**1990**
9.00	8.75	8.61	8.55	8.48	8.31	**1991**
8.07	7.95	7.92	7.99	8.10	7.98	**1992**
7.17	6.85	6.66	6.67	6.93	6.93	**1993**
8.11	8.07	8.34	8.57	8.68	8.46	**1994**
7.41	7.57	7.32	7.12	7.02	6.82	**1995**
7.65	7.46	7.66	7.39	7.10	7.20	**1996**
7.14	7.22	7.15	7.00	6.87	6.76	**1997**
6.55	6.52	6.40	6.37	6.41	6.22	**1998**
7.19	7.40	7.39	7.55	7.36	7.55	**1999**
7.65	7.55	7.62	7.55	7.45	7.21	**2000**
7.13	7.02	7.17	7.03	6.97	6.77	**2001**
6.53	6.37	6.15	6.32	6.31	6.21	**2002**
5.49	5.88	5.72	5.70	5.65	5.62	**2003**
5.82	5.65	5.46	5.47	5.52	5.47	**2004**
5.06	5.09	5.13	5.35	5.42	5.37	**2005**
5.85	5.68	5.51	5.51	5.33	5.32	**2006**
5.73	5.79	5.74	5.66	5.44	5.49	**2007**
5.67	5.64	5.65	6.28	6.12	5.05	**2008**
5.41	5.26	5.13	5.15	5.19	5.26	**2009**
4.72	4.49	4.53	4.68	4.87	5.02	**2010**
4.93	4.37	4.09	3.98	3.87	3.93	**2011**
3.40	3.48	3.49	3.47	3.50	3.65	**2012**
4.34	4.54	4.64	4.53	4.63	4.62	**2013**

MOODY'S SEASONED
CORPORATE Baa*

	JAN	FEB	MAR	APR	MAY	JUN
1950	3.24	3.24	3.24	3.23	3.25	3.28
1951	3.17	3.16	3.23	3.35	3.40	3.49
1952	3.59	3.53	3.51	3.50	3.49	3.50
1953	3.51	3.53	3.57	3.65	3.78	3.86
1954	3.71	3.61	3.51	3.47	3.47	3.49
1955	3.45	3.47	3.48	3.49	3.50	3.51
1956	3.60	3.58	3.60	3.68	3.73	3.76
1957	4.49	4.47	4.43	4.44	4.52	4.63
1958	4.83	4.66	4.68	4.67	4.62	4.55
1959	4.87	4.89	4.85	4.86	4.96	5.04
1960	5.34	5.34	5.25	5.20	5.28	5.26
1961	5.10	5.07	5.02	5.01	5.01	5.03
1962	5.08	5.07	5.04	5.02	5.00	5.02
1963	4.91	4.89	4.88	4.87	4.85	4.84
1964	4.83	4.83	4.83	4.85	4.85	4.85
1965	4.80	4.78	4.78	4.80	4.81	4.85
1966	5.06	5.12	5.32	5.41	5.48	5.58
1967	5.97	5.82	5.85	5.83	5.96	6.15
1968	6.84	6.80	6.85	6.97	7.03	7.07
1969	7.32	7.30	7.51	7.54	7.52	7.70
1970	8.86	8.78	8.63	8.70	8.98	9.25
1971	8.74	8.39	8.46	8.45	8.62	8.75
1972	8.23	8.23	8.24	8.24	8.23	8.20
1973	7.90	7.97	8.03	8.09	8.06	8.13
1974	8.48	8.53	8.62	8.87	9.05	9.27
1975	10.81	10.65	10.48	10.58	10.69	10.62
1976	10.41	10.24	10.12	9.94	9.86	9.89
1977	9.08	9.12	9.12	9.07	9.01	8.91
1978	9.17	9.20	9.22	9.32	9.49	9.60
1979	10.13	10.08	10.26	10.33	10.47	10.38
1980	12.42	13.57	14.45	14.19	13.17	12.71
1981	15.03	15.37	15.34	15.56	15.95	15.80
1982	17.10	17.18	16.82	16.78	16.64	16.92
1983	13.94	13.95	13.61	13.29	13.09	13.37
1984	13.65	13.59	13.99	14.31	14.74	15.05
1985	13.26	13.23	13.69	13.51	13.15	12.40
1986	11.44	11.11	10.50	10.19	10.29	10.34
1987	9.72	9.65	9.61	10.04	10.51	10.52
1988	11.07	10.62	10.57	10.90	11.04	11.00
1989	10.65	10.61	10.67	10.61	10.46	10.03
1990	9.94	10.14	10.21	10.30	10.41	10.22
1991	10.45	10.07	10.09	9.94	9.86	9.96
1992	9.13	9.23	9.25	9.21	9.13	9.05
1993	8.67	8.39	8.15	8.14	8.21	8.07
1994	7.65	7.76	8.13	8.52	8.62	8.65
1995	9.08	8.85	8.70	8.60	8.20	7.90
1996	7.47	7.63	8.03	8.19	8.30	8.40
1997	8.09	7.94	8.18	8.34	8.20	8.02
1998	7.19	7.25	7.32	7.33	7.30	7.13
1999	7.29	7.39	7.53	7.48	7.72	8.02
2000	8.33	8.29	8.37	8.40	8.90	8.48
2001	7.93	7.87	7.84	8.07	8.07	7.97
2002	7.87	7.89	8.11	8.03	8.09	7.95
2003	7.35	7.06	6.95	6.85	6.38	6.19
2004	6.44	6.27	6.11	6.46	6.75	6.78
2005	6.02	5.82	6.06	6.05	6.01	5.86
2006	6.24	6.27	6.41	6.68	6.75	6.78
2007	6.34	6.28	6.27	6.39	6.39	6.70
2008	6.54	6.82	6.89	6.97	6.93	7.07
2009	8.14	8.08	8.42	8.39	8.06	7.50
2010	6.25	6.34	6.27	6.25	6.05	6.23
2011	6.09	6.15	6.03	6.02	5.78	5.75
2012	5.23	5.14	5.23	5.19	5.07	5.02
2013	4.73	4.85	4.85	4.59	4.73	5.19

* Source: Federal Reserve Bank of St. Louis, monthly data calculated as average of business days

MOODY'S SEASONED CORPORATE Baa* BOND YIELDS

JUL	AUG	SEP	OCT	NOV	DEC	
3.32	3.23	3.21	3.22	3.22	3.20	1950
3.53	3.50	3.46	3.50	3.56	3.61	1951
3.50	3.51	3.52	3.54	3.53	3.51	1952
3.86	3.85	3.88	3.82	3.75	3.74	1953
3.50	3.49	3.47	3.46	3.45	3.45	1954
3.52	3.56	3.59	3.59	3.58	3.62	1955
3.80	3.93	4.07	4.17	4.24	4.37	1956
4.73	4.82	4.93	4.99	5.09	5.03	1957
4.53	4.67	4.87	4.92	4.87	4.85	1958
5.08	5.09	5.18	5.28	5.26	5.28	1959
5.22	5.08	5.01	5.11	5.08	5.10	1960
5.09	5.11	5.12	5.13	5.11	5.10	1961
5.05	5.06	5.03	4.99	4.96	4.92	1962
4.84	4.83	4.84	4.83	4.84	4.85	1963
4.83	4.82	4.82	4.81	4.81	4.81	1964
4.88	4.88	4.91	4.93	4.95	5.02	1965
5.68	5.83	6.09	6.10	6.13	6.18	1966
6.26	6.33	6.40	6.52	6.72	6.93	1967
6.98	6.82	6.79	6.84	7.01	7.23	1968
7.84	7.86	8.05	8.22	8.25	8.65	1969
9.40	9.44	9.39	9.33	9.38	9.12	1970
8.76	8.76	8.59	8.48	8.38	8.38	1971
8.23	8.19	8.09	8.06	7.99	7.93	1972
8.24	8.53	8.63	8.41	8.42	8.48	1973
9.48	9.77	10.18	10.48	10.60	10.63	1974
10.55	10.59	10.61	10.62	10.56	10.56	1975
9.82	9.64	9.40	9.29	9.23	9.12	1976
8.87	8.82	8.80	8.89	8.95	8.99	1977
9.60	9.48	9.42	9.59	9.83	9.94	1978
10.29	10.35	10.54	11.40	11.99	12.06	1979
12.65	13.15	13.70	14.23	14.64	15.14	1980
16.17	16.34	16.92	17.11	16.39	16.55	1981
16.80	16.32	15.63	14.73	14.30	14.14	1982
13.39	13.64	13.55	13.46	13.61	13.75	1983
15.15	14.63	14.35	13.94	13.48	13.40	1984
12.43	12.50	12.48	12.36	11.99	11.58	1985
10.16	10.18	10.20	10.24	10.07	9.97	1986
10.61	10.80	11.31	11.62	11.23	11.29	1987
11.11	11.21	10.90	10.41	10.48	10.65	1988
9.87	9.88	9.91	9.81	9.81	9.82	1989
10.20	10.41	10.64	10.74	10.62	10.43	1990
9.89	9.65	9.51	9.49	9.45	9.26	1991
8.84	8.65	8.62	8.84	8.96	8.81	1992
7.93	7.60	7.34	7.31	7.66	7.69	1993
8.80	8.74	8.98	9.20	9.32	9.10	1994
8.04	8.19	7.93	7.75	7.68	7.49	1995
8.35	8.18	8.35	8.07	7.79	7.89	1996
7.75	7.82	7.70	7.57	7.42	7.32	1997
7.15	7.14	7.09	7.18	7.34	7.23	1998
7.95	8.15	8.20	8.38	8.15	8.19	1999
8.35	8.26	8.35	8.34	8.28	8.02	2000
7.97	7.85	8.03	7.91	7.81	8.05	2001
7.90	7.58	7.40	7.73	7.62	7.45	2002
6.62	7.01	6.79	6.73	6.66	6.60	2003
6.62	6.46	6.27	6.21	6.20	6.15	2004
5.95	5.96	6.03	6.30	6.39	6.32	2005
6.76	6.59	6.43	6.42	6.20	6.22	2006
6.65	6.65	6.59	6.48	6.40	6.65	2007
7.16	7.15	7.31	8.88	9.21	8.43	2008
7.09	6.58	6.31	6.29	6.32	6.37	2009
6.01	5.66	5.66	5.72	5.92	6.10	2010
5.76	5.36	5.27	5.37	5.14	5.25	2011
4.87	4.91	4.84	4.58	4.51	4.63	2012
5.32	5.42	5.47	5.31	5.38	5.38	2013

COMMODITIES

OIL - WEST TEXAS INTERMEDIATE CLOSING VALUES $ / bbl

	JAN	FEB	MAR	APR	MAY	JUN
1950	2.6	2.6	2.6	2.6	2.6	2.6
1951	2.6	2.6	2.6	2.6	2.6	2.6
1952	2.6	2.6	2.6	2.6	2.6	2.6
1953	2.6	2.6	2.6	2.6	2.6	2.8
1954	2.8	2.8	2.8	2.8	2.8	2.8
1955	2.8	2.8	2.8	2.8	2.8	2.8
1956	2.8	2.8	2.8	2.8	2.8	2.8
1957	2.8	3.1	3.1	3.1	3.1	3.1
1958	3.1	3.1	3.1	3.1	3.1	3.1
1959	3.0	3.0	3.0	3.0	3.0	3.0
1960	3.0	3.0	3.0	3.0	3.0	3.0
1961	3.0	3.0	3.0	3.0	3.0	3.0
1962	3.0	3.0	3.0	3.0	3.0	3.0
1963	3.0	3.0	3.0	3.0	3.0	3.0
1964	3.0	3.0	3.0	3.0	3.0	3.0
1965	2.9	2.9	2.9	2.9	2.9	2.9
1966	2.9	2.9	2.9	2.9	2.9	2.9
1967	3.0	3.0	3.0	3.0	3.0	3.0
1968	3.1	3.1	3.1	3.1	3.1	3.1
1969	3.1	3.1	3.3	3.4	3.4	3.4
1970	3.4	3.4	3.4	3.4	3.4	3.4
1971	3.6	3.6	3.6	3.6	3.6	3.6
1972	3.6	3.6	3.6	3.6	3.6	3.6
1973	3.6	3.6	3.6	3.6	3.6	3.6
1974	10.1	10.1	10.1	10.1	10.1	10.1
1975	11.2	11.2	11.2	11.2	11.2	11.2
1976	11.2	12.0	12.1	12.2	12.2	12.2
1977	13.9	13.9	13.9	13.9	13.9	13.9
1978	14.9	14.9	14.9	14.9	14.9	14.9
1979	14.9	15.9	15.9	15.9	18.1	19.1
1980	32.5	37.0	38.0	39.5	39.5	39.5
1981	38.0	38.0	38.0	38.0	38.0	36.0
1982	33.9	31.6	28.5	33.5	35.9	35.1
1983	31.2	29.0	28.8	30.6	30.0	31.0
1984	29.7	30.1	30.8	30.6	30.5	30.0
1985	25.6	27.3	28.2	28.8	27.6	27.1
1986	22.9	15.4	12.6	12.8	15.4	13.5
1987	18.7	17.7	18.3	18.6	19.4	20.0
1988	17.2	16.8	16.2	17.9	17.4	16.5
1989	18.0	17.8	19.4	21.0	20.0	20.0
1990	22.6	22.1	20.4	18.6	18.2	16.9
1991	25.0	20.5	19.9	20.8	21.2	20.2
1992	18.8	19.0	18.9	20.2	20.9	22.4
1993	19.1	20.1	20.3	20.3	19.9	19.1
1994	15.0	14.8	14.7	16.4	17.9	19.1
1995	18.0	18.5	18.6	19.9	19.7	18.4
1996	18.9	19.1	21.4	23.6	21.3	20.5
1997	25.2	22.2	21.0	19.7	20.8	19.2
1998	16.7	16.1	15.0	15.4	14.9	13.7
1999	12.5	12.0	14.7	17.3	17.8	17.9
2000	27.2	29.4	29.9	25.7	28.8	31.8
2001	29.6	29.6	27.2	27.4	28.6	27.6
2002	19.7	20.7	24.4	26.3	27.0	25.5
2003	32.9	35.9	33.6	28.3	28.1	30.7
2004	34.3	34.7	36.8	36.7	40.3	38.0
2005	46.8	48.0	54.3	53.0	49.8	56.3
2006	65.5	61.6	62.9	69.7	70.9	71.0
2007	54.6	59.3	60.6	64.0	63.5	67.5
2008	93.0	95.4	105.6	112.6	125.4	133.9
2009	41.7	39.2	48.0	49.8	59.2	69.7
2010	78.2	76.4	81.2	84.5	73.8	75.4
2011	89.4	89.6	102.9	110.0	101.3	96.3
2012	100.3	102.3	106.2	103.3	94.7	82.3
2013	94.8	95.3	92.9	92.0	94.5	95.8

* Source: Federal Reserve

OIL - WEST TEXAS INTERMEDIATE
CLOSING VALUES $ / bbl

JUL	AUG	SEP	OCT	NOV	DEC	
2.6	2.6	2.6	2.6	2.6	2.6	**1950**
2.6	2.6	2.6	2.6	2.6	2.6	**1951**
2.6	2.6	2.6	2.6	2.6	2.6	**1952**
2.8	2.8	2.8	2.8	2.8	2.8	**1953**
2.8	2.8	2.8	2.8	2.8	2.8	**1954**
2.8	2.8	2.8	2.8	2.8	2.8	**1955**
2.8	2.8	2.8	2.8	2.8	2.8	**1956**
3.1	3.1	3.1	3.1	3.1	3.0	**1957**
3.1	3.1	3.1	3.1	3.0	3.0	**1958**
3.0	3.0	3.0	3.0	3.0	3.0	**1959**
3.0	3.0	3.0	3.0	3.0	3.0	**1960**
3.0	3.0	3.0	3.0	3.0	3.0	**1961**
3.0	3.0	3.0	3.0	3.0	3.0	**1962**
3.0	3.0	3.0	3.0	3.0	3.0	**1963**
2.9	2.9	2.9	2.9	2.9	2.9	**1964**
2.9	2.9	2.9	2.9	2.9	2.9	**1965**
2.9	2.9	3.0	3.0	3.0	3.0	**1966**
3.0	3.1	3.1	3.1	3.1	3.1	**1967**
3.1	3.1	3.1	3.1	3.1	3.1	**1968**
3.4	3.4	3.4	3.4	3.4	3.4	**1969**
3.3	3.3	3.3	3.3	3.3	3.6	**1970**
3.6	3.6	3.6	3.6	3.6	3.6	**1971**
3.6	3.6	3.6	3.6	3.6	3.6	**1972**
3.6	4.3	4.3	4.3	4.3	4.3	**1973**
10.1	10.1	10.1	11.2	11.2	11.2	**1974**
11.2	11.2	11.2	11.2	11.2	11.2	**1975**
12.2	12.2	13.9	13.9	13.9	13.9	**1976**
13.9	14.9	14.9	14.9	14.9	14.9	**1977**
14.9	14.9	14.9	14.9	14.9	14.9	**1978**
21.8	26.5	28.5	29.0	31.0	32.5	**1979**
39.5	38.0	36.0	36.0	36.0	37.0	**1980**
36.0	36.0	36.0	35.0	36.0	35.0	**1981**
34.2	34.0	35.6	35.7	34.2	31.7	**1982**
31.7	31.9	31.1	30.4	29.8	29.2	**1983**
28.8	29.3	29.3	28.8	28.1	25.4	**1984**
27.3	27.8	28.3	29.5	30.8	27.2	**1985**
11.6	15.1	14.9	14.9	15.2	16.1	**1986**
21.4	20.3	19.5	19.8	18.9	17.2	**1987**
15.5	15.5	14.5	13.8	14.0	16.3	**1988**
19.6	18.5	19.6	20.1	19.8	21.1	**1989**
18.6	27.2	33.7	35.9	32.3	27.3	**1990**
21.4	21.7	21.9	23.2	22.5	19.5	**1991**
21.8	21.4	21.9	21.7	20.3	19.4	**1992**
17.9	18.0	17.5	18.1	16.7	14.5	**1993**
19.7	18.4	17.5	17.7	18.1	17.2	**1994**
17.3	18.0	18.2	17.4	18.0	19.0	**1995**
21.3	22.0	24.0	24.9	23.7	25.4	**1996**
19.6	19.9	19.8	21.3	20.2	18.3	**1997**
14.1	13.4	15.0	14.4	12.9	11.3	**1998**
20.1	21.3	23.9	22.6	25.0	26.1	**1999**
29.8	31.2	33.9	33.1	34.4	28.5	**2000**
26.5	27.5	25.9	22.2	19.7	19.3	**2001**
26.9	28.4	29.7	28.9	26.3	29.4	**2002**
30.8	31.6	28.3	30.3	31.1	32.2	**2003**
40.7	44.9	46.0	53.1	48.5	43.3	**2004**
58.7	65.0	65.6	62.4	58.3	59.4	**2005**
74.4	73.1	63.9	58.9	59.4	62.0	**2006**
74.2	72.4	79.9	86.2	94.6	91.7	**2007**
133.4	116.6	103.9	76.7	57.4	41.0	**2008**
64.1	71.1	69.5	75.6	78.1	74.3	**2009**
76.4	76.8	75.3	81.9	84.1	89.0	**2010**
97.2	86.3	85.6	86.4	97.2	98.6	**2011**
87.9	94.2	94.7	89.6	86.7	88.3	**2012**
104.7	106.6	106.3	100.5	93.9	97.6	**2013**

GOLD $US/OZ LONDON PM
MONTH CLOSE

	JAN	FEB	MAR	APR	MAY	JUN
1970	34.9	35.0	35.1	35.6	36.0	35.4
1971	37.9	38.7	38.9	39.0	40.5	40.1
1972	45.8	48.3	48.3	49.0	54.6	62.1
1973	65.1	74.2	84.4	90.5	102.0	120.1
1974	129.2	150.2	168.4	172.2	163.3	154.1
1975	175.8	181.8	178.2	167.0	167.0	166.3
1976	128.2	132.3	129.6	128.4	125.5	123.8
1977	132.3	142.8	148.9	147.3	143.0	143.0
1978	175.8	182.3	181.6	170.9	184.2	183.1
1979	233.7	251.3	240.1	245.3	274.6	277.5
1980	653.0	637.0	494.5	518.0	535.5	653.5
1981	506.5	489.0	513.8	482.8	479.3	426.0
1982	387.0	362.6	320.0	361.3	325.3	317.5
1983	499.5	408.5	414.8	429.3	437.5	416.0
1984	373.8	394.3	388.5	375.8	384.3	373.1
1985	306.7	287.8	329.3	321.4	314.0	317.8
1986	350.5	338.2	344.0	345.8	343.2	345.5
1987	400.5	405.9	405.9	453.3	451.0	447.3
1988	458.0	426.2	457.0	449.0	455.5	436.6
1989	394.0	387.0	383.2	377.6	361.8	373.0
1990	415.1	407.7	368.5	367.8	363.1	352.2
1991	366.0	362.7	355.7	357.8	360.4	368.4
1992	354.1	353.1	341.7	336.4	337.5	343.4
1993	330.5	327.6	337.8	354.3	374.8	378.5
1994	377.9	381.6	389.2	376.5	387.6	388.3
1995	374.9	376.4	392.0	389.8	384.3	387.1
1996	405.6	400.7	396.4	391.3	390.6	382.0
1997	345.5	358.6	348.2	340.2	345.6	334.6
1998	304.9	297.4	301.0	310.7	293.6	296.3
1999	285.4	287.1	279.5	286.6	268.6	261.0
2000	283.3	293.7	276.8	275.1	272.3	288.2
2001	264.5	266.7	257.7	263.2	267.5	270.6
2002	282.3	296.9	301.4	308.2	326.6	318.5
2003	367.5	347.5	334.9	336.8	361.4	346.0
2004	399.8	395.9	423.7	388.5	393.3	395.8
2005	422.2	435.5	427.5	435.7	414.5	437.1
2006	568.8	556.0	582.0	644.0	653.0	613.5
2007	650.5	664.2	661.8	677.0	659.1	650.5
2008	923.3	971.5	933.5	871.0	885.8	930.3
2009	919.5	952.0	916.5	883.3	975.5	934.5
2010	1078.5	1108.3	1115.5	1179.3	1207.5	1244.0
2011	1327.0	1411.0	1439.0	1535.5	1536.5	1505.5
2012	1744.0	1770.0	1662.5	1651.3	1558.0	1598.5
2013	1664.8	1588.5	1598.3	1469.0	1394.5	1192.0

* Source: Bank of England

GOLD $US/OZ LONDON PM MONTH CLOSE

JUL	AUG	SEP	OCT	NOV	DEC	
35.3	35.4	36.2	37.5	37.4	37.4	**1970**
41.0	42.7	42.0	42.5	42.9	43.5	**1971**
65.7	67.0	65.5	64.9	62.9	63.9	**1972**
120.2	106.8	103.0	100.1	94.8	106.7	**1973**
143.0	154.6	151.8	158.8	181.7	183.9	**1974**
166.7	159.8	141.3	142.9	138.2	140.3	**1975**
112.5	104.0	116.0	123.2	130.3	134.5	**1976**
144.1	146.0	154.1	161.5	160.1	165.0	**1977**
200.3	208.7	217.1	242.6	193.4	226.0	**1978**
296.5	315.1	397.3	382.0	415.7	512.0	**1979**
614.3	631.3	666.8	629.0	619.8	589.8	**1980**
406.0	425.5	428.8	427.0	414.5	397.5	**1981**
342.9	411.5	397.0	423.3	436.0	456.9	**1982**
422.0	414.3	405.0	382.0	405.0	382.4	**1983**
342.4	348.3	343.8	333.5	329.0	309.0	**1984**
327.5	333.3	326.5	325.1	325.3	326.8	**1985**
357.5	384.7	423.2	401.0	383.5	388.8	**1986**
462.5	453.4	459.5	468.8	492.5	484.1	**1987**
436.8	427.8	397.7	412.4	422.6	410.3	**1988**
368.3	359.8	366.5	375.3	408.2	398.6	**1989**
372.3	387.8	408.4	379.5	384.9	386.2	**1990**
362.9	347.4	354.9	357.5	366.3	353.2	**1991**
357.9	340.0	349.0	339.3	334.2	332.9	**1992**
401.8	371.6	355.5	369.6	370.9	391.8	**1993**
384.0	385.8	394.9	383.9	383.1	383.3	**1994**
383.4	382.4	384.0	382.7	387.8	387.0	**1995**
385.3	386.5	379.0	379.5	371.3	369.3	**1996**
326.4	325.4	332.1	311.4	296.8	290.2	**1997**
288.9	273.4	293.9	292.3	294.7	287.8	**1998**
255.6	254.8	299.0	299.1	291.4	290.3	**1999**
276.8	277.0	273.7	264.5	269.1	274.5	**2000**
265.9	273.0	293.1	278.8	275.5	276.5	**2001**
304.7	312.8	323.7	316.9	319.1	347.2	**2002**
354.8	375.6	388.0	386.3	398.4	416.3	**2003**
391.4	407.3	415.7	425.6	453.4	435.6	**2004**
429.0	433.3	473.3	470.8	495.7	513.0	**2005**
632.5	623.5	599.3	603.8	646.7	632.0	**2006**
665.5	672.0	743.0	789.5	783.5	833.8	**2007**
918.0	833.0	884.5	730.8	814.5	869.8	**2008**
939.0	955.5	995.8	1040.0	1175.8	1087.5	**2009**
1169.0	1246.0	1307.0	1346.8	1383.5	1405.5	**2010**
1628.5	1813.5	1620.0	1722.0	1746.0	1531.0	**2011**
1622.0	1648.5	1776.0	1719.0	1726.0	1657.5	**2012**
1314.5	1394.8	1326.5	1324.0	1253.0	1204.5	**2013**

FOREIGN EXCHANGE

	JAN		FEB		MAR		APR		MAY		JUN	
	US / CDN	CDN / US	US / CDN	CDN / US	US / CDN	CDN /US	US / CDN	CDN / US	US / CDN	CDN / US	US / CDN	CDN / US
1971	1.01	0.99	1.01	0.99	1.01	0.99	1.01	0.99	1.01	0.99	1.02	0.98
1972	1.01	0.99	1.00	1.00	1.00	1.00	1.00	1.00	0.99	1.01	0.98	1.02
1973	1.00	1.00	1.00	1.00	1.00	1.00	1.00	1.00	1.00	1.00	1.00	1.00
1974	0.99	1.01	0.98	1.02	0.97	1.03	0.97	1.03	0.96	1.04	0.97	1.03
1975	0.99	1.01	1.00	1.00	1.00	1.00	1.01	0.99	1.03	0.97	1.03	0.97
1976	1.01	0.99	0.99	1.01	0.99	1.01	0.98	1.02	0.98	1.02	0.97	1.03
1977	1.01	0.99	1.03	0.97	1.05	0.95	1.05	0.95	1.05	0.95	1.06	0.95
1978	1.10	0.91	1.11	0.90	1.13	0.89	1.14	0.88	1.12	0.89	1.12	0.89
1979	1.19	0.84	1.20	0.84	1.17	0.85	1.15	0.87	1.16	0.87	1.17	0.85
1980	1.16	0.86	1.16	0.87	1.17	0.85	1.19	0.84	1.17	0.85	1.15	0.87
1981	1.19	0.84	1.20	0.83	1.19	0.84	1.19	0.84	1.20	0.83	1.20	0.83
1982	1.19	0.84	1.21	0.82	1.22	0.82	1.23	0.82	1.23	0.81	1.28	0.78
1983	1.23	0.81	1.23	0.81	1.23	0.82	1.23	0.81	1.23	0.81	1.23	0.81
1984	1.25	0.80	1.25	0.80	1.27	0.79	1.28	0.78	1.29	0.77	1.30	0.77
1985	1.32	0.76	1.35	0.74	1.38	0.72	1.37	0.73	1.38	0.73	1.37	0.73
1986	1.41	0.71	1.40	0.71	1.40	0.71	1.39	0.72	1.38	0.73	1.39	0.72
1987	1.36	0.73	1.33	0.75	1.32	0.76	1.32	0.76	1.34	0.75	1.34	0.75
1988	1.29	0.78	1.27	0.79	1.25	0.80	1.24	0.81	1.24	0.81	1.22	0.82
1989	1.19	0.84	1.19	0.84	1.20	0.84	1.19	0.84	1.19	0.84	1.20	0.83
1990	1.17	0.85	1.20	0.84	1.18	0.85	1.16	0.86	1.17	0.85	1.17	0.85
1991	1.16	0.87	1.15	0.87	1.16	0.86	1.15	0.87	1.15	0.87	1.14	0.87
1992	1.16	0.86	1.18	0.85	1.19	0.84	1.19	0.84	1.20	0.83	1.20	0.84
1993	1.28	0.78	1.26	0.79	1.25	0.80	1.26	0.79	1.27	0.79	1.28	0.78
1994	1.32	0.76	1.34	0.74	1.36	0.73	1.38	0.72	1.38	0.72	1.38	0.72
1995	1.41	0.71	1.40	0.71	1.41	0.71	1.38	0.73	1.36	0.73	1.38	0.73
1996	1.37	0.73	1.38	0.73	1.37	0.73	1.36	0.74	1.37	0.73	1.37	0.73
1997	1.35	0.74	1.36	0.74	1.37	0.73	1.39	0.72	1.38	0.72	1.38	0.72
1998	1.44	0.69	1.43	0.70	1.42	0.71	1.43	0.70	1.45	0.69	1.47	0.68
1999	1.52	0.66	1.50	0.67	1.52	0.66	1.49	0.67	1.46	0.68	1.47	0.68
2000	1.45	0.69	1.45	0.69	1.46	0.68	1.47	0.68	1.50	0.67	1.48	0.68
2001	1.50	0.67	1.52	0.66	1.56	0.64	1.56	0.64	1.54	0.65	1.52	0.66
2002	1.60	0.63	1.60	0.63	1.59	0.63	1.58	0.63	1.55	0.65	1.53	0.65
2003	1.54	0.65	1.51	0.66	1.48	0.68	1.46	0.69	1.38	0.72	1.35	0.74
2004	1.30	0.77	1.33	0.75	1.33	0.75	1.34	0.75	1.38	0.73	1.36	0.74
2005	1.22	0.82	1.24	0.81	1.22	0.82	1.24	0.81	1.26	0.80	1.24	0.81
2006	1.16	0.86	1.15	0.87	1.16	0.86	1.14	0.87	1.11	0.90	1.11	0.90
2007	1.18	0.85	1.17	0.85	1.17	0.86	1.14	0.88	1.10	0.91	1.07	0.94
2008	1.01	0.99	1.00	1.00	1.00	1.00	1.01	0.99	1.00	1.00	1.02	0.98
2009	1.22	0.82	1.25	0.80	1.26	0.79	1.22	0.82	1.15	0.87	1.13	0.89
2010	1.04	0.96	1.06	0.95	1.02	0.98	1.01	0.99	1.04	0.96	1.04	0.96
2011	0.99	1.01	0.99	1.01	0.98	1.02	0.96	1.04	0.97	1.03	0.98	1.02
2012	1.01	0.99	1.00	1.00	0.99	1.01	0.99	1.01	1.01	0.99	1.03	0.97
2013	0.99	1.01	1.01	0.99	1.02	.098	1.02	0.98	1.02	0.98	1.03	0.97

Source: Federal Reserve: Avg of daily rates, noon buying rates in New York City for cable transfers payable in foreign currencies

US DOLLAR vs CDN DOLLAR
MONTHLY AVG. VALUES

JUL		AUG		SEP		OCT		NOV		DEC		
US / CDN	CDN / US	US / CDN	CDN / US	US / CDN	CDN / US	US / CDN	CDN / US	US / CDN	CDN / US	US / CDN	CDN / US	
1.02	0.98	1.01	0.99	1.01	0.99	1.00	1.00	1.00	1.00	1.00	1.00	1971
0.98	1.02	0.98	1.02	0.98	1.02	0.98	1.02	0.99	1.01	1.00	1.00	1972
1.00	1.00	1.00	1.00	1.01	0.99	1.00	1.00	1.00	1.00	1.00	1.00	1973
0.98	1.02	0.98	1.02	0.99	1.01	0.98	1.02	0.99	1.01	0.99	1.01	1974
1.03	0.97	1.04	0.97	1.03	0.97	1.03	0.98	1.01	0.99	1.01	0.99	1975
0.97	1.03	0.99	1.01	0.98	1.03	0.97	1.03	0.99	1.01	1.02	0.98	1976
1.06	0.94	1.08	0.93	1.07	0.93	1.10	0.91	1.11	0.90	1.10	0.91	1977
1.12	0.89	1.14	0.88	1.17	0.86	1.18	0.85	1.17	0.85	1.18	0.85	1978
1.16	0.86	1.17	0.85	1.17	0.86	1.18	0.85	1.18	0.85	1.17	0.85	1979
1.15	0.87	1.16	0.86	1.16	0.86	1.17	0.86	1.19	0.84	1.20	0.84	1980
1.21	0.83	1.22	0.82	1.20	0.83	1.20	0.83	1.19	0.84	1.19	0.84	1981
1.27	0.79	1.25	0.80	1.23	0.81	1.23	0.81	1.23	0.82	1.24	0.81	1982
1.23	0.81	1.23	0.81	1.23	0.81	1.23	0.81	1.24	0.81	1.25	0.80	1983
1.32	0.76	1.30	0.77	1.31	0.76	1.32	0.76	1.32	0.76	1.32	0.76	1984
1.35	0.74	1.36	0.74	1.37	0.73	1.37	0.73	1.38	0.73	1.40	0.72	1985
1.38	0.72	1.39	0.72	1.39	0.72	1.39	0.72	1.39	0.72	1.38	0.72	1986
1.33	0.75	1.33	0.75	1.32	0.76	1.31	0.76	1.32	0.76	1.31	0.76	1987
1.21	0.83	1.22	0.82	1.23	0.82	1.21	0.83	1.22	0.82	1.20	0.84	1988
1.19	0.84	1.18	0.85	1.18	0.85	1.17	0.85	1.17	0.85	1.16	0.86	1989
1.16	0.86	1.14	0.87	1.16	0.86	1.16	0.86	1.16	0.86	1.16	0.86	1990
1.15	0.87	1.15	0.87	1.14	0.88	1.13	0.89	1.13	0.88	1.15	0.87	1991
1.19	0.84	1.19	0.84	1.22	0.82	1.25	0.80	1.27	0.79	1.27	0.79	1992
1.28	0.78	1.31	0.76	1.32	0.76	1.33	0.75	1.32	0.76	1.33	0.75	1993
1.38	0.72	1.38	0.73	1.35	0.74	1.35	0.74	1.36	0.73	1.39	0.72	1994
1.36	0.73	1.36	0.74	1.35	0.74	1.35	0.74	1.35	0.74	1.37	0.73	1995
1.37	0.73	1.37	0.73	1.37	0.73	1.35	0.74	1.34	0.75	1.36	0.73	1996
1.38	0.73	1.39	0.72	1.39	0.72	1.39	0.72	1.41	0.71	1.43	0.70	1997
1.49	0.67	1.53	0.65	1.52	0.66	1.55	0.65	1.54	0.65	1.54	0.65	1998
1.49	0.67	1.49	0.67	1.48	0.68	1.48	0.68	1.47	0.68	1.47	0.68	1999
1.48	0.68	1.48	0.67	1.49	0.67	1.51	0.66	1.54	0.65	1.52	0.66	2000
1.53	0.65	1.54	0.65	1.57	0.64	1.57	0.64	1.59	0.63	1.58	0.63	2001
1.55	0.65	1.57	0.64	1.58	0.63	1.58	0.63	1.57	0.64	1.56	0.64	2002
1.38	0.72	1.40	0.72	1.36	0.73	1.32	0.76	1.31	0.76	1.31	0.76	2003
1.32	0.76	1.31	0.76	1.29	0.78	1.25	0.80	1.20	0.84	1.22	0.82	2004
1.22	0.82	1.20	0.83	1.18	0.85	1.18	0.85	1.18	0.85	1.16	0.86	2005
1.13	0.89	1.12	0.89	1.12	0.90	1.13	0.89	1.14	0.88	1.15	0.87	2006
1.05	0.95	1.06	0.95	1.03	0.97	0.98	1.03	0.97	1.03	1.00	1.00	2007
1.01	0.99	1.05	0.95	1.06	0.95	1.18	0.84	1.22	0.82	1.23	0.81	2008
1.12	0.89	1.09	0.92	1.08	0.92	1.05	0.95	1.06	0.94	1.05	0.95	2009
1.04	0.96	1.04	0.96	1.03	0.97	1.02	0.98	1.01	0.99	1.01	0.99	2010
0.96	1.05	0.98	1.02	1.00	1.00	1.02	0.98	1.02	0.98	1.02	0.98	2011
1.01	0.99	0.99	1.01	.098	1.02	0.99	1.01	1.00	1.00	0.99	1.01	2012
1.04	0.96	1.04	0.96	1.03	0.97	1.04	0.96	1.05	0.95	1.06	0.94	2013

FOREIGN EXCHANGE — U.S. DOLLAR vs EURO MONTHLY AVG. VALUES

	JAN		FEB		MAR		APR		MAY		JUN	
	EUR / US	US / EUR	EUR / US	US / EUR	EUR / US	US / EUR	EUR / US	US / EUR	EUR / US	US / EUR	EUR / US	US / EUR
1999	1.16	0.86	1.12	0.89	1.09	0.92	1.07	0.93	1.06	0.94	1.04	0.96
2000	1.01	0.99	0.98	1.02	0.96	1.04	0.94	1.06	0.91	1.10	0.95	1.05
2001	0.94	1.07	0.92	1.09	0.91	1.10	0.89	1.12	0.88	1.14	0.85	1.17
2002	0.88	1.13	0.87	1.15	0.88	1.14	0.89	1.13	0.92	1.09	0.96	1.05
2003	1.06	0.94	1.08	0.93	1.08	0.93	1.09	0.92	1.16	0.87	1.17	0.86
2004	1.26	0.79	1.26	0.79	1.23	0.82	1.20	0.83	1.20	0.83	1.21	0.82
2005	1.31	0.76	1.30	0.77	1.32	0.76	1.29	0.77	1.27	0.79	1.22	0.82
2006	1.21	0.82	1.19	0.84	1.20	0.83	1.23	0.81	1.28	0.78	1.27	0.79
2007	1.30	0.77	1.31	0.76	1.32	0.75	1.35	0.74	1.35	0.74	1.34	0.75
2008	1.47	0.68	1.48	0.68	1.55	0.64	1.58	0.63	1.56	0.64	1.56	0.64
2009	1.32	0.76	1.28	0.78	1.31	0.77	1.32	0.76	1.36	0.73	1.40	0.71
2010	1.43	0.70	1.37	0.73	1.36	0.74	1.34	0.75	1.26	0.80	1.22	0.82
2011	1.34	0.75	1.37	0.73	1.40	0.71	1.45	0.69	1.43	0.70	1.44	0.69
2012	1.29	0.77	1.32	0.76	1.32	0.76	1.32	0.76	1.28	0.78	1.25	0.80
2013	1.33	0.75	1.33	0.75	1.30	0.77	1.30	0.77	1.30	0.77	1.32	0.76

Source: Federal Reserve: Avg of daily rates, noon buying rates in New York City for cable transfers payable in foreign currencies